PRAISE

KARL BARTH'S CHU[...]
FOR EVER[...]

This exciting new volume makes Karl Barth's *Church Dogmatics* accessible for pastors, students, and laypersons in a whole new way through an interactive reading guide that is both engaging and easy to navigate. Whether you are new to Barth's theology or a seasoned reader, this volume offers valuable resources for everyone.

—**Kait Dugan**, managing director for the Center for Barth Studies, Princeton Theological Seminary

Like a Mozart symphony, Karl Barth's *Church Dogmatics* has motifs and recurring themes that weave through its pages. However, it takes a gifted ear to hear the themes of Barth's thought in his often paragraph-long sentences. Dr. Marty Folsom is one who has that ear for Barth's music, with the added gift of helping the ungifted to hear it too.

—**Richard Keith**, pastor, Corowa Presbyterian Church, NSW, Australia

I would recommend this helpful book as a companion for the church when picking up Barth's *Dogmatics* for the first time. Barth needs to be read; this resource can provide the encouragement to do so!

—**Cherith Fee Nordling**, sessional lecturer, Regent College

Pope Paul VI said that Karl Barth was the greatest theologian since Thomas Aquinas. That is praise enough to support serious study of Barth's theology. Marty Folsom encourages just that in this new introduction. *Karl Barth's Church Dogmatics for Everyone* provides an accessible and commendable initiation into the theology of Karl Barth.

—**Paul D. Molnar**, professor of systematic theology, St. John's University, Queens, NY

Folsom couldn't be more right! Barth has been admired, and criticized, more than he has been read. In this breakthrough series, Folsom is taking *Church Dogmatics* down from the upper shelf it often fills in the pastor's study, blowing off the dust, and illuminating its pages for the benefit of parched souls and practical living.

Restoring deepest meaning to theology as "queen of the sciences," I hear Torrance and Macmurray applauding as Folsom provides us a lens to introduce us not only to Barth but more importantly to the God who is revealing God uniquely in Jesus Christ, the God apprehended (not comprehended!) in faith, the God who loves us more than He loves himself, the God who is truly *for us*!

One of Folsom's greatest contributions in this series is to provide not only an accessible entre to Barth but also an infrastructure that can be easily utilized for personal or group study. Such a format is only fitting for the discovery of the triune God, who is, in unity, persons in community!

—**Jeff McSwain**, founder, Reality Ministries, Inc.

This series sets out to communicate with clarity and imagination the insights that define the work of the greatest theologian since John Calvin. Written for nonprofessional theologians, its lucidity makes it accessible to a very wide audience. The additional essays by Julie Canlis and others are no less easy to read than Marty's text and are, without exception, outstanding. This series opens a door to the thought of Karl Barth for people who might otherwise miss out on the insights into the faith of this theological giant. This would be an ideal series for church discussion groups who wish to think through the Christian faith in great depth.

—**Alan J. Torrance**, emeritus professor of systematic theology and founding director of the Logos Institute, University of St Andrews, Scotland

KARL BARTH'S *CHURCH DOGMATICS* FOR EVERYONE

VOLUME 2

The Doctrine of God

A Step-by-Step Guide for Beginners and Pros

MARTY FOLSOM

With additional essays by:

Chris Tilling

David Guretzki

Earl Palmer

Wyatt Houtz

James Houston

Andrew Howie

Ross Hastings

Jeremy Begbie

Illustrations by Abigail Folsom

ZONDERVAN ACADEMIC

ZONDERVAN ACADEMIC

Karl Barth's Church Dogmatics *for Everyone, Volume 2—The Doctrine of God*
Copyright © 2023 by Marty Folsom

Requests for information should be addressed to:
Zondervan, *3900 Sparks Dr. SE, Grand Rapids, Michigan 49546*

Zondervan titles may be purchased in bulk for educational, business, fundraising, or sales promotional use. For information, please email SpecialMarkets@Zondervan.com.

ISBN 978-0-310-12570-9 (softcover)
ISBN 978-0-310-12571-6 (ebook)

Cover design: Brand Navigation
Cover art: Dreamstime
Interior design: Kait Lamphere

Printed in the United States of America

23 24 25 26 27 28 29 30 31 32 /TRM/ 15 14 13 12 11 10 9 8 7 6 5 4 3 2 1

Dedicated to Richard Dawson,
Friend, companion in
theology and ministry,
ever faithful to the Word of God
and the upbuilding of the Church

CONTENTS

PREFACE

We are continuing a journey that began when Barth rang a bell on the playground of the theologians. The playground has not been the same since. In this book, you are invited to come and hear more deeply the One whom Barth made center stage. The echoes are still ringing today.

In volume 1 of this series, we used the image of entering and exploring Earth from outer space, slowly zooming into the landscape. This approach engaged how we come to know God.

Volume 2 will portray God as vocal, and use the imagery of music. If we listen, we will hear that God has spoken and continues to speak. We will listen with a sense of awe to all of the dimensions of God's life, including God's intention for His creation. But we must not lose our focus; knowing God is our priority.

In *CD* 2, Barth prepares for our investigation by providing tools and questions to explore God's being and attributes. We must meet God as a subject—to know God as a personal being who wants to know us and be known by us. Four questions will engage our attention:

1. What is real about God that can be known? What's the reality, possibility, and actual realization of our knowledge of God based on God's revelation? This revelation is not mere information; instead, we learn to listen to God and all He intends for His creation.
2. How can we talk about God? How can we make statements that can both contain and truly express the reality of God?
3. How do we live with the God who comes to us? How do we engage the unfolding of God's freedom toward humanity in the actuality of God's choice to extend grace to us?
4. How do we live well in response to God's presence? How does God's freedom for humanity imply a claim and a command over humanity that creates a theological ethic of command and free response?

This is a book for learners. Its musical theme gives a new perspective on how God is the creative source and ongoing composer, crafting the art of living together. Further, God gives His creation and creatures the room and freedom to play and work in joyful response to His gospel tune.

Invite others into the conversation as you read this book. Just as harmony requires more than one voice or instrument, the proper play of theology needs discussions. We need a community that embodies unity, with distinct contributors who attentively work together. We call the outcome *improvisation*. This style is not about singing in unison. Dogmatics is not about conformity; it's more like respectful play so everyone can join in the graced space created by the triune God.

> This is a book for learners. The musical theme gives a new perspective on how God is the creative source and ongoing composer, crafting the art of living together.

This book conveys the melody line that God provides. It invites us as persons into communities to respond to and innovate in light of the love and freedom of God in our place and time.

INTRODUCTION

> I still believe that the *Gotteslehre* [doctrine of God] of *Church Dogmatics* II/1 and 2 is the high point of Barth's *Dogmatics*.
> —T. F. Torrance, "My Interaction with Karl Barth" (1986)

Welcome to the second volume of *Karl Barth's* Church Dogmatics *for Everyone*.

We will continue the basic structure but with new expressions in the content. The layout helps us on our tour through this wonderland of discovery.

As in volume 1, the big picture perspective will start in chapter 1—hearing a voice in the distance. This captures *CD* 2 in two words since it is the second volume. The voice will come closer and closer. What we hear will become more distinct as a melody, a chorus, a hymn, and then a symphony. All this prepares us to listen to the whole of *CD* 2.1 and 2.2. We will move from being part of an audience to one who joins the musical event as a participant.

This book contains twenty chapters, five of which are introductory. From chapters 6 through 20, we continue looking at the "paragraphs" in Barth's *CD* 2, from § 25 to § 39. The § symbol means paragraph. In these volumes of the *CD*, they are pretty significant. The first book of this series covered § 1 through § 24. This book explores *CD* volume 2, "The Doctrine of God."

TOOLS FOR THE JOURNEY

Like volume 1, each chapter in volume 2 offers a set of tools to help you understand the *Church Dogmatics*. What follows is similar to being at a music camp and engaging the art as a participant in a learning adventure. The chapter structure orients you to where you are in the process.

Chapter Titles: Begin by looking at the chapter titles. Each chapter title helps you adjust your sensibilities to hear the God who is encountered.

Focus Statement: The focus statement will feature a bolder and larger print size to bring our attention to the revealed point of each chapter. It tunes us in to hear the music of God, who is revealing Himself. This statement will employ a music metaphor for engaging with *CD* 2. In Barth's *Dogmatics*, we are learning to listen to the heart of the triune God, who wants to be known and invites loving responses. Metaphors open our eyes and ears to see and hear more clearly. In this section, metaphors will illuminate Barth's point.

Introduction: The introduction highlights the purpose of each chapter, helping to attune our hearing so that we can harmonize with God in each section under consideration. These may be compared to a session with the conductor, preparing us to play together.

Context: Next are some helpful details to discern where we are in the symphony of God's life as depicted in *CD* 2. This section shows the context of each chapter, which *CD* volume we are in, how many pages we are listening to, and so on. In addition, there is a list of subsections within the paragraph. In this book, we will cover the text of the second pair of books shown in the image below as II/1 and II/2.[1]

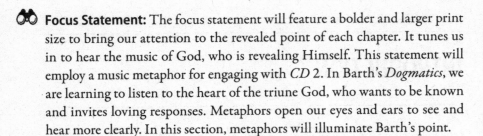

---

1. This illustration in all its forms through this and following volumes are created by Wyatt Houtz.

Text: In this section, we engage the text in a simple form. Starting in chapter 6, this section notes Barth's synopsis at the start of each paragraph in the *CD*.

Chapters 1–5 make up part 1 and provide an overarching survey. They engage and introduce the two volumes that make up *CD* 2.

Starting with chapter 6, chapters cover the contents of *CD* 2.1 and *CD* 2.2, discussing the introductory text that Barth provided to begin each "paragraph," as they are called. Remember, when we say a *paragraph*, we do not mean a small selection of sentences. Each paragraph in the *CD* can range from 15 to over 200 pages in length. The whole of the *CD*, including the fragment he did not finish, contains 78 paragraphs. This book will cover fifteen paragraphs of *CD* 2 (§ 25–39). A helpful collection of essays then connects this work to other disciplines.

 Summary: Next is a summary of each paragraph. The text is simmered down to short sentences and paragraphs. These concise statements express the heart of the section being considered. Like much of social media, these are snapshots for easy viewing. Each statement attempts to provide simple language for the complex beauty you will engage. Each is one or two sentences long and yet could be a sermon as they develop the flow of Barth's thoughts. Each has that invigorating punch that makes you want to talk about it or share it on social media. This book is all about nutshells.

The survey of the larger sections is like a concert or symphony performed before you. From there, you will be better able to read these smaller statements like the lyrics or themes within a song.

 Commentary: A few closing comments clarify the key concepts in each chapter.

 Conclusion for the Church: This is *Church* dogmatics. Thus, this section includes helpful conclusions for the Church.

Insight for Pastors: This note for pastors invites those in ministry to consider the value of each section for leading a church to encounter and know the living God.

Insight for Theologians: These proposals clarify how we use theology to participate in life with God, the Church, and with the humans God so loves. The intent is to discover how to serve others in hearing and responding to the living God.

? **Clarifying Questions:** Clarifying questions allow us to assess whether we align with Barth as we see the "Yes" of God and the implied "No."

A MAP OF WHAT FOLLOWS

Part 1 of this book, "Attuning to the God of the *Church Dogmatics*, Volume 2," surveys all of *CD* 2 as an introduction to tune you in.

Part 2 and part 3 of this book focus on specific paragraphs of the *Church Dogmatics*. Part 2 engages *CD* 2.1, and part 3 covers *CD* 2.2.

Finally, part 4 of this book contains a collection of short essays by extraordinary thinkers who appreciate the *CD*. As those who excel in their fields of study, each has been asked to articulate in a punchy essay why they value *CD* 2 and how Barth's work is of great importance for their discipline.

I have maintained the masculine for God (He, His, Him, etc.) because we will encounter this in the *CD*, and it is best to clarify its use here. Barth does not think of God in male terms; only humans have these gendered attributes. The pronouns help maintain that God is personal and not a force, power, or idea—not an *It*. Jesus was male, but that in no way elevates the masculine. Jesus came in the most humble and lowly way possible. Thus, these pronouns are to be read merely as referring to the personal being of God in three persons.

PART 1

ATTUNING TO THE GOD OF *CHURCH DOGMATICS*, VOLUME 2

Author	Work	Volume	Year
Karl Barth	Church Dogmatics	I/1	1932 (1936 ET)
Karl Barth	Church Dogmatics	I/2	1938 (1956 ET)
Karl Barth	Church Dogmatics	II/1	1940 (1957 ET)
Karl Barth	Church Dogmatics	II/2	1942 (1957 ET)
Karl Barth	Church Dogmatics	III/1	1945 (1958 ET)
Karl Barth	Church Dogmatics	III/2	1948 (1960 ET)
Karl Barth	Church Dogmatics	III/3	1950 (1961 ET)
Karl Barth	Church Dogmatics	III/4	1951 (1961 ET)
Karl Barth	Church Dogmatics	IV/1	1953 (1956 ET)
Karl Barth	Church Dogmatics	IV/2	1955 (1958 ET)
Karl Barth	Church Dogmatics	IV/3.1	1959 (1961 ET)
Karl Barth	Church Dogmatics	IV/3.2	1959 (1962 ET)
Karl Barth	Church Dogmatics	IV/4	1967 (1969 ET)

CHAPTER 1

THE VOICE HEARD FROM A DISTANCE

👓 **FOCUS STATEMENT:** In the beginning was the Voice. We hear the living voice of God. We must learn to listen to it. God speaks so we may know Him as the living God. However, right now, we need the big picture.

We will start with all creation as our auditorium. This One voice stirs in the distance within all of space and time, faint from where we stand. Our awareness comes like the dawn. God is speaking, but we can only tell that He is there and that His voice is speaking to us. He knows us. He expresses Himself so we will know Him!

This first chapter attunes us to hear the simplicity of *all* of *CD* 2 in *two words*: living Word. Think of hearing *CD* 2 from a distance. Imagine we are in a vast garden meadow, and we hear a sound coming across the expanse. This melody comes with a unique voice, not yet entirely distinct. Nevertheless, it is personal, not a mere sound. This voice is alive. We are not alone. There is another, drawing us with an invitational mystery.

We are invited to hear the voice singing from before the creation of the world, revealing as it wills life into being from the loving heart of God freely at work.

🖋 **INTRODUCTION:** In this chapter, we are attuning to the two books that combine as the second volume of the *Church Dogmatics*. We are preparing to hear from the living Word. Instead of a "landscape" setting the context for our exploration, we have a soundscape, and God's voice fills it. We venture on by listening. We attend to the sound and content of what is said to attune to the mystery. In this way, we come to know the personal God who precedes us and comes to us.

These volumes of *CD* 2 (2.1 and 2.2) tune our ears to hear who God is as God wants to be known—this is the doctrine of God. God must speak for this encounter to happen. We must learn to avoid both heeding imitation voices and projecting human ideas onto God. Care to avoid projection and imitation clears the way to listen and respond to God attentively. The gospel becomes music to our hearts when this happens. God's self-presentation opens dynamic new ways for relating to God and each other.

IIIiI CONTEXT: Let's get oriented to where we are in the *Church Dogmatics*. We have seen *CD* 1, "The Doctrine of the Word of God," which clarified the manner of God coming to be known. It further outlined the task of the Church in reflecting on God's coming to be known.

Church Dogmatics 2, "The Doctrine of God," consists of two books divided into four chapters and expressed into fifteen paragraphs (remember they are more chapter length!). Barth engages the God who is made known and our response to God's choosing to come to us in love and freedom.

Volume 2 will prepare us for *Church Dogmatics* 3, "The Doctrine of Creation." The God we are coming to know in volume 2 reveals His work in making the world, our place in it, and the nature of His relation to His creation. For now, we will focus on the God who speaks.

📖 TEXT: *CD* in two words: living Word

✝ SUMMARY:

The message of *CD* 2 can be summarized in two words: living Word. This Word is the living Jesus, God in person. He is the speaking address of God to humanity. He is also the content of that Word, displaying His free and loving choice to be *for us and with us*. He empowers us to live in a freeing response.

Outside attentive listening to God, our thoughts about God are likely to derive from what we think is good, faithful, and beautiful in the world. However, human sensibilities never provide authentic engagement with God.

Only God can reveal God. All else is casting ideas upward to paint God large with human brush strokes or to cast a human voice like a ventriloquist. This move creates a severe problem.

The living Word who is *speaking* is the Word who is a *person*. He speaks to address us with *communication*. Thus, the Word in the first sense is the Son of God—He is the "text" to understand. He speaks and reveals God. He is God. He is an active Person, who utilizes words so we will know God, the Father and Spirit. When His voice speaks to us, it creates a massive opening for discovery.

As we read, His voice conveys His Father's heart to us through Scripture, the written Word that enables the living communication of God to engage us.

Through this ancient document, He calls us to respond today. By His Spirit, He speaks personally concerning our whole life. Having heard God, we reply to the invitation to live with deep and penetrating knowledge. We come to know this God who wants to be known.

COMMENTARY:

Already in these two words, *living Word*, we hear:

> Only God can reveal God. All else is casting ideas upward to paint God large with human brush strokes or to cast a human voice like a ventriloquist.

- **The personal.** We are addressed by a person in our study of God.
- **The verbal.** We are met by One with a voice who speaks our language.
- **The intentional.** This Word speaks to us with a motive of love and a desire for a response.
- **The means.** God has already made the way to know God personally.
- **The historical.** This Word is spoken in space and time.
- **The active.** This Word does not remain distant or abstract but comes to act in an embodied manner that lives what He says.

CONCLUSION FOR THE CHURCH: The Church is to listen to one voice. In this chapter, we prepare to *apprehend* the mystery of God simply by acknowledging, "Oh, there you are; now I can hear you." To fully understand would be to *comprehend*. More humbly, to *apprehend* is to become aware and ready to discover. The whole of *CD* 2 affirms that God is there and speaking to be *apprehended*. This opens the way for relationships.

- **Living.** To say His voice is "living" points out that it is alive *from* Him, both then and now. Subsequently, His voice speaks today. It connects with our deepest emotions, like a melody line we have never known. Now we hear and love that voice and yearn for more.
- **Word.** This Voice is Jesus, the Word who still reveals God to His Church. We are not untouched; He elicits a loving response that frees us. His life provides His address to us to hear this Living Word. It enables the task of theology for the Church: to know God personally, not merely to know about God. Jesus reorients the Church as its high priest who intercedes. He creates a dialog between heaven and earth.

We need more than a figurehead Jesus in the Church; we need the living God named Jesus. We need more than a figurehead Jesus in the Church.

He spoke the universe into being. His Word reawakens the call to live as those chosen because we are dear and gifted to answer His heart.

INSIGHT FOR PASTORS: We must get clear about what we mean by doctrine. Doctrine is the fruit of learning to hear and respond to an authentic Word from Jesus. It is not a definite and final opinion. If anything, it is a commitment to an ongoing, clarifying conversation to be true to whom or what we are engaging. This approach is not about programs or positions. It is a posture of listening and responding with deepening love and alignment. Doctrine should not lead to definitions and arguments. It must lead to dynamic relationships.

Do not read these texts (*CD* 2.1 and 2.2) to make up an outline for an adult education class. Study to enter into deep prayer. Prepare to gather the community so that Jesus Himself will create a yearning for profound hearing. Let the voice of Jesus be what is offered, in word and deed. We are stewards of this Word.

Election needs rethinking and is a significant part of *CD* 2. *Election* has become a confusing term used to refer to who is in and who is out of God's care and concern. However, this discussion of election with Barth will be more like discovering the will of One who loves us. This person determined that we be taken care of for the rest of our lives, we and our families. Election affirms that, as a gift, we already belong as family members. We were ignorant of this fact. Now, we need only live within the gift and share in its benefits. Election is God choosing to be for all of us as God and to be the Human who brings us home to belonging again.

For this to happen, a change of mind is required in the Church. Knowing God does not mean going on individual spiritual journeys. We need to respond to the election of Jesus—His choice to be for us and with us. From this place, we may become a community of creativity. We have been gifted to be caring stewards of the gracious provision of God. He has supplied us, as a people chosen, both to receive and give as a delighted family in a darkened world. We do not need to learn to get better at living; we need to become who we are as beloved children who know the fearless play of love. From that comes the outworking of the freeing love of God in daily activity.

INSIGHT FOR THEOLOGIANS: These two volumes are some of the most significant theological texts in the history of the Church. They serve the vital task of moving us away from fear-based interpretations used to control or motivate parishioners.

These volumes are about hearing the Word in living stereo. They are intended to grab the theologian by the ears. They redirect us to a deep and explosive hearing of the self-giving of God in Jesus. There is a givenness of God's presence in these pages. As God's being resonates in our being, it will reorder our thinking. Jesus displays what is real about God, ourselves, and the world. Thus, as demonstrated here, theology does not focus on human ideas, points of view, definitions, and applications. It is a form of listening and reflecting: God's commitments, choices, and ways of being come to shape our here and now. Doctrine cannot be done at a distance. It lives within the dynamics of the discovery. When God is known in this way, it changes everything.

? **CLARIFYING QUESTIONS:** Is your doctrine of God an outline with points and subpoints, seeking to get the correct answers? Or is your doctrine of God a constant focusing of your attention on the voice of One Person, to live within the sphere of His love and activity?

CHAPTER 2

HEARING THE MELODY

FOCUS STATEMENT: This chapter introduces the motif of *CD 2* in a sentence. As we come closer to the approaching One who is speaking or singing—we know not which, nor in what language—we come to hear a melody line that seems to descend from above.

In this chapter, we learn to listen, becoming more closely attuned to the One who is singing to us. Through the song, we begin to distinguish the speaker's melodious presence. Something is awakening in us as we hear this newly discovered song. Its simple phrasing penetrates our hearts; the tune resonates with the character of the other who is singing. The simplicity and depth of the singer and song enthrall us. It is like hearing fantastic news in the morning—full of hope.

The voice is a person, now coming into view. What we hear begins to clarify the life of the singer.

INTRODUCTION: This chapter is an entryway to meet the living God. Its simple message broadcasts the voice of Jesus, who announces God's actual, historical, living reality. *CD 2* clarifies the intent of God, who wants us to know Him and intends for us to know that we are known. The One who made us pursues us.

In this short overview of the two volumes of *Church Dogmatics* 2, we find that we are deaf and that God still loves us unconditionally. Encountering the reality of God, we find that God profoundly loves us with unstoppable freedom. Hearing the way God orchestrates His love compels us to respond to His call.

This pair of books takes us on an adventure. We come to know we have been chosen, seen for who we are, and invited to step into a divine embrace that will never leave us alone.

 **CONTEXT:** There are thirteen volumes in the *Church Dogmatics*. We are exploring volumes 3 and 4.

    Pages in Church Dogmatics 2: 1448 pages (pp. 1–667 and 1–781)

TEXT: *CD* 2 in *one sentence*: "In Jesus, God actively elects us through His love freely expressed, and we answer with our freeing response."

SUMMARY:

God wants to be known.

God intends for humans to hear and embrace what He makes known, namely Himself.

Knowing God is a participation in His life, made possible by the revelation of Jesus and through the Holy Spirit.

Only God knows God. We must keep the source of our knowing God in what He makes available.

God is love. This is not a theory; it is the demonstration of God's presence in the world.

All God's ways live out the freely given grace embodied in Jesus.

God chooses to be *for* humanity.

God, by grace, overcomes alienation and estrangement with humanity.

God does not just choose individuals. God chooses whole communities like Israel and the Church.

God gifts every person with unmerited grace that embodies freeing love.

God commits to the well-being of humanity. Thus, He calls humans out of their alienation to move in response to His choice to be *for* us.

God elects from love, and we answer with a freeing response.

 COMMENTARY:

In this one sentence, we see:

- God is the focus of theology.
- Jesus shows us God.
- When God elects, God is choosing to be consistent with God's freeing love. We cannot condition God into loving us. It is His nature.
- Election is not a lottery or a vote of confidence in humans; God chooses to act from love for the other.
- God chooses to be for humanity from eternity.
- God acts in history to be with humanity.

- God's election creates space for a human response.
- God's election does not exclude human action and response, but makes space for joyful responses.

CONCLUSION FOR THE CHURCH: God has acted and is still acting. His choice to act for us is called election. He is still in this business. The Church is not a separate business or a franchise. It is a servant of the God who loves and elects. If we think that election is a grand scheme to get some into heaven and reject others, we have missed knowing God revealed in Jesus. He elected Himself to birth the Church and be its living head. This body is a family participating in the reality of God's love. The Church's call is to help humans know that Jesus is God's act of love to include all and bring them to His Father. Any church activity should leave people walking out the door with joy and love, confidently knowing God's love and able to live without worry or shame.

INSIGHT FOR PASTORS: To pastor is to know Jesus, the head of the Church, and to point others to Him. This knowledge should lead to intimacy, confidence that one is known, and response to God's loving embrace. God has elected to be the very fountain of life for His people. Our service as ministers is to convey that powerfully. As people exit our gatherings, we might ask, "Do these people know that God has chosen to be for them and loves them unconditionally? Can they leave here resonating with God's love because they've been infused with the love of God?" *CD* 2 is a launch into the extraordinary mystery of God. Jesus creates the possibility for human restoration within His life of love.

INSIGHT FOR THEOLOGIANS: Theology, as defined in these volumes, attends to the will and acts of a personal God. Theology is human reflection on personally knowing the living God. Jesus provides a dynamic touchstone for reality; He becomes the context for the meaning of life. This focus is especially true for the doctrines of revelation and election.

As theologians, we must learn to listen to the person who is the voice of God. No one is a surrogate or representative in God's absence. We are more like messengers who know the One we serve. Coming to know God refreshes our minds to correspond with His personal reality. Prayer and study facilitate delving into a person, not just improving classic positions in theology. Theology that functions in this mode is vibrant and attentive, both to God and the human life lived in response.

? CLARIFYING QUESTIONS: Does your theology build on defenses and arguments to serve and protect the reputation of God? Or is your theology the outcome of sitting in silence and learning to hear God speak, to listen to His heart and voice? Are you preparing for constructive theology that lets God talk about His choice to act in love and freedom toward our time and place?

Theology, as defined in these volumes, attends to the will and acts of a personal God. Theology is human reflection on personally knowing the living God.

CHAPTER 3

HEARING THE CHORUS OF THE SONG

FOCUS STATEMENT: This chapter introduces the theme of the two volumes of *CD* 2 as a chorus. This functions as a prelude to what is coming, expressed as the chorus of God's loving address. This chorus is what we hear coming across the landscape. It has harmony, as this chapter is about the triune God to whom we are learning to pay attention.

Sometimes a song has a chorus that captures the point developed in the verses. This chorus focuses on God as sung by His singer. This singer, as God, loves to sing about His companionship with humanity. This chorus will repeat throughout the movements of *CD* 2.1 and 2.2. It is our first moment of catching this invitational tune, with God revealing God as only God can.

The triune life of God is a dance of God's love and grace that is simple and yet profound. This movement is imaged as a unified dance of joy that calls to humanity to join in.

INTRODUCTION: As we survey the doctrine of God in *CD* 2, we need to attune to the God who speaks (and sings!). To hear clearly, we need to resist how people sing their own songs and fail to listen to whether God is speaking or has spoken. Fortunately, God can sing us His song, which is an invitation to bring us home to Himself. We come to know Him because He never stops singing. In addition, His music reveals His heart; it tells about His intentions and how He wants to be with us. Unfortunately, we often miss God. This chapter enables us to gain clarity about God from God's perspective. We want to hear the theme of God crisp and clear. It makes the point to which we will continually return.

CONTEXT: *CD* 1 is the context for *CD* 2. The living Word, the written Word, and the preached Word open the way to know God. Now, we intend to know the God *CD* 2 sings out to us by acknowledging that only God can properly know God. We need to listen. Only He can connect us with

His reality, as the One who loves in freedom. This is foundational. God's revelation to humanity sounds forth God's intent. This reveal on God's part becomes the context for our human response. God's free and loving choice to be Creator and covenant companion attunes us with God's purposefulness in our responsive lives.

📖 **TEXT:** *CD* **in a Chorus:**

> Ask not whether God is known,
> In the Word, My love is shown;
> Choosing freely from above,
> My gift for you, those made for love.

�҂ **SUMMARY:**

We must not hurry past the fact that theology is about God, from God.

We must just as quickly clarify that all our ideas about God to this point may not have been informed by God. Human ideals, moral values, religious attitudes, practices of spirituality, and the quest for meaning often form a cloud of confusion that looks like it is pointing to God but is a hall of idols—meaning human-made gods. We must learn to listen to His Word.

God being *actually* known means "as God appears in history." This means God as known in the person of Jesus. All knowledge of God comes from Him because He walked the Earth in time and space. Because He was present at the beginning, in history, and now as the ascended Lord, we can speak of all that He made accessible to human knowledge.

God's reality is not the abstract thought of philosophy or mythology. God's reality is personal, as shown in the person of Jesus. He has chosen to let us into His life.

As Creator of the universe, God freely operates within the cosmos to fulfill God's intention. This commitment includes choosing to be for and with His creatures as companions.

His command to love compels us as God's companions to live freely in loving response to His freeing judgments.

🔬 **COMMENTARY:**

In this chorus, we see that:

- Theology is not a word about God as much as God's Word to us.
- We are deaf and blind when we merely listen and look for God—He gives Himself when and where He chooses.

- We should not attribute anything from our experience to God's way of being. That method ends up taking human values and descriptions and then casting God in that shape.
- Election is God's endgame of love. He does not predetermine who is in and who is out. Instead, God chooses to be the winner for everyone. By His embrace of the human race, in Jesus, He embraces and deals with all divine judgment. He elects to be the One who restores humanity in relation to Himself.
- Discovering God means we consequently find out who we may be in the context of God's love. This affirmation does not give us a mere status; it opens the way for transformation. What we value, how we act, and the corresponding of our lives with His life all follow from the intention to love. This love is born from being the people of God by His choice.

INSIGHT FOR PASTORS: Theology is not apologetics; it is not answering the questions of the doubtful; it is attentiveness to God. Pastors are servants of His Word. This emphasis means that you, as a pastor, do not primarily appeal to what makes sense to your congregation. Selling the value of Christianity is not your mission. Do not make your church "interesting," like a museum showing relics of the past, like a zoo offering animals otherwise unavailable. Your people would become observers separated from the objects of their interest.

In coming to church, people should expect to meet with the God who speaks. It is best to come with a sense of wonder, but not wondering what is in it for them. The goal is to know the reality of God and to connect deeply with the God who made them and loves them. Hopefully, they will leave as those who didn't even know what they were missing. They become adventurous participants. This new perspective is because the God who shows up is so surprising.

Barth's two-volume set is a classic in theological thinking. It unravels old possibilities in the Christian experience and constructs the possibility of engaging in Christian life in response to God. It unclogs ears. It opens the arteries to the heart. When God addresses us, God will be heard, loved, and obeyed in the awakening of passionate love born from God's self-giving.

Consequently, the freeing love of God calls forth daily acts of love that confirm that the reality of God is blossoming into a myriad of possibilities. This is the logic of *CD* 2.

INSIGHT FOR THEOLOGIANS: Science is a human reflection on the nature of the reality in which we live. It is a reasoned process of knowing. It is developed by appropriate attention to the object of study. Through proper attentiveness, one learns about and clarifies the nature of the reality engaged. Science includes the process of discovery and the revisable conclusions that serve humanity to live in the light of truth. Science is a human activity reflecting on reality.

In Barth's volumes, God is studied. We cannot capture God in theories or propositions. However, God may be known in person as a person. This perspective expands our scientific field to include studying persons as personal beings instead of impersonal objects. Theology explores God properly when it does not try to fit Him into our categories of knowledge. God appropriately occupies a realm of learning only by letting God take the initiative in coming to us. This presentation of God by God invites further exploration on our part. This revelation is the basis of theological science.

Having come to contemplate, explore, and dwell within the scope of God's activity in Jesus, the theologian must gather insights and clarify within the limits of God's revealing. Subsequently, a theologian may think about the dynamics of God's speaking in the present context. In a sense, this is like an oceanographer penetrating the depths of the sea. One knows the surface with an immediate sense of observation and anticipation. However, wonder calls for exploring all that is unknown in the expanse extending for fathoms in all directions. This curiosity includes the future of our relationship to what we discover as those who are stewards. God, unlike the ocean, does not need our protection. Instead, we need to dispel the illusions and delusions that lead to our destruction because we lack appropriate wisdom for living in the spaces opened to us in knowing God and ourselves as His creatures.

CLARIFYING QUESTIONS: When you think of knowing God, do you think of categories and descriptions that fit God into the world of the "known"? Or do you proceed with wonder in knowing God? Do you find that every presentation of God is transformed in the light of who God actually is?

🗺️ **CHAPTER 4**

HEARING THE HYMN OF GOD

👓 **FOCUS STATEMENT:** Now, we expand to see the four chapters of *CD* 2 as a revealing hymn, played in verses. As the singer comes nearer, we begin to notice His features as well as His song. We hear His divine words and see His dazzling, earthy face. All our surroundings fill with exhilaration in His presence.

As His hymn encounters us, we feel as though we are inhabiting Adam's first breath—He has chosen to give us life. In Him, God is addressing all humanity. We feel known as we come to know His freely offered love for us. He gives meaning to the word communion in the most creative, embodied, captivating way. We feel fully embraced, like He chose to love us, particularly because of who He is. Further, we sense that He embraces us and our complexity, and He knows us with extravagant clarity. The whole cosmos seems to dance in response to His self-offered singing. This hymn of God makes God available and ourselves responsive.

Hymns are rich with tradition and tell a story of God's love. The image of the triune God, sitting at a table of love, gathered in a harmonic intertwining that cannot be separated, bespeaks the richness of what God reveals and compels in response.

🪶 **INTRODUCTION:** Within *CD*, seventeen chapters create a flow of logical progression. In *CD* 1, we explored:

Chapter 1: The Word of God as the Criterion of Dogmatics
Chapter 2: The Revelation of God
Chapter 3: Holy Scripture
Chapter 4: The Proclamation of the Church

These chapters prepared us to hear the living Word. We now move beyond preparation for the Word of God, ready to listen to the God to whom all that pointing brings us. A hymn is a community engagement sung among a family to celebrate the personal God.

God is not bashful and wants to be known. He provides an encounter that conforms human knowledge to the mystery and majesty of God, who loves freely and unconditionally. God graciously and unconditionally chooses to be for humanity, the community of the Church, and each person through the electing of Jesus. God claims us as beloved children, and we say "yes" in word and deed to the invitation to love that is God's command.

The chapters of *CD* 2 are:

Chapter 5: The Knowledge of God
Chapter 6: The Reality of God
Chapter 7: The Election of God
Chapter 8: The Command of God

These chapters enable us to hear the heart of God. He is the One who loves in freedom as the intent of His very being. His love is expressed in expansive ways to address and restore humanity, fulfilling the gospel's gist.

Pages in Chapters of *CD* 2:

Chapter 5: 254 pages (*CD* 2.1: pp. 1–254)
Chapter 6: 423 pages (*CD* 2.1: pp. 255–677)
Chapter 7: 506 pages (*CD* 2.2: pp. 1–506)
Chapter 8: 275 pages (*CD* 2.2: pp. 507–781)

📖 **TEXT:** *CD* 2 in a *hymn*
The Hymn of God
Jesus sings to us:

Verse 1:　I belong to you and you to Me,
　　　　　　　Available in time, from eternity.
　　　　　Acting in your space so you might know My face
　　　　　　　As I unfold embodied grace.
Chorus:　*Ask not whether God is known,*
　　　　　In the Word, my love is fully shown;
　　　　　Choosing freely from above,
　　　　　My gift for you, those made for love.
Verse 2:　I live in love that frees your life,
　　　　　　　Acting in beauty to restore from strife.

My gift of love displays My heart,
> My steadfast presence will never depart.

Chorus: *Ask not whether God is known,*
> *In the Word, my love is fully shown;*
> *Choosing freely from above,*
> *My gift for you, those made for love.*

Verse 3: My choice to love is a gift bestowed,
> My determined embrace never lets you go.
I healed our rift, now My mystery shines,
> Good News indeed, "I have made you Mine."

Chorus: *Ask not whether God is known,*
> *In the Word, my love is fully shown;*
> *Choosing freely from above,*
> *My gift for you, those made for love.*

Verse 4: My focused love will engulf your ways,
> You're a partner in My dance of freeing grace.
Feel love's sweet release as I call your name,
> With love's transforming work, you'll never be the same.

Chorus: *Ask not whether God is known,*
> *In the Word, my love is fully shown;*
> *Choosing freely from above,*
> *My gift for you, those made for love.*

✛ SUMMARY:

This is a very personal song, sung by a lover to His beloved.

It addresses our most fundamental questions: Are you there for me? Do we have a relationship?

It affirms the eternal decision of God in Jesus to be for us before we can do anything. This is unconditional love.

The nature of God relating to humanity is one of gift. The gift is not separate from God's self, like power, a remote control, or blank check; or giving us the master key that He hands over to us and then leaves. God gives Himself. The gift is God's freeing self that will never abandon us.

God's love is not an abstract idea. God's love is lived in action. The life, death, and resurrection of Jesus demonstrate His love. This evidence informs us of God's reality established in human history.

All that can be known of God is consistent with God's free and freeing love. This love meets the needs of broken relationships to bring renewal and awakening connection.

God has decided how to heal the broken relationship that stretches back to Adam and Eve.

In Jesus, God chooses to be the One who embodies and embraces the loss of the first Adam. He takes the nakedness, shame, and curse and decides to be the new Adam. In Him, shame is erased, the gift of love is bestowed, and the blessing of being family is restored.

The good news is that God has done all that could ever be done to restore all that could be wrong. He compels us to stop living in the falseness of old illusory stories and conceptions. He invites us to live in the reality of love fulfilled.

We are children of God by God's choosing. Our response to accept being chosen does nothing to change God's relation to us. It is our awakening to love that has chosen us.

> The good news is that God has done all that could ever be done to restore all that could be wrong.

When we enter a relationship with an adoring, loving other, this creates a response of love—and we act like it.

COMMENTARY:

- Theology is not so much about understanding God through a set of descriptors. It is about God speaking so that He might be known personally and dynamically.
- We know little of God by surveying our present historical context. We know much of God in the person of Jesus, who speaks to us across the centuries.
- The freedom of God is not necessarily free *from* the powers that surround us and infringe on our lives. Freedom is experienced in the embrace of One who is *for* us.
- Election will never be a choice made because we are worthy of being chosen.
- Election will always be an act of love.
- Election is a free choice of God. God chooses God. God desires to be for us before we can do anything. God chooses to stand in for us on our behalf.
- Election is unconditional and eternal: it is all about the eternal God choosing to do in Jesus what we cannot do.
- The calling of God is to live freely within the choice God has made to be our God.
- When we speak of God and what He is like, we must see that our words pale in comparison to His actuality. Our terms are like shadows that point to a concrete reality.

- In Jesus, we know the character of God as light that comes into the world so we can see. Therefore, in that context, we see what God is actually like and come to understand all He has made.
- The ethical response to God is a human response to the Word spoken to us. We do not get a set of rules; we encounter the Lover who will not abandon us. The new dynamic displaces the old patterns.

 INSIGHT FOR PASTORS: Many go to church to become better Christians. However, the task of the Church is to know the living God. Often people walk away knowing about God's characteristics, definition, and descriptions and have ideals in their heads. These conceptions lead to an abstract and distant God. We have starved people.

God wants to be known. The Church has often neglected God simply because of a desire to be successful by human standards. Nevertheless, the success of the Church is in understanding the reality of God. He has chosen to be freely and lovingly present. He is speaking to those who listen. Having heard from the heart, they will be transformed from alienation to conform to what they already are, the children of God. The Church fulfills its calling when doctrine moves from lecture-focused to becoming a word that welcomes a family. This orientation cultivates response in a personal manner. God enjoys overwhelming us with His kind of love. The life of a Christian becomes an experience of freedom that is like coming home afresh every day.

INSIGHT FOR THEOLOGIANS: Theology books are essential, but coming to know the One they point to is much more valuable. Theology cannot be a purely reflective activity; it must also engage the people of God.

The science of theology requires active engagement, an encounter through which we know the reality that has been revealed. Through acts of reflection on Jesus, we align with His mediation, His actions that facilitate God-human relationships. He opens our awareness to God. He speaks to people in particular places and times. This requires us to learn the skills of language, history, and rhetoric to apprehend the unveiled presence of the hidden God. The goal of theology is to be lovingly met by God's freeing embrace. We then go with Him to love the world in action. The test of a theological method is whether people exhibit the DNA of God's Trinitarian life in the community and beyond. Being reborn by His Spirit, we apply our academic study to life as we are shaped by God's presence that grows us to maturity. In our classrooms, we help others to do the same.

? **CLARIFYING QUESTIONS:** Do you think of election as
God choosing some for heaven and some for hell as a decree
from eternity? Or do you see the love of God in Jesus as
His choice, decision, decree, and election? Can you see that
to be "in Him" is to be within the One who is elected on
our behalf?

The goal of theology
is to be lovingly
met by God's
freeing embrace.

CHAPTER 5

HEARING THE SYMPHONY

FOCUS STATEMENT: This chapter displays *CD* 2 with its four chapters and fifteen paragraphs set in the format of a symphony. A traditional symphony has four movements or parts. The movements of the symphony of the revealing God echo the four chapters of *CD* 2. Each movement will orient us to interact with God's movement, disclosing Himself with His love that freely releases us to loving response. Welcome to His outdoor space for this grand event.

In this chapter, we will listen to God's music, directed toward our hearts as much as our ears. Heard properly, it frees us to embrace the gift of God's love that has embraced us. We will listen to God's personal self-presentation and a consequent penetration into our hearts, freshly tuned for a life of responding.

This chapter will survey § 25–39, set in an outdoor event location. All creation listens in, as it hears the Creator's music that put it in motion. This symphony is a Creator-creation harmonization.

Remember, paragraphs are not the usual short units of thought on a page. Here, they are excursions of ingenuity that can go on for hundreds of pages, full of history and intricate detail. These echoing engagements allow discussion of the grace of God to run free in recounting specifics. In a sophisticated interplay of themes, the motifs reveal the soundscape we will encounter in the two volumes that make up *CD* 2.

The image invites us to participate, to pull up a chair and release ourselves into rapt attention to the grandeur of God in symphonic expression.

INTRODUCTION: *CD* 2 focuses on the doctrine of God. For Barth, this means carefully attending to the Christian God known in the person of Jesus Christ, especially concerning His creation.

In the fifteen paragraphs of *CD* 2, inner logic and dynamics will unfold as thematic elements of a symphony. God is known in action, not abstraction. His way of being extends concretely from His love. The dynamics of His love have many facets that wash over us with a transforming effect.

His intent to love is expressed in His choices; these choices extend His will or what He elects to do. Each of these words reflects God in a continuous personal display, becoming the gospel in living color or, in this case, vibrant music. His central actor, Jesus, plays out God's self-determined grace. He commands our attention and affection. We will leave feeling something beyond inspired and enthused. We have connected, and we have been drawn to a life of responsive love with listening hearts.

Barth loved Mozart and began each day listening to his music. Thus, we can easily imagine the inner structure of *CD* 2 through the lens of a symphony with its design of four movements and a unique score to play out God's brilliance. Oriented in this way, we can listen to the interplay that builds within his themes of knowing, reality, election, and command. The interaction of the refrains, moods, and melodies produce a cohesive reflection on God's being, heard in relation to His creation. We are being prepared to savor the uniqueness of each element of God's ways and works in the world.

CONTEXT: *CD* 2, "The Doctrine of God," follows *CD* 1. The first volume focused on the address of God to us. The speech came as the living Word was made known through the written Word. That Word is now preached in the Church. We discovered that God is revealed in Jesus Christ, who shows the whole of the triune God. Jesus tells of the Father who sent Him. Through the Spirit, we hear and share in the community of the Church as His body. The Bible provides an ongoing witness for the Church and personal connection with Jesus. As the Church speaks, it equips its members to know God and share His mission to know the One to whom we belong.

In the current volume, we move from the manner of God's address to us in *CD* 1 to now know the God who has addressed us as the theme of *CD* 2. In discussing the doctrine of God in *CD* 2, we are concretely positioned to sit where we have access to God's personal revealing. Doctrine is more about engaged discovery than a study of complicated words or unbending statements. Think about sitting as a child full of wonder, ready to enter an exciting unknown moment, with all the mystery of meeting a person full of promise. As we listen, we will need to muffle competitive noises that intrude. Listening well will attune us to know the intent (election) of God at play in the world and our obediently playful response (ethics).

When we get to *CD* 3, we will engage the activity of God as Creator and God's intent for His creation, especially the creation of humans as covenant partners.

For volumes 1–3 of the massive *Church Dogmatics*, think of this mapping:

> **CD 1:** Preparation to meet the actuality of God (we *were* here)
>
> **CD 2:** *Encountering the God who freely chose us for reconnection* (we *are* here)
>
> **CD 3:** The God-human relation as played out with God as His covenant-partners (*coming* down the road)

Pages in Paragraphs of *Church Dogmatics* Volume 2:

Paragraph 25: 60 pages (pp. 3–62)
Paragraph 26: 116 pages (pp. 63–178)
Paragraph 27: 76 pages (pp. 179–254)
Paragraph 28: 64 pages (pp. 257–321)
Paragraph 29: 29 pages (pp. 322–50)
Paragraph 30: 89 pages (pp. 351–439)
Paragraph 31: 138 pages (pp. 440–677)
Paragraph 32: 91 pages (pp. 3–93)
Paragraph 33: 101 pages (pp. 94–194)
Paragraph 34: 111 pages (pp. 195–305)
Paragraph 35: 201 pages (pp. 306–506)
Paragraph 36: 43 pages (pp. 509–51)
Paragraph 37: 79 pages (pp. 552–630)
Paragraph 38: 101 pages (pp. 631–732)
Paragraph 39: 49 pages (pp. 733–81)

📖 **TEXT:** *CD 2 in a Symphony*

1. **The first movement** of this symphony is brisk and lively (*CD 2*, chapter 5). The opening section reveals the active and personal movement of God. It has the feel of approach, the coming near of One who was mysterious and hidden, not yet seen face-to-face.

    a. **Paragraph 25**. The themes of this paragraph reveal the One who comes with mystery and clarity. Jesus is the One whom we may love and fear above all things. We hear mysteriously muted tones at points, but they exhibit penetrating clarity.

    b. **Paragraph 26**. Here we find the development of the theme of knowing God.

        i. We hear the clarity of the Son of God, who owns the stage. He is the master musician, voicing joy descending

from above. The Spirit brings our hearing to attune to
His majestic message.

    ii. Joy is coming to the world. The original voice now
expresses themes that engage, embrace, and invite all to
participate in the musical dance for a lifetime with the
One who is its very source and sustainer of life.

  c. **Paragraph 27**. We hear the interplay of two melodies. The
variations play out the hiddenness and revealedness of God.
These themes counterbalance human attempts to replicate the
music of God.

    i. The themes present the clash between human attempts
to create faith and the faithful provision of God.

    ii. As the themes develop, false intrusions are removed, and
pseudo-inventions that subvert God's themes of grace are
silenced.

    iii. A final recapitulation on the themes of love and grace,
balanced with limitation and exclusion, finishes this
movement in the comfort of God's embrace.

2. **The second movement** is slower and more lyrical (*CD* 2, chapter 6).
This symphonic section interweaves the loving freedom of God, displaying the harmonious abundance of God's being and action.

  a. **Paragraph 28**. Attention turns to the supreme soloist. In hearing Him, we feel His voice and the depth of His Spirit. This
performer exudes love freshly given, which frees us to move like
never before. He is movement—love in action.

  b. **Paragraph 29**. This section expands into gorgeous harmonics
(loving), playfully improvised (freedom) from the lead of the
one voice. The unity of what we hear magnifies into a rich,
diverse liveliness.

  c. **Paragraph 30**. The simplicity of the last section spills now
into a balance between God's majestic outpouring of love and
responsive human themes to create beauty.

  d. **Paragraph 31**. This second movement ends with swelling
vitality into the deep stretches of God's love. It couples together
a trio of themes: symphonic unity, constancy in love, and the
complete unfolding of God's personal presence.

3. **The third movement** is energetic music for dancing (*CD* 2, chapter 7). This splash of creativity arrives as an enthusiastic expression,
exploding out from a unified, single, powerful chord. This Jesus song

is the fullest expression of the plan to stretch to the zenith of the God-human relation.

  a. **Paragraph 32**. The dancing music begins. The gospel theme rings out clear, surging with intentionality right from the start.
  b. **Paragraph 33**. With one small step for the deity of Jesus, He comes robed with humanity. He reverberates as the Song in action. He sings of woe and worship. He gives a command performance that leaves all others speechless.
  c. **Paragraph 34**. A trio. Jesus engages in a lively interchange with Jewish temple music and Black soul music, with Jesus on electric guitar.
  d. **Paragraph 35**. A minuet. In this section, we hear a melodic and harmonic contrast, the rejected and elected brought into accord in Jesus for a culminating dance.

4. **The finale movement** brings everyone to their feet, and they offer a rollicking response to whatever is called out (*CD* 2, chapter 8).

  a. **Paragraph 36**. We find Jesus invigorating our blood and bones as His vigor revitalizes our capacity to respond like never before.
  b. **Paragraph 37**. The power of Jesus' composing and conducting comes together in a way that brings us to our feet afresh—no longer as an audience, but as unashamed participants moved by grace.
  c. **Paragraph 38**. This section heads toward the end of the symphony. Yet it has the character of a sonata, the opening of a new movement. The ending awakens a new dimension of listening and responding never thought possible.
  d. **Paragraph 39**. Rondos pair one theme with a contrasting theme. Here we delve into the depths of human darkness contrasted with the resurrection lightness of Jesus that raises us above the roofs to hear by the Spirit the music of eternity.

COMMENTARY:

- This symphonic overview of *CD* 2 is focused on personally knowing the God who loves in freedom.
- Like any good musical score, it opens with a compelling theme, Jesus, and weaves around Him to the end.
- Barth's work has long held a reputation for its majesty and mystery, echoing from his daily listening to Mozart. This current book lives within this symphonic image.

- In Barth's obituary in April 1969, John B. Logan said, "Loving music, especially Mozart, Barth presented the Gospel as a great orchestral symphony. God's Word was its theme, especially in his magnificent series *Church Dogmatics*. His work forms a symphony of several progressive movements, blossoming into human understanding latterly in works like *The Humanity of God*. Generations to come will find in his writings a quarry for re-statements of the everlasting Gospel."[1]
- Those who follow in Barth's wake have echoed Barth's musicality, including Ray S. Anderson. "It has been said that while other theologians can tell you what Barth *says*, Anderson's lively, pastoral interpretation makes Barth *sing*!"[2] This view provides an appropriate mode for listening and responding.
- Knowing can now be seen as a provision by God, gifted in personal self-giving. We do not know God as an object to be described but as a relating subject to be heard. We may appropriately respond to Him in a symphonic encounter.
- Reality refocuses us from truth statements about God, now pointing us to the actual God who loves in freedom, washing over us with symphonic unity in particularity.
- Election is the amplification of the single rhythmic heart of God that includes rather than divides and excludes. Election is the heart theme of the symphony as it is revealed. This motif picks up from ancient themes. It accentuates the intent of God's "Yes" to humanity so that it rises and falls, appropriately encountering the limits of human existence and speaking to them with His "Yes" that may include His "No."
- *Command* does not mean barked orders. It is more like the attention-grabbing address of God and His loving presence. He calls us all to reenter His meaningful and active life. He sounds forth His intention and conduct, through which He invests in the good of all. He brings His work of love to a finale.

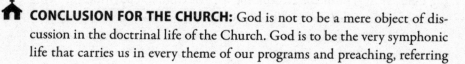 **CONCLUSION FOR THE CHURCH:** God is not to be a mere object of discussion in the doctrinal life of the Church. God is to be the very symphonic life that carries us in every theme of our programs and preaching, referring

---

1. John B. Logan, "Looking Back: Thank God for Karl Barth," *Life and Work: The Magazine of the Church of Scotland*, April 1969, https://www.lifeandwork.org/features/looking-back-thank-god-for-karl-barth.

2. Christian D. Kettler and Todd H. Speidell, introduction to *Incarnational Ministry: The Presence of Christ in Church, Society, and Family* (Eugene, OR: Wipf & Stock, 1990), xv.

us back to God. The doctrine of God should not give us dictionary definitions of God's nature and attributes. Barth expandingly calls the Church to become clear and convinced that God is still alive and at work in dealing with humanity. The Church may think it can use God's creation (the beauty of nature) to begin a discussion about what God is saying to us, but this may be a sleight-of-hand move that reorients the interpretation of God's Word to what interests humans. But God is the theme and the voice of His own unveiling. We need transformation in meeting Him, not information so that we can talk about Him. We must allow ourselves to be apprehended by God so that the Church may find itself in concert with its composer and conductor, who is still at work and calling us to follow.

 INSIGHT FOR PASTORS: As this is *Church Dogmatics*, it speaks to pastors. It calls us to go beyond being sources of information to become vehicles of transformation. This change occurs as people are invited to come, hear, and become involved in God's symphonic life. The developing life of a community of faith needs to meet with a living personal God, not only with humans or our church programs. Rather than learning Christian principles for self-directed living, we must learn to hear that the Creator speaks and gathers His children around Himself.

As pastors, we are privileged to join our people in philharmonic participation, where each person is invited to contribute and listen to others. We must always listen to the prelude of God's electing to be for humanity. This preparation means that in each gathering we must expand on His themes. These become movements of grace that swell through our loving activity in everyday life. Interludes ought to be charged with enthusiasm and anticipation for the continuing symphonic movement of God's life with us. We must repeat God's themes. Creativity must be embraced. Total congregational involvement must be pursued. We do not merely seek an audience with God; we need to get out on the dance floor and move. When the Church lives with the resounding love of God, a reputation for being a people of harmonic love will convey the glory of God echoing out into the world. God is the good news, and He needs to be heard each week and listened to every day.

 INSIGHT FOR THEOLOGIANS: Theological work points to the reality of God in symbols and references that ought to direct us back to the reality of God. In conceiving *CD* 2 as a symphonic work, we see the ebb and flow of themes born of the life of God in Jesus. As theologians, we may gain insight into the construction of Barth's witness, leading to an intricate and expansive presentation. That composed life, like any masterpiece, may become etched in a person's memory. This deep awareness will attune the thoughts and emotions of learners to find consonance with God. As Jeremy Begbie suggests in many of his works, we may do best to pursue theology *through* the arts. This pursuit is especially true when listening sustains human interrelationship, presented to invite participation.

All that follows in this book keeps God as the focus. We share in what God is doing. Theology, as a discipline, moves toward becoming an act of interdependence with God. Theology is not an independent task in serving the academy, our careers, or for writing as spectators more books about God. Theologians are to be virtuosos who know how to feature others, especially God, but also those God gives us who help us focus on the object of our study: Jesus. In this, we give glory to God. We still play with gusto under His direction as we follow His lead.

? CLARIFYING QUESTIONS: Does your theology fill books and create arguments to win a war of truth about God? *Or* does it cause you to keep listening and looking to see what God is doing? Are you oriented to the revealing of His heart in His actions, seeing Him as for us and with us so as to evoke a transformed response?

PART 2

CHURCH DOGMATICS 2.1

Revelation and Freedom in the God-Human Relationship

Karl Barth	Church Dogmatics	I/1	1932 (1936 ET)
Karl Barth	Church Dogmatics	I/2	1938 (1956 ET)
Karl Barth	Church Dogmatics	II/1	1940 (1957 ET)
Karl Barth	Church Dogmatics	II/2	1942 (1957 ET)
Karl Barth	Church Dogmatics	III/1	1945 (1958 ET)
Karl Barth	Church Dogmatics	III/2	1948 (1960 ET)
Karl Barth	Church Dogmatics	III/3	1950 (1961 ET)
Karl Barth	Church Dogmatics	III/4	1951 (1961 ET)
Karl Barth	Church Dogmatics	IV/1	1953 (1956 ET)
Karl Barth	Church Dogmatics	IV/2	1955 (1958 ET)
Karl Barth	Church Dogmatics	IV/3.1	1959 (1961 ET)
Karl Barth	Church Dogmatics	IV/3.2	1959 (1962 ET)
Karl Barth	Church Dogmatics	IV/4	1967 (1969 ET)

CHURCH DOGMATICS, CHAPTER 5

"The Knowledge of God"

STANDING BEFORE THE SYMPHONY THAT CONNECTS

§ 25. *The Fulfilment of the Knowledge of God*

FOCUS STATEMENT: We now enter the grandeur of the Symphony as we engage the first paragraph (§ 25) of *CD* 2.1. We must learn to hear the music and the Voice that fills our listening space. God speaks and sings. We come to listen, learn, and belong.

Imagine being before this symphony of God, playing in the wilderness of the world. Complex crafting has shaped the dynamic, internal structures of the music that washes over us in this divine performance.

Our ears attune to the voice that spoke creation into being. The singing has depth and vitality that is profoundly present. At the same time, it is mysteriously beyond us. Our "here and now" moment is enriched by the composer, who approaches the stage. He has come to guide us into interactive participation. He will not pursue passivity in this event. He facilitates dynamic involvement, awakening all to discover what He intends.

The whole symphony flows from one divine source. The percussion provides the rhythm, complexity, and color of the Father's undergirding contribution within its unity. The woodwind section adds the tone and texture of the personal breath of the Spirit in voiceless expression and emotion. The string section is the most defining section of the orchestra, closely approximating the human voice. And the strings are led by the first violinist—Jesus, our leader in the song and symphony.

This symphony we are about to hear is not in a hall. It has been heard from eternity, before the first day of creation. It is still available for all of creation, as it resonates with the eternal musicality of God. View the image as the beginning of a much broader experience, awakening anticipation as the symphony begins.

Jesus holds our attention. He is "The Fulfilment of the Knowledge of God." He is the visible and audible One through whom the symphony soars across the world. His voice awakens us to enter the space made possible for this intimate encounter. The point of this chapter is to orient us as we stand before God. All that follows is about coming to know this personal God who is ready to be known.

INTRODUCTION: We have finished the prelude to prepare us for the symphony. Now we engage the first chapter of *CD* 2.1, chapter 5, "The Knowledge of God."

This chapter begins with paragraph 25, "The Fulfilment of the Knowledge of God." It aims for deep listening, to hear what God intends for us as we begin to encounter each other.

In knowing God, we seek "the real," exploring that which we encounter. We may not comprehend all that is at work in the complexity we engage, but being where God is available begins our discovering this other who is God.

This first paragraph unveils the juxtaposition of God and humanity. We exist together in actuality and with a readiness to know and be known. God, in Jesus, says, "You are mine," but we are not ready to answer. We fall prey to many kinds of mishandling in getting to know God. We must learn to allow the reality of our knowing to be faithful to God.

God is not just a thing to be known as a silent object; God is a speaking person who opens our ears. He tells us His name that we might know Him as the most personal other, the creator of our personal existence. In the power of His presence, we yield to that which He makes available to us—Himself. In Jesus, we come to know all that is to be known of God.

To study the music and miss its performance and message is to be deaf to it all. With God, reality is finally experienced in hearing the news that we may know, and are already known, by the One who calls us His own.

CONTEXT: *CD* 2.1
Pages in Paragraph: 60 pages (pp. 3–62)

Subsections
1. Man before God
2. God before Man

📖 **TEXT:** § 25. The Fulfilment of the Knowledge of God

OPENING SUMMARY: The knowledge of God occurs in the fulfilment of the revelation of His Word by the Holy Spirit, and therefore in the reality and with the necessity of faith and its obedience. Its content is the existence of Him whom we must fear above all things because we may love Him above all things; who remains a mystery to us because He Himself has made Himself so clear and certain to us.[1]

✠ **SUMMARY:**

1. Man before God (pp. 3–31)

Speaking and hearing in the Church of Jesus Christ is to be attentive to God alone.

In the Church, humans stand before God to know God. But we must learn what it means to listen beyond the empty soundlessness of the world.

The Church left to its own shallow devices could conjure up all forms of faddish images of God to suit its fancy.

Through His Word, God is known and will be known again.

Where God is known, God is knowable.

We begin with concrete realities, not abstract possibilities, when we engage the actuality of God.

When we say knowledge must be *a posteriori*, we focus on what is already established, available for subsequent reflection. This ordering deals first with actualities that might be investigated, such as a person standing in front of you or a natural phenomenon.

To work with an *a priori* method is to have prior commitments in the pursuit of knowledge, as when we say, "It doesn't make sense in light of what I have seen before." One's past defines what is possible. To say, "I do not see God; therefore, there is no God" is based on the *a priori* commitment that the real must be seen.

To ask whether God is knowable is only to pursue a possibility, not acknowledging the actuality of Jesus in history.

Legitimate questions include asking how far God is known and then how far God is knowable.

This section answers how God is known in God's actual fulfillment of God's intention to be known.

---

1. Karl Barth, *Church Dogmatics: The Doctrine of God, Part 1*, ed. Geoffrey William Bromiley and Thomas F. Torrance, vol. 2 (London; New York: T&T Clark, 2004), p. 3. Henceforth, *CD*.

The fulfillment of the knowledge of God takes place in the Church as the Church is bound to the Word of God, the God of the Bible.

We are not free to think of God as the man upstairs or the unmoved mover, as we might casually characterize Him in our imagined thoughts. Those are merely human imaginings. He is not the power in the world, the absolute being of existence, the ground of being, or any other abstract concoction.

Biblical concepts point with clarity to God. Knowing God through His Word is not one among many choices to know God.

We are constrained to be true to the object of our study if we are to make truthful statements.

We are not "free" to choose this or that reality; we are bound to the actualities that present themselves to us.

Since God is the true God, all others who claim to be God will be false gods.

Good apologetics can only build on the actuality of God's self-building; all other foundations are built on false grounds.

To know God is to stand before God and to resist all others.

We can only honestly know ourselves as those with God and cannot truly know ourselves apart from this relation.

We are those who stand opposite God but are not opposed by God.

Only God truly knows God and has access to the full knowledge of God.

We know God in His revelation and thus in a mediated manner. But God, not human capacity or ingenuity, provides the medium.

In our knowing as persons, the Spirit makes God accessible through hearing the Word who has come to us.

The knowledge of God is the knowledge of faith.

- Faith describes the relation of humans to God as God has made actual.
- Having God before us, we are turned to face God; this is faith as a response to the actuality.
- Saying "yes" to reality as it appears before us is faith.
- In saying "yes," we acknowledge that we belong to God because God has called us to Himself.
- Faith describes a specific knowledge of God that is created by God, not humanly constructed.

Faith is an orientation to God created by God.

Biblical faith excludes human, religious self-help.

In recounting the history of God, our faith comes into being. We are sanctified, meaning "set apart" from all others. As those who encounter the coming of God, we are set apart from those who have not. Those who have encountered God's reality "to be for us" are distinct from those who have not.

God knew Godself before human knowing existed. Godly self-knowledge is primary knowledge, faithful knowledge of God by God within God's triune being.

> We must seek God where He has sought us—in Christ.

Secondary knowledge is made possible in that God makes Godself known to us in revelation to another. In this secondary knowledge, God gives Himself to be known by us in a manner consistent with how He knows Himself.

God the Father is mediated to us in the Son who reveals God to us. This mediated revelation is the basis of faith that God has given God's true self to be known by us.

Jesus is the garment of God's objective reality, by whom God is known, and God knows humanity.

God is known in His works but only in the works of God by which He chooses to be known. We cannot select the pieces we think reveal God.

The works of God in Jesus reveal God, unlike the musings or idols with which we clothe our ideas of God, elevating the works of creation as the image of the Creator.

We must seek God where He has sought us—in Christ.

The New Testament is the gracious passing of God before humanity so that God may speak His being as He did before Moses on the mountain.

Only because God shows up to be known can humans claim to be knowers of God.

In the Bible, the witnesses who tell God's story are not stellar or self-confident. They face difficulties that challenge their belief. The God who calls by the Spirit motivates their faith.

What becomes of the person who comes to know God? Having been made distinct by God as one who knows God and as one called, this person is changed because of God's action and direction. They can never be the same—but only because God has come to them.

The human response to the coming of God is obedience as a correspondence to the act of God.

The life of prayer turns us toward the reality of the One who is gracious to us, not to the temptations and idols that turn us away.

The knowledge of God begins with God's voluntary choice to be known and continues with a voluntary response by humans.

The knowledge of God must be bound to God's self-giving, in the specific person where God has made Himself available.

This knowledge comes from God's side—giving—and not from the human side—seeking.

When we say that humans stand before God, we affirm that God has actively come to establish this situation. By showing up in God's unique, personal way, it is God who determines and limits what may be told.

Human speaking can only be valid as a second act, as a response to God's action that acknowledges and confirms what God has said in a manner consistent with God's self-giving.

God opens human eyes to see and know Him. Because of this, humans can know God.

2. God before Man (pp. 31–62)

God is to be loved above all things.

We may love God because He permits us to love Him and authorizes the permission as the intention of His will so that we may be liberated to perform what completes us.

The permission, "may," is threefold:

- God is worthy of our love and will not disappoint us.
- God offers Himself to us so that it is obvious and gives us a reason to love Him.
- God creates the willingness and readiness to love Him.

To love includes wishing not to be any longer without one's beloved other. God is also the One whom we must fear above all things.
The compulsion, "must," is also threefold:

- We must fear God in that we possibly "may not" love God, which would be our end in terror.
- We may and must love and fear God so that there is no other. To love God is to fear losing Him.
- We must love and fear God in that He has willed to be loved and feared, and He holds our existence in His hand.

Love, in this case, must be identified as the basis of fear, in that to lose love is a cause of fear.

When we truly love someone, we fear the loss of them.

Obedience is not a form of slavery; it is the form of a child. It is honest and free obedience to the One who loves us.

Faith is a serious knowing and acknowledging of God's mystery in revelation.

We know our existence only in relation to Him whom we find loving us and who is to be feared.

To say we know Him "in His mystery" is to say we know Him as He gives Himself for our understanding of Him.

Mystery means that He remains the One we know solely because He gave Himself to be known.

Jesus is the light that comes into the world with clarity. He also comes as a mystery, even for those who walked with Him.

To know God is to love God, which is to say we know God knows us.

Having come to know God, it is impossible to turn back to the unreal, the idol, and the shadowy things of this earth.

Because we do not begin with ourselves, we do not end up with ourselves. We end up with Him who has called us to Himself.

When questions arise concerning the knowledge of God, we answer in light of the work of God, before whom we stand.

Therefore, God is known through God and God alone.

It is about Himself that God speaks in His Word. He is revealed as the essence and criterion of truth and reality itself.

In the fullness of God's Word, God turns toward humanity, creating a covenant-making basis for the relation between God and humanity.

God's covenant is created by His Word about Himself, engaged with humans who have turned away from Him.

God is revealed as the Lord, who has the right and might to be the Lord of His covenant.

- He is known as the Creator.
- All belongs to God; humans owe all to Him.
- God is gracious to humanity not for what they deserve but for God's own sake and based on God's unmerited promise.

God's truth is the truth by which all other proposed truth is measured. God stands before humanity as the triune God.

- The Father, Son, and Spirit know each other in the unity of their life.
- We know this internal relation of God by the revelation of the Son.

- Humans become participants in this knowing in a manner impossible outside God's revelation.
- Revelation is not based on humanity's self-evidence, but on the external expression of God's inner truth.
- Primarily and comprehensively, God speaks about Himself. Human knowledge of God is derived and secondary.

Only by beginning with God and not ourselves can we understand how God stands before us. Otherwise, we will only know human words about our experience of God without hearing God.

God shares Himself in the manner He thinks proper to human knowing and partaking in God's life.

Human eyes, ears, and hearts are opened by God's address in a manner not humanly or previously possible before God unveils Himself.

God's unveiling invitation excludes human attempts to conjure images or claims of knowledge of God.

No separate part can be thought of as providing an accurate picture of everything God revealed. Even God's uniqueness, or the person of Jesus, must be considered and known in relation to the entirety of God's revelation.

When speaking of Jesus, either we know Him rightly in relation to all He reveals, or we do not know Him at all.

To say that God gives Godself to be known is the limit to our knowledge of God. Attempts from other sources are disqualified.

In taking on the human form, God veils Himself in a form which He is not, to unveil who He is as God for humanity.

Revelation becomes a sacrament through words, works, and signs—a creaturely knowledge made possible by God's self-provision.

A fuller knowing, a face-to-face possibility, exceeds our present limitations.

As a child begins with partial knowledge of the magnificence of reality, we too have a starting place and grow.

Our knowledge of God grows into knowing who God is. We discover the manner and depth in which we are known and loved by God.

The fact that we know God here and now does not mean that we know Him in the manner that He knows us.

Faith is not an absence of the other for our minds to construe; faith is knowledge of a greater depth to come, knowledge that deepens hope instead of fabricating to fill in the gaps.

God already "sees" us in His true knowledge. We are coming to know God by seeing beyond the reflection—seeing face-to-face, "in person."

We must be clear about the limitations of our knowledge of God as acts of faith based on God's revelation.

1. God allows some of His creatures to speak for Him at particular times and places.

    The most basic form of God's speaking in creaturely form is in Jesus Christ.

    Wherever revelation is given, it points to Him. This is true of prophetic expectation or traditions of recollection in the practices of the Church.

    Based on the reality of Jesus, a sacramental continuity extends from Him back to Israel and forward to the apostolic Church.

    The humanity of Jesus is the first sacrament of the Church. All secondary sacraments are grounded in and point to Jesus.

    When God makes Himself visible through humans, He accepts that He will remain invisible to humans regarding who He is to Himself.

    Faith can see, despite the hiddenness, the intention of God in the act of His self-giving.

    Willingness to listen opens the way to understanding. This is faith seeking understanding.

    The cross is foolish to those who do not believe. But to those who are open to its intent, it reveals the face of Jesus. He becomes for them the light of God. In response, the human becomes a new creature.

    Jesus comes as a stumbling block to those who see a mere man or refuse to see Him at all. The hiddenness of God continues in their thinking even with His openness in the historical revealing.

    The gift of the self-knowledge of God given in Jesus is always a gift of participation.

    We do not create the experience of faith; it is a response to the work and word of God spoken to us.

    Faith does not bring an immediate knowledge of God; it is mediated through revelation that both veils and unveils.

2. God is available, within the limitations of our knowledge of Him, in the sphere He has created.

    Revelation means that God meets us as Father, Son, and Spirit in an inward encounter and even now encounters us.

Consequently, reciprocity of relationship exists between God and His creatures.

God's revelation enables and calls us to live within God's determination to practice life with reciprocity.

In Jesus, God comes before humanity to address us as "thou," that is, as persons, who may address God as "Thou" in response.

Humans, as created "*I*'s," have received provisional *I*-ness that is understood only in relation to the Creator with a measure of approximation.

Humans attempt to observe and reflect on themselves and then approximate what we may understand in others, as though that were a suitable analogy.

Yet we cannot apply human analogies to our knowledge of God, seeking to reverse the order by using our knowledge to understand God.

We may know God, but only as God has approached us and made known what is proper to God's being and intention.

We cannot name God as we name creatures, by corralling them in our categories.

Moses meets God in the burning bush and tries to figure out how to fit the phenomenon within the realm of created things.

The voice from the bush brings the presence of God. God speaks. Moses cannot look, but he can hear.

God comes to call Moses to the task of deliverance from bondage and release to the promised land that God has prepared.

God, revealed as Yahweh, is who He is and does what He does.

Yahweh is the Lord who acts. He gives Himself to be known.

Yahweh will not be reduced to a creature and must be maintained in His *I*-ness as the Lord who acts, which points to His revealing Himself as I.

3. When God gives Himself to be known, He must lower Himself into creaturely time.

Our knowing of God is in creaturely time.

God allows Himself to be known as He truly is, but in a humble, temporal state, and not in the fullness of the way He knows Himself in eternity.

Our time happens in succession, beginning afresh in every present. God's time occurs in the single stroke of eternity. We are not equipped for knowing like that.

Our truth always has a context of temporality. Times are inter-connected. At the center, at the heart of time, stands Jesus.

God has given us time so that we may respond, even though it is a time of sin; hence, our alienation. But God has also given us divine time so that He may have time for us—revelation time.

COMMENTARY:

- As we begin to speak of God, attention needs to be given to distinguishing what is true of God from what sounds good but is false.
- To say that only God can know God and that our knowledge is mediated does not shut us out of the knowing process. It means we depend on God to reveal Himself; we do not build on what seems reasonable to us.
- It is logical to say that we can only know a person appropriately when they give us insight into who they are in themselves and who they are to us. An idol is an image of our own shaping that does not accurately reflect the other.
- When developing a doctrine of God, we are obliged to avoid abstractions based on predetermined suppositions or caricatures that fail.
- God is accessible to humanity but not manageable.
- While the Father, Son, and Spirit have an immediate, divine connection to one another, we humans always live with a reflected image. When we look into a mirror, we see the real thing, but the picture is affected by the reflecting process. This is mediated knowledge.
- To know God is to know that He speaks and to learn to listen.
- We come to a frontier of knowing when we become aware that we need skills and tools appropriate to the task of knowing God.
- Faith is not a human creation or choice. It involves seeing what (or who) is there. It is often mediated; we respond to reality by being aligned to the reality presented to us. The sun does not rise; Earth turns. Earth is not flat; we observe only a fraction, so it looks flat. The world is not motionless; it is spinning at about 1,000 miles per hour. We develop faith through discoveries made from a better point of view.
- God is personal. God can say I. Who He is will be presented in His self-giving address. God can be a Thou, a "who" that we may address. But we must not think He is just another *thou* like us. God can be a He, an object to whom we refer. We must be careful. As an *object* for us, we often think about God in ways that miss the personal God we now find in the Trinity.

CONCLUSION FOR THE CHURCH: God stands before the Church as the God who speaks it into being. As long as the Church sees the source of its life and purpose in this Lord, it will live within the dynamic that allows it to be the body of Christ. But if it listens to other voices that claim to know about God and a godly life, it will build idols and false religion. The Church must fear this false choice. False faithfulness is an act of betrayal to the One who sustains faith and gives it life. The Church ought to not just talk about God in doctrines that become litmus tests of conformity. The Church is called to make known this one living God so that faith is born in the hearts of those who hear themselves addressed and called beloved.

INSIGHT FOR PASTORS: The first thing for a pastor to understand in this section is that Barth is not creating a written faith statement. We are learning to help people know the triune God in a personal way. This learning happens by letting God have the first say in who He is and what He is up to. It means that when we lead a congregation, we are calling people to allegiance to Jesus. This response comes into being because they have let Him speak. An openness develops to let Jesus lead His Church, in which we are servants. We do not just repeat the words Jesus said; we also allow the Spirit to bring those words to speak to the context we are in today. We begin by affirming that God wants to be known and by getting to know Him. Your job as a pastor is to allow God to make Himself known. The Bible reveals God as loving and speaks about who He is to us in our current context. In time, your people's faith will be developed by hearing the voice of God. This encounter creates trust and attunement to this personal God who is always at work. You do not need to generate faith in people. You need to mediate the Word of God so that the speaking God is faithfully heard and encountered. Trust develops faith. The more you know and can speak of God as self-gifting, the more confident your people will be in God because they encounter a God worth trusting.

> Your job as a pastor is to allow God to make Himself known.

 INSIGHT FOR THEOLOGIANS: As a theologian, your task is to know God and what is not God. This first section of *CD* 2.1 prepares you to understand what it means to stand before the object of your study and learn by listening. All the theories and arguments that are standard fare are likely to blur your hearing if you start with them.

Begin in attentive silence. Believe God has spoken concretely. He has spoken in Jesus and the witness of the Bible. Do not begin thinking that

God is a larger version of you. Start a journey of investigation, rethinking who you are in light of what you discover. Begin by shedding or questioning all that has been told you and start over. Ask afresh, "Who are you, Jesus?" Then let Him answer you, correct you, and open new insights. He is as One who opens the heart and life of God, making life fulfilling when shared with someone who loves you. Theology in this mode is a personal adventure. You are a person, exploring a personal God, finding language to invite other persons into this involved kind of knowing. This exploration is a call to faithful, loving connection, opening you to be a theologian. Discovering God, knowing and being known by Him, is to stand before the God of invitation to participation. Following Him fulfills your call as a professional theologian.

? **CLARIFYING QUESTIONS:** Does your theology seek to build a doctrine of God based on human logic, experience, and complex descriptions? *Or* do you begin by clearing your schedule and mind, shedding past claims, to hear from God Himself? Do you want to know what He has been up to, is doing right now, and what He intends to do in the future?

📍 **CHAPTER 7**

THE WELLSPRING OF THE SYMPHONY

§ 26. The Knowability of God

👓 **FOCUS STATEMENT:** By now, we should be getting excited for the grandeur of the music to unfold. It is appropriate to wonder where all this beauty comes from. We enter this paragraph (§ 26) to discover the source—hence, "The Knowability of God."

We want to get the most out of the magic of the music. We want to be ready to soak it all in. We know the musicians have prepared, but we have no idea about the event's origination or nature of those preparations. We want to be ready to hear but cannot imagine what is coming. Fortunately, beauty will do its work in overwhelming us. We hope that our limitations in hearing will be removed and our being will resonate with the music.

The image depicts the composer/conductor (Father) leading the way. His Son (Jesus) is center stage, the first violin leading the flow of philharmonic (love of music) performance, attuned to His Father. The unseen sound engineer (Holy Spirit) ensures all have an extraordinary experience of divinely orchestrated revelation. The unity of the experience resonates from the collaboration within the one God.

All three divine persons were a part of the composition; they now contribute to the performance and make it possible for us to hear. Their collaborative work creates the unique experience of each audience member. God's preparation informs the joy of our participation.

It is hard to imagine, but there are people in the audience with headphones on. Why? They didn't want to be bored or disappointed, so they brought their own music. They are satisfied with previous experiences and are not open to enjoying what is right in front of them. It is a deaf presence—bodily present but checked out.

This section tries to help people remove their soundproof headphones and be ready to listen to the revelation of music itself. Even more, Barth wants readers to be overwhelmed by the persons who are present, making this encounter profound and transformative.

INTRODUCTION: This paragraph is legendary. It includes Barth's confrontation with natural theology, which is when people read their ideas onto God from their observations of nature. Think about someone glancing at you and quickly judging you. Based on their experience and observation, they try to fit you into a boxed category. That is the essence of natural theology. It is a complex form of prejudice—prejudging based on experience, whether good or bad.

In Barth's view, natural theology occurs whenever humans look first at their experience, intuition, reasoning, or perceptions and then say, "God must be like that." One has a wisp of human imagination, of course, made large and loud. But we miss God entirely.

Natural theology often includes concluding that there must be a God because sunsets are beautiful. But taking what is good, beautiful, or true *to us* and then thinking God *fits into those categories* reduces God to our perceptions. Our illusions replace the actual God.

Barth wants us to know that God is ready to be known. He has made Himself known. In Jesus, by the Spirit, He gives us ears to hear. In the Church, we come to meet the reality already given by God. Many want to argue for "reasonable" ways to talk about God. Barth says, "No! Nein!" If we want to know God, listen to Jesus. If we want to know who we are, listen to Jesus.

Are humans ready to hear God? Not by themselves. Humanity is self-focused and inattentive to the God who is speaking. But in Jesus, God has made a way to know and hear God. He brings us to listen to the symphony of heaven.

CONTEXT: *CD* 2.1
Pages in Paragraph: 115 pages (pp. 63–178)

Subsections
1. The Readiness of God
2. The Readiness of Man

TEXT: § 26. The Knowability of God

OPENING SUMMARY: The possibility of the knowledge of God springs from God, in that He is Himself the truth and He gives Himself to man in His Word by the Holy Spirit to be known as the truth. It springs from man, in that, in the Son of God by the Holy Spirit, he becomes an object of the divine good-pleasure and therefore participates in the truth of God.[1]

 SUMMARY:

1. The Readiness of God (pp. 63–128)

The knowability of God is possible because God has come. We reflect on His coming to us in human history.

A backward gaze at actual events is quite different from attempting to find God through our own means.

Responding to God's self-giving is an act of gratefulness. It is obedience in action.

We cannot ask, "Is God really known?" He has given Himself to be known.

We cannot ask, "Is God really knowable?" His being known is based on being knowable.

We cannot ask about abstract possibilities when we have concrete actualities to consider.

The Church's investigation into the knowledge of God must be carefully and critically engaged. It must wisely clarify its speaking about God so that it represents God's speech.

Outside of what God has said, and hence actual knowledge of God, is an empty domain of conjectures and proposals that humans believe may be true of God.

The glory of God is known in His genuine, explicit, visible, and clear expression.

For the sake of the Church, valid expressions of God must shut the door on false expressions attempting to commandeer the conversation.

We know God is ready to be known in that He does not merely stand at the door. He has entered our space and time in Jesus.

God can be known as He has already turned to us in His activity. When He took on human form, He affirmed His readiness and His availability to be known.

God's readiness to be known is not based on a human capacity to know God as just another object in the world.

---

1. *CD* 2.1, § 26, p. 63.

God decided from eternity to be known. We cannot enter the sphere of space and time that exceeds our human capacity. That eternity is closed to us.

God has opened a way from eternity to be like us, among us, and for us.

If we stay within the truth mediated to us by God, we need not fear intruding into God's sphere of self-knowing. We will attend to the sphere of His self-giving.

Dishonest knowledge results from resisting God's truth as though there is a superior and more general truth.

Grace is God giving Himself to be known.

Suppose our human knowledge is occupied with ourselves and not focused on God, knowledge that is resourcing from human nature and projecting onto God. In that case, those thoughts will be mere reflections of the human self and empty regarding knowing God.

Projecting human knowledge onto God is a game for humans and self-deception regarding God.

In the nineteenth century, Protestants got irritated with revelation as they entered an era of disillusionment with the idea of listening to God. But those illusions were built on humanity in its religious forms.

In Jesus, God's being in unreserved good pleasure extended mercy and grace to us and thereby readied us to respond with gratitude.

No idea of a lord that we can conceive matches the magnitude of the Lord, who is over all things in life and death.

In the end, our inadequate analogies point us to our alienated existence. In the process, we exclude knowing God as He is. We fumble with scanty illusions and only think we know God.

Additionally, we lack an adequate analogy to capture the meaning of *God as Creator*.

As the Creator of all things out of nothing, God made the sphere of our existence and the universe—from nonexistence to existence. How can we find a parallel to that?

By excluding God's truth, human understanding defaults to a cosmos that moves itself. But it is not because God is hidden that other explanations are preferred.

We also have no proper analogy for *God the Reconciler*.

God makes peace with the alienated world through His Son.

God overcomes the disagreements that cannot be overcome and heals the wounds that cannot be resolved.

Of His own initiative, God has made peace with us, and all we can do is be thankful without boasting or contributing to the reconciliation.

Finally, there is no adequate analogy for *God the Redeemer*.

Just as God is not the *image we create* of God the Creator, God also is not the Redeemer who perfects all things *as we imagine* them at the end.

Redemption means eternal life as deliverance from eternal death.

Confident, joyful, active hope can only be the work of God the Redeemer.

Our human hopes and dreams, our expectations and ideals, cover over and obscure God's future.

Our sole task is to visualize our being grateful for what is to come from God in the future.

Barth now introduces an unnamed opponent: the Roman Catholic belief that God can be known from created things through the natural light of reason.

But Barth says that God can only be known as the Christian God through revelation as the triune God.

Humans have no ability in themselves to know God outside God's self-giving.

Understanding God as Lord and Creator based on human knowledge rather than that from Jesus is a construction of human thinking. This approach leads to the belief that humans can know God without revelation.

The unity of God as Lord, Creator, Reconciler, and Redeemer must be taken seriously. To say God is logically the Creator and not affirm God as Reconciler and Redeemer is to divert to another knowing and another god.

The Roman Catholic view looks away from and above the God among us and for us. This view holds God as Creator, *affirmed without revelation*, looking to the nature of being and the natural human being before listening to God's being revealed to us.

This is the *analogia entis* debate, attempting to discern the starting point for theological thinking. To know God, the *analogia entis* position begins with analogies from our human experience, the being of the world as perceived through our senses. This is a human-based interpretation of what is available through creation, rather than beginning with what God reveals.

For Barth, *analogia entis* can only be subordinated to *analogia fidei*, the analogy of faith.

With the analogy of faith, the ground of knowledge comes from God and is then apprehended within human experience or being. This ordering is necessary for faithful learning.

As God assumes or takes on human nature, this becomes the analogy (i.e., another word) where God's triune being takes on human being to heal and to clarify the being of God so that we may have true participation in the hearing and responding.

Our actual being is also discovered as we hear ourselves addressed as creatures of God, as beloved children of God.

Jesus taking on human flesh provides for us the analogy of faith (a faithful reflection) of God that becomes and informs our analogy of being (who we are).

Our *participatio fidei* (participation by faith) is based not on human ability but on God coming to us in Jesus.

If, in knowing God, we begin with the *analogia entis* as the focus, looking at the actuality of our human being as the source of knowledge, then we have a problem.

By not attending to Jesus' faithful reflection of the substance of God, we have accepted the "invention of the anti-Christ." This human replacement of knowledge informs our thinking and speaking, instead of listening to God's self-given knowledge.

If we make our human ways of being the context of understanding God's being, we detach our knowledge from God and merely reflect ourselves, calling creation god. This stance is the essence of idolatry.

When we construct a theology that elevates human reason, we echo the making of a golden calf and call it Yahweh—or the use of Greek philosophy and call it the wisdom of God.

Why is it that "God speaking for Himself" is not so clear that it automatically excludes all other attempts to know God, those based on knowledge from human origins?

1. Some claim that knowledge of God is possible and practicable. Is natural theology so self-evident that we are forced to accept it?

   It is undoubtedly possible to practice what is called natural theology. By natural theology, the human attempts to master the world. With this goal of mastery, natural theology succeeds in being a form of control of the natural world.

   But is this knowledge really of the God of the Bible? No. In that scenario, Jesus, the Bible, and therefore the Church of Jesus Christ are abandoned.

   The ability to have a general knowledge of "God" is arbitrarily granted to the natural human with reasoning capacities, as though competence and trustworthiness are a given.

Some kind of knowledge of gods is possible and practicable and can have a certainty to it; it is just not connected to the God of the Bible.

This approach would be a second revelation of God, where we are able to naturally know God from reasoning and experience. Nothing compels us to believe this "natural" knowledge of the actual God is possible.

The actuality of God's given knowability renders a "natural" ability impossible for Christian theology.

2. Is the practical necessity of this form of theology so crucial that we must set aside the gracious self-giving of God to us in the Word and Spirit? Does it serve pastoral and apologetic needs so successfully?

Some offer reasons to introduce "natural" human knowledge of God to the conversation between the Church and the world, hoping to make "contact" with those outside the church, giving them something familiar.

The reasonable individual steps forward to fulfill the duty of love as a natural human. But it is a trap. Natural theology is only a human attempt to master self and world.

This move becomes a game as a preliminary stage to lead the individual to a self-affirmed decision. The human decision commands the field and becomes the focus of theology.

If we must proceed with natural theology, we have to consider all the possibilities for theological thinking. All that is not real must then be laid aside.

The goals are that the actual God becomes knowable and that false thinking is rejected or corrected.

We would never pursue natural theology for the sake of a faithful theology of God. Natural theology leads us to ourselves—what makes sense to me—and not to the living God.

If we become blind to the real God, laying down our own foundation in reality, we become God's enemies and lead people away to another god.

Seeking natural knowledge of God, we keep the real God hidden from the world. We become blind to God.

It is worth asking how we point away from ignorance to a proper knowledge of God for the Church and the world. This is the highest and most comprehensive work of love.

Anselm is not the patron saint of natural theology. He begins with faith, not human rationality. Faith informs rationality and understanding. They are not equal or reversible in order.

Sound theology makes faith intelligible as it speaks to the other.

Natural theology aims to disguise and pretend to share in the ordinary life of the natural human. It is then guilty of falsifying knowledge of God, the unbeliever, the nature of the world, and the heart of unbelief. Therefore, natural theology violates every sense of truth and love for neighbor.

Only one thing can be treated more seriously than unbelief: faith in God.

The knowledge of faith is the consequence of God coming down to our level.

Faith is a witness to our being sinners with nothing to hide. This attitude is a counterwitness to the unbeliever that we take our sinfulness seriously and honestly, not as self-aggrandizement.

We bring love to the conversation with no guarantees; we do not send unbelievers on the way to hardening of their hearts.

Those who claim to need natural theology are wearing masks to disguise their intentions to not believe in God and to serve another master.

3. Suppose that God gives us another way alongside of or instead of revelation. This tactic would be the voice of the knowledge of God "from elsewhere," but somehow seen as acceptable by Scripture.

God is knowable in the revelation of His Word and Spirit as acknowledged through Holy Scripture.

If there is "knowledge from elsewhere," we are released from the authority of Jesus Christ and the Holy Spirit.

This option puts us under the authority of our thinking, pursued without grace, mercy, revelation, Jesus, or the Holy Spirit.

Because the Bible itself does not adequately endorse natural theology, we are not forced to give way to its intrusion.

Some biblical passages raise the question of whether natural theology is possible.

Does the Holy Spirit speak independently from the Father and Son about who God is? Do humans? Does the cosmos? Is an independent voice that truly speaks about God possible from these sources? If not, they are excluded along with their resulting natural theology.

In this independent "natural theology," there would need to be an *immediate and direct* confirmation that it is consistent with revelation.

There would also need to be a *mediate and indirect* confirmation of the witness of revelation based on human capabilities, independent of revelation.

The Holy Spirit is the confirming witness to the prophetic and apostolic word.

There is, in a sense, a "Christian natural theology" that is a preparation, a pointing away, but it is minor. It gives no authority to the person in the cosmos. Having listened to God, it points only with Him to what He has made in the creation. *It does not look at creation to find God.*

The Psalms are sometimes appealed to for evidence of natural theology. Psalm 19 is the first example.

The gospel of the Psalter begins by declaring the glory of God, referring to the exodus and the choice of the patriarchs, Moses and beyond. They do not start with heaven's declaration.

The biblical gospel works from the knowability of God in His revelation. It does not argue from the starting point of God being known from a general revealedness in the cosmos.

The witness of the Old Testament is that no one understands or seeks God; all have become corrupt.

Paul's letter to the Romans confirms the inability of humans to operate independently of God without divine opposition. Paul does not point anywhere but to God's self-revelation.

The unknown god on Mars Hill is the human abstraction that Paul sees as ignorance.

To find a "biblical basis" for natural theology, one must do some severe amputations, cutting off the material from its living source.

The light of God's revelation shines on the world so that it can be seen as the work of His hands. It is all understood in the light of who He is, not otherwise.

The human witness to the glory of God is coordinated with God's revelation. So, too, all creation gives witness in subordination to the speaking and acting of God upon the earth.

God's testimony as Creator is confirmed by humans as the priests of creation on behalf of the speechless voice of creation.

Where many speak wickedly or falsely about God and His relation to creation, we speak faithfully of Creator and creation. This is the work of dogmatic science.

The Bible points to humans in the cosmos, but the universe does not point of its own accord to God.

From whence does the Bible point? Does the prophet or apostle point from their own authority? Do the writers of the Bible have any source other than God to inform their witness?

The "main line" of the biblical witness must come from God and meet humanity as it exists in the cosmos.

God does reach humanity. God's revelation does come to us with God's authority and makes possible human hearing.

When God's revelation engages a human being, the human transforms into a different person.

When the light of God's Word meets a human being's hidden darkness, the truth of humanity and the truth of the cosmos are revealed.

The Bible presents humans as living in the cosmos, the natural world—this sets the context for God to speak to humans in their natural, veiled condition.

Revelation brings light into the dark. Light born from darkness is utterly irrational.

To gain knowledge about God redirects our attention to the God-Man, who is the revelation of God. In His covenant with Israel and as the head of His body, He brings people to participate in and be grasped by God's good desire to be known.

Jesus presents humans as they exist, both beloved by God in Christ and needing to connect with the truth they cannot see.

Humans find themselves surrounded and upheld in the universe, although they cannot see this simply with their eyes.

Job gives us the best answer regarding how to think about interpreting the natural world in relation to God: I need to remain silent and listen to You. You tell me, and I will listen. I will drop all my complaints and construed insights. I repent. You alone hold the truth and reveal as You see fit.

As independent witnesses, humans are disqualified from being right about who we are as we always take ourselves out of context, hence misrepresenting reality.

Seeing true humanity in the cosmos can only point us to Jesus Christ. We become faithful witnesses when we stand with Him, belong to Him, and serve with Him.

Jesus stands as the truth teller about humanity, whom He loved to death and stood for in resurrection. He will stand for us regardless of our response.

Humanity is given a place within God's care as a partner to love and cherish.

The good realm God created for humans is adapted for God's revelation, which is particular as an act of grace—Jesus Christ.

What does Romans 1:18 point to? This verse is often used in favor of natural theology. But it accuses humanity of seizing and subverting the truth that only God's revelation can give.

The theme of the letter to the Romans is not about human capacity; it is about the necessity of God's inbreaking into human history to be known in contradiction to profound human ignorance and its consequences.

The light of God's wrath confronts the shadows of humanity in its darkness.

God's light for the world came to darkened humanity so we could know who we are. He came to reconcile us to our actual being as God's partners, reoriented to know God and ourselves for the first time.

The "point of contact" between God and humanity is God's self-proclamation, the gospel of God's givenness, not human abilities.

The Bible always confronts false sources of knowledge and then points to the living Word of God already given.

4. There may be further questions to be asked.

Why does natural theology continually arise, claiming to be new (even after being refuted) like a weed clinging to the healthy stalk and finally killing it?

Are we willing to accept God's grace? Does the Bible present humans in this state of ready receptivity? *Nein*!

Augustine and Aquinas contributed to the positive side of Christian theology. But on the negative side, they did not prevent the infiltration of "another revelation" via natural theology in their systems of theology.

In the end, natural theology witnesses to how humans are closed off from God and how they prefer to pursue self-sufficiency.

2. The Readiness of Man (pp. 128–78)

The knowability of God depends on human readiness to know God.

Natural theology centers on the problem of human readiness to know God. It elevates humans to an independence that neglects to explain God's revelation.

Humans need the miracle of grace to know God, to be open to this definite knowledge of God, and to be willing to accept this grace.

Out of God's grace comes human readiness, alongside the need, openness, and willingness to know God.

Humans can doubt their existence and live in fear and despair. This state is not living in light of reality; it is living a lie.

An openness for grace, built into the nature of humans, is missing.

The most profound human reality is that God addresses us. Yet we are absent of openness to God's gracious self-giving.

Natural theology is the most robust evidence that the revelation of God is often rejected, and another starting point will be initiated, maintained, and exclusively followed.

The core of natural theology is that "a truth" can be had without having the truth itself. The human believes he has the facts apart from the truth of God and therefore thinks himself the measure of truth.

Humans often want to control everything. They resist being carried or controlled or needing anything from God.

Natural theology goes on to play Monopoly with the truth about God and humans as it takes over the board and defaults to human values and perspectives. If truth is self-evident to a person, why consider another option?

Natural theology domesticates theology to make it fit within the human sphere of understanding. It cannot disturb or transform the human. Like a rude houseguest, God will be asked to conform to the house rules and not speak with confrontation or a call to obedience.

The human now determines what is possible, acceptable, valuable, and able to be accommodated in a manner relevant to human desires and reasonable existence.

We must say "no" to the question of whether humans are ready to know God by themselves, with their capacities alone.

Born again by the Word of God and the Spirit of God, a human may become an obedient child of God by His grace, but this is not a human work.

People will be led astray if they begin with the idea that humans are ready to know God or have an ability waiting to be realized to pursue God. This leads people down the wrong road in the following:

- **Dogmatics.** We make theology into anthropology.
- **Preaching.** We preach something other than the Word of God.
- **Teaching.** It is not scientific; it follows a method of projection, not theological science.
- **Pastoral work.** It directs us to ourselves to heal our problems, separating us from the Healer.

The natural human being strives against grace in the pursuit of reason, self-preparedness, strength, and an appealing human point of view, which excludes the readiness needed to hear God.

Humans create knockoffs, trying to build a bridge to knowing God. All such bridges are cheap imitations and do not even begin to engage the real. Case in point is the golden calf named Yahweh. The idol is an affront against God.

What is the truth from which illusions are constructed about the Christian person? Who is deemed ready for God? When existing as a natural person, we are not ready for God.

We do know a human ready for God, but He is not everyman, although we think we are similar.

There is one human who is ready for God. If that human was revealed, He would bring freedom to all who look to Him. He would grant truth and life, freeing humans from their attempts to know God.

The readiness of humans to know God can only be pursued christologically.

We cannot speak of any human other than Jesus to affirm the proper knowledge of humanity and the human ability to be ready for God.

Humanity is ready because Jesus is ready. God is ready because Jesus is ready. Jesus is the meeting point and the point of meeting.

Humanity stands outside the knowability of God. But God becomes a human and is human. In Him, we are no longer outside but indwell God's life.

To say we participate in God's life is to say that in Jesus we have gained access to hear and respond to God's address.

Jesus has taken our flesh, our hostility, and our rebellion, making it His own to take away all that stands between His Father and us.

Jesus stands before the Father in our place. He suffers in our place. He accepts grace in our place. He is obedient in our place.

Jesus is the human ready for God. Jesus is the real human. If we are to speak meaningfully of human readiness for relationship, it must be pursued through Him.

In every age the Church is called to repentance. That means returning to Jesus, who has been so easily forgotten, and allowing Jesus to once again be the head from whom the body's members draw life.

Every question in our minds regarding knowing God must presuppose and work with the givenness of its answer in Jesus alone.

In Jesus we participate in the life of God, who enduringly was, is, and will be.

Our participation in the person and work of Jesus is the work of the Holy Spirit.

The Bible speaks of the presence in time of the eternally present God, who comes in the outpouring of the Holy Spirit working for us and in us.

All is made alive by the Spirit, including the Church, human persons, and the life of the children of God.

Life in the Spirit is the life of faith. We can already live here because of what He does.

The Church lives by the work of the Spirit and faith in Jesus. The Church is included in God's life in three ways:

1. by the strength of Jesus, who is for us eternally,
2. by the work of the Spirit, and
3. by faith.

Where the Spirit is, there is faith.
Where faith is, there is the Church.
Where the Church is, there are humans gathered in common life.
Where humans gather in time and space, Jesus is their foundation.

With this foundation, humans gather around Jesus for service, hearing, and teaching.

This gathering around His Word is for building up, renewal, and proclamation.

> The Bible speaks of the presence in time of the eternally present God, who comes in the outpouring of the Holy Spirit working for us and in us.

If the Church lives in and for itself, it is a religious community like any other and is against God's grace.

The Church is the historical form of the work of the Spirit.

Because of Jesus, the Church is already the tabernacle of God among humanity. It is through the Church that we come to participate in the person and work of Jesus.

Jesus has accomplished everything necessary for our inclusion; He intercedes for us by His unanimous work with the Spirit and Father.

At first glance, it was not apparent how to assess natural theology. It appeared as no more or no less than a discussion of what is evident to the natural human observer.

But in that natural state, there is no openness to God, and therefore no readiness for God's self-giving in His revelation.

Natural theology is self-justifying as the human asserts that what is known must be based on what is accessible to human experience.

Even in the life of the Church, natural theology domesticates the knowledge of God. In seeking to be reasonable and relevant, it breaks away from lordship to the living God.

We are confronted with a choice in knowing God. We can come to know God in Jesus (revealed theology)—a human who knows God, is God, shows us God, and shows us our state of ignorance. Or we can attempt to look at ourselves to know God (natural theology). This is futile.

Why does natural theology persist with such vitality? It has not shed new light on God. It has not given a better way of learning about God. It has not been shown to have a biblical contribution or approval to exist independently.

If we make the "natural" human with natural theology the mouthpiece of God in church, we set aside the One who is, in fact, the face of God and the head of the body.

We should not look elsewhere than to Jesus. We should not evade the work of the Holy Spirit. We should not step outside the sphere of faith and the Church as they depend on and focus on Jesus.

We may be merciful and understand that natural theology is the only comfort the natural person has in life and death outside of knowing Christ. It is a false, untenable, harmful, and petty comfort to replace the possibility of absolute comfort.

"The illusion that we can disillusion ourselves is the greatest of all illusions."[2]

One thing cannot be granted to natural theology: that it has a legitimate role in the Church. All it should do is disappear. It is an illegitimate voice claiming to speak of God, which it cannot do.

Proper theology can only take Jesus Christ seriously and examine humans as they are known in Him.

The serious work of the Spirit is to point us to Jesus and have nothing to do with any other sources for knowing God.

---

2. *CD* 2.1, § 26, p. 169.

The German Church engaged a new myth in 1933, a masked form of the human spirit knocking on the Church's door.

The Barmen Declaration purified the Church of natural theologies.

The emphasis of everything said in this section is that Jesus has said something. He has said it about Himself: "I am the way, the truth, and the life." The Church lives as it hears the voice of this "I" and chooses this way, knows this truth, lives this life, and goes through the door that is Jesus Christ alone.

COMMENTARY:

- Natural theology is a controversial topic, a result of a human urge to control information and the means to power.
- The reason natural theology is so hard to give up is that it seems so natural to us. We want to use our natural senses to observe the natural world. We easily conclude that God must have been at work in the design and beauty of creation, the development of conscience, and the sense of morality shared by most humans. It all "makes sense" to us.
- Barth argues that God must grant authentic knowledge of God. If it comes from another source, it will be alien and limited, human thoughts foisted onto God.
- Theology helps avoid idolatry. All those elements of the world we call idols, including statues, money, prestige, power, and so on, are objects to which we have given value and acclaim that belongs to God.
- The cultural dream of any people is easily perceived as God's blessing. This idea is expressed in the form of possessions, control, influence, or any set of ideals that serves those at the top.
- Barth was dealing with Nazi Germany when he wrote this section of the *CD*. He had the Barmen Declaration in hand, which was written in response to Hitler. His declaration vowed to accept only One as Lord (*führer*). He would not accept any God other than Jesus.

CONCLUSION FOR THE CHURCH: If the Church in the world today is to remain faithful to God, it must resist trying to be relevant by appealing to the values of the culture. When God is domesticated, meaning being made to fit our comfortable intuitions, the Church loses its focus. We must recognize that the Church is a theological community. It has one task with a million implications. We are to know the living God. This means to know Jesus, His Father, and His Spirit. In this context, we find ourselves as Jesus' body, those brought daily to adore and exist as companions of this God. He brings us to His home, lived within the human experience as His family. We must not try to squeeze God into a temporary seat of honor. With humility, the Church must pursue authenticity in knowing God and exploring life together.

INSIGHT FOR PASTORS: Barth is intent on helping the Church find its proper source and direction by being attuned to God's authentic self-expression and the fulfillment of God's purposes without being laced with human agendas. The problem with natural theology is that it is not good news; it is fake news. It claims to be about God but supports cultural agendas that direct the Church away from Jesus. When we preach, we stand as those who represent the voice of God in Jesus. If we want people to like us, our church, or Jesus because we grant their desires, we crumble into a "deepfake" of Jesus. We claim to be His servants, but we are speaking and giving false information. If we polarize the Church over issues instead of pointing to Jesus, we misrepresent the One who calls us to follow Him. Check your sermons and programs to see if they are intended to give information to better control our lives or if they lead people to listen persistently to Jesus.

INSIGHT FOR THEOLOGIANS: The validity of a science is found in its authentic engagement with reality. Barth finds a widespread deficiency in theology and the Church. The desire to make theology appealing to the modern mind has, in the same act, meant a turning away from the reality of God's self-revelation. The integrity of the science of God is to remain faithful to the One we are coming to know. He is the source for our exploration. Significant figures of the past, such as Augustine and Aquinas, have not guarded the door. For Barth, this has been the failure of theological thinking ever since. Theology has let in a germ that contaminated the lab. As a result, much of theological reflection looks a lot like the cultural context in which it thrives. Jesus becomes a figurehead who is not Lord. He is not the leader of the Church, nor is He the object of discussion in scientific thinking, even though He is the Creator of all the sciences engaged. To be a theologian, faithful to the discipline and to God, one must understand what is at stake in this section of the *CD* or become a servant of some other regime (as happened with the Church in Germany).

? **CLARIFYING QUESTIONS:** Does your theology seek to be reasonable, convincing, or relevant to the needs of the people, intent on selecting what will be attractive to those with whom you work? *Or* is your theology a serious and joyful confession that you are incapable of knowing God outside Jesus, and you are willing to focus on Him alone to know the living God?

CHAPTER 8

ATTUNING TO THE MUSIC OF GOD

§ 27. The Limits of the Knowledge of God

👀 **FOCUS STATEMENT:** This paragraph (§ 27) tunes us to hear God, corresponding to how God has improvised to meet us. We must also know how being out of tune relates to getting in tune. As Barth puts it, the goal is veracity, meaning to be true to someone or something. In our case, to be faithful to God in our concepts is to be attuned to God with integrity.

The image above has the musicians getting in tune, but consider that our ears and hearts also need to be attuned.

The music of God is unique. Our ears and hearts must adjust to discern the majesty and mystery of what is given to us. As we sit in readiness, past symphonic performances may preemptively fill our minds in anticipation of what is to come. Our experience formats us up to this point. What is coming is new and will change everything.

Only in silent readiness may we begin to wash away the past musical experiences and be readied to hear the symphony that is unparalleled by human performances.

As the music begins, we need to release previous conceptions. That way, the complexity, simplicity, and wonder of the musician and His music will awaken us to a new, life-giving, auditory experience. We accept God's provision intended to draw us in. In the process, we discover "The Limits of the Knowledge of God."

We cannot conjure up this experience; it is beyond imagination. We can only respond in thankfulness to what we hear. Possibly more astounding yet, this experience feels like what the "real thing" was originally meant to be.

INTRODUCTION: This third paragraph in *CD* 2.1 clarifies how we may be true in our talk about God. We must acknowledge the limits and possibilities of any claims we make about God.

This section focuses on our inability to speak truthfully about God when our claims are human creations. This kind of mistake happens quite easily because, in some ways, God is not immediately available to human experience—God is hidden in the absolute otherness of God, quite distinct from us. Once we understand this point, we need to listen to the newness that God provides. When God speaks, He speaks as only God can. If we do not listen to God where and how He speaks, we will become mistaken. We will default to old categories and descriptions that are profoundly inadequate to refer to God.

If we do not safeguard our language about God, we will import all manner of false images and analogies. Our substituted concepts will eventually replace God in our thinking. Analogies can provide a bridge if appropriately used. The meaning of the analogy must first arise in the life of God. Only then can an analogy find a derivative and reflected meaning for us. In the sphere of human conversation, to say "a father" is appropriate for our human fathers. But if we say, "God is Father," we must not begin with the idea of human fathers to understand the Father of Jesus. However, having met the Father, we can ask how our fathers reflect the original source of fatherhood. The analogy must be grounded in God. To miss this leads to fashioning God in a human image, and ignoring God.

CONTEXT: *CD* 2.1
Pages in Paragraph: 76 pages (pp. 179–254)

Subsections
   1. The Hiddenness of God
   2. The Veracity of Man's Knowledge of God

TEXT: § 27. The Limits of the Knowledge of God

OPENING SUMMARY: God is known only by God. We do not know Him, then, in virtue of the views and concepts with which in faith we attempt to respond to His revelation. But we also do not know Him without making use of His permission and obeying His command to undertake this attempt. The success of this undertaking, and therefore the veracity of our human knowledge

of God, consists in the fact that our viewing and conceiving is adopted and determined to participation in the truth of God by God Himself in grace.[1]

 SUMMARY:

1. The Hiddenness of God (pp. 179–204)

Barth offers clarifying questions as to where we have come from and where we are.

How far is God known? He is known as far as God knows God and no further. This focus limits our knowledge of God, keeping us from human encroachment in making claims in knowing God.

God is hidden from us because of the unique nature of God; God cannot be grasped outside God's self-giving.

How far is God knowable? God is knowable as far as He makes Himself known in His revelation. The actuality of God's self-giving allows and demands that we recognize God as being knowable.

God's knowability is affirmed as truthful when based on God's faithful self-disclosure. This clarifying is like confirming, "Is this Your Word, and is this what You meant?"

We are asking questions regarding the starting point and ending point for precise knowledge in our theology. In this way, our language will point to God and not our perceptions.

God is knowable as Father, Son, and Holy Spirit. Their revealed life is the basis of a love that comes to us and awakens praise expected of us.

Without a revelation of the reconciliation of God restoring what was lost, there would be no knowledge of God and no doctrine. Consequently, there would be no Church, children of God, human honoring of God, or godly salvation for humanity without these.

The growth of the Church and the children of God find a proper basis in God's absolute, simple, and indisputably certain starting point.

God has spoken; this is the first speaking. Human speaking is a secondary event, which is taken up to participate in the first event.

Human thinking arises when we view objects. Having perceived them, we form images in our minds. We form conceptions as counterimages from reality in the form of images, mirrored mental images that reflect reality.

By arranging and naming the concepts in our minds, and keeping them in proper correlation to the objects to be known, we become capable of expression through words. In this manner, humans may speak of God.

---

1. *CD* 2.1, § 27, p. 179.

We are equally capable of creating images of God in our minds and forming idolatrous images as projections from our capacities. We live with this vulnerability.

Our knowledge of God is not passive. God puts it in our hands, and we work with it. We do not produce it.

We have insufficient means to know God with human capacities. The first act of faith is acknowledging that God is hidden and taking this so seriously that we stop searching. Then we may start listening to God's manner of giving us knowledge of Himself.

When we speak of God as *hidden,* we speak of God, not of ourselves and our capabilities or limits. We are speaking of God revealing to us the absolute *uniqueness* of His existence.

Our task in theology is to understand more rationally that God is incomprehensible.

God does not belong to the set of objects that can be submitted to a process of viewing, conceptualizing, and then expressing in words.

God does not belong to any category or fit any human definition.

We know *that* God is but not *what* He is.

We do not possess, nor can we discover, any attribute in ourselves upon which to build a claim that we know how to think about God appropriately.

What humans can apprehend we come to master and call for submission. Therefore, we become "masters of the world."

Between God and all God creates, there is no unity; creation's existence is distinct from God's existence.

By ourselves, we will never be one with God. By the grace of God, we are made like Him and one with Him.

God is invisible to the physical eye and spiritual eye of humans.

God is not invisible and inexpressible in the same way other infinite, absolute, and indeterminate things are unavailable. His way is always unique.

God is present in the world created by Him. This presence occurs in His revelation in Jesus, in the proclamation of His name, in His witness, and in the sacraments.

The hiddenness of God is a proper asserting of the truth about God.

The hiddenness of God is not a cause for despair. It is the beginning point for fundamental human knowledge of God. It grounds our knowledge exclusively in what was begun by God—His revelation.

Proper knowledge is founded and ordered by God, and this does not cancel His hiddenness.

If we forget the limitation of only allowing God to speak honestly of God, we depart from God.

If we begin in the wrong place, our thinking ceases to be a mirror of God's revelation. "God" becomes a mirror image of our own reflections.

Knowledge of God must be referred back to God as its trustworthy source (God gives), object (God is known), and freely given origin (God gives in grace to be known).

Are we to remain silent in our limitations? No, we are to speak as a deaf person who has been given the gift of hearing and cannot keep from telling of the One who, in His healing, spoke and brought forth our hearing.

God is hidden from us. God is also known and available within the gifting of the Father, Son, and Holy Spirit.

The first act of worship is to give thanks for the grace of His revelation and to confess Him as the hidden One. This gratitude is bold in our humility, to let God be God beyond our control, and acknowledge Him beyond our achievements.

That Jesus was made flesh is the first, original, and controlling sign of all other signs.

The human creature has been commissioned to represent Him, to bear witness to Him.

God's revelation is His condescension to His creatures. That is, He comes to them in the act of His Word in Jesus. His capacity meets us in our incapacity as a pure gift.

God encounters us in the witness of His revelation, in the human form of historical occurrences, and through our relationship to these happenings. We are invited to know Him as the One who has acted toward us in these events and has established our relationship.

The *goal of our knowing* reaches its climax only in knowing God Himself and in faith as our grateful response.

God's goal is that we participate in His life by entering His self-knowledge as extended to us.

Within this context, there is no reason to depreciate human words about God. They simply need an ongoing critique.

Theology can be vain when it is not humble in submitting to God. But when it commits to making the exposition and explanation of revelation its complete task, it becomes profoundly pertinent.

If the Church is to live as the people of God, it must be informed *from* God and finally lead the Church *to* God.

Knowledge of God occurs in an event in which humans are embraced in the bosom of the Trinity.

We need to clarify the biblical concept of truth. Truthfulness affirms the authenticity and validity of knowledge as faithful to the state or process being claimed.

Human truthfulness in being, thinking, speaking, and acting can consist of nothing more than a response to God's faithful way and work, which are permanent, valid, and trustworthy.

God is the truth, and our truth can only come from truth itself.

> If the Church is to live as the people of God, it must be informed *from* God and finally lead the Church *to* God.

We are on a journey as theological pilgrims.

2. The Veracity of Man's Knowledge of God (pp. 204–53)

The veracity, or truthfulness, of our knowledge of God is grounded in God's self-disclosure. We must affirm that veracity is firstly rooted in God's truth and never our truth.

In God's revelation, God lays claim to our thinking and speaking. Our thinking is our responsibility to ourselves. Our speaking is our responsibility to others. In both cases, our commitment is to God, to be faithful to what God has told us.

The veracity of our knowledge about God will make us humble.

Humility before God is not resignation; it is an acceptance of grace and a continual inquiry into God's revelation.

Our truthfulness in knowing comes from receiving from our *goal*, namely from the God we desire to know, who gives us proper knowledge. Also, this actual knowledge is limited from the beginning and acknowledges its *source* in God alone.

We begin in the veiling of the hiddenness of God and end with God unveiled in Jesus, a goal witnessed in the Bible.

In what ways do we participate in the truthfulness of our knowledge of God?

1. We participate in God's revelation by giving thanks. God evokes this gratitude.

   We offer thanks as a sacrifice, participating in the faithfulness of His being. He calls out the best in us as we are reordered by His revelation, acknowledging His self-giving.

Thankfulness that has dread, constraint, restraint, or is forced is not the true sacrifice of thanksgiving.

We come to God not as slaves but as children filled with exuberance.

2. We participate in the truthfulness of God by acting with wonder and awe.

Participation is a consciousness that cannot stand back and observe.

This is not amazement at ourselves for the clarity of our thinking and speaking. Astonishment comes as the force of God's presence impacts us; we are compelled to wonder.

As a result, we speak because God has enabled us, not because we are wise and crafty.

Awe refers to a recognition of the immense difference between ourselves as knowers and God as known. We sense the magnitude of the absolute difference between God and humanity.

There is a positive relationship between our views, concepts, and words in relation to the reality of the God whom we hope to know.

If this relationship is negative, there is no relationship between God and humanity. Revelation would be denied. Grace would be empty. Faith would be baseless. We would not be participating in the truthfulness of God's self-giving.

We are quite aware of the meaning of words when applied to humans. Objects, emotions, body parts, and so much more are naturally a part of the sphere of our existence.

Do our words mean the same thing when used of God? No.

We know God by the means given to us, or we do not know Him at all.

The concept of analogy may be used to bridge the two fields of use—the divine and the human.

Analogy means similarity, a restricted correspondence, and agreement—with the exclusion of the problematic mode of natural theology.

The truthfulness, origin, and constitution of an analogy must rest in God alone.

The similarity of God and humanity, expressed in human words, is a form of human participation in the divine way of life as revealed in God's revelation.

Analogy must be explained as God's Word coming to meet us,

selecting human words to which we then attach ourselves in responsive obedience.

God is pleased to be known within the limits of our comprehension.

God first lives in the way of being true to Himself. Second, He is for us and becomes involved in our work and way of being. He is the same person in both instances.

We cannot reverse the relationship, to make what is human apply to God.

The words *father* and *son* are not valid of human generations first. They are first terms of the Father and Son in the Trinity. All human uses are derived and secondary.

Secondarily, we can understand *our truth* as the reflection of *His truth*—the analogy is one of the relations of reality and its reflection.

The words that form in our mouths have contact with the reality of God because He has enlisted them so that they may serve in our participation in the truth—this is a resurrection of words, a miracle of God's doing alone.

When we think that analogies can give proof or knowledge of God without revelation, we abandon their faithfulness to God and look to the inadequate capacities of the human—this is the error of natural theology.

There is genuine correspondence between our words and the being of God. However, there is also a necessary limit, if we are to be faithful to our task.

An analogy is not a ladder of knowledge by which we climb to God; it is more of an auditorium where we acknowledge with listening hearts the speech and acts of God. Our language follows from what is heard.

God is One. This unity of being does not correspond to any set of human definitions, qualities, or characteristics.

All knowledge of God begins by acknowledging the hiddenness of God and then receives the grace of God given in His revelation.

The gospel is a witness to a restoration in which God brought alienated humanity to know God. He brought humanity back to love Him, the hidden God who becomes unveiled, known, and reconciled in this revelation.

In a *univocal* analogy, one word appropriately bridges two fields. Think of the word *love* as applied to God and to humanity. God's love is radically different, yet we use the same word; they are not univocal because God's love is essentially distinct. The urge to make our terms of God mean the same as our terms of humans is the origin of much of our confusion.

The analogy of love is *equivocal*. This means that the same name or word may be used to describe something, but what it refers to is different. For example, Jesus is human while remaining Creator God, and we are humans as creatures, reliant on God's grace. To use the word *human* in both cases is equivocal. They are not equal.

God is Spirit in a unique, uncreated manner; humans exist with a created spirit.

Analogy, properly applied, refers to the same thing occurring in two different objects in different ways, giving insight from the original to the derived.

In an analogy of attribution, the similarity consists of the common element properly existing, first in one object and secondarily and dependently attributed to another.

This analogy of attribution is not a general concept; it is specifically theological. It refers to the language of the relation of God and humanity. We must begin with God's revelation for a proper beginning.

We begin on the wrong path if we insist that our understandings be firstly acknowledged when studying the "being" of what is other than ourselves.

God is not a part of the "being" of reality. If we claim so, we then diminish God as only sharing in reality rather than creating it. "Being" cannot be the bridge to knowing God as though we both share the same nature.

The return to a doctrine of *analogia entis (analogy of being)*, as in Roman Catholic and liberal Protestant theology, is a return to the flesh pots of Egypt (see Exodus 16:3). The analogy begins with human experience and not the provision of God.

Grace is God's determination to be oriented to us. The analogy of grace begins with God's self-giving in Jesus, who speaks to our experience.

Our orientation, regarding the relation of God to the human creature, is established in the Bible.

Our task is to know God through human strategies and to explore how successfully we can (1) have our concepts be of *God,* and (2) have our concepts be *true.*

Knowledge of God is actual and possible. But is this knowledge of God circular?

Our faith has its origin in God. Its establishment, limits, and possibilities come from Him alone.

If we dispense with faith, what can God do when He finds us with ears and eyes shut? He can leave us to our frivolous self-questioning, self-criticism, and doubt.

In acknowledging God, confidence grows in our faith, which must come to us and not be created by us.

We cannot grasp after God to create certainty for ourselves. He has grasped us; in faith we accept His embrace.

Any systematic approach in experience, organization, logic, or reason that we think will help us know God becomes a substitution for faith.

Our line of thought can only be valid as the consequence of trusting in Jesus.

Jesus is the place we meet with God and know God.

In the dynamic unity of the Father and Son, fulfilled and expressed in the grace of the incarnation, we come to authentic knowledge.

What is temptation? It is the urge to question God and turn away in self-work instead of faith. Jesus has endured this and set it aside on our behalf. He has become our judge.

We are called to accept the validity of His taking our place. His judgment is set against claims to consider our work in faith.

What is comfort? It is the confirmation of the good pleasure of God that has come in Jesus Christ that does a work in us. It means He is our Savior.

Jesus gives us living faith, awakening it from the dead, to acknowledge and affirm our being made right with God, which we cannot do ourselves.

We must believe *in* and *with* the risen Christ. He has restored us to the Father and brought God's comfort.

The correctness of our line of thought is answered in Jesus. He is the place and the limit of our knowledge of God in truth.

COMMENTARY:

- Proper theology is not given in proper doctrines alone. Doctrines merely point to the living God. Unfortunately, we may end up with shared ideals, but miss hearing them from God.

- Improper theology is not theology at all. It is often a set of human values and ideals projected onto God. This projection is the "known god," an echo of ourselves who would "do the right thing," value as we value, and fits us like a glove. He becomes the personification of what we hold dear. This impersonation is not God; it is an idol made in our image.

- This paragraph in *CD* is all about getting knowledge of God in a pure form. By doing so, we avoid a God who is more of a cultural icon than the God revealed in Jesus.

- In trying to make God "reasonable," Barth recognizes that natural theology is attempting to employ human reason to talk about God. We speak about justice, the conscience, or love *as we know it*. Then we show that God has these concerns as well. We neglect to recognize that these terms could either refer to what is genuinely true of God or arise from entirely human concepts. The latter is the most tempting option by far.

- When we say that God is hidden, we do not mean to say God hides from us in a game of hide and seek. Instead, we are pointing out that the Creator of the universe is not physically accessible for observation like a rock or a neighbor. But God has come in space and time to know and be known.

- The clarity and purity of our thoughts about the Christian God have been sacrificed on the altar of pragmatics. Humans are more interested in God working in their lives than knowing the heart of God. Thus, God has judged us as self-seeking sinners and chose to act by saving us.

- All faithful thinking about God must come from Jesus. Knowing Him is the goal. Everything else remains hidden; what is known of God is limited within the sphere of His self-giving.

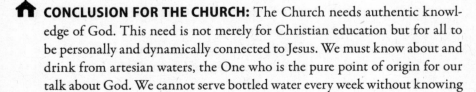 **CONCLUSION FOR THE CHURCH:** The Church needs authentic knowledge of God. This need is not merely for Christian education but for all to be personally and dynamically connected to Jesus. We must know about and drink from artesian waters, the One who is the pure point of origin for our talk about God. We cannot serve bottled water every week without knowing its source.

People may want relevance in their sermons, with the message focused on them. But in that quest, the result will be an abandonment of Jesus speaking in the Church. "Fitting Jesus into our lives" corrals us to format our sermons to meet the needs of a tradition or our congregation. In that mindset, analogies easily begin with human values and stories and then connect with God. The classic example is family. We want good families (as God values). But they usually end up looking like the ideal of our culture, where "good kids" follow the rules and become successful as measured by human standards. Considering what it means to be part of God's family as revealed in Jesus is largely unexplored. Our knowledge of God and our faith response have been hijacked in their source, goal, and methodology. We must learn all over again the corrective limitations of knowing God, or we will produce cheap imitations and miss the real thing.

 INSIGHT FOR PASTORS: There is a difference between seeing Jesus as the "friend of sinners" and seeing Him as a "buddy for the neighborhood." In the first instance, Jesus shows up as God with His agenda to bring people to know His Father. The hidden God is to be known in presenting Jesus and creating a community that comes to learn from Him. He is truly a friend of sinners, who deems them worthy of reconciliation.

In the second instance, we make Jesus into a person who shares the interests and agenda of the neighborhood's people. He defaults to their interests. If you love motorcyclists, Jesus is a leather-wearing road warrior. If your neighborhood is garden focused, you talk about Jesus and gardens. In these cases, we have collapsed Jesus into the interests of the people. Jesus loves motorcyclists and gardeners, but only in seeing them as beloved, without the alternate identities.

A pastor is called to filter out hijacking human beliefs, such as self-sufficiency, self-empowerment, or living a life where blessings are all about acquisition. If one filters out what conforms us to the world, then the focus for the Church's mission statement can be formed around faithfulness to Jesus. We stop thinking that the best definition of success is counting the people in the pews and collected dollars. Instead, we help people become attuned to the person of Jesus and follow the lead of the Holy Spirit in making real connections and allowing an authentic life of response.

INSIGHT FOR THEOLOGIANS: Each of the sciences needs to clarify the source of its knowledge, as well as the goal of its discovery process. Suppose a lumber company offers to study the forests surrounding a community. One might ask if they are committed to agendas representing the good of the people in stewardship or if they are driven by self-interest.

Likewise, in theology, one can easily find a history of theologians who were attempting to present God in a manner that would appeal to human concerns, a standing tradition, or a reasonable approach that fit the philosophy of a people. They affirm the idea of humans taking control of their lives. In these cases, the theologian has defaulted to serving humans and not the God revealed in Jesus. This problem was the case on the black day when Barth's former teachers marched in support of a German agenda that had little to do with the Jesus of the Bible.

A theologian must learn what to filter out and what is a proper theology by determining its appropriate source. One must bring people to a genuine sense of knowing and being known by God. If we miss this step, our trajectories become political, philosophical, and heretical, having started by heading in the wrong direction.

? **CLARIFYING QUESTIONS:** Does your theology seek to help people believe that God is reasonable and relevant *or* to discover afresh the God revealed in Jesus? Do you always start with what Jesus is doing to facilitate the mission of the triune God?

CHURCH DOGMATICS, CHAPTER 6

"The Reality of God"

📖 **CHAPTER 9**

THE MUSIC BEGINS: SONG, DANCE, AND COMMUNITY

§ 28. The Being of God as the One Who Loves in Freedom

👀 **FOCUS STATEMENT:** This paragraph (§ 28) gives us the melody line for all that follows. This melodic tune of God cannot be merely hummed. This is the love of God as the music of God, God's own singing of the song that He uniquely sings in Jesus.

The singer and the song are inseparable. The melody does not merely create emotion in the present moment. This outpouring is God's music that creates the world. It is the personal harmony of Father, Son, and Spirit. Their love in action freely causes God's handiwork to come into being. It sings with "The Being of God as the One Who Loves in Freedom."

The love of God moves all God's children with all their being and with one another. This freedom may be imaged as a dance of loving response.

God's dynamic song moves what is other than God. Creation responds to the love God freely sings. This transforming movement by God sustains and liberates what God creates. The world resonates with God's freeing grace carried in the Song. There is a clear danger that what God has created could pursue dissonance. With closed ears, humans may seek a "freedom" from God that arises from and limits itself to human hopes and desires.

When God's internal singing—as personal, creative harmony—extends to His dancing people, it creates community. These are people formed to experience God's freedom as a gift by His gift. Thus, community cannot merely be an idea or a theory. He transforms His children through the exercise of His loving way of being, freeing others for love—God's unique love.

INTRODUCTION: This paragraph begins our excursion into the reality of God as defined by God. This investigation requires us to lay aside dependence on the senses and human understanding in pursuing "reality." It asks the reader to respond to a reality that is God-given in the person of Jesus Christ: God in action, or we might say, God in actuality. *God is*—this is a basic entry into all that follows, giving meaning to all other existence.

In Jesus, God acts in the world with His character of love. We cannot default to other ideas of love to understand Jesus. We must let the activity and self-giving of Jesus fill out for us what *love* looks like, especially if we are to use the term of God.

> We must let the activity and self-giving of Jesus fill out for us what *love* looks like, especially if we are to use the term of God.

Finally, in this section, God's love does not try to fit any logic as to *why* God must love. God loves unconditionally and, hence, freely, expressing the very character of God's being as Father, Son, and Holy Spirit. This commitment to clarity requires that we shed conditional forms of freedom. True freedom brings the fulfillment of love. This freedom is distinct from the world of "freedoms" that bind and imprison humanity. God's personal being is the origin of love that ultimately frees humanity, fulfilling that love.

CONTEXT: *CD* 2.1
Pages in Paragraph: 65 pages (pp. 257–321)

Subsections
1. The Being of God in Act
2. The Being of God as the One Who Loves
3. The Being of God in Freedom

TEXT: § 28. The Being of God as the One Who Loves in Freedom

OPENING SUMMARY: God is who He is in the act of His revelation. God seeks and creates fellowship between Himself and us, and therefore He loves us. But He is this loving God without us as Father, Son and Holy Spirit, in the freedom of the Lord, who has His life from Himself.[1]

---

1. *CD* 2.1, § 28, p. 257.

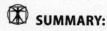 **SUMMARY:**

1. The Being of God in Act (pp. 257–72)

God is.

This short sentence speaks volumes. First, it talks about the *specific God* known in Jesus as the Trinity of Father, Son, and Holy Spirit.

Secondly, the *is* refers to the concept of being, to have existence, a very particular actuality.

We must proceed with a clear remembrance that only God can provide knowledge of God. It is made possible by God alone (and not humans). It is limited to what God makes known (and not any human capacity to know).

The Church has a commission to serve in its own sphere as a science. It lives by listening to the object of its study, acknowledging one simple fact— God is.

The Word of God uniquely reveals the actions and workings of God, asserting that God is and how far God acts.

We cannot begin by looking at the benefits of knowing God or investigating a general concept of God.

God is who He is *in His works*. His works are bound to Him.

But God is who He is *without His works*. Their existence depends on Him; His existence in no way depends on His works.

While God reveals Himself in His works, He is distinct from them, and He remains superior to them.

God has not withheld Himself from humanity. He has given Himself to overcome human neediness, coming as the Father in His own Son by the Holy Spirit.

Humans, as sinners, are called back to God from their wayward journey. He desires that humans answer His call, discovering that He is the source of life, comfort, and love who has power over all things.

God's act is His revelation, proclaiming His reality to be for us within His own proper life.

God's being is life. The voice of the living God is our starting point.

The work of the living God, as well as our share in worship and fellowship with the living God, offers the only adequate means to fulfill the task of knowing God.

The Father has life in Himself and gives His Son to be the author of life. We are brought to share in this divine life by the Holy Spirit.

God's revelation is a particular event; it is not identical with any other event in human history.

God's action is a specific action, one that is different from human actions.

God is separated from all other actualities, and yet He is connected to them.

God is both present to the phenomenon of the world (immanent) and separated from it (transcendent).

God is not dependent on what is other than Himself.

Metaphors that describe God and God's attributes often use content based on human experience, shaping God into human perceptions. This approach is called anthropomorphism—shaping God into the form of human experiences and ideas.

We must cleanse the meanings of words intended to speak of God. We must make sure they are not unsuitable, plastering false definitions onto God. With careful preparation, we are ready to speak of the triune God and not unconsciously speak of other beings.

The genuine person is God. We as humans are impacted and transformed by God's "personalizing," which brings us to live in response to God's decision and act to be for us. Only God is entirely a person; we are being made persons in Him by His act.

Our task is now to apprehend the quality of His livingness as seen in His revelation.

2. The Being of God as the One Who Loves (pp. 272–97)

True statements about God must be linked to the fact that God is who He is in His act. God's actions must grasp all our thoughts to inform our being and not allow us to collapse into self-contained illusions.

If we begin with the word *love* and human concepts attributed to this word, we will have abstracted the word to mean whatever fits each person.

To generalize is to make an abstract. Therefore, we must be very specific with terms where God uniquely gives meaning to the term. Each word must be distinguished so it applies originally and appropriately only to Him.

The act that becomes visible to us is God's revelation, from which we may discuss what God is and how He is in the world in the way He is manifest to us.

This God freely creates and seeks a relationship with us.

God wills that we belong to each other. He does not will for us to be without each other.

There is death and damnation within the scope of His relationship with us, but His attitude and action always seek to connect us.

God does not will to exist for Himself or alone. God exists as Father, Son, and Holy Spirit, fully alive in this unique being with and for and in another.

God receives us into fellowship with Himself through the Son. This reception is God's blessing for us, and there is no more excellent gift because God has nothing greater to give.

In defining God's loving, we must begin with the specific act that reveals God's essence in expressing love.

We must resist any counterfeit or general idea of love to substitute for the real.

If we say that God is love, as we ought, we must also resist the idea that love is God. Only when love is mediated, expressed, and performed by God on our behalf is it genuinely love, clearly identified with God.

We must clarify and explain the love of God in the light of God's being.

1. **God's loving is a giving of Himself.** It is not just seeking love for its own sake, but in God's act, He gives us everything *in Himself.* All other love flows from His loving.
2. **God's loving is not conditional.** We need not measure up to any standard or reciprocate God's love for His love to be given to us. He does not love us because we are lovely or loveable.
3. **God's loving has its source in God's being.** Love flows from God, and its goal is in His good pleasure. God is not bound to a higher reason than His love.
4. **The only necessity of love lies in God Himself.** He is not bound to higher principles or decrees. Nothing outside God requires or compels God to love. God wills, in His love, to be for the other, for us, and not only for Himself.

"God is" means "God loves."

The loving being of God centers our exploration when we work out the attributes of God.

God is a person as One who has His being in His act. God informs us what a person is—He acts as a person.

A person is a knowing, acting, willing I. God loves uniquely in this manner and is, therefore, *the* person.

Humans become persons based on being loved by God and loving God in return.

To be a person is to be what God is as one who loves in God's way.

When we speak of humans as persons, we speak as an echo of what God is in reality.

The only One we can honestly know as a human person is Jesus Christ.

God is not something but someone, who therefore reveals the personal nature of God.

To speak of persons within God's being, we must begin with the Trinity. We must resist all manner of human constructions that precede listening to God.

In the nineteenth century, discussion regarding persons departed from the school of Scripture and entered the school of heathen antiquity.

God was depersonalized and elevated to a philosophical ideal, a conceptual absolute that lost touch with the personal God revealed in Jesus.

Understanding God's nature went through an inversion. Rather than understand humanity from God, humanity became the focus, and God became a derivative of human reason.

For Hegel, God's personality became the highest good, the spirit we know as the highest rationality in the conception of humans, known by looking at the self as a person.

The Enlightenment influenced intelligent persons so that they became locked into an abstract world of ideas created by reason. On these premises, Romantic and Idealistic opposition to exploring the actual personality of God could not be avoided. Concepts replaced the Creator.

With this mistaken approach, God simply came to be understood as the content of the highest human values.

Feuerbach acknowledged that rationalists create god in their own image, whom they then worship, imagining their creation as a being independent of their thinking.

To experience God as "personal" became a manifestation of subjective feelings, losing touch with the real God. That approach abandoned the objectivity of God, the very One who came in person to be known.

The neo-Protestants of the eighteenth and nineteenth centuries tried to create a rational God. This method was a path toward paganism—life without the actual God, pursuing a creative imitation until God became unnecessary.

We do not simply proclaim that God is a person but make known the particular person He is.

We must not make the mistake of thinking that there are three separate personalities in the Trinity—there are not three egos or separated subjects in the Trinity.

We reject all tritheism. We affirm that within the one God, God exists in three ways.

As Father, Son, and Holy Spirit, God is this One who lives and loves. As one God, He meets us and addresses us as Thou.

There are not three faces, wills, words, and works: One is revealed to us in Jesus.

This One triune God is the personal God.

3. The Being of God in Freedom (pp. 297–321)

God's being is uniquely His own; He does not share in a larger field of being.

God's act is His own; it is not motivated from anywhere but God Himself.

God's love is His own and self-sourced, not compelled to respond to any other thing.

The uniqueness of God is the one thing we must affirm and respect.

Clarifying the vital distinctions, we must carefully dismiss any presumed, general, or universal knowledge of God.

Our full attention must be concentrated on God's revelation alone. Otherwise, we will speak of what is not God but appears to be proposed as God.

In asking, "What is God?" we must recognize that God is not an *it*, a thing to fit into any category of being.

We may ask, "Who is God?" God is a subject who may answer our question in self-revelation of His mystery.

There is no necessity, requirement, or obligation in the loving being of God. He is free in love for His creation and creature.

Freedom is more than the absence of limits, restrictions, or confines.

In its proper quality, freedom is self-moved, unlimited, unrestricted, and unconditional being and acting in love.

The *I Am* is the free Lord of the Bible. He alone is God, and besides Him there is no other.

God is pleased to establish and maintain fellowship with His created reality. Therefore, He may be present within His creation, acting with His characteristic freedom to love what is distinct from Himself.

God's freedom is unique to Him. It is constantly displayed through His good pleasure to have and hold this sphere of reality other than Himself. To this sphere, He grants its own created form of freedom.

No need or necessity causes God to be. He exists freely with no external compulsion.

God is free from origination, conditioning, or determination from outside Himself, by any other than Himself.

God's freedom is understood primarily as the freedom to be Himself.

God's freedom can be understood secondarily as the freedom to relate to others.

God is independent of all other things. All other things are related to God and to each other.

Every external relationship into which God enters must be interpreted as occurring between two utterly unequal partners.

The second partner (humanity) can have no determination in affecting the first (God).

However, God's self-determination does not override the self-determination of humans. It is God's choice to act in sovereignty for this second partner, to grant them freedom.

God has not determined to be synthesized with the universe in any form of *pantheism* (believing God is identical with all reality). He is distinct from it and sustains its very existence.

God has not determined to be the "spark of life" in creation. He cannot be identified with what He creates in any form of *panentheism* (God as interrelated with the world's being). It takes elevated human ideas about what is spiritual and names it *god*. Pantheism and panentheism can never lead to the Christian God.

To say that God is absolute affirms that He is separate from the world in His being and acting. This distinction does not prevent Him from initiating a relationship with the world.

God has the freedom to be present to that which is not God. He can communicate and unite Himself with the other (His creation) and the other with Himself.

God has the freedom to be *immanent* in the world, *present* in a way that is impossible for other beings.

There is always a tentativeness in how created beings relate to each other, communicate, and make promises to each other.

There is no true *transcendence* in these relationships, no freely and unreservedly *going out to meet the other*.

True immanence is also missing. This may be described as the ability to achieve a unique inwardness that is with and for the other from an authentic being of the heart.

God can indwell His creature as its Creator and Giver of life. He gives His presence to those who are different from His life.

God will not detach Himself in aloofness. With His eternal faithfulness, He is present in a manner of which no other creature is capable.

God is free to work within what we call the laws of nature, or outside them in the form of a miracle.

In God's revelation in Jesus Christ, He meets us in a manner that embraces all the contradictory possibilities imaginable by us—all things lie within His possibilities.

It is not appropriate for us to imprison God within the limits of human reason. That creates an idol.

Scripture recounts all the various modes with which He has engaged the world from Creation to promised Consummation. This recounting includes His speaking through the prophets, apostles, and life of the Church.

The *primary freedom* of God has its reality in the inner life of God as Father, Son, and Holy Spirit.

In the mode of the Son, the *second form of freedom* comes to humans. He approaches us as this One who shares the divine communion as an extension of the original freedom.

Before all worlds, the Father extends otherness in the Son so that His loving freedom is from eternity to eternity.

The Creator became a creature so that there could be a relationship between God and the world. This connection is the highest form of all possible relations.

In the freedom of Jesus being for us, we see the meaning, norm, and goal of the loving activity of God with humanity.

Jesus is the one work of unvarying wisdom. In the abundance of His life, He wills one thing—ordering all things for the life and healing of the other.

The world's religions come about because they do not or will not acknowledge the ground of divine presence in Jesus. Christian heresies spring from the same neglect.

The legitimacy of every theory regarding the relationship of God and humanity can be tested by evaluating whether it is an interpretation of the relationship created and sustained by Jesus Christ.

God's being is independent from theories. God's being is in Himself as freedom in love.

God does not have or fit into the category of love as an idea; love is the very act of His existence.

God does not first live and then love. God loves and in this act lives. Living is the freedom to be Himself.

The *event* of revelation has a natural, bodily, outward, and visible component. This event is seen in the history of God from creation through to the resurrection of the body.

What we call *spirit* is no less a creation than what we call *nature*. When we describe the nature of spirit, we cannot think of it as an exclusion or denial of nature.

The connection between the spiritual and the natural world depends on the proper place and proportion of the spiritual to biological reality. This connection is implied when we think theologically of God as Father and Son and of ourselves as children of God.

The nature of God must be allowed to be seen above the categories of spirit and nature. They must also be seen to overlap and comprehend our nature.

Acts happen in the unity of spirit and nature. If this unity is denied of God, then there can be no true history of His doings. We would exclude the decisions and workings of God. We would eliminate God's revelation and reconciliation. Creation and redemption could not be regarded as God's decision and true happenings.

The freedom of God is known in the event, act, and life of God in His revelation to humanity. This is the freedom of the Spirit in knowing and willing in the particularity of being a person.

The peak and point of revelation is that God speaks as an *I* and is heard by the *thou* who is addressed.

We must be careful in discussing how spirit and body exist in revelation. We will not be describing reality if we divide spirit and nature, inner and outer, soul and body, in any dualism that splits and separates.

We reject false spiritualizing (rejecting nature) and false realism (dividing the natural from the spiritual).

God's nature must be understood as *being-in-person*. This concept is not the same as a personified being. It maintains the unity of spirit and nature, with superiority of its spirituality and inferiority of its naturalness.

God is always an *I* (spirit) and never an *it* (natural).

Natural being, the being of objects, are unmoved by themselves.

Spiritual being, in distinction from nature, is an unobservable and incomprehensible being.

God is a self-moved being and self-motivating. This assertion is not about an abstract unmoved mover or deistic power outside the universe. God acts freely in love as the act of His very being.

God has no larger context or source of movement than Himself.

Our viewing and conceiving of nature and spirit is a human work. All science is a human construction that results from engaging the world.

When we, as living beings, are subjects perceiving the world, we are functioning as spirits. Our perception is a concrete embrace of what surrounds us.

Nature, then, provides a tangible, material structure of what appears as real. Spirit provides the form, as formulations and meaning ascribed to concrete reality.

We must not confuse the self-moved being of God with our human being or our sense of self-movement. Nor should we think that God is a more complex version of our existence.

Kant built on the idea of the rational capability of humans as the necessary presupposition for reasoning about God's being and pure reason. But this is no more than a program of exalting the human and calling the outcome "God's," all while speaking strictly about humans.

Hegel appears to speak of God and the process of absolute spirit. In the end, his description of the movement of nature and spirit arises from and returns to ourselves. This proposal is veiled humanity being projected onto eternity.

Schleiermacher speaks of God as the ground of our self-consciousness and our absolute dependence. He takes little notice of God's self-moved force engaging us and instead proposes a self-made Christian self-consciousness. With this move, the human usurps the being and place of God in Christian belief.

In proper theology, we are not left with our thoughts and ideals. We encounter God's promises, grace, and commandment—set apart from fragile, human foundations.

God's work precedes our work in such a way that we may follow in it. But for the setting right of all things and the fulfillment of the covenant in God's work—only God is needed. All is grace. However, we may be moved by His grace.

God personally wills to act in an executed decision initiated in eternity. He also acts afresh in every moment of our time.

All human sense of self-motivation is sin at work, an illusion of our humanity as self-contained, self-moved beings who think about the world's reality only as a projection of human experience because we resist God's Word of revelation.

COMMENTARY:

- Concepts that attempt to speak of God but lack a grounding in the life and work of Jesus are figments of our imagination.
- Barth wants to have this discussion about God in space and time—in reality. We cannot reduce God to the confines of our thinking. God acts in history. Love is not an idea; it is all that is seen in the life and work of Jesus.
- What we see in Jesus is the love of God in action. His love extends from the Father to meet us, arising out of His agenda and not our own.
- Real love is active. It cannot just be felt; it must be actualized in the relation between persons.
- God is the source of all true love; all fulfilling human love is an outworking of His gift.
- When human acts do not correspond to God's intentions, we have departed from Him and have struck out on our own.
- True freedom is not conditioned, constrained, or limited. It is the character of God's love. It is at work in the world today. He is at work here and now.

CONCLUSION FOR THE CHURCH: Throughout the ages, the Church has wrestled with speaking truthfully about God. In its attempts to be relevant, it easily defaults to cultural values or human concerns. It then considers God as an answer to human needs and desires. Barth calls the Church to clear away the wreckage of past proposals, contending that their synthetic conceptions of God are not God at all. He clears the room, preparing the Church to engage the reality of God. As a bouncer, Barth exposes all the modes and forms of supposedly speaking about God, which actually are talking about humans. He pulls back the curtain on all exaggerated extensions of human philosophies that try to fit God into the cloak of an idealistic view. The problem is that they bypass Jesus, who brings true love and freedom to the human race as God with us.

Barth calls the Church back to reality. This reality is based on the incarnation of Jesus, with Him as our dynamic touchstone. This strategy is not an optional point of view. Only in Jesus do we encounter the work of the personal God who loves. Too often, the Church utilizes "successful strategies" to bring people into the pews, appealing to human priorities. For Barth, reality happens when love comes to town and the Church refocuses on the living God, offering freedom in a whole new mode of relatedness.

INSIGHT FOR PASTORS: This chapter is a call to pastors to redirect the task of the Church *from* thinking about what we do and how God helps us. It directs us *to* the reality of God, who makes His loving intentions active in His Church. We do not call people to church to discover new techniques to live a better life. We invite them to experience God's love that can only come from knowing God.

Something radically new is possible. Old habits of attending a church service and hearing sermons will not have the same impact as when we commit our services to serving the reality that God is, God is here, and God is here to love. God's love may correct or revitalize our lives. God will bring authentic love to do what He does best—love.

God has no other reason to engage us than that it is His nature to love. It is His heart. And His love freeingly divests human fears. When we embrace the reality of who Jesus is and shed the illusions that invade human lives with fear, actual freedom is possible. God is love; we ought never to stop being amazed at all that can mean.

Recovering the reality that God is the One who loves in freedom is like using a compass that is not influenced by all manner of magnetic forces that cause malfunction. While true north orients us properly, another magnetic field or object will turn us astray. Our cultures and their values can have this effect. We require to be guided by the love of God. The Church needs to respond freely to that present, personal love in all its activity. This will be a transformative experience because God will be the agent of change. We will freely share in His concern for others and end our infatuation with self-improvement or proving ourselves worthy. Whom the Son sets free is free indeed within loving relationships.

 INSIGHT FOR THEOLOGIANS: Any science must clarify the object of its study. Suppose a scientist has an agenda that is shaping an investigation. In that case, they will have inaccurate results about reality—their conclusions will look like what they went looking for. If practitioners take shortcuts or present an imposter god, we will miss the truth.

If people want God to give them success, happiness, or power, they find a way to import their ideas onto God to get their way. Science will be neglected, and a self-serving agenda will skew the results.

Theologians need clarity that begins with actualities—the truth of God made known in Jesus. If we try to reason our way to God by other means, we will have a god constructed by reason. This step may be perfectly reasonable to us, but the reasoning will not reflect God. If we study a lake for the hidden purpose of building a resort, our "scientific findings" will be influenced by our hoped outcome. If we are to study God, we must be willing to acknowledge all assumptions and agendas for success and be willing to question our questions to see what results they are inclined toward.

Science investigates what exists as reality. But reality must discover complex depths. We must be humbly open as we come to know and be ready learners. This humility is especially needed as we come to see the One who is beyond human comprehension but more genuine in love than we could imagine.

? CLARIFYING QUESTIONS: Does your theology seek to fit God into existing language, with definitions and descriptions as to what is real, including definitions of love and freedom? *Or* does your theology begin by listening to let God fill out the meaning of every act and word to unfurl the glory of God?

CHAPTER 10

THE MUSICAL PRISM

§ 29. The Perfections of God

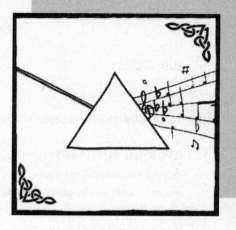

👀 **FOCUS STATEMENT:** In this short paragraph (§ 29), we prepare to explore the prism of God's love and freedom. These are "The Perfections of God." Think of the term *perfections* as descriptive of the spectrum of color always present in light, seen when hitting rain or a prism. This paragraph is brief, preparing us for the grandeur of § 30–31. Beginning with the prism of love and freedom, we discover the variety within God's light. The image above considers how this paragraph could be the cover of the album of God's love.

Light has unity, but also complexity; it creates rainbows. Within its character, light contains a spectrum of colors. In the prismatic encounter, the whole array is displayed. Similarly, the perfection of the one God is manifested in a multiplicity of perfections.

For our purposes, we will say Jesus prismatically reveals the fullness of God's being in the freedom of His loving, acting, and speaking.

This section reveals the character of God, using the term *perfections*. Barth wants the whole content of these terms to be informed by God, not from human designations.

🖋 **INTRODUCTION:** This section opens the way to talk about the attributes of the loving and free God. However, we ought not "attribute" anything to God. That method would borrow from human experience and attach that meaning to God. Love, our starting point here, easily defaults to human concepts. Thus, we miss hearing *God's* form of love. So, when love takes on godly expressions, Barth uses the term *perfection*. The word *perfection* serves to focus us on using the terms in such a manner that they could *only* be true of God.

ᚾ CONTEXT: *CD* 2.1
Pages in Paragraph: 29 pages (pp. 322–50)

Subsections

No subsections

📖 **TEXT:** § 29. The Perfections of God

OPENING SUMMARY: God lives His perfect life in the abundance of many individual and distinct perfections. Each of these is perfect in itself and in combination with all the others. For whether it is a form of love in which God is free, or a form of freedom in which God loves, it is nothing else but God Himself, His one, simple, distinctive being.[1]

✠ **SUMMARY:**

The One, incomparable, unified, complete being of God is known in God's acts.

All God's acts are inseparable outworkings of His being, and therefore are manifestations of His love.

We can only know the perfections of God as we know His loving freedom in His acts.

What we discuss here have been called designations, virtues, attributes, and properties, as well as perfections.

For our purposes, the term *perfections* serves in pointing to something specific of God and not to general attributes that may be aspects of the human. *Perfection* sustains their uniqueness, as faithful to God alone. *Attributes* collapses into features shared by all living beings.

There is a oneness in God and also a manyness.

- God is One as the being who loves in freedom.
- God is many, as the outworking of the perfections, expressed as His love in action.

God does not have perfections in the way we think of humans having attributes. God *is* His perfections; they cannot be separated out as something detached from His being.

The *glory of God* opens an explanation of God's way of being.

In speaking of the Lord of glory, there are two dangers, two aspects of separation:

---

1. *CD* 2.1, § 29, p. 322.

- God's glory may be limited to God's engagement with *us* and not the reality of God. This revelation is only an *economical glory of God*.
- God's glory may be so perceived as *separated* from God, becoming a caricature of God and a collection of forces and powers that miss His actual person. God becomes a set of values without personhood.

The God of the Bible is unified. He is the God of glory in Himself and in all His dealings with His creatures.

We must look at the possibility, legitimacy, and necessity of looking at the multiple perfections in God's One being.

While it is proper to think of divine simplicity referring to the unity of God, this does not mean our thinking can avoid the multiplicity of divine perfections.

We cannot let the simplicity of God become an idol, an all-controlling principle that swallows up all other ways of God's being and acting.

The perfections *belong* to the divine being, *express* the divine being, and therefore *reveal* the actuality of God.

We may use human words to describe God as long as we allow God to be the interpreter of what they mean.

Three points of view should be avoided:

1. We will avoid a *psychological framework*. This view thinks of God as a person and defaults to human conceptions of thinking, knowing, and willing. But how will we avoid just talking of human traits and actually speak of God?
2. Schleiermacher proposes the *religion-genetic* form. Beginning with the religious self-consciousness of the human, one characterizes these attributes and then applies them to God. God is forced into the world of nature with humanly constructed ideas of God.
3. The third form to avoid is the *historico-intuitive*. This proposal argues that the attributes of divine being entered into Christian thinking from ancient forms of philosophy and piety, interpreting the divine spirit from the human spirit.

Correct discussion of God's perfections begins where God is fully revealed and concealed in self-disclosure at the same time.

By the grace of revelation, our human views and concepts come to share in God's truth.

We need humility in our ignorance and obedience to what we know in truth.

In God's self-disclosure, God has become an object of human knowledge. At the same time, God is unknowable.

In all our thinking and speaking about Him, we can never become His masters. We will always be servants.

We must be attentive to each perfection as they are emphasized, known, and unknown as expressions of God's grace.

God loves in the unity of His being. At the same time, He loves in the distinctiveness of His freedom. In this way, the acts of God's love also act as the perfections of His being.

We can only speak rightly of this one holy God in the mutual understanding of His love expressed in His freedom and His freedom as an outworking of His love.

Three decisive points are at stake before we proceed:

1. We must hold God's love and freedom together. When we think of God's love, we tend to think of God in relation to the other—what God loves. When we think of God's freedom, we tend to think in terms of what is over against God.

   Inadvertently, we think of God's loving relationship *with* the world and His freedom as *over against* the world. We assume God cannot be one who loves and, in distinction, also be free.

   However, when God loves, He does not surrender His freedom. He exercises it. God's freedom can never be a limitation of His love.

2. We must distinguish between human and divine love and freedom. We must resist confusing the human form of love and freedom with God's. That introduces the *way of human transcendence*—transcending from the created world to speak of God in the form of superlatives.

   Likewise, we cannot negatively state that God is the opposite of what we are—also using the human starting point. This is the *way of negation*—rejecting the created world to speak of the uniqueness of God.

3. We must understand love and freedom as shown in Jesus. This way attends to the being of God revealed in Jesus, resisting projection and abstraction based on humans. This methodology is the *way of revelation*.

Theologians often begin with the *general* nature of God (abstract) and then consider the triune God. Unintentionally, one may bypass or neglect the *specific* self-revelation of God.

We begin our exploration by acknowledging the God who is for us. Only then may we talk about God in Himself without abstraction. With each perfection, we see more deeply that He is the One who loves in freedom in the unity and diversity of His being.

COMMENTARY:

- We may say that just as a single diamond has many facets, the perfection of God as One who loves in freedom presents many qualities.
- Barth corrects explicit or implicit perspectives that default to human attributes. We may be tempted to think our understanding of love, wisdom, and so on point us to Him. Barth rejects such strategies.
- Barth affirms the unity and simplicity of God. As well, he will not exclude the diversity of biblical terms exhibiting the complexity of God's activity in the world.
- Many theologians explain God and His activity through separate chapters. Barth presents God's particularities within the freeing love of the one God, whose unity is filled with wonders of His love.
- Discussing God's perfections may sound like a dialog based on human philosophy. Rather, we engage the myriad ways God's love freely acts. Perfections are God's way of being God for the other.

CONCLUSION FOR THE CHURCH: The Church has a unique opportunity to clarify all the wrong first steps people take in thinking about God. Beginning with statements like "If God is good, how can He allow..." builds on assumptions that a category of "goodness" exists into which God must be fitted based on human judgments and assumptions. This is also true with ideas like "being loving" or "being real." Ever so easily, human categories are assumed as primary, and God is questioned and measured by them.

The profound affirmation in this section is that we reject any prior categories into which we try to fit God or by which God is measured. The Church is called to be a myth buster here. This means removing the myths that produce an abstract and unreal god or idol. Israel made a golden calf because they wanted a present, physical god. God becomes conformed to our images and ideals. Only by removing the human measuring tape—forgetting what God is supposed to be like—may we know God as He has made Himself available. In discovering God in Jesus, we are set free for love's communion, not rebellious delusions.

INSIGHT FOR PASTORS: It is easy to want people to know God and use a lot of noble terms to describe God. However, if our terms are imperceptibly magnifications of human ideas, we have made God smaller. If we say God is holy and think that God must be separate from all we are, we have taken human intolerance and projected it onto God. God is holy in sending Jesus as a holy human who reconciles our sinfulness. He sends His Holy Spirit to redeem us and bring us home. God's holiness challenges our forms of holiness by calling us to see it as a form of loving, not limiting.

Every single word we use of God must be rethought, considering who God is, to challenge what our definitions tell us. Jesus must be the walking dictionary to fill out what love, wisdom, peace, goodness, and all the other terms mean. Jesus' love gets angry at religious judgmentalism. Jesus is free when love calls Him to embrace women and children. Our pastoral role is to allow the reality of God to strip the prejudgments about who God is and what God should do—in that way our prejudices may be exhumed from us, and Jesus' resurrection life begins.

INSIGHT FOR THEOLOGIANS: This short section is like washing our hands before preparing a meal or performing surgery. It calls for the careful removal of all that infects and contaminates our thoughts about God. By being adamant that only God can define our terms, we relinquish all the false forms of God. All the untrue terms of God that we may try to attach to Him are like gargoyles. They are interesting to look at, but they reflect little of the actuality of God. They scare people away.

In getting a laser-beam focus on what God is like, we allow the light of God to open the way for the science of God. Good science clarifies as it explores in search of the truth. Jesus did not align with religious institutions that missed the lesson of this section. They were terrible scientists. They used religious language but did not allow it to carry wisdom that came from His Father's heart. They did not align with the restorative work of His Spirit. This section appeals to humility. It calls for theologians to wash and sanitize our minds, words, and acts. This cleansing must happen every time we communicate the grace of God.

CLARIFYING QUESTIONS: Does your theology seek to find definitions, descriptions, charts, and categories that characterize the nature of God?

Or does your theology call you to return again and again to see how Jesus acts and speaks in a full spectrum of love's outworking?

GUIDE TO THE PERFECTIONS OF GOD

We will be exploring the *perfections* of God, a term related to the attributes of God, but without placing any of our ideas onto God. Perfections are like all the colors contained in white light. They cannot be discerned within the unity of white light but can become a rainbow. This chart helps clarify the freeing spectrum within the love of God.

The Perfections of God God as the One Who Loves in Freedom		
The Perfections of Divine Loving		
Grace – God's gift of extending fellowship to His beloved with unconditional favor and forgiveness	**Mercy** – God's compassionate readiness to remove the distress of another, His creature	**Patience** – God giving space and time to allow humans a free response, providing for development in a space alongside God's own
And **Holiness** – God's purifying love that overcomes our resistance to Him with corrective judgment in love	And **Righteousness** – God's being right and true to His being, in love, which judges in order to bring repair to those He loves	And **Wisdom** – God's steadfastness to maintain the inner clarity of God's life of reason, meaning, and order, working out in love to sustain the world
pp. 351-368 18 pages	pp. 368-406 38 pages	pp. 406-439 34 pages
The Perfections of Divine Freedom		
Unity – God is unique, one of a kind in the universe, and simple in His singularity, faithfully free in all His ways within His complexity as One God	**Constancy** – God's consistency in directing all He creates, while freely acting in love with creativity in knowing, willing, and acting	**Eternity** – God in His eternal duration that lacks time, simultaneously present as Himself to the otherness He created as time
And **Omnipresence** – God is consistently and freely present to all that is not Himself, as its Lord in a togetherness with distinction	And **Omnipotence** – God's ability to do what He wants, the focused power to fulfil His loving will	And **Glory** – God's glory is shown in His freedom to love, making Himself known, creating an honored recognition of Himself, attracting us in His beauty, bringing all into a fulfilled relationship with Himself
pp. 440-490 50 pages	pp. 490-607 117 pages	pp. 608-677 69 pages

CHAPTER 11

SURROUND SOUND IMPROVISATION

§ 30. The Perfections of the Divine Loving

FOCUS STATEMENT: As we enter this paragraph (§ 30), we must imagine sound, instead of light, surrounding us in free and loving expression. "The Perfections of the Divine Loving" will be displayed as a spectrum of sound. This presentation allows for attentive *listening*. In this encounter, we will hear the distinguished elements of God's love—we could call this *harmony* within God's loving.

Imagine we are entering a sound booth to distinguish God's "perfections." We will hear six tracks that constitute God's loving. These interplay and cannot be heard as essentially separate. They are "rainbowed" expressions of God's love.

Think of the music that flows from God, initially creating the universe by singing with enriching tones, synchronization, and complexity. Even today, God's single heart of love streams out from the dynamic interplay of Father, Son, and Spirit. Within the whole of the cosmos, an expansive gamut of harmony continues to breathe life into the world that sustains us.

Listen for the orchestra to highlight specific thematic pairs. In this section, we will hear three complementing combinations together in tandem. Through it all, the entirety of God's love plays, accentuating the fullness of God's love sounding forth.

INTRODUCTION: This section distinguishes elements of God's love as articulated by God. Barth called these *perfections*, a term displaying God's perfect fullness in His ways of being. Barth's method discerningly presents how God loves in freedom, starting with God's loving in § 30; § 31 will explore God's freedom. This process of revealing the pairings of perfections clarifies and unifies them within the whole. Together, they express the triune life depicted in the Bible as dynamically engaged with humanity.

We have three pairs to explore. The pairings of *grace* and *holiness* unveil God's turning toward us and the purity of His love. *Mercy* and *righteousness* reveal God's compassion for His creature, acting rightly and truly in accordance with His love. *Patience* pairs with *wisdom* to clarify that God makes space and time for us to fulfill His freeing, meaningful purpose.

As these elements reveal God's complexity, we hear the dynamics of God being faithful to Himself. God faithfully loves His creatures, as concretely displayed in Jesus.

▐▐▌ CONTEXT: *CD* 2.1
Pages in Paragraph: 89 pages (pp. 351–439)

Subsections
1. The Grace and Holiness of God
2. The Mercy and Righteousness of God
3. The Patience and Wisdom of God

▭ TEXT: § 30. The Perfections of the Divine Loving

OPENING SUMMARY: The divinity of the love of God consists and confirms itself in the fact that in Himself and in all His works God is gracious, merciful and patient, and at the same time holy, righteous and wise.[1]

✠ SUMMARY:
1. The Grace and Holiness of God (pp. 351–68)
God is.

God is love.

God is love in Jesus Christ.

God is love in Jesus Christ, loving all His children.

God is love in Jesus Christ, loving all His children to love all humanity.

God is love in Jesus Christ, loving all His children to love all humanity and together loving all creation.

God's perfections exist in the continuity of the single love of God.

---

1. *CD* 2.1, § 30, p. 351.

God's love always begins with Jesus, and He works it out in us. By the Spirit, we participate in this love.

Love always has a *whence* in the heart of God: From whence did this love come? It also has an objective movement forward: Where is this love leading? In both cases, God acts and speaks with a freedom that fulfills God's love, actually expressed with specificity.

Our choices in knowing God must not be based on a form of reasoning alien to God. They must not serve the human, validating selfish love or a desire for narcissistic freedom.

We must determine how the love of God in Jesus, as witnessed in the Bible, becomes an event and a reality. From this, we may come to conclusions regarding the actuality of God's love.

We begin with divine *grace* in our consideration of divine love. Grace will not stand alone. It will be met, purified, and controlled by its interface with divine *holiness*.

When God loves, He seeks and establishes fellowship, extending love manifested as grace.

Grace acts with a free inclination of God's love to unconditionally favor His beloved. This approach overcomes any sense of worthiness or opposition to God's love on our part.

Grace is a gift—the epitome of all the gifts of God—in revelation, reconciliation, redemption, and even creation.

God makes Himself the gift, offering Himself to us as the One who loves us.

Grace cannot be separated from God as though it has a mediatorial role that stands between God and humanity.

God's turning to us is the move of a superior to an inferior. It is condescension, the act of the greater coming to the lesser, embodying all the benefits He intends to bring.

The biblical conception of grace contains within it the logic that humanity is utterly unworthy of this gift. Not only have we not earned it, but we have also violated God's offer as we resist God's goodwill.

The focus of grace is God's persistence in *overcoming* human sin. This commitment is distinct from God's response of mercy, which is God's sympathetic *removal* of sin.

Grace claims and cleanses us, even as it is judging and redeeming us.

Even when God is unknown and hidden, denied and hated, or provoked and at enmity with His creature, God is always graciously for us.

The distinction between worshiping God and worshiping an idol is critical. The difference exists in whether we have found grace as offered by God—living in His presence, or following an abstract concept of grace—detached from God's personal being.

From the sphere of God's Trinitarian loving, God turns toward His creature. He comes to overcome human resistance.

Our gaze now turns to the place of *holiness* alongside grace.

We cannot cling to *our* ideas of grace and holiness if we hope to know the actuality of God.

God maintains His will over and against every other will. He validates His own true love in the actuality of His fellowship with humanity.

Holiness is the purity of God's love toward us.

Holiness is the freedom to turn toward the other while remaining true to Himself so that His own will prevails.

With holiness, God's favorable inclination overcomes creaturely resistance.

"To say grace is to say the forgiveness of sins; to say holiness, judgment upon sins."[2]

Both characterize and distinguish God's love in action as the Lord of His covenant.

The acts of God performed for His people extend on their behalf as loving acts in helping, blessing, and restoring. This acting includes a sign of judgment against that which needs to be separated as a threat or intrusion. Thus, holiness becomes resistance in these encounters.

The person, toward whom God is holy, will sense their resistance overcome. Therefore, God's holiness is experienced as opposition.

The holiness of grace is God's corrective in the case of conflict between God and His creature.

In the act of opposing human waywardness, God is turning toward us to restore fellowship.

The law is not separate from the gospel; it is contained within it as the outworking of the gracious will of God in our lives.

When we look at the cross, we see the holiness of God and the love of God poured out as God takes our place as the recipient of God's holy wrath. We can see the result of our opposition to God in Jesus' broken body.

Grace, turning to help the other, means opposing with holiness that which destroys the other.

---

2. *CD* 2.1, § 30, p. 360.

Sin disturbs fellowship with God. Holiness removes or rectifies what stands in the way. In this way, holiness restores relationships.

The Holiness Code in Leviticus is for humans, reminding them that God is present and active to correct and restore all along the way.

The Holiness Code is a means for humans to dwell within God's glory, so that He may fulfill their holiness. This awareness involves gratitude for the gift of the covenant. It also brings the attentiveness to avoid moving into opposition against God's grace.

It is because God is good that He is holy. It is because He loves that He is angry. Love corrects and disciplines.

Some see the holiness of God receding into the Old Testament, replaced by love and grace in the New Testament.

However, God forever meets us in person with holy jealousy. He had this same passion for Israel. Holiness is also expressed in the crucifixion of God's Son.

As with Isaiah, holiness is seen in the manifestation of wrath and judgment. It comes with the purging, pardoning, reconciling, calling, and grace entrusted to those who speak a word of salvation.

We accept God's holiness with reverence and thankfulness that replenishes us.

Christ was made sin in our place. He took our resistance, rebellion, opposition, ignorance, and sinfulness and acted on our behalf.

In our place, the holiness of God was completed as love was manifested in Jesus. He confirmed the rightness of God's wrath and restored us with love and grace. In all this, cleansing was poured out to reconcile us back to the Father.

In accepting the faithfulness of Jesus on our behalf, we accept both the divine judgment and the forgiveness that restores.

There remains for us only recognition and adoration of Him who is gracious and holy, awakened to the way God loves.

2. The Mercy and Righteousness of God (pp. 368–406)

Following the Bible, we now continue with the *mercy* and *righteousness* of God.

Divine love bears the character of *mercy* as it sees the creature in distress. God is ever ready to share in sympathy with the distress of the other.

God takes the initiative to remove distress; He is present in the midst of it and wills to remove it.

Mercy is not merely a feeling; it is an action that is initiated by a feeling.

God's love and grace are not merely mechanical relations but have their true origin and movement from the heart of God.

Some would reject that God has feelings. "But the personal God has a heart."[3]

God can feel. God can be affected. Another cannot move God, but He can move Himself in His own free power.

No cause outside God can cause Him to suffer, unless He wills it to, but there is no suffering in Himself.

There is an original, free, powerful compassion rooted in God. Thus, God is open and ready to respond to the other's needs, distress, and torments.

The "affections" of God are different from human affections or emotional responses. God has mercy in Himself, not ignited by the other.

The impassibility (inability to suffer) of God does not imply the impossibility of the compassion of God.

In Jesus Christ, grace stands in opposition to the resistance of God's creatures concerning consequences and punishment.

In Jesus Christ, mercy also deals with the opposition, focused on creaturely distress, misery, and suffering.

Humanity plunges itself into the ills of suffering through arrogance, rebellion, and lust that result in bondage, foolishness, and torment.

God seeks to overcome by removing, consoling, and helping amid the pain and suffering.

No human sin or guilt can suspend or invalidate the powerful, manifest compassion of God.

God does get angry but sets limits to His anger. At the same time, His compassion is active to make alive, renew, and enlighten as the dynamic reality of His mercy.

We cannot prove God's mercy by human logic. We can only acknowledge its reality in Jesus Christ, through whom we know that God is merciful.

To let God be God is to accept, with joy and gratitude, God's merciful substitution on our behalf. He removes what destroys us. We answer His love with our love.

God extends free and compassionate actions that arise from His heart and being.

We now turn to the *righteousness* of God, which we cannot understand apart from the *mercy* of God. The two are intertwined and must be distinguished as they augment each other.

---

3. *CD* 2.1, § 30, p. 370.

Mercy precedes righteousness in that the love of God acts in grace and mercy to create fellowship with humanity, which determines what His righteous actions will be to make this fellowship in love.

Theologians often divide the unity of God, holding that God rewards on the one hand and punishes on the other. This worldly way of measuring justice misses the working out of the love of God toward us.

The *justice* of God is that by which we are justified. We do not have an exacting judge; we have a gracious and forgiving Father.

If we begin with God's righteous will, removed from God's loving being, this move will extract "God's will" from outside God Himself. God's will must not only be consistent with God's love; God's will is determined by that essential love.

God is merciful and righteous to the wicked and the good; there is no disorder in God's kingdom.

God demonstrates His righteousness in that He is right and faithful to His being, in love, not right according to an external or impersonal law of justice. Therefore, in His righteousness, He shows mercy.

The God of the Bible is the judge.

The God of the Bible is the judge revealed in His law.

The God of the Bible is the judge revealed in His law as righteous and merciful.

God's activity is the fulfillment of His law flowing from the One who loves in freedom.

Both the Old and New Testaments portray the outworking of God's ministry of righteousness, displaying God's glory.

God's law is not a law of impersonal justice by which we are *measured*. It is not a law to create fear to *constrain* us. It is not a rule of divine guidance to present a *criterion* for salvation.

God unconditionally maintains the right to be the judge and to let love determine the faithful outworking of love as well as its violations.

The God seen in Jesus is just, justifying what had gone awry. His grace forgives sin. His law is not removed. In Jesus, God acts unconditionally to fulfill the law.

Humans are not saved *from* the hand of God but *by* the righteous hands of God.

The *righteousness* of God is revealed in Jesus, as is God's *mercy*—both are seen in the cross.

God reveals Himself as One bound to His nature. He is faithful to Himself and also to the object of His covenant love.

God's righteousness is the source of all comfort, and at the same time it reveals God's jealousy.

In righteousness, God summons us away from all the ways we wander, pursuing our own ideas of justice. Rather, He calls us to accept His righteousness.

In choosing God's righteousness rather than ours, we condemn our old view of justice. We instead have faith in God to be loving, gracious, and merciful.

We flee from ourselves and take refuge in Jesus. We acknowledge we are condemned sinners and accept the life offered. There is no longer separation from God.

His love now nourishes us as the entrance to our freedom.

Faith for humans is to grasp that we all stand as widows and orphans, poor and outcasts before God. We have confidence in His mercy as those in need of what we do not have.

With Job, we stand and profess that we are sinners before God. We claim God's righteousness as our own. We confess our sin, and He cleanses us from all unrighteousness.

By forgiving our sins, God makes known His righteousness. He becomes our Redeemer as we cast our needs on Him.

We stand trusting the judgment of God. He stands against all human accusations and the judgments of our own self against us. We stand by the faithfulness of Christ. Thus, we give ourselves to Him.

Jesus' righteousness compels Him to see and condemn our miserable state. It also includes His act to resolve our humble state in pardoning and restoring.

God still stands against unrighteousness. This commitment means He is for us and against what destroys us.

Full of gratitude, we have found our hope in the One who lives for us.

We do not stand at a crossroad with God's glory in one direction and fiery damnation in the other. We give ourselves to God, who has given Himself for us.

In our intrinsic being, we are in collision with the faithfulness of God.

The wickedness of humanity at the time of the flood has been repeating ever since the flood.

We must look seriously at the fact that the God of the Bible condemns and punishes because of His righteousness. We must see that He does get angry, reprimands, and disciplines. We must also appreciate that even here, His love is at work.

The resurrection of Jesus from the dead is God's righteous act of divine pleasure, acquittal, and reward.

The divine "No" of the cross is met by the "Yes" of the resurrection. Both fulfill the righteousness of God.

We cannot understand the "No" of Good Friday without seeing the "Yes" of Easter within it. We cannot see the "Yes" of Easter morning without presupposing the righteousness of Good Friday's cross.

The "No" of Good Friday addresses all the sins of Israel and all of humanity collectively. The sin of humanity becomes the object of divine wrath and retribution.

The awfulness of the crucifixion of Jesus connects with all the biblical executions of judgment.

What happened at the cross did not happen *to* us; it happened *for* us.

God offered divine judgment out of the righteousness of God and accepted mercy, in unity with humanity, as the fulfillment of the same righteousness.

1. The fact that God Himself, in the Son, took our place on the cross and freed us from divine judgment, reveals the *implications* of God's punishing justice.
    - Humans are alienated from God, living in rebellion against Him.
    - Humans ought to be punished in a way that involves our destruction.
    - It costs God the death of Jesus to remain righteous and not to annihilate us.
    - God enters our opposition and bears the pain of it.

2. Because the Son of God took our place on Good Friday, what had to happen to deal with this situation *could* happen there. It was carried out by the only One able to take the path necessary to deal with our sinful condition.
    - The divine majesty of God's love could take on human likeness and bear divine wrath without annihilation.
    - In God's severity, He was faithful to Himself as One who stands against the true nature of humanity, standing in opposition to its failure.
    - This kindness is what happened on the cross—God did not lay aside the demands of His righteousness. He showed Himself equal to His own wrath.

- God showed mercy in humility and absolute strength. He was unquestionably righteous.
- Righteousness triumphed in the death of Jesus—in love freely given. He maintained perfection in righteous love and expressed loving mercy to deal with our failure.

3. Because it was God Himself who suffered for us, His suffering could *satisfy and fulfill* the righteousness of God.
    - If God does not correct or discipline the rebellious opposition of humanity, He will be unhelpful and thus unfaithful to humanity and unfaithful to Himself.
    - To be faithful to Himself, God must resolve the conflict of the trespass of humanity. This correction comes through a proportionate response to what humanity has committed.
    - The One who is injured is the Lord and judge. Should He be righteous in judgment? He is the wounded and offended party, yet He is also the measure of righteousness against which humanity rebels.
    - If God were bound to an abstract concept of right, superior to Himself, forced to judge us by its standards, He would not be free to be faithful to Himself. He would sacrifice being a righteous God to submit to this other law.
    - God is righteous because He is free to be righteous in His loving mercy, true to Himself and to us as well.
    - God maintained the nature of His glory. God allowed righteousness to have proper influence.
        - God was merciful but also just.
        - He was faithful to His nature and practiced the pleasure of His goodwill.
        - He did not conceal, deny, or ignore the reality of the conflict.
        - God bore the conflict to the bitter end.
        - He took the conflict to heart—His heart—even though the battle was between us.
    - In Jesus, we have One who represents the divine judge and who also represents us as the judged.
    - Jesus suffered our distress as the distress in the heart of God— bearing the guilt and shame, worthy of condemnation.
    - We reject the distortion that God is indignant, enraged, and

angry, and takes this out on one innocent man whom the rest of us happily hide behind—unchanged!
- Only the concrete righteousness of God does not change. It includes judgment and mercy worked out on the cross.
- God offers vicarious suffering. Humans may accept this vicarious suffering as a gift of love, grace, and mercy. However, this is not hiding (like Adam and Eve in the garden). It is an honest confession regarding the state of the relationship and gratitude for God's action.

4. Because it was the Son of God Himself who took our place to attain our reconciliation with God, the victory of God's righteousness could then be our own righteousness before God.
- Jesus alone could restore what was lost, so we are righteous as He stands in our place.
  - Jesus could do it physically: He became human.
  - Jesus could do it lawfully: He was obedient, fulfilling the justice of God.
  - Jesus can do it effectually: His suffering is reckoned to us.
- We can be free from fear. We may cling to Him who has done what is necessary to reconcile us to God.
- Jesus had the power and freedom in His humanity to become the head and representative of us all.
  - Jesus speaks to us in God's name.
  - Jesus speaks to God in our name, as flesh of our flesh.
- The Father hears the Son and holds that there is no more condemnation for those for whom His Son became flesh.
- Jesus is the Word of God's pardon. This Word is spoken to us, and we hear it. Judgment has passed, and fear is relinquished.
- Jesus intervenes on our behalf and makes effective the love, grace, and mercy in which He has turned to us sinners, all without self-betrayal to His righteousness.
- Only by overlooking the resurrection of Jesus could it be thought that we are still dealing with the judgment of God. All was completed in Jesus as the judge and judged.

3. The Patience and Wisdom of God (pp. 406–39)

We now attend to God's *patience* and *wisdom* that circle within God's being in action.

We are expressing the same truth again—God is *gracious* and *holy*, *merciful* and *righteous*—and we include now that God is *patient* and *wise*.

We are not leaving the first sets of affirmations. This discovery process is cumulative.

The confession of Exodus 34:6 is a series of echoes, confirming the patience or long-suffering of God, as well as God's faithfulness.

Human grace or mercy could be impatient. However, we speak here of the extraordinary patience of God.

God's grace is merciful because we creatures are in a position of need and distress. God takes on our creaturely cause, taking us into His own heart.

The God revealed in Jesus loves in grace and mercy; now we see that this extends to His character of patience.

Patience means that God gives space and time to fulfill His intention, to allow freedom for a response.

While it is reasonable that God should be impatient, He gives Himself as patient.

Patience is deep-seated in the will of God's being and actions.

God fulfills His own will in such a way as to sustain and accompany, allowing the other to develop in freedom.

God is powerful in His actions. He is just as powerful in holding Himself back from acting.

In God's gracious will, God waits for each person, giving them freedom and opportunity. This patience is an outworking of God's freedom, power, and activity. This work adds to God's love rather than taking anything from God.

God takes up the cause of His creature. God accepts the full impact of the state of the human condition and intervenes in the reality of its severity.

God is severe with Himself in the offering of Jesus on the cross.

Human freedom lives in an encounter with God's love working in space and time.

God controls His creation by His grace so that it does not lead to the catastrophic destruction of His creation.

Rather than destroy His creature, God comes to share in its warped existence. This embrace is the meaning of God's mercy.

God's heart is so deep and expansive that it can contain all the darkness at the depths of human failure.

The mark of Cain and the rainbow for Noah are signs of God's promise to make room and time for fallen humanity to know God's mercy and long-enduring patience. These are protective promises. These signs are tokens of the gift of life for the undeserving.

All the covenants of God are outworkings of the patience of God, worked out in grace and mercy.

Jonah complained against God for being too patient, but the problem was that Jonah was impatient.

God's patience upholds all things by the Word of His power, achieved by God's Son, who has spoken to us.

God has time for us. Therefore, all of God's activity is an exercise of His patience toward us.

God's patience does not leave humans to their own devices.

The zeal of God for His creature, manifested in the incarnation, is a display of God's activity, not passivity.

If God gives humans time, freedom, and long periods of patient waiting, He does so because He has already acted for them, walked with them, and all this in His own time.

Humanity has already fallen into God's hands. One named Jesus stands in their place. He accomplished what was expected of them all.

God is not self-deceived, nor does He turn a blind eye to human sin. He is sincere in His love as He faces the thoroughness of human failure and patiently waits for us. God is not shortsighted or filled with optimistic illusions.

Jesus Christ is the power that upholds and sustains all things. He exercises the power of self-restraint, the forgiveness of sins, and speaks as the eternal Word that clarifies the testimony of God's patience.

The open secret of the whole Bible is that the Word of God becomes the protector and avenger, the covenant maker, who judges and disciplines, and who establishes signs of fellowship with His creatures.

To have faith is to live in the time and space that God has provided. This is God's reality for our existence, to be with Him and not without Him. He waits for us to accept His reality so that we may enter the life He has made available.

We may balance the *patience* of God with the *wisdom* of God. This pairing is another expression of the love of God.

God's will gives sense, purpose, and reason to our lives as His wisdom.

To choose other than God's will is to choose senselessness, purposelessness, and unreason.

Jesus is the one sense, purpose, and reason of human life. To choose anything or anyone other than Him is to walk into the darkness.

God is wise. He knows the end for which He purposes His gracious and merciful actions.

God does not act by whim or chance inspiration. He is in every respect a God of order.

God is wise in Himself. Therefore, God's wise order informs and affirms the expressions of His holiness and vindicates His righteousness.

Our confidence in God is based on our appreciation of His reason, meaning, and order—His wisdom.

Our recognition of God's wisdom informs our freedom, following God's wise activity with its completeness as intelligent, reliable, and liberating.

The *wisdom* of God is the inner truth and clarity of God's life. It establishes and confirms the source, entirety, and criterion of all that is true.

God's demonstration of His wisdom in action is the manifestation of His glory.

The wisdom of God is not merely a quality, skill, or proper interpretation of right action. The wisdom of God is the steadfastness of God.

In Jesus, God's sense of what will serve His purposes directs in His activity.

In the Bible, the *wisdom* of God is tied to God's *patience*.

By God's wisdom, He creates, sustains, and oversees the workings of the world.

God's patience has determined that all creation is made and fit to be the theater of His wise action.

God's wisdom is prophetic, speaking in the streets on behalf of God. When wisdom's preaching of repentance, judgment, and salvation is accepted, the promises of peace and fearlessness become true.

God's wisdom is not an intermediary; it is the self-explanation of God giving meaning to the world.

"Divine wisdom is obviously the meaning and ground of creation and therefore of the sphere in which man can live. The whole art of living and understanding life consists in heeding and accepting divine wisdom and in this way becoming wise."[4]

In the Old Testament, the wisdom of God contrasts with the foolish idolatry of the people.

The unique contribution of the concept of wisdom is that God has freely given us time and space to clarify the actualizing of His grace and holiness, mercy and righteousness.

---

4. *CD* 2.1, § 30, p. 430.

Jesus is the meaning of God's patience, the visible form of God's wisdom in the world.

Wisdom has to do with the art of living.

Wisdom is a gift from God that has to be sought, springing from divine grace and favor.

Wisdom is not a private desire to discern between good and evil or the skills to rule over people.

Love of the other rules among the faithful people of God. This love is revealed in public. It shows hope in God dearer than life itself. This wisdom holds hope for the good of the other by the grace of God.

Jesus Christ, who is greater than Solomon, stands amid His people as the embodiment of Solomon's wisdom.

Jesus is the patience of God shown for us within the time given to us. He gives meaning to patience as the One who is with us and making us wise.

Whatever the world's wisdom may be, it is not the art of living; it is the opposite.

Christians participate in the folly of this world on the one hand. On the other hand, they participate in authentic divine wisdom over false human wisdom.

Paul proclaimed God's wisdom in the word of the cross. This event is the wisdom of God to bring all humanity into reunion through one man.

Jesus Christ is the wisdom of God who fulfills the goal of God's wisdom. Through His resurrection, He aligned humanity with the patient love of God, fulfilling God's wisdom for us.

God is the only wise One. Humans realize wisdom only by having faith in Him.

The wisdom of God is known in the mystery of His will. He wills to gather all things together in heaven and on earth in Christ as their head. In Him, God's wisdom is made visible and fulfilled.

The wisdom of God is God's own turning to humanity in grace and mercy, as His love is freely fulfilled in Jesus.

 COMMENTARY:

- God is One, yet God has complex ways of acting. These express a spectrum of forms of God being faithful to Himself and considerate of alienated humanity.
- Grace can never be separated from God. It is God being with humanity in a particular manner.

- Holiness has to do with separateness. But God has separated Himself to be *for* us; He is not separated *from* us. Thus, His holiness makes us whole and is about restoring relationships.
- Mercy cannot merely mean withholding judgment; mercy is active in saving the alienated.
- Righteousness is not a standard of success or failure; it is God making all things right in accordance with Himself.
- Patience makes God's enduring acceptance available, creating space for humans to grow and develop. This fortitude is not passivity; it is timely and persistent unconditional support.
- Wisdom is not knowledge, information, or human achievement. It is God's love expressed in action. When we align with Him, we act in wisdom.

 CONCLUSION FOR THE CHURCH: Having bathed in the outpouring of God's grace and holiness, mercy and righteousness, patience and wisdom, the Church is ready to participate in the outworking of God's character. There can be no formulas here, only faithful compliance with the love of God in the character of church communities.

Only in knowing God's outpoured grace can a church ask how to live. Aligning with God's heart results in an extended turn to the needy and the neighbor with selfless love. In sharing God's mercy, a church can extend God's compassion and restorative justice. Finally, each church can give time and space for imperfect people to find the meaning of God's life and purpose in loving relationships. We need not create synthetic forms of God's perfections. Knowing the living God in Christ is the trustworthy source of this fruit that grows only by deeply knowing the triune God.

 INSIGHT FOR PASTORS: No set of doctrines or definitions of God's attributes can ever fulfill what this chapter provides. It unveils the intervention of God's love into the human situation. God, and hence His Church, deals with human alienation and brokenness, self-seeking, and impatience. Engaging the personal life of God opens the possibility of character transformation that depends entirely on knowing God. The Church is to serve in bringing a community to the source of this life-altering process.

In discovering God, we encounter the possibility of yielding to His profound work for us and with us. For leaders, this section offers no upward climb to perfection. It offers God. What follows is the fruit of knowing and being known by Him in all His glorious, resplendent love. Ask yourself if this is the God you have come to know and are making available to your people. Assess how your vision for the Church is helping your church to develop the character of a loving family, simply out of knowing God. Have other goals taken priority for programming? Wrestle through a conversation with your people as to what your church would look like if God's perfections were the heartbeat of the community. Learn to listen to God through these perceptible perfections. Let Him do the development as the Spirit guides each person to be a particular reflection of the perfections.

 INSIGHT FOR THEOLOGIANS: This section could be conceived as descriptively talking *about* God. But it is better to see a theological shift that defies theology as definitions and descriptions and discards all human categories into which God might be placed, with characteristics attributed to Him, sourced out of the human experience. No more God-in-a-box-of-chocolates—God does not have separate "flavors," some favorites, some to be avoided. Like assessing a masterful meal with intricately woven components, we are feasting on the living Word of God to discern all the complexity within. But the parts never distract from the wonder of the whole.

Barth's perspective places our thinking into a new manner of engagement. All of God's ways of being are to be seen as dynamically cast within God's outworking of love. Each portrays God's consistency within God's life and love. Each element of God's love is to be brought to clarity so that the academy and the Church might share the life and mission of Jesus. The academy is to clarify God's ways of being so that the Church can adequately live in relation to Him.

Our pursuit of academic endeavors should break down any destructive, petrifying schemes regarding God's attributes. Instead, we must explore the Spirit's creative undertakings. The Spirit opens us to work out the perfections of God by meeting God. Critiquing and correcting inadequate theology helps us embrace the actuality of God as He comes to us.

 CLARIFYING QUESTIONS: Does your theology seek to describe the nature and character of God's attributes with concise definitions? *Or* do you see that God's love is like the sun, in that it does distinct, consistent, and creative work in many ways and places? Do the attributes flow from God, or do you try to paste them onto God like placards of historical information in a museum?

CHAPTER 12

RESONANCE AND REFLECTION IN THE OCTAVES OF GOD

§ 31. The Perfections of the Divine Freedom

FOCUS STATEMENT: In this paragraph (§ 31), we continue with the perfections of God. We now hear the freedom with which love is expressed. This is not a separate topic. "The Perfections of the Divine Freedom" echo the first set, reverberating from God into the world.

Double rainbows, as well as reflected rainbows, are likenesses with echoed interaction. Reflecting light from a common source, they create various visions of beauty. Wet ground or a lake may capture the glory of this reflective meeting of light and water. These watery essentials enter playful moments to further the collaboration with color.

The perfections of divine freedom express love in action. They reveal the scope, reliability, impact, and outworking of God's freedom. These perfections are not separate from divine loving. They expand the reflections of God's love into the many dimensions of space, time, and God's ongoing involvement in the universe.

God's freedom is akin to the playfulness of light as it fills and illuminates space over time. Barth expands our vision to see that God exceeds our experiences of space, time, power, and presence. We are embraced by the music of the spheres, the harmony of all things sustained by God, and all things transfigured in the light of the glory of God.

Music, like light, takes on indescribable dimensions in the hands of the masters. The invitation of this section is to resonate with the musicality of the living God. He takes us to octaves beyond our imagination. He unleashes the power of His grand symphony. His love bounces and reflects beauty in previously unimaginable ways within His providential care.

119

INTRODUCTION: This section is much longer than the previous section. In this section, the pairings of *unity* and *omnipresence* convey that God is indivisible in the unity of His love. These perfections stand in intimate and direct relation to all He has made. Further, the *constancy* and *omnipotence* of God's love affirm that He has the freedom to act from a consistency of love, and the power to fulfill His love in every act. Finally, the *eternity* and *glory* of God connect us to the profound scope of God's enduring love that freely acts before, during, and after the time of creation. In that duration, He reveals the glory and beauty of God, which awakens and invites our participation in His glorious life of love.

The light of God's love resounds, reflects, refracts, recreates, and reveals the love of God in freedom. These are discussed in long, sometimes almost book-length, sections. Nevertheless, they shed light on God's love that originates beyond the time-space continuum and powerfully acts within it.

CONTEXT: *CD* 2.1
Pages in Paragraph: 238 pages (pp. 440–677)

Subsections
1. The Unity and Omnipresence of God
2. The Constancy and Omnipotence of God
3. The Eternity and Glory of God

TEXT: § 31. The Perfections of the Divine Freedom

OPENING SUMMARY: The divinity of the freedom of God consists and confirms itself in the fact that in Himself and in all His works God is One, constant and eternal, and therewith also omnipresent, omnipotent and glorious.[1]

SUMMARY:
1. The Unity and Omnipresence of God (pp. 440–90)
God in His freedom is constant in His being. He confirms that His love is freely given to humans.

Divine freedom is engaged second, not in *subordination* to divine love but in *correspondence*.

God's love will *be implicit* in all we say as we go forward. It will be *made explicit* for us in God's freedom.

---

1. *CD* 2.1, § 31, p. 440.

God is One.

God is One who loves.

God is One who loves in freedom.

God is One who loves constantly and eternally in Himself.

God is One who loves constantly and eternally in Himself and in all His actions.

God is One in such a way that He is omnipresent—always present in unity.

God is constant in such a way that He is omnipotent—always constant in His power.

God is eternal in such a way that He is glorious—eternally coming.

God's love is attested to in events that express the reality of God's freedom.

This loving freedom is explained in the series revealed as unity, constancy, and eternity.

We must clarify what compels us to conclude that our understanding is properly from what God has given. These are discussed in the sections on omnipresence, omnipotence, and glory.

By saying that God is One, we have summed up all the perfections of divine freedom.

God's oneness can have two meanings. It can refer to God's *uniqueness* or *simplicity*.

By saying that God is *unique*, we mean that He is the only one of His kind. Any "god" set alongside Him is a false god.

God is the origin, the creator of all that is created, dependent, derived, and contingent.

God does not face competition, nor does He fear contradiction or opposition. His Word needs no supplementation, assistance, or authorization.

By saying that God is *simple*, we affirm that God is undivided in Himself. God is not composed of something distinct from Himself.

God is One, even in the distinctions of the divine persons of the Trinity.

God is One, even in the wealth of His distinguishable, divine perfections.

In God, there is no separation, distance, contradiction, or opposition. He is the one Lord in every relationship.

In God's relation to the world, there can be no combination, amalgamation, or identification of God with the world. He is not drawn from it, mixed into it, or seen as part of it. He is genuinely distinct as its Creator.

God cannot be seen as having left a residue of Himself in the world as an effluence, emanation, effusion, or irruption into the world.

God's creation of the world caused what is other than Himself in every aspect.

The early Church affirmed the *homoousion* (same being) for the Son and the Spirit with the Father. This confirms the simplicity of God as a unity.

We cannot construct an absolutized, perfect idea of oneness in being and then try to fit God into this mentally constructed category. We can only see that the God revealed in Jesus reveals one God in three inseparable persons.

If we imagine that "the One," the wholeness of the universe, is God, we will be reflecting creaturely ideas of unity onto God. Those are empty imaginations, projections foisted onto God. They are caricatures void of reality.

When used of God, *simplicity* cannot mean the same as any other simple thing or philosophical concept—it can only refer adequately with the unique meaning that arises from God to refer to His being as the one triune God.

One can speak of the simplicity of God as the indivisibility of God.

The testimony of the prophets and apostles affirmed that this one God creates, reconciles, and redeems as the one Lord, using all the perfections of God's loving in freedom, originating from within His one being.

God is trustworthy. Therefore, He is indivisible, unbreakable, and uncompromising.

God is faithful. He keeps covenant with His people. He is faithful to His word. This constancy is the basis of saying that He is the God of truth.

The "Yes" of God to humanity affirms that our existence falls within the full spectrum of God's faithfulness as seen in Jesus Christ, witnessed to by the prophets and apostles.

Because God is One, unique, and simple, He is *omnipresent*. He exists and acts consistently with His being, present to everything that is not Himself.

To say that God is sovereign over all things is to say He is present to all things.

The concept of God's omnipresence sets the idea of God with reference to the universe, standing in an intimate and direct relationship.

God is present to the universe but distinct from it. However, even here, we cannot say God is limited by the presence of the universe, as though He were defined in relation to it.

God is not only existent; He is coexistent. His existence has priority over all other existence. Particularly as the God of love, He is present to all under Him as His creation.

Without divine love, there would be nothing other than God, nothing for God to be present to or reveal to, and no coexistence with another.

Time is the form of creation in which the acts of divine freedom have a theater as the context of God's love.

Space is that form of creation that is truly distinct from God as the object of His love.

We encounter God in space and time as One who is not defined or limited by time and space.

Heaven and earth, nature and spirit, and the whole realm of human existence function within this created reality.

To say that God is infinite, measureless in space and time, does not mean we can exclude or deny God as the One who has created all beginnings and endings, who sustains all measures and limits within space and time.

God's infinity does not contradict His being the One who loves in freedom. He is freely present to all He creates.

Inwardly, God's togetherness is the life of the Father, Son, and Spirit with a distance that exists in their distinction as the unity of one God.

Outwardly, there exists a togetherness that is the distinction between Creator and creation, including His creature.

God possesses His own space in love and creates space for the other as a work of His love.

A general definition of divine spatiality is as simple as saying that God occupies space as Himself. In the fullness of Himself in this space, He is the One who loves in freedom. Consequently, He loves all that He makes.

We cannot say that God is nowhere and also say that God is everywhere. Revelation reveals presence.

God is always somewhere. He is here as the One who is seeking us and who may be sought.

God is here, there, and everywhere as Himself in and with His creation —known in His revelation.

God is neither lifeless nor loveless as the fulfillment of His life and the expressed freedom of His love. He is present and active, fundamentally free in love as befits His triune being.

The word differentiation encompasses the full complexity of withness and distinctness. God is with us, yet distinct. This distinction is freedom manifestly expressed as the One God loves in freedom, engaged with that which is utterly different.

God gives all things other than Himself their space as a gift.

God has space for Himself.

God is present in wrath and grace.

God is present in hiddenness and revelation.

There is no absence of God in all His creation.

God's presence to the whole world is by His Word, who creates, sustains, and upholds the world, and is God's unique presence in it.

The dwelling places of God may occur at locations within the life of humanity, especially with His people, Israel.

The gods of the heathen dwell in arbitrary and accidental places.

God's definite, distinct dwelling among us is in the Word become flesh dwelling among us.

Jesus is the fulfillment of the Old Testament predictions, and so salvation is from the Jews. It is from the Jews but for all humanity, as the Father wishes it to be.

The tabernacle of God dwells among humankind as God Himself with us.

Set-aside places, like those seen in the Old Testament sacrifices, have now passed. We do not look to Jerusalem, but to Jesus.

Jesus has entered heaven, is now present in the world from heaven, and calls persons to Himself to move them back to the Father, who desires their worshiping embrace as His children.

We were strangers and sojourners in this world. We have been called back to our home country—not to a building, but to the personal God.

We find a home by being in Christ and He in us. He is the availability of God's space made welcome to us.

It is only through the Word of God, in self-revealing and acting for all-that-is-other than God, that we understand God appropriately.

Beyond God's general and special presence in creation, there is a third distinction.

This third clarification of God's presence is in His Word, Jesus Christ. He is the center of God's special presence, giving meaning to His general presence.

The whole of the Bible's witness points to Jesus as the presence of God's dwelling in the world.

Jesus' presence is the origin and goal, the basis and center of all God's self-representation; Jesus is the one, unique, simple, and proper presence of God in His creation.

God's people become the children of God through being accepted by Jesus. This status comes through participation that comes by Him, from Him, and with Him, fulfilling the possibility of His divine presence.

God's personal work engages and aligns our thinking to the presence of the triune God, who presently oversees heaven and earth.

In one way, the whole of Jesus is properly in heaven at the Father's right hand. In another way, the totality of the same Jesus is present in Israel, the Church, and the entirety of the world.

Where His Spirit and grace are, Jesus is present, very God and very man. He is present in heaven and earth, in both places with His human and divine nature.

2. The Constancy and Omnipotence of God (pp. 490–607)

We now turn to God's constancy and omnipotence.

The word *constancy* refers to God's perfect freedom.

The word *omnipotence* refers to God's perfect love, in which He is free.

All the perfections of the One God, expressed in freedom and love, only make sense if He is constant.

As the One God constantly directs all that is other than Himself, He is also omnipotent.

In God's *constancy*, God cannot be moved or changed by anything outside Himself.

Regarding the question of whether God is immutable, we need clarification. If we are speaking of anything *outside God*, we must say nothing changes God. But God can change within the constancy of His freeing love *in Himself*.

God is not immobile, fixed, or noninteractive. If He was, He would not have a relationship with anything other than Himself. The pagan idea of immobility is death. This does not apply to God.

If we are to say that God is immutable, we must let God fill in the meaning. He is consistent and has always been who He is: the God who lives and loves.

God's constancy is the form of God's limitless immutability. Constancy is not a constraint to require changelessness. He exercises liberating freedom to always be the God who loves freedom and is creative in His dynamic activity.

God's personal revelation is always a fresh demonstration of His constant, eternal life.

God's constancy is the continuity of His knowing, willing, and acting as His specific person.

God maintains all of creation distinct from Himself as a confirmation of His constant vitality.

In a *monistic* view, the world collapses into God. The world may appear separate from God but is integral to Him. Or the world may be thought of as the essence of God Himself. God as God erodes into a dream, hidden within or subsumed into the reality of the world.

It is a grave error to not maintain a clear distinction between the Creator and creation.

One must not see, as with a dualistic version, the relation between the Creator and creation as essentially separate. With that division, God is seen as immutable and not involved in the world.

In this fractured reality, the human is deprived of participation in God's life. In that scheme, God is perfectly separate in detached untouchability.

In *dualism*, God and creation live in semidetached houses. There is no door in the wall between them to allow them to be a part of one another's life.

In a semidetached house, humans live with a sad face, their conscience tortured by their helpless place in a changing world without God. This detachment creates a pessimistic view of life.

God is safely separated, perfect in unchangeable, unaffected superiority. Such is the tragedy of the dualistic vision.

With God sequestered away, it would be logical to assume God might be dead. There is no awareness of the living God. This loss is the consequence of rejecting revelation.

Another consequence of dualistic thinking is to see a wall protecting humanity from God. The unaffected, unchanging God is simply excluded from our vision. Humans are left to their own devices and values in a changing (mutable) world. This view is optimistic toward human self-rule.

When God is seen as absent from the world, humans are left to enjoy an agenda of self-satisfaction. Life becomes self-made to suit secular, godless goals. The changing world becomes an occasion for human control, intoxicated by the power to guarantee one's own triumph in life (and turn a blind eye to death).

Yet both the pessimistic and the optimistic views miss the divine love that intervenes in God's creation. Consequently, both also miss any understanding of the relation between the Creator and His creature.

Humans consequently miss honoring and accepting the loving life of God.

God's constancy is the very basis of the life of the world. The world's life cannot be lived without the presence and activity of the Creator in whom and by whom the world exists.

The world is distinct from God. He made it that way. But the life of the world derives from Him and returns to Him.

Both dualism and monism fail to provide a proper concept of God. God's constant love for His distinct creation is missed or misconceived. One presents a false unity; the other, false separation.

Only the constancy of the love of God as Creator, given in freedom for His beloved creation, holds the relation appropriately.

In the face of human defection, God acts to restore what would be lost, a relation God has made through free and freeing love with His creature.

There is no conflict within God's constant, loving, triune being. The conflict exists between the Creator and His creature, who pursues the possibility of self-destruction in the face of God's love.

If humans did not have the possibility of falling away from God, they would not be living creatures. To be unable to fail is to be forced without freedom.

God grants the possibility to oppose His loving meaning for which humans were intended. This status is a possible impossibility. It is possible in that humans choose it. It is impossible in that the constancy of God's love is irrevocable. The reality is greater than the illusion of self-sufficiency.

Evil is opposition to the love of God on the part of the creature. God opposes this opposition to Himself.

God is constant.

God cannot cease to be God.

God will not cease to be Creator and Lord.

God will not cease His work of revelation and His reconciliation of the world.

God will not be drawn into conflict but will be constant in love freely given.

God will be the judge and helper of alienated creatures as the One who is peace in Himself.

God will maintain Himself in relation to the world, binding Himself afresh.

God will reveal His constant being as One who is present and active in His world.

God is in opposition by being opposed to the world's opposition and contradictions. He exercises His love to maintain the constancy of His being and the hope of future redemption.

Humans think God is changeable and can be manipulated. Thus, they do not trust in the constancy of God's faithful decision as the basis for a trusting, faithful response.

God has befriended humanity in their sinfulness. He continues to be a friend extending grace and mercy, making a new creation by restoring sinful humanity to Himself.

The constancy of the faithfulness of the Creator does not exclude; in fact, it *includes* the freedom of the creature. The creature has freedom distinct from God.

The relationship between God and humanity does not take place in a general way. God works through specific humans. To preserve the human race, He makes a covenant with Noah. For the sake of all nations, He chooses Israel. For the sake of the world, He chooses the Church.

Grace is the hidden meaning of nature. However, a more meaningful connection is made available as nature becomes the theater of grace in the constancy of God's self-expression.

The special act of God entering creation engages a partnership. God chooses to work on behalf of humanity within the sphere of creation.

God interrupts human self-destruction and resistance to His love. While heaven and earth proceed in continuity with what has gone before, the miracle of a new heaven and new earth comes with the entrance of the Son and the Spirit.

We live now in a provisional form of creation. We live in light of a truth yet to be fulfilled.

While God alone exercises the right to rule over creation, those who are His people stand beside Him like Moses or the disciples whom He called friends—this brings the freedom of friendship.

The meaning of the world is found in Jesus Christ. The preservation of the world fulfills the secret of His unchangeable work to restore it to His Father.

Because Jesus is alive in the history of reconciliation as the special act of God, He can be seen as belonging to Israel and the Church as the constancy of divine love.

Jesus is the constantly living God. The immutability of God is seen in Him and no other.

God has become a creature. He has become one with us, enabling fellowship with His beloved creatures.

Jesus does not just speak about God; God speaks through Him so that God speaks to us. He acts as God, lives, dies, and suffers as God on our behalf.

God has befriended His fallen creation. He will lead it back to redemption in faithful love.

If God did not bind Himself to His creation, He would not be faithful to His love for what He makes.

Jesus taking on human flesh does not alter divine being. It confirms that God joined our human nature with His divine nature in one person. He did this to reveal to us that He is constant as Creator, Reconciler, and Redeemer.

In Jesus, God was ready to accept a position in which He would be in the world and not be known as God.

By self-emptying in Jesus, God puts Himself in the position to take on the rebellion of humanity against Himself. This action was no surrender of His deity. This achievement was God's self-offering on behalf of humanity.

For a while, Jesus kept His divinity hidden. Only the Father knew the Son. Other humans did not know Him. He kept His divinity even when concealed in the form of a human.

In Jesus' revelation, we see the constancy of God's freedom in action. There is no obligation in this matter, only a free choice to display His love.

Consequently, we are bound to respond to His free love and not decide to go our own way. His freedom is the context in which we are to live. To walk away is to reject His gracious freedom.

The relationship between God and creation is not a fixed one. God is constant but not bound to act according to a script.

God's divine commitment does not remove the contingent freedom of the world.

In God's relationship to humans, God's dealings are not only actual but also provisional.

Problematic shadows hang over some depictions of the divine will and decree.

- In some depictions, God may remain hidden, immovably ruling from a *distance*. We relate to the decree, but not to God Himself.
- Others have a general doctrine of God that is *abstract*. By decree, God preserves and rules the world. These views miss the event of God coming to rule the world in Jesus. The general overrides the particular in God's relation to the world.
- Some turn the covenant of grace into a *legal or eternal testament* of God in relation to the world. This view misses and distracts from the direct and specific revelation of God in Jesus Christ as the revelation of the will of God.
- If Jesus had been seen as the decree of God, the doctrine would not have become a *vague philosophical outline*. The idea of a nonliving God could not have been sustained.

In Jesus, we have the will of God as it exists for us and is extended in time and space.

We have established that God is constantly the One He is. He does what He is. Now we look at how He can fulfill what He wills.

God's *omnipotence* is God's ability to do exactly what God wants.

As God loves in freedom appropriate to His love, He is not bound by necessity or wild in changeableness.

God is constant in love and completely able to meet His creation freely, without wavering from His essential being.

God does not default into a vault of eternal decrees that are not loving to the creature.

God does not accommodate to His creatures by violating His own will.

God has real possibilities that can be fulfilled as actual possibilities.

God is the source and sustainer of all life.

We must look at the power of God as real power. We cannot begin with human concepts of power. Otherwise, we will reduce God to human categories.

Power apart from God is evil. As human potential, power is a freedom from restraint that supports suppression, revolt, and domination. That is the power the devil would like to have. Might, detached from God's love, is a path to tragic wielding of power.

Scripture leads us along a path to God's power, which is discovered only by coming to the God revealed with this unique power.

Beginning the creed with "I believe in God, the Father Almighty" acknowledges the uniqueness and priority of God's personal being in power. We must distinguish this from human applications and abuses of power, particularly those by fathers.

God the Father is the proper source for understanding power. He stands in opposition to every preconception brought from our human, abstract, and abusive forms of power.

God's power acts with a command and a promise directed toward humans who are called. The response is faith, an acknowledgment of God's faithfulness to fulfill His good and loving will.

When we say that God is almighty, we depart from the Bible if we look anywhere other than to the Father.

Our *first* assertion is that God alone can define the meaning of God's power.

A *second* affirmation is that God's power can never be seen as a potential, a mere physical possibility in God.

God being right means the righteous application of His might so that

His acts flow from His love freely expressed. This alignment informs God's holiness, righteousness, and wisdom.

A *third* statement to clarify is that God is almighty. This affirmation refers to what He has done and will do. This capability is not merely the ability to cause things to happen or affirm what has occurred.

God is almighty in His work, but this does not exhaust what we know as His power. He is almighty in Himself before and beside His work.

In turning His love toward us, God does not expend His power in a diminishing way. All that God does for us is a continuation of His free love in grace, mercy, and patience.

God did not merely cause the world and then withdraw. God did not become a part of the world to be dissolved into it.

We cannot present the attributes of God as a supreme world power that may later lose its connection with God and be reduced to philosophical principles. They collapse into the self-evidence of the human in the world apart from God's power and presence. Barth is thinking of Schleiermacher.

We absolutely must not say that God's omnipotence corresponds with what is experienced in the human consciousness. God's omnipotence is not to be understood as the power of God in nature and morality.

The problem for Barth lies in the distinction between what God can do (omnicausality) and does (omnipotence). The first is an ideal concept; the second, the actuality of God's love in freedom.

The first concept identifies a general power in the world as humanly conceived, a mere set of potentials. However, God's omnipotence is uniquely His free, loving activity. Therefore, God's power is about God alone, not deduced from human categories. God's power is power over everything.

The *fourth* point is that God's omnipotence is a very specific capacity with real content, wholly and utterly concrete.

Omnipotence is the power of God as Father, Son, and Spirit being Himself.

That which denies God's reality stands against it. Or it tries to be like God as an imposter, a supposed reality. These realities become demonic, but their capacity is unreal—this is the impossible possibility. Demonic attempts exclude the divine possibility, which is the standard of everything possible. Therefore, it is a fake impossible possibility.

The conditions and limits of what is possible for God must be found in God.

Absurdities in creation are not the substance of God's omnipotence; they are contradictions.

God can do everything in His power, but this is a power unique and authentic to Him alone.

Since God is the Creator of all creaturely powers, He is the basis and limit of all creaturely possibilities.

Proper confidence regarding human ability and possibility is best grounded on the reliability of God, not on the unreliability of creatures.

The *fifth* point to maintain is that "God's power is power over everything."[2]

God's power is not the accumulation or combination of all other powers.

God permits other powers to exist beside and distinct from Him. This permission includes powers that correspond to His work but also those in opposition. He allows for powerlessness and the impossible possibility of what He has excluded.

It is by God's power that He tolerates other powers. God is not limited or determined by these other powers. He limits them.

Barth distinguishes between absolute power and ordered power.

Absolute power is that which God can choose to do but does not have to.

Ordered power is the power that God does use.

God's omnipotence is His free power, asserting that God could do what He has not done. He is bound to nothing but being Himself. We must be careful of other interpretations, such as the distinction between supernatural and ordinary power, which misses the point.

The only valid order in this world belongs to God and His Christ.

God orders all things. God's power is seen, not primarily in the miraculous interruptions but in the ordering by God of everything that reveals the power of God.

In freedom, God revealed His absolute power as His ordered power. It is ordered according to His love and plays out in His sovereign freedom. God must always be the context and content of His exercises of power.

So far, we have only distinguished divine and human power. Now, we need to explore the characteristics of the power of God in detail as divine knowledge and will. This is how we meet God's power in the Bible.

In the freedom of God's personality, He expresses a sovereign and comprehensive capacity to know and decide with superior and penetrating ability.

God's nature is spiritual and personal. God is expressed in His knowing and willing in a manner absolutely unique.

---

2. *CD* 2.1, § 31, p. 538.

This God is "the personal Creator of all personal being, the spiritual Creator of all spirit."[3]

God's personal power, being His own master and not a separable capacity, is not mere potential; it is power in the form and being of the personal God.

God's power has a definite direction and content. He judges what is wise and what is foolish. He determines what is possible and impossible.

Sin may be understood as that which God does not will. Such things as sin, folly, and the devil are the objects of God's knowledge, with which He deals in the freedom of His omnipotence.

God stands above all other powers in freedom. All other powers exist in a limited way.

While surrounded by His knowledge and will, creatures still have independence and the freedom of self-determination.

Holding in mind all we have said about God's being in love freely expressed, we now turn to God's spirituality, meaning His knowing and willing.

The personal God is omnipotent in His knowing and willing. Those are expressions of His power.

God speaks.

God speaks in His revelation.

He speaks about Himself.

He speaks to us.

In speaking about Himself, God speaks about us.

Thus, God speaks about all things as they exist between Him and us.

He speaks about all things as the One who knows them all.

God speaks and lets Himself be heard as the One who is a person—a spirit.

God discloses to us in such a manner that we know ourselves as those known by God.

God's revelation uncovers a vast wasteland of falsehood.

God's revelation shatters the illusion that we can successfully tell lies and deceive God—God cannot be deceived.

God opens the way for fellowship despite our errors and lies.

In sharing His self-knowledge, God actively loves us. He draws us to Himself and holds us so we will never fall from Him again.

In knowing God and knowing ourselves as God's, our conscience is awakened. Our confession is the outward manifestation that the sleep of death is overcome by the knowledge of Him for us.

---

3. *CD* 2.1, § 31, p. 543.

Once awakened, we can never deny or forget that God knows and that He knows us.

God's love allows and commands us to know Him and follow Him in love.

"God knows" is to be inscribed on our hearts. To live with this knowledge is to live with God.

To know God's revelation is also to know His will. It is a place of divine reconciliation.

We do not deserve coming to know Him; it is an act entirely of His free self-determination.

God's meeting with us in Christ enables us to understand Him. Through Christ, we look back and see His action as our Creator. Looking forward, we see His action as our Redeemer. He has decided how He will be toward us in Himself.

God wills, and in this, He reveals and confirms that He is a person.

In the outworking of His will, we see the Word of God and the work of God. He is to be sought and found in His Word and work, and nowhere else.

God loves us. This does not *merely* mean that He knows us; it means that He chooses us.

In responding to God's action, we become what He has willed—His children.

To understand that God knows us, we must meet Him in His divine revelation.

To understand the God who wills, we must meet Him in His reconciliation.

God is God omnipotent.

God is God omnipotent in that He wills.

God is God omnipotent in that He wills specifically *what* He wills in the unique *way* that He wills and toward the *end* that He wills.

1. God's omnipotence affirms the two statements "God knows" and "God wills." This is God's essence.
2. God's will is His knowledge, and His knowledge is His will, although each is a distinctive characteristic of His omnipotence.
3. Divine knowing and willing are free, superior in relation to all that is distinct from God. This self-determination is the working out of God's omnipotence in loving freedom.
    a. Divine knowledge is complete and referred to as *omniscience*. This is unique and all-embracing knowledge. The realm of the

      knowable is finite for us, but for God, it is infinite. He knows all things. What is not knowable or known by Him does not exist.

   b. Divine willing is complete and exhaustive and called *omnivolence*. God embraces and controls all things without detracting from the character of their wills.

There is no will beyond God, none that hinders God or conditions God's will.

1. Divine knowledge possesses the character of foreknowledge in relation to all God has created.
2. The essential nature of God's knowing and willing must be known concretely. It is the whole of the personal God at work in freely loving what He creates. Thus, God's being, knowing, and acting are original in God.

God knows not only Himself but also all created things in His free, practical, and visible knowledge. He becomes the Creator, Ruler, and Upholder of all things in the acting out of His will.

Ascribing autonomy to created objects leads to the great danger of limiting divine knowledge. This misstep explicitly happened with the "possibility and actuality" of the creature's will. Broken from its proper context, it is called *free will* and becomes the cause of human sin.

The sinning of humanity is neither fate nor fortune. It is the human use of the will *to depart* from the freedom of connecting with God's will.

God has not authored sin, and while knowing the contingency of all things, He permits what He knows will happen without causing the human to will it.

God's will is not compulsory or obligatory. It does not coerce or force the human will.

Some have conceived of a "middle way" in thinking about the relation to God's knowledge and human use of the will.

By foreknowing what the creature would do, it was proposed that God had a choice to save or condemn. God has provided "prevenient grace," but it lies in the creature's will to use or reject this grace. Everything depends on the creature's willingness to align with God's grace. Problematically, all conditions fall to the human.

The result of the noncooperation of will and grace is a conditional future known only to God—a middle way. God has not chosen it; God does not will it. In this case, this future is not the object of God's free knowing in that it becomes conditioned by the human in this "pact."

When God is seen to make provisional and conditional agreements with humanity, God's knowledge can only be assumed to follow as a consequence of human willing and acting.

God's freedom appears lost when it is constrained by human choice.

This view hands God's power to humans. We must reject this. It loses the actuality of remaining free as God's gift in all things.

In making human willing crucial, we end up knowing systems of conditions and not the absolute knowledge of God, who knows and wills in accordance with Himself. This view defaults to human free will.

God wills the good and only the good. Sin is the defect, the lie that occurs in the creature. God's positive will grants permission, not a cause, of this defect. It is a human misuse of freedom. It is betrayal and revolt.

God's goodwill permits sin, which neither excuses humans nor invites humans to sin.

Humans have no autonomy outside God's power and knowledge. Therefore, God is not kept waiting for any human happening so that He can come to know it. He knows unconditionally.

Any attempt to build a creative tension between the will of God and the human ends up making God equal to humans. We make God like us and then default "the will of God" to our own inclinations.

Human free will becomes autonomy. This act begins by neutralizing the impact of God's will, making it an equal humans may resist. Then, thinking God's will is subdued, one pursues a human kind of freedom.

We must cease to think of God as being in a God-creature system that allows the human will as an equal to God's will.

A proper approach to knowing God's will must follow from the fact that God took on human flesh in the person of Jesus. He reveals God's knowing and willing, embracing the human and divine.

A human will opposed to God has no freedom. Jesus alone exercises the human freedom to know and act with the power to love in freedom.

God establishes and maintains a relationship with humanity—this is the outworking of grace. This grace includes knowing, competing with, and cooperating with humankind.

Human freedom is not asserting ourselves in relation to God.

God's choice to be for us did not destroy human freedom in choosing.

Human choice is a responsible choice. Our wrong choices are not without consequences.

God's knowledge of who we are includes a choice for genuine human self-determination.

To exist with free will, we must be thankful for God's choice to unconditionally grant free will to us. We cannot condition God by our acts or attitudes to give us freedom.

Gratitude is our freedom to live within God's unconditional grace. To be free is to be governed by God's love in freedom for us. To assert free will as our own self-determination in resistance to God is to abandon God's freedom.

Human autonomy over and against God is enmity against God's grace, a repetition of the fall.

Any middle way that tries to include and equalize both God's and the human's will collapses into human failure and rejects God's unconditional provision.

We now turn to discuss the *genuineness* of the divine will. This focus is to explore the character of God's true will, all-embracing and free. He fully acts as God in this living act.

God's will is His living act and is wholly free.

God's knowing and acting meet us as a personal will, and not as blind force like gravity.

His will is not merely an event but is a personal action with intention.

When the all-powerful God says, "I am the Lord thy God," He is unconditionally binding Himself to us because of who He is in unreserved mercy.

Where there is a will, and not merely an event, there is One who wills.

God wills to be Himself with love that freely exists within the Trinity. At the same time, God wills to love His creation with the same love and freedom.

God's powerful knowledge is creative, productive knowledge that wills what He knows.

We may say that evil, sin, death, and the devil exist by the will of God and not without it. There is no sphere outside God's will. There is not another competitive realm, implying dualism, or some battle between two great powers.

These elements exist in their own way within the will of God. God does not cause them. God disavows and condemns them as His enemy, which He has conquered.

God has not created, caused, or produced the sphere of resistance. He only creates what is positively the outworking of His will and fulfills His intentions.

God chooses to give independence to humans. This choice makes a way for freedom and consequential blessedness.

God does not make impossible the misuse and abuse of freedom and independence.

God wills to be permissive. He permits opposition to His will.

He eternally stands against the revolt of creation against Him. Creation also revolts against itself, producing its self-created distress in the form of sin and wickedness. God stands against this as well.

God does not permit resistance without condemning and overcoming this willfulness to self-destruction. In this way, God brings the negative to be subordinated within His positive will by His own freedom in love.

God's permissive will must be taken seriously within the scope of His positive will.

God is glorified when we seek Him and when we avoid what keeps us from Him.

We avoid pursuing what He merely permits when we desire what He in loving freedom desires for us. God loves us uncompromisingly with His divine will in either case.

A proper understanding of omnipresence must be free from any sense of a natural capacity or blind force. It must affirm the power of God as unique, personal, intentional, and consistent with God's willing and knowing made effective by His Spirit.

Omnipotence must never be thought of as impersonal power. It is always the personal being of God in knowing and willing in the free act of His love.

In our thinking about human freedom, we must not believe that God's omnipotence is limited in any way.

Any sense of competition between God's self-determination and human self-determination is unnecessary and inconsistent with God's actual self-giving. Humans do not have to struggle against God to have the ability to exercise their power.

God's knowing and willing are not merely figurative or metaphorical.

God's love is actual in the personal knowing and loving where God is present in His revelation and reconciliation.

When God speaks to us, we recognize that He knows us.

The Bible witnesses to God's omnipotence by referring to the hand of God.

The exercise of God's hand is the actualizing of His personal power to be Himself in what He knows—and does by His freeing love—concerning specific situations.

The Old Testament is the memory of the story of God's power worked out in the covenant and liberation of His people.

The hand of God acts to reveal Himself as God, King, and Lord for those whom He intends to benefit with His love.

The whole Bible points to this powerful person, directing our attention to Him, not first to His acts by themselves.

The power of the Lord of history sustains the stars, stirs the sea, and sends the lightning. All the power in the universe is His power, the fruit of His choosing and calling.

We see God's power in His mercy for Israel. His love is expressed in making a covenant, comforting, and judging those He calls His own.

By His Word, God created the heavens and the earth. That speaking of God is a command and a promise. By this Word, all things came into being and have being.

God's power is set in motion on the first page of the Bible. The personal power of the One who is Spirit begins the history of the world, and He comes as its Lord within history.

God takes a specific historical location, a concrete point from which He knows, wills, and exercises His power over all ages.

That place in time and space marks the site where the Bible focuses us to know the personal power of the true and living God. From that location, He loves the world in all places and times.

From that centered place, He stands against rebellion and restores the world to Himself.

As the Messiah, He is born in His own time, as the fulfillment for all time.

The gospel is the power of God. This news reveals God's power to engage His love. It is the power to create, restore, and commune with His creatures.

Jesus does what He does by the power of God. He has this power as the Son of God and does nothing without His Father.

Jesus has the power of God because He is the power of God. He is also the wisdom of God.

In Christ crucified, the wisdom of the love of God is revealed.

The Son is crucified for us. He is offered up by the love of God, by the Father who raised Him from the dead. This act fulfills the intention of divine love through divine power as an expression of divine wisdom.

Only in recognizing and acknowledging Jesus as the power of God for us can we be transformed to inhabit reality. This awakening is called salvation.

By missing the fullness of Jesus, one defaults to limited human reasoning instead of conforming to God's reality. Then, one will walk in darkness and miss who God is toward us.

We must be set free by the true love of God. Then we can know the actuality of God.

3. The Eternity and Glory of God (pp. 608–77)

God's *eternity* is the duration of God's love, a function of God's freedom; all this is inseparable.

When we speak of God's eternal duration, we recognize a beginning, succession, and end.

We must be clear that the beginning, succession, and end are not three separate occasions. They are three simultaneous occasions as beginning, middle, and end.

God is beginning, middle, and end without separation, distance, or contradiction—that is all His simultaneity.

Eternity is God in the sense that God is Himself in this eternal duration and is simultaneously present in its fullness as Himself.

Eternity is not time.

Time is a form of God's creation.

With time, the beginning, middle, and end are distinct.

Past, present, and future are features of time and not of eternity. Eternity is the duration that lacks time.

The middle point of time is the present. The present is set in opposition to the past and future. Present is not past or future, but it has a relationship with them.

Eternity is nontemporality, and so we say God is, not was or will be. He is eternally present to time as His creation. Nothing contains God, but all things are contained in God.

God exists in pure duration from everlasting to everlasting, in distinction from humans who live from one time to another in the sequence of time.

God is free in the duration of His existence. God is constantly and reliably loving in determining His freedom in relation to His creation.

Time has no power over God. God has control over time to be constant in His love.

In the act of God's love, He lifts what is created to share His eternity.

For this reason, there is now an eternal life in which we hope and an eternal fire we may fear.

Time, as the eternal God's creation, is God's free activity outward.

Eternity is God's free activity inward—God is uniquely One with Himself. He is omnipresent to Himself.

God's freedom is clearly expressed when the Bible speaks about God as eternal. The limits of history and nature that constrain humanity do not bind God.

As eternal God, He is independent of human necessities and is constantly faithful to Himself.

Where Greek philosophy focused on the concept of being, the Bible focuses on the eternal God.

The "being" of the world, as we know it, is preceded and followed by God's eternity. All the perfections of God's being envelop and engage the contingent being of the world as the outworking of His love.

Eternity, the fullness of God beyond time, includes being and time as created by Him.

Real things have a relation to the will of God, who is their maker from eternity. Unreal things are those that resist and rebel against God and that can only hold an illusion of reality.

It is inadequate to understand eternity as the negation of time.

Eternity's duration, as the simultaneity of the beginning, middle, and end, is only properly understood when we see that God Himself is the beginning, succession, and end.

As it passes over various periods, the Bible understands space and time as created together by God. As the "speed of light" implies the time it takes light to travel through space, a place is fixed by God in the Bible's presentation of created time.

As God's life, eternity is the "now," the complete present of His life including, but also beyond, space and time.

One cannot understand eternity simply by expanding on our concept of space and time.

We come to know eternity not by the negation of time but by the knowledge of God who possesses and is this eternal life.

God existed first and then creation came into being with the inclusion of time. We must not think God fits into or adapts to preexisting time. God created time.

God has time for us.

God has time to reveal Himself to us.

God has time and enters into time for us in Jesus Christ.

God has time to be patient. He has time for our lifetime, our turning to Him, and our faithful life together.

Time is included in God's duration so that we may know He meets us, that we may have faith and trust Him in our time as He has given it to us.

Time exists with space as the form of God's creation.

Eternity has time; it merely lacks the fleeting nature of the present and the sequential separation between before and after.

God is personally present at every point of our time.

God coexists with the time He created in a manner similar to the North Star, which is the pivotal point among the stars and yet does not move with them. This is an imperfect illustration.

Eternity is perfect and coexists with time and all that it contains. It has a superiority that the North Star cannot have over the starry sky.

The triune God is eternally the *Father*. He is the origin and begetter. He is simultaneously the beginning, succession, and end in His own essence.

The triune God is eternally the *Son*. He is begotten of the Father and one essence with Him. He is also simultaneously the beginning, succession, and end in His own nature.

The triune God is eternally the *Holy Spirit*. He proceeds from the Father and the Son and is of the same essence as Father and Son. As the Spirit of the Father and Son, He is simultaneously the beginning, succession, and end in His own essence.

The unity is in the movement of God in the once-for-all unique relations of the triune God. The distinctive movements of God proceed sequentially as the One God, irreversibly and intentionally, acts coherently in time.

Jesus does not just embrace our time. He submits to our time and permits temporality to become the form of His eternity.

- God is pretemporal in that He precedes time.
- God is supratemporal in that He accompanies time's duration.
- God is posttemporal in that He exists after time's ending.

God has the power to exist before, above, and after time.
Eternity surrounds time on all sides and includes all its dimensions.

- In relation to all space, God is the original and proper space — omnipresent.
- In relation to all power, God is the original and proper power — omnipotent.
- In relation to all unities, God is the original and proper One — unique and simple.

God is ready for time. He creates, preserves, and rules it.

- Creation is the basis of human existence, established by God.
- Reconciliation is the renewal of human existence, accomplished by God.
- Redemption is the revelation of human existence, consummated by God.
- Redemption is the revelation of the meaning of creation.

Our existence stands under God's past, present, and future.

God Is Pretemporal

His existence acts physically in the creation of the world.

God stands before the existence of His created universe.

God's freedom in love, grace, mercy, and patience can only be understood if we start at this point.

At this "pretime," God decided to call the world into being in the power of His eternal Word.

He called humanity into being and determined to send His Eternal Word to the humanity He created.

All that God intended, He willed from before the foundation of the world. He intended good for the world in giving Himself and freedom to His creation.

It was then that the Son was appointed from eternal time to be for the temporal world.

Then and there, free grace was shown to resolve and personally manifest God's goal toward us in Jesus—God with us and for us.

The eternal presence of God over time and in time was established before time.

God Is Supratemporal

We could use terms like *cotemporal* or *intemporal* to express the embracing of eternity on all sides of time.

We must reject any sense of eternity as timeless. Eternity and time have a positive relationship.

Eternity accompanies time. This relation can be compared to a single stretch of the sky that accompanies us (eternity) as we travel from one point to another (time).

God's before and after are not separated but are the whole duration of His being that endures.

He wills to be with us in His freedom in our favor. He wills to be God among us.

In being with us, God's one message is: "Do not be overanxious."

In the coming of the Messiah, God's eternity is revealed in time. His accompanying of time in eternity becomes His presence in time.

Jesus comes as One who connects to our past and overcomes the rupture born in Adam. On the cross, He buried the old man of disobedience and ended the power of death.

In the resurrection, Jesus brings to light that He is the new man of the future. He makes humanity the object of God's favor.

At the same time, we are both *sinners*, who bear the scar of the past, and the *righteous*, to whom righteousness comes as a gift.

Our sin is our past, and our righteousness is coming. God's righteousness negates our sin.

The past is that from which we are set free; the future is that for which we are set free by Him.

There is no sense in looking back with tears and complaints concerning the past. The only reason to look back is to remember God's benefits for our life.

The future is a new time in which we enjoy the benefits for which we are set free in Jesus.

The life of faith is not blind to time. Faith allows us to understand that from eternity God's purpose was to fulfill in Jesus that which is complete and being finished in time.

Faith is seeing time and history in the light of Christ.

God Is Posttemporal

Just as God is before and accompanies all time, He is also after all time.

We come from God. We may be companions of God. We move toward God.

When time is no more, He will still be.

All roads lead to eternity. Any other road leads to nothingness.

Eternity is God's Sabbath rest after the completion of His works.

The revelation of the kingdom of God consists in the fact that God is all in all. This fulfillment lies in the future, and thus is posttemporal.

God embraces time and us within it, as He stands in front of us and provides what we do not have.

He is the first, and He is the last. His is the kingdom coming.

Veiled in time, we see the Godhead; we must not complain, but may live in hope.

There is no rivalry between the three forms of eternity.

Focusing on God's *pretemporality*, as some do, makes God's eternal decrees a set of completed actions that remove the ongoing involvement of God with humanity. In that proposal, eternal decrees were complete and finished in a selective approach. God becomes bound to a set preamble. This proposal was a problem for some Reformers.

Sixteenth-century theology overemphasized God's supratemporal, overarching role in eternity. In reaction, eighteenth-century theology focused too much on humanity in time. This reaction included human problems, but even more the possibilities for human progress.

The word *eternal* was removed from God and given over to a grand ideal. The "eternal good of the people" or "the idea of eternal love" replaced honoring God.

The replacement of God with human ideals turns our concept of God into preferences and prejudices. This turned Christian truth toward the road to secularism. God became a faint echo of human ideals.

In the nineteenth and twentieth centuries, we have seen a form of overemphasized *posttemporality*. These take on a form of eschatology.

An emphasis on the kingdom of God as primarily future-focused eschatology may override the present involvement of God. Faith becomes diluted to an individualistic hope for the future. The prominent focus is on an ending when all things will be set right.

Human help in ushering in the kingdom gradually turns to socialism, a human attempt at bringing in God's eternal fulfillment. Focus on "God's end ideal" justifies the means of human management toward a supposed higher order.

After the First World War, Barth was compelled to push past all human expectations attempting to usher in the kingdom of God. These occur at every level, for individuals, nations, and political parties. Their stated pursuit was to seek God's future and Jesus Christ as the fulfillment of time. Barth bellowed a resounding "No" against all human attempts to fulfill God's ends.

The problem was in the lack of a "Yes." Only Jesus brings in the legitimate affirmation, as promised in the Bible, of the means to fulfill God's hope.

Eternity is the living God Himself. Eternity is not a quality He possesses, nor a space in which He dwells.

To think of eternity is to think of God. To think of God is to think of eternity.

God does not statically *exist* eternally; He dynamically *lives* eternally.

The living eternal God exists in a relationship of *perichoresis*—all of God mutually and personally indwells each other. This interworking with each other is the unity of all three forms of eternity we have been discussing. In this, we see the unity and distinction of God throughout eternity.

In our final consideration of the perfections of God, we will discuss what it means to say that God has and is *glory*.

The eternity of God opens the view to see the glory of God.

God's glory is explicitly shown in His freedom to love. It is His dignity and right to manifest Himself in a variety of ways to create a recognition of Himself.

God's glory is His competence to make use of all His perfections to make Himself known.

In God's glory, God seeks and finds fellowship, personally involved in every aspect.

God exists in relationship to Himself.

God exists in relationship to everything outside Himself.

God exists as the basis and prototype of every kind of relationship.

All this relating displays the fact that in His glory, God loves.

We must understand the Greek word *doxa*, translated as glory.

In secular Greek, *doxa* refers to an opinion someone has of another person, their standing, or their reputation.

In the New Testament, the word took on a new meaning. It became the honor a person has, a dignity accepted by others. It can refer to the splendor a person has and is displayed. This glory of God revealed in Jesus unveils this sense.

Glory becomes an unquestionable recognition, which could not be otherwise.

In the Old Testament, *kabod* is an inner strength that expresses itself in one's appearance and activity. It is the radiance and the source of light that shines from a person.

Only God is light in the sense of spreading brightness across the earth in contrast to darkness. In this sense, God alone is glorious.

Jesus glorifies the Father and is glorified by the Father.

Jesus is the reflection of divine glory. In Him, God's love comes in person and powerfully creates the event of fellowship with humanity as a fact in human history. He brings God to shine in history.

The glory of God is the sum of God's self-revealing perfections as they emerge, express, and manifest the reality of God.

The glory of God opens the eyes of questioners—the very brightness of His glory opens blind eyes.

The majesty of His glory meets our inability to know God. Our ability to know Him is restored by His glory as He meets us.

With God's glory set in the primary place of our attention, a secondary focus arises. Our worries and the riddles of our existence become shadows. In the light of Jesus, these issues are illuminated, clarified, and resolved.

We come to see that we have no independent reality from God. In having Him, we have all that could be had. He may not do as we would wish, but He will be consistent with His loving will as He nurtures fellowship with us.

Humanity exists in opposition to God. But when we are aligned with the glorious being of God, His glory covers us and removes our shame. His transforming presence removes our fear and death.

With threats gone, we turn to look at the glory of God. We are comforted by His glory, which brings true contentment. We come to recognize that we lack nothing.

Human existence and meaningfulness are not essential to humankind. Humans respond to the movement of divine self-glorification as God transmits His internal joy.

Humans may humbly submit a response of jubilation. That which was lost between God and humans is restored by personal participation made possible by Jesus Christ.

All creation is to overflow with gladness, ignited by the glory of the One who is their source.

We must describe the glory of God with reference to God's *beauty*—this is how He enlightens, convinces, and persuades us.

The nature and form of God's beauty facilitate a power of attraction, which speaks to us with a divine beauty unique to God.

Beauty is not a leading concept in the doctrine of God.

Beauty helps us explain God's glory. It enables us to clarify and emphasize what is essential to God's glory.

Glory includes and expresses what we call beauty. It contains the ideas of the pleasant, desirable, and enjoyable. This wonder is the outflowing of God's self-communicating joy.

God's love gives meaning to His glory, as seen in His grace, mercy, and patience. The effect is that it persuades and convinces, calling for a response of love. We see its power in giving pleasure, awakening desire, and creating enjoyment.

It is possible, allowable, and indispensable to have joy standing before and in the living God. Glory awakens joy.

Glory is not gloomy and solemn. The being of God justifies our finding joy, which attracts us with desire and pleasure toward Him.

For the gospel to be good news, it must have the sparkle and radiating joy of the glory of God made evident in His revelation. It must attract.

Beauty yields and instills pleasure. In discovering God's beauty, we find the basis and criteria of everything else that is beautiful.

God's revelation is beautiful, and from it, we learn beauty.

Theology, when properly seen and grasped, is a particularly beautiful science. It is the most beautiful of all the sciences.

"The theologian who has no joy in his work is not a theologian at all."[4]

We *affirm the triunity of God*, the unity of the Father, Son, and Spirit. From this one unity flow the many perfections.

The relationship of the three persons is *perichoretic*; each is in the others and cannot know or act without the others.

From the inner life of connection in truth and power comes the active life of Father, Son, and Holy Spirit in their outgoing distinctiveness.

God does not exist with three divisions. God is whole and undivided.

God is radiant with joy that is beautiful and attracts. The form of God's life as a triunity, particular to God, is the extent of His beauty.

We also *affirm the incarnation* as the focus and goal of God's work. Jesus reveals the beauty of God in a special and supreme way.

God comes to us in the glory of His Word to arouse joy. We are attracted to the beauty of God's being, His triunity, the delight of His inner life, and our adoption into His life.

God condescends to humanity. God embraces, indwells, and fully shares in the nature of humanity so as to be their partner. This undertaking involves union with a stranger or one estranged.

God has determined that humanity should again share His glory, for which we were created—He does this through the union *He* creates and in no other way.

Solomon had a human beauty connected to his wisdom, exhibiting a promise of beauty.

---

4. *CD* 2.1, § 31, p. 656.

The promise of Solomon was finally resolved in the beauty that came in the personal form of God's image in Jesus Christ.

The beauty of Jesus is the beauty of God, the expression of what God is and does in Him.

In Him, we see the majesty and condescending of God.
In Him, we see sublimity and holiness.
In Him, we see mercy and patience.
In Him, we see faithfulness to Himself and His creature in action.
In Him, we see the love in which God is free, as well as the freedom
     with which He loves.

Barth feels that artists should leave the face of Jesus to mystery, for no art can capture Him. The art ends up serving humans and not God.

God has provided His very being with a beauty intended to create His joy in His creatures with an inviting musicality.

In manifesting His love, God is fully satisfied in making Himself known as the One He is. He is this life of love internally (immanent) and externally (transcendent).

God chooses not only to exist but to coexist as the outworking of God's glory.

God's glory incorporates the glorious answer awakened in humans by God Himself, included as the echo of worship offered by His creation in response to God's voice.

Only in light of the beginning, center, and goal of creation found in Jesus can we say there is an echo in creation. Glorification springs from the glory of God, and not the self-will of our own voice.

Looking to Jesus, within the community of His children, we look away from ourselves and all that is created. We see the Son of God, who has accepted what He made and has brought its fulfillment.

Creaturely glorification, while limited, is genuine. It looks to God's redemption and fulfillment even as it waits. The world is not without God's glory.

The creature is free *because* of God's glory, to *extend* God's glory, and to *enjoy* God's glory.

The glory of God includes not only the Father and Son but also the Spirit. The Spirit is the unity of love in the Godhead. He is also the activity of God in the world. He opens hearts to God so they may receive Him.

The Spirit is the unity between God and His creature. He is the bond between time and eternity.

Humans serve God's glorification as a wall echoes and repeats. Human gratitude, created by the Spirit, shares in the glory of God in its activity. The honoring extends into actions of thanksgiving and service.

God's part in worship is primary, decisive, and comprehensive. The human component is derivative—the overflowing of God's glory.

The mercy of God permits His creature to praise Him as the fruit of His befriending humans.

God loves humans, seeking to be with them and not without them. He draws humans to Himself so they will not be without Him. His glory comes to us in Jesus, and this is the sum of the doctrine of God.

As a divine gift, the creature is liberated. This release is liberation from powerlessness and the limits of human existence. It is a liberation to the praise of God.

Human freedom comes in coexisting with the Creator. The creature acquires a new form and freedom to praise God.

We are awakened to Jesus Christ, and in Him we are being restored to the image of God, who glorifies God.

God has a reflection of Himself in creation. Jesus is this true reflection. In Him, the Creator is revealed.

God wills to have another reflection of Himself in His creature. For this, Jesus comes in the flesh. For humans, to be born again is to participate in Him, to be His reflection, the renewed image of God.

This reflective relation is the call to walk in love, as Jesus has loved us.

God calls us. God awakens us. We confirm Him as we conform to Him. We honor Him as our words and actions conform to His existence.

Freedom comes with living in harmony with God's way of being, and not in opposition.

To honor God is to live from the heart. By the heart's readiness and willingness being given to God, we may live a life of honor, thanksgiving, and service. This readiness is liberation into the life of loving in freedom, as we have been loved.

The Church is comforted in glorifying God's future, where all will be brought into conformity with His glory. The Church lives in the tension between what will be the restoration of God's eternal purposes and the realities of here and now.

We live in a time of limitation. God's self-giving is not limited. Our knowledge of and conformity to God's freedom and form of life in Jesus Christ are limited. Freedom is still found in Him. Yet the limits remain.

We stand on earth needing a holy place to stand. In that place, proper reverence directs our minds to Him while we live in this provisional time.

In the here and now, the form of our participation is the Church. We express glory in our proclamation, faith, confession, theology, and prayer. In this temporal form, God's glorification takes place here and now.

COMMENTARY:

- Beyond the perfections of God, this chapter paints an even more dynamic picture of God, known in the light of His free action in the whole of the cosmos—and beyond.

- This section continues to discuss the unity of God's love and freedom. It considers God's robust relation to space and time to fulfill His purposes. It reconceives abstract concepts, making them practical and unique ways of God's being.

- God's unity is not just holding together many parts within God. Unity affirms the absolute uniqueness of God. God cannot be divided; His being has an inseparable wholeness. When we attempt to isolate any aspect of God from the whole, we lose the meaning of the whole.

- Omnipresence is God's intimate and direct relation with the whole universe, beyond space and time. Humans work within God's created sphere. Our question is often whether God is here, and if there is any limit to His loving presence. The answer is that God is present with us right now.

- The constancy of God transforms the limitation of God. Barth affirms God is constantly faithful to Himself and His love rather than using the awkward language of *unchanging*. His mercies are new every morning.

- The omnipotence of God is the ability to accomplish what God thinks and wills as the outworking of His love. His love is unstoppable.

- The eternity of God is not timelessness, what we call infinity—without time. Eternity is God's kind of time. It makes space for created time and is present to it all at once. This space includes the beginning, progression, and culmination of our time.

- God's glory is the way God shines on, embraces, and includes His creation in reflecting His love and devotion.

- This section is a rainbow of insights. Each topic reflects into the life of the Church and Christians who share in His glory, enjoy His beauty, and maintain humor.

CONCLUSION FOR THE CHURCH: Barth's concern in this long section is that we shed our human misconceptions about the character of God. Instead, Barth wants us to become informed by God's self-giving in all the expressions of His love. Barth clarifies the language so that it is not merely an expanded form of our human use of terms. He wants to extend our boundaries beyond our recognition so that God's profound distinction may be exposed in Jesus. The Church is most alive when it opens to absorb the light of God's love and action toward it and in its life together. The Church ought not be in the business of replicating the character of God. Instead, the Church forms a sacred space to indwell God's loving glory and reflect the love proceeding from God into the world that remains ignorant of God's grace.

 INSIGHT FOR PASTORS: So often, our presentation of theology is densely abstract, like a cloud that gives no rain to water a parched land. Talk about God as omniscient, omnipresent, omnipotent, eternal, and immutable make God distant and silent—out of touch. An honest person might ask, "If God is omnipresent, is He here for me? If God is omniscient, does He really know me? If God is omnipotent, can He really help me?" In attempting to protect the grandeur of God, we may simply make God unapproachable.

Barth wants us to see that God is not only amazingly distinct from our created world but also present and active in it in the way God has chosen. Barth presents us with an opportunity to see that God is distinct from us and yet desires intimacy. He is not far away. He is not near in the way we want. We must apprehend God as He chooses, as the presence of loving care. As leaders, we can serve people by reminding them that God is present. He is persistent in loving us just as we are. All of Him is present all the time. He has time for us, indwells our space, and brings beauty to attract, align, awaken, and reflect His freedom in love. We must not gaze inwardly to look for God or our own self-improvement. We must create a church culture that beholds the face of the One who loves us moment by moment, lived in His embrace.

 INSIGHT FOR THEOLOGIANS: As theologians, it can be tempting to corral the attributes of God into stalls that allow us to manage our God-talk. The language of attributes can become a sleight-of-hand move. We *say* we are thinking of God's holiness, but we may *actually* be describing a sanitized life that looks nothing like Jesus. We use philosophical terms of God as terms of description, such as omniscience, omnipotence, omnipresence, and aseity. Unfortunately, they remain reflections of *human attributes* of knowing, acting, presence, changeability, and so on. They do not bring us into God's embrace. Barth takes abstract theological terms and sees them all concretely related to Jesus. This is how theology becomes a science.

If Jesus is the One who informs theology, then terms of abstraction need to be seen as terms of distraction—Jesus must reboot them in lived engagement with our humanity. Jesus shows us the *simplicity* of God as the true revealed image of the invisible God, the inseparable God. Jesus shows us the *presence* of God in human flesh; in His ascension He never stopped being human or present. Jesus is the *constant* love of God from whom nothing can separate us. Jesus lives the *power* that overcomes death and brings us into His eternal life—*beyond* our space-time context. Jesus is the One who shows us the *glory* of His Father in human blood and bone. He reveals what that glory looks like in shaping a community and makes possible the Spirit's work of reflecting the glory of God in us.

This section is a massive shift into playing in a new key. The same notes take on unimagined octaves that were previously unheard and unhearable. Now, the music of heaven moves from being unnoticed elevator music to become the accompaniment of human life. This is the science of God as the context for human existence.

? **CLARIFYING QUESTIONS:** Does your theology seek to find definitions and descriptions of God's power that label every aspect of God into a neat system that is unrelated to human experience? *Or* does your theology step up to the Bible and look for the empowering face of Jesus?

PART 3

CHURCH DOGMATICS 2.2

Election and Ethics in the God-Human Relationship

Karl Barth	Church Dogmatics	I/1	1932 (1936 ET)
Karl Barth	Church Dogmatics	I/2	1938 (1956 ET)
Karl Barth	Church Dogmatics	II/1	1940 (1957 ET)
Karl Barth	Church Dogmatics	II/2	1942 (1957 ET)
Karl Barth	Church Dogmatics	III/1	1945 (1958 ET)
Karl Barth	Church Dogmatics	III/2	1948 (1960 ET)
Karl Barth	Church Dogmatics	III/3	1950 (1961 ET)
Karl Barth	Church Dogmatics	III/4	1951 (1961 ET)
Karl Barth	Church Dogmatics	IV/1	1953 (1956 ET)
Karl Barth	Church Dogmatics	IV/2	1955 (1958 ET)
Karl Barth	Church Dogmatics	IV/3.1	1959 (1961 ET)
Karl Barth	Church Dogmatics	IV/3.2	1959 (1962 ET)
Karl Barth	Church Dogmatics	IV/4	1967 (1969 ET)

CHURCH DOGMATICS, CHAPTER 7

"The Election of God"

CHAPTER 13

GOD IS HIS OWN MUSE; ALL OTHER MUSIC COMES FROM HIM

§ 32. The Problem of a Correct Doctrine of the Election of Grace

FOCUS STATEMENT: This paragraph (§ 32) launches us into one of the symphonic highpoints of the whole *CD*. We will spend significant time listening to the heart of God (election, will, and intent are words that reveal the heart commitment of God lived out in His choices). This experience is like listening to soulful gospel music played with boundless philharmonic proportions.

God's revealing music is illustrated above as the tree of life. It provides as it produces what is needed. God's harmonious being is lived through self-giving that keeps on giving.

God's election is complex. Therefore, we must carefully engage "The Problem of a Correct Doctrine of the Election of Grace." We must listen and learn from the sound source.

For many, a muse is the source of inspiration for their music. God does not use others' music. His music courses from Himself as its source. He is its form and content, its melody and meaning. He is active in its initiation, reverberation, and reception for the hearer. God's election fills the universe with His intentional musical presence. The sweeping themes engage our ears with good news. The intensity will not leave us alone.

God is not a soloist. He makes music to include others. The song God sings, the reason He sings, and the lyrical content are original to Him. His election is an expansive invitation to participation. To say God elects is to reveal God's choice to be for and with those He loves. Election sets His grace in action. His music ignites a response, causing all creation to join in joyful participation.

159

God's song does not exclude imperfect voices, although He has perfect pitch. He makes space for creative and chaotic instruments all to join in. When we hear His song aright, it invites us to join His Choir and Orchestra as we are—He chose it to be that way.

Election is Jesus' song. It is Jesus singing His song. It's the good news He sings. He is a song for all communities and every person. He values the uniqueness of each person. In Him, the theater of creation contains and resonates with His acoustic bliss—He elected Himself as the source of the good news song extending across space and time.

INTRODUCTION: This section begins chapter 7, which deals with election. Barth does not argue that God chooses some for heaven and some for hell. Instead, he engages God's eternal decision in Jesus to be for all humanity— whether or not they respond. The doctrine of election is not an eternal decree that binds God's hands, keeping Him from further involvement with humankind. It is God's choice to be for and with humanity as the Lord who loves in freedom. The chapter explores the unequal relationship in which God's choice creates the context within which humanity responds.

This section points us in the right direction—oriented by Jesus. It argues for the importance of election as foundational for understanding God's inclusive, gracious decision. Election is not a subpoint within the doctrines of creation, anthropology, or salvation, intended to determine who is in and who is out. Those shortsighted views miss the point. Election is God's choice, from before the world was made, to love His creation in Jesus. It is only responsively about us living in reply to His intention.

CONTEXT: *CD* 2.2
Pages in Paragraph: 91 pages (pp. 3–93)

Subsections
1. The Orientation of the Doctrine
2. The Foundation of the Doctrine
3. The Place of the Doctrine in Dogmatics

TEXT: § 32. The Problem of a Correct Doctrine of the Election of Grace

OPENING SUMMARY: The doctrine of election is the sum of the gospel because of all words that can be said or heard it is the best: that God elects man; that God is for man, too, the One who loves in freedom. It is grounded in the knowledge of Jesus Christ because He is both the electing God and elected man in One. It is part of the doctrine of God because originally God's election of man is a predestination not merely of man but of Himself. Its function is to bear basic testimony to eternal, free and unchanging grace as the beginning of all the ways and works of God.[1]

SUMMARY:
1. The Orientation of the Doctrine (pp. 3–34)

It is by God that God is known.

It is by God that God is known as the One who loves in freedom.

It is by God that God is known as the One who loves in freedom displayed in the wealth of His perfections. From this loving freedom, God elects to act for His creature.

The voice of the Church is only to be measured by the Voice attested to in the Bible who can reign in the Church.

Jesus Christ is the voice by which God taught us.

When theology is jostled away from Him, it creates an idol from a human image that nudges Jesus out of our attention.

- Theology must *begin* with Jesus Christ, not generalized principles.
- Theology must *continue* with Jesus Christ as the root and origin of the Word of God.
- Theology must *end* with Jesus Christ, not self-evident conclusions taken from Him.

When we speak of God, we must talk about His free decision. We must also tell of His relationship to this other whom He loves.

Jesus is God moving toward humanity, embodied in His covenant with His people, acting among and toward them.

Jesus is the decision of God enacted in this relation—He is the relation.

This covenant is an irrevocable relation. Once God entered it, He could not be God without it.

The partner of God is not humanity in general, nor in the totality of their individuality gathered.

The partner of God is Jesus and those represented in Him.

---

1. *CD* 2.2, § 32, p. 3.

Everything that takes place between God and humanity takes place in Jesus Christ. This relationship is the dynamic of the union formed through His covenant with those who belong to Him.

In this relation, He acts as the Lord of His covenant. He is its author. He determines its ordering and content. He oversees it in every aspect to move it toward its goal. He decides who will be His covenant partner.

This choice is an election on God's part to originate, sustain, and guide His covenant. It is the expression of His perfections freely extended in love for humanity in His Son.

God's love is merciful, meeting the other in the plight of their being.

This love is patient, giving a place for the other to exist and grow into fulfilling the goal God intends in His covenant.

In making His covenant, God establishes and invests Himself, and He is the beneficiary.

In His majesty, God establishes fellowship even with those opposed to Him.

God's election of grace is the entirety of the gospel.

Election emphasizes and explains the word grace. In love, God elects another for Himself.

We must emphasize that this is *God's self-choice to be God* and not motivated by the other.

God determines never to be without the other whom He will maintain in covenant.

Grace is unconditional and impossible to earn.

In electing Jesus, God is free in what He does and permits. He is Lord in His unconditioned sovereignty and in helping the other He loves.

God's covenant-relation in Jesus fulfills the doctrine of God but does not exhaust it.

In response to God's unconditional covenant, there is an unconditional response when God encounters humanity in love.

In freeing love, God becomes the companion of humanity. That is His self-determination.

In Jesus, grace favors, claims, and rules us by the love that frees us.

Grace makes a claim on our lives. We do not merely know about it and receive it. Grace implies an ethical response to the commanding grace of Jesus as Lord.

Within the field of theology, we are entering into the topic of *predestination*.

The predestination of God is good news. It is not an abstract truth to only consider, nor a theory that does not affect our lives. Its contents are a proclamation of joy.

Predestination is not a mixed message of joy for some and terror for others. It brings light, which of course, creates a shadow. But the light is the *focus*, and the shadow a *consequence*.

The final word of predestination is not a word of warning and fear. It speaks a "Yes" from God to humanity that says "no" to what is contrary to His freeing love.

God's election is "Yes" to humanity, and that means it must acknowledge the "No" to what is contrary without giving the negation the power of its own existence.

The doctrine of predestination has a tragic history. The shadow side that awakens fear has often been brought to the fore.

The doctrine has been made an abstract theory engendering hostility and confusion toward God. We must let the light of the gospel shine in election to disperse the shadow of misrepresentations.

The doctrine of predestination is the gospel as a "Yes" and not a "No" to humanity. It is not "Yes" and "No," in some kind of balance. It is not "No"; it is in every way "Yes."

God's work as Creator, Reconciler, and Redeemer benefits humanity with all the joyful blessings and promises God has declared. All this is included in the eternal election of God's grace.

Whatever contradictions may appear, when we see them in the light of the reality of God's grace, the shadows are dispersed, fear is dispelled, and our connection to truth prevails.

If the preaching of the gospel brings despair, it is teaching blind human reason.

Election in the Bible begins with God electing Israel. In the end, the whole Bible is a divine "Yes" to Israel. Indeed, it is the divine "Yes" to the true Israelite, Jesus. He suffers the divine "No" to all that oppose God's intentions only to reaffirm the eternal "Yes" in Jesus' crucifixion and resurrection.

In the New Testament, election is the call to disciples forming a community sent out to participate in the Messiah's future.

A problem arises when we think of the Book of Life as having two columns, a death column and a life column, as though election and rejection were interconnected.

God's decision precedes human choice and is independent of human decisions.

God's free decision is a mystery. He has left us out of the council room of God. We cannot question the purpose or validity of His election.

We must acknowledge that God will always be consistent with and worthy of Himself. His election is wisdom before which we can only be silent.

God determines what is orderly; we cannot measure by our standards. He teaches us what order is. We measure our sense of order by the decisions He has made.

Violence is done to the doctrine of God's election when we do not begin by listening to God in His righteous wisdom. Thinking themselves wise, some set conditions on what God is free to do, measuring God based on human considerations instead of beginning with listening to God. These people are seeking a school other than one instructed by the Holy Spirit.

The election of God precedes His other choices. This choice is eternally fulfilled in Jesus and continues through Him for His creatures. This decision is not an absolutized choice in eternity, as a pronouncement distinct from Jesus.

In this election, the inner life of the triune God expresses the freedom of God's love outwardly.

In this election, God is for us. God is for the world created by Him, distinct from Him, and yet maintained by Him.

The movement of election is an active demonstration of God's love. In this election, God loved the world.

God ordained and constituted Himself as friend and benefactor of the world He created.

The world contains opposition to the love of God. Opposition is rejection by humans. God does not will this negation of His affirmation.

God wills the affirmation of salvation, not damnation.

Even in rejecting God's election, descending into the abyss, we are still in the hands of God and His decision. Even then, we are not alone, but God goes with us, true to His "Yes." Even in hell, one can only think of the love and grace of God.

The gospel affirms God's love for us in God's unshakable resolve to be for us regardless of our acceptance or resistance to His loving election.

We have three questions to explore in understanding a gospel-interpreted view of God's gracious election:

1. What is the meaning of God's freedom in election?

    God unconditionally precedes His creature. Human choices can only follow.

Humans cannot produce goodness in themselves.

There is no human reason to expect divine election and favor; that was lost.

The creature is intended to know its need as it discovers God's freedom to love one in such a state.

Despite human opposition and resistance, God elects to be for His creatures.

"Grace is the Nevertheless of the divine love to the creature."[2]

In that it all is grace, it is free. If it were not free, how could it be from divine love?

Against our "no," He responds, "Nevertheless."

God allows humans to fall. God has also decided that humans shall stand.

Humans are free to obey Him, live in Him, and be released from the bondage that leads to death.

We are given the freedom to cling to the grace of God. This blessing is held out to all who hear.

2. What is the meaning of the mystery of God's freedom in election?

God's election arises out of His pure good pleasure.

We cannot force God to give an account for His act, as though it could be reasoned by a higher logic than the freedom of His love.

A proper hearing will lead to joyful obedience, the aim of freeing grace.

The One who has handed us His decision to elect Himself on our behalf is right in His love. He is beyond questioning by human standards.

God's verdict releases us from the accusation against us. He stands against the curse and death's shadow over our lives.

The past of our self-determination is laid behind us.

The future is decided for our salvation as the mystery of the life-giving God.

God's election disturbs our will. The compelling power embraces us as His "Yes" that disrupts our lives.

Within the sphere of God's grace, we are quieted.

The sphere of disquiet is outside God's grace, where creatures resist the love of God.

---

2. *CD* 2.2, § 32, p. 28.

Entangled in the web of our untrustworthy relation toward God and the world, we are rescued from the sphere of unrest. We are brought into the rest of the mystery of the life-giving God.

Anxiety is cleared by God's "Yes." Acceptance permeates our unrest as we find we are affirmed in the "Yes" of God.

What is left is wonder. We are filled with reverent astonishment before the mystery of life affirmed by God.

The one demand of us now is that we should worship. God is both the God we must worship above all things and the God we may love above all things.

3. What is the meaning of divine righteousness in the event of God's election?

In God's election, He exercises judgment. He is the only One with the right and wisdom to engage the task.

God creates order. Who can discuss what constitutes order? All other order is disorder.

In the righteousness of God's election, we are made aware of our limitations in our disorder.

Standing within the embrace of God's gracious election, we can see the abyss we had chosen apart from God.

God regards it worthy of Himself to be the judge who speaks truth and order. He is also worthy as the One who releases and frees those who have gone astray to their destruction.

God's lovingkindness avenges sin by forgiving it.

2. The Foundation of the Doctrine (pp. 34–76)

What is the source of the truths and realities to which we are pointed in the doctrine of election?

What is it that makes this doctrine possible to talk about and necessary to bring specific clarity?

The most common failure in theological thinking is a lack of investigation as to the starting point from which we are to think.

Supposed "self-evident answers" have led to many conjectures and systems that turn the investigation astray.

The basic rule of Christian dogmatics is that no element is legitimately proposed unless explained within the context of the listening Church, singularly oriented toward God's self-revelation as presented in the Bible.

Some initial concerns:

1. We cannot develop doctrine by *beginning with the tradition of the Church* to be our guide. The Church cannot set the norms of understanding. In each case, we must ask regarding the origins of held beliefs.

   Our formulations cannot be reformulations of great traditions that are unexamined, and none can become the measure or norm of Christian theology.

   We must follow Calvin by doing what he did, beginning with the Bible, to which we must repeatedly address ourselves.

2. We must not lay a foundation based on what we think will be *most beneficial* for teaching or healing people's hearts.

   It is tempting to construct doctrines based on their usefulness. This approach ends up complying with our human valuing of what is useful. It abandons the trustworthy source found in the living Word, where real usefulness emerges.

   Systemization becomes more desirable over time and asserts the value of "useful" principles in the form of axioms.

   Human sensibility can filter out the actual stand of God for us.

3. A third concern is with those who make election *dependent on human response*.

   If we go to the Bible as judges, working from our sensibilities in discerning who has responded appropriately, do we not take judgment into our own hands and neglect the judgment of God?

   The Bible refers to God's judgment; it does not permit us to usurp the judgment of God.

   The Bible determines to give us the right questions before it gives us its answers. Unfortunately, Calvin looked first at the questions of his own experience as to whom was elected based on his judgment.

   In the end, human judging concerning who is elected was a problem. Theologians began to replace God's judgment with their own, speaking for God regarding who He preordained in acceptance and rejection.

   Humans unconsciously determine that God must predetermine some to be saved and some to be sent to hell—on a one-by-one basis.

   Once we have our categories of the two groups (the blessed and the damned), we may take the next step to inquire about the nature of their private relationship with God—although we have no basis to pursue this judgment.

We easily presuppose a natural connection between the doctrine of election and the private life of a relationship with God for every person.

Having affirmed our place in the judgment, the doctrine of election turns into a filter.

Private relationships with God do exist. But God has determined who He will be in these relationships—He is Lord in every relationship.

God's election is vital for every person. This does not mean that each person's specific outcome is decided beforehand.

God intended His free love for every person. This choice does not necessitate that each individual is elected or rejected in advance.

The divine election of grace has a definite goal and limit. It is not for individuals generally; it is for One in particular. In Him, people are called and unified in relationship with God. Their particularity arises within the scope of His activity.

Only Jesus can properly be understood as "elected" or "rejected."

Other humans are elected *in Him* and not as individuals.

We cannot discern the nature of humanity based on our views. We cannot set up an opposition between those deemed Christian or heathen in a manner that is grounded in our experience and judgments.

4. We ought not begin with a view that God's omnipotent will *randomly directs every person* to heaven or hell. An abstract God, making arbitrary decisions about specific people, is not consistent with the gospel of grace in Jesus.

God's decisions are *prior* to any other conclusion. However, God's decisions are not abstract or arbitrary; they concretely work to fulfill His love in freedom.

The doctrine of predestination must not be part of a deterministic scheme. This clarification does not mean we reject all determinations on God's part. However, He must reveal those according to His purposes.

We must always begin with the superior reality in the activity of Jesus as the demonstration of God's election.

When God's power and free will are separated from God's revelation, His providence becomes a logical principle instead of His personal overseeing of creation.

The providence of God can be turned into a plan by humans. In that case, it appears God determines everything from outside time and space as an eternal decree. History is just playing out the plan (like watching a movie already made).

We cannot speak of God's love and freedom abstractly, leaving it to a generalized view of sovereignty.

God's love is displayed concretely in the freedom to act specifically in history. We may have confidence in His election as an actuality.

God rules over all things by His will. But that does not imply that He is a being who rules absolutely.

God's presence and activity in the world include His self-limitation within a definite sphere and power to be with and for His creation.

We are dealing with the true King, not a tyrant. His decisions align with His self-limitation and loving determination.

Where God is revealed to us, we may begin to speak about who He is, how He wills, and the manner of His ruling.

Either we attend to the concrete, self-given God, or we create false gods and idols.

By beginning with the particular, we come to know the general of humanity. One acts on behalf of the many.

The One revealed *God* acts on behalf of *humanity* as true God who elects. The One actual *human* who is elected in our stead for *God* is the One man Jesus.

God's election is the basis of the relationships between God and humanity.

The doctrine of God would be incomplete without God's decision to give Himself to another.

The problem with election has two poles: one on the side of God and the other on the side of the human. Each pole needs to be seen in its particularity (Jesus) and not in a general sense (the divine or humanity).

The Bible gives us a precise focus on God as the "I" who addressed Moses, the patriarchs, the prophets, and the apostles.

The God of the Bible wills to be known and adored in a relationship of fidelity.

The event of Jesus in human history is the fulfillment and substance of all the preceding history of God's expectation in Israel and the following history of the Church.

When entering human time, Jesus became the covenant partner of God on our behalf. He became the invitation, the hope, the promise, and the question set against every human and all humanity.

Jesus is the "I" who introduces every perfection in the character of God, revealing the free and loving sovereignty of God.

In election, we have to do with Jesus, who reveals God's decision as the active presence of God in the world, as God's eternal decree bursting forth toward us with God's self-determination.

In Him, God makes His choice specific in a historical form and actuality.

It is God's choice to have this focus.

It is God's choice to move toward humanity, to be our covenant partner.

It is God's choice to give Himself to His people as Lord and Shepherd.

It is God's choice to act in this age on behalf of all times and places.

It is God's choice to create and to make Himself head of a people. He chose that they would be His body and the instrument of His love.

Adam cannot tell us what we need to know about the human race.

The Bible speaks in the sphere of the particular, giving us stories of specific humans so we know the intent of God toward us.

From these specific people, a whole people came. Together they formed the whole of the developing story with God.

We must come to see that individuals do not stand alone. In Adam is all humanity. In Abraham are all the families of the earth. In Jacob is all Israel.

As a flesh and blood people, Israel is a sign within humanity.

The Word that created Israel became the Son of David.

All the hope of Adam, Abraham, David, Solomon, and the prophets were fulfilled in Jesus.

God's Son is the king of His people. In and through His election, all people were elected.

If we are to follow the Bible, our attention must turn to One elected man. In Him, all other humans are united and represented as an elect people. This uniquely elected person is how we come to understand elect humanity.

By looking at the same person, we come to know the electing God. This person is God's revelation, revealed as a man.

If we want to know what it means to be elected by God, we must look to Jesus, in whom the beginning and end of this mystery are enclosed. All else is conjecture.

Election is the center of divine revelation.

Knowledge of election is a distinctive form of our knowledge of Jesus Christ.

Except for Aquinas, all the great teachers of election have paid attention to election "in Him."

For Calvin, Christ is the mirror of election. He is the prototype of all divine election and human election.

There is no basis for election in any human. It is all grounded in Jesus Christ.

Both Augustine and Calvin would have understood the human decision to stand wholly under the *prior* decision of Christ.

When asked a pastoral question regarding God's election, are we to direct people to a mysterious eternal decree or to Jesus as the revealed decision of God?

The pastoral provision is to give assurance of the declaration of God made known in Jesus for our favor.

We can rejoice in God's electing of us because we can see Him as the place He has made it known.

We may not begin with focusing on Christ, and then look away to eternity to specific souls who are elected. This approach would fabricate another decision in eternity, sorted out beforehand, based on secret speculation.

When looking away to another judgment, the cross becomes merely instrumental to the distant decision. We lose our focus on God's determinative act for humanity in Jesus. He alone offers humanity what is needed for salvation.

Can the Father make a preliminary choice as to who is saved outside Jesus? No. Christ is the author and finisher of salvation.

The Arminians held that the criterion of the measure of all things is the human—the human conception of what is right and rational—things worthy of God and humanity.

The dignity of humanity is held over and against the sovereignty of Jesus Christ, arguing for autonomous human freedom in decisions. Jesus becomes an instrument of salvation, not one who elects some and leaves the rest to fate. This theology drifts away to human control.

We must learn to think of election as "in Him," as referred to in Ephesians. That makes God's decision a specifically Christ-focused reference rather than a hidden decree.

Our task is to understand the gospel in the light of this person, not to understand this person in light of principles or propositions.

A "foreseen faith," conceiving of a person making a choice that God acknowledges and affirms, defaults to human choice. Holding the idea that "because I knew you would choose Me, I elected you" focuses on the human choice, not the loving freedom of God.

We must not reduce God's will to ratifying the future choice He knows humans will make.

Abstract ideas are in danger of missing the concrete givenness of God. The Father is merciful, but that is seen concretely in Jesus.

Jesus is electing God and elected human. When we speak of Him, we speak of both elements—He is electing God, freely and in love. He is elected humanity, providing our free and loving response to God. In Him, we are elected.

3. The Place of the Doctrine in Dogmatics (pp. 76–93)

Why should we place the doctrine of election at the beginning in the doctrine of God?

May we discuss it before creation, reconciliation, and redemption? Yes, we may.

To know God is to know Him electing from eternity as the triune God who elects Himself in His Son, and in the Son elects His people.

We must understand all the acts of God revealed in revelation, which informs our knowledge, as the subsequent outworking of God's divine election in love.

God cannot be other than the One who elects. Therefore, all faithful doctrine will attend to God's election as the basis of God's actions in our coming to know God.

We must clarify what other positions have been taken in placing the doctrine of election and how we differ in the current placement.

1. In classical Reformed orthodoxy, *election followed the doctrine of God and preceded creation.*

   Although called a *central dogma,* election was not the basis of the doctrines that followed.

   The basic tenet for that tradition was *the decrees of God* rather than God's election.

   Election became part of the providence of God; the absolute governance of God primarily focused on the salvation of humans.

We must reject this because it begins with God's *general relationship* to the world, and reduces election to one function. Instead, we must start with God's electing in His *specific relationship* established in Jesus Christ.

We must be able to follow the forms, direction, and aims of the divine will. We must not ascribe abstractions to God that reduce Him to conceptions and ideas.

God's internal action in election is consistent with His external ways of loving in freedom in expressing the fullness of His perfections.

2. The arrangements of other theologians proposed speaking of *creation and providence before speaking of election.*

    Election became the *completion* of God's providence in the world rather than the *initiating* act of His love.

    Appropriate ordering places the first work of God as the electing in Jesus Christ preceding creation.

    This election is the eternal love of God freely choosing to create and to love His creation.

    Suppose we subordinate election to creation and providence. In that case, we introduce limitations and considerations that divert from the clear, consistent act of the election of Jesus as God's determining action for all His works.

3. In other proposals, *election is detached from the doctrine of God.*

    Election is often disconnected from God's providence and moved into the doctrine of reconciliation, where election becomes a confusing key to determine who is saved and who is rejected.

    Election gets tied to the Church. It encompasses those who were chosen to be included, as well as those not chosen. The Church becomes the company of the elect, a preselected group.

    Nevertheless, before there were elected people, there was an electing God.

    Any assurance of faith is grounded in the knowledge that the electing God preserves true humanity in grace and mercy.

4. The arrangements that follow place *predestination as the key to reconciliation* and what it means to be saved.

    A first consideration has predestination immediately following Christology. The effect is to focus on how the individual subsequently appropriates Christ's reconciliation and election.

In this organization, we first look back to Christ to give Him some credit. Then we look forward to the status of the Christian and the Church where salvation is applied.

5. When *predestination is linked with reconciliation* by conjoining it with sin, it dominates Christology and the nature of salvation, emphasizing the *problem* rather than the *determination* of God.

Beginning with human *sinfulness* on center stage, the issues of reconciliation and salvation and the place of the Trinity stand further down the line. They become a response to the human problem.

6. A final consideration in linking predestination to reconciliation is to *make it the final word that makes sense of all that has gone before*. Election then shines a light back down the trail to make sense of what God has been doing.

Rather than understanding election as the *final word*, we should see it as the *first word*, as in Romans 8:30. God's predestining starts the discussion.

Election does not merely underline grace as a reflection on God's free and eternal self-giving. No, He chose us in Him before the foundation of the world.

The most profound word in dogmatics is that God was in Christ reconciling the world to Himself.

God's election is initiated, enacted, and completed in His act of reconciliation. The source is in God's being. All subsequent activity has its context in God's election.

To say *the mystery of the event* points to God's election to act in love toward what He creates. Creation, reconciliation, and redemption are these acts expressing God's intent.

If we begin with His works selectively, what keeps us on course? How will we avoid defaulting in a manner that prioritizes our concerns? How can we stop fashioning a God who conveniently responds to our questions with answers acceptable to us?

When we begin with the Word of His decision, we submit to the mystery of God's being for us and with us in Jesus.

We cannot introduce election too early—it is the presupposition of God's work.

Election is a self-ordaining of God toward creation. His works are the outcome of that orientation and commitment. Therefore, election is a constituent element of the doctrine of God before it plays out the drama of God's act in the world.

From the start, God is gracious.

This gracious God is self-determined to move purposefully toward humanity.

The reality of this movement is in the revelation of Jesus Christ Himself.

The movement is from eternity and embraces the time frame of humans.

Every created thing has its nature and purpose as determined by God's grace, which God has elected to extend to all in His ways and works.

 COMMENTARY:

- Election is adequately oriented when its beginning and ending all point to Jesus.
- Election is simply God's choice to be for us in person.
- In God's predestination, God does not choose winners and losers before the game starts. That would make salvation occur outside of the cross of Christ.
- All are elected in Jesus. There is no decision other than the one made in His choice to embrace humanity.
- When teaching on election elicits fear, God's part is almost certainly being misrepresented.
- The single foundation of election can only be found in Jesus. It has nothing to do with human choice.
- The story of God includes choosing specific people and whole peoples in the narrative of the Bible. This is the outworking of God's mission in history.
- When we discuss election in the context of doctrine of the Church or individual salvation, we misapply our judgment. We select based on how we judge what we think the Church "should be." We view heaven as filled with people who meet with our approval.

 CONCLUSION FOR THE CHURCH: The Church needs clarity on what it means to live within God's act regarding God's intended relation to humanity. A local church is a vehicle of the message of God's profound "Yes" to humanity. God speaks "Yes" through Jesus, the Bible, and the local church so that humans will respond "yes" with their lives.

Election is a controversial topic that divides churches. If we suppose that election plays a critical role in predetermining who God loves and who is rejected, churches will quickly become judges, abandoning their role as gospel-bearers, creating fear about who has not been elected. God may appear as an indiscriminate judge who makes decisions before a person is born or because they didn't appear worthy. Whatever the case, churches may easily miss the actuality of the love of God's election in Jesus, in whom we all are elected.

Election, when seen as a predetermined choice by God regarding who goes to heaven and who goes to hell, has left serious confusion in the Church. The Church tragically focuses on the worthiness of the human. Elsewhere, churches simply stop talking about election and miss the heart of God. Some others come as the bearers of a hard truth that God is sovereign, and we must wait without knowing.

Barth sweeps those roles away. He calls the Church to live in continuity with God's eternal choice to be for and with humanity and awaken people to this reality. The Church needs to be a gospel community, making clear this one choice of God above and before all others—God has chosen already who is elected, and it is Himself.

INSIGHT FOR PASTORS: As an act of God, election opens a gulf of mystery. Many Christians think that God chooses some, and based on their failure, others will be omitted. The pastor's place is to point to Jesus as the One who has been elected on our behalf. As all died in Adam, so we are dead to God in our estrangement and alienation. But that is only part of the story. In Jesus, all are made alive—that is the point of election. He elected to be for us, all of us. This option is not forced on us; it is simply the actuality of God toward us.

What are we to do? We are called to surrender to His love. In acknowledging His choice to accept us before we could accept Him, we respond with unconditional devotion to the unconditional love offered in returning home with Him.

Can we resist God's election? Yes and no. No, we cannot do anything to stop Him from loving us unconditionally, even in hell. Yes, we can live the illusion that His election is not for us, and we will be living in denial of reality. We will join the disordered life of those who walk away. It is adequate to say that this is a taste of hell here and now. That is the result of living with the deception that we are alone and independent. Yes, we can resist; no, we cannot stop God from loving us.

If humans believe that Jesus has not elected to fulfill God's mission of restoration, they will experience logical consequences. Detachment creates depression, anxiety, insecurity, anger, and trauma in our disordered lives. Election is God's reattachment that heals. It does not magically make our humanity go away. Pastors are privileged to tell every person the good news that Jesus is the elect One who has already embraced them. The election of Jesus is a transposition to live in the new key of the gospel, attuning to the love of God for us.

INSIGHT FOR THEOLOGIANS: This critical section recenters the theologian from arbitrary beliefs about divine decrees that appear random and worrisome. Barth appropriately refocuses us to fix our eyes on Jesus as the decision of God. We begin with the heart of God, who loves in freedom. In all our theological thinking, we must follow the eternal decision of God to be for and with His creation.

If we depart from discussing election from within the heart of God and for His beloved creation, we will fracture our whole understanding. This mistake will lead us along a bewildering detour, missing all the ways and works of God.

Once we see God's election as the defining act of God in Jesus, all other doctrines follow from this sure foundation. All subsequent doctrines become expressions of this electing act in Jesus. Election becomes concrete and not abstract. Complex, conditional systems become obsolete. Election becomes about one person: Jesus. All humans are elected within the scope of His choice. However, this is not universalism (God choosing all to go to heaven). Rather, this is an unconditional love from God that leaves no room for wondering whom God chooses and whom He rejects. His freedom still allows room for human rejection. He does not prevent human freedom from choosing the nothingness that is folly.

? CLARIFYING QUESTIONS: Does your theology of election seek to figure out who is in and who is out with God? Do you think this was a choice that happened in the deep recesses of God's eternal life? *Or* do you believe that God's election is an unconditional commitment in Jesus to be God's love in action? Do you understand election as unveiling human need by showing that God's love from eternity already meets it?

CHAPTER 14

THE SINGER WHOSE VOICE IS NEVER SILENT, EVEN WHEN WE ARE DEAF

§ 33. The Election of Jesus Christ

FOCUS STATEMENT: This paragraph (§ 33) centers us on recognizing that God's election is not a distant decree or hidden, locked, and unchangeable in some vault of eternity. We are stirred to hear God's voice in Jesus revealing "The Election of Jesus Christ." He carries the intent and content of God's love from eternity into our present time. He addresses and embraces the rejected and the accepted.

Jesus is the song that resounds before a darkened and tone-deaf world. He chooses to be the light and melody whose singularity sings a "Yes," which stirs a dissonant world to life.

God's election is embodied in the person of Jesus. He does not just sing the song of God's unwavering love; He is the song. He is One who fulfills all God's promises and commitments. His heart, voice, and song are inseparable from His mission to be God with us and for us. He is the virtuoso who precedes all singers. He carries us to share in His life, inviting us to harmonize within His singing, making His song "our shared song." What is in His heart and on His lips resonates within our hearts.

Initially, we humans are deaf to His voice and song. Our deafness does not stop the power and accomplishment of Jesus' grand performance. That is the song of His reconciliation, still playing on behalf of the impaired humanity He freely loves.

INTRODUCTION: This paragraph focuses on the main point of election: Jesus is the electing God and the elected human on our behalf. In this duality, Jesus becomes the personal bridge between God and humanity. This is a proactive eternal role, not a reactive move to solve the problems of fallen humanity.

Election has been problematic in the past. We must not think of election as a hidden, eternal, out-of-sight decision. It is *not* a choice where some humans are arbitrarily or logically determined to be saved and some damned. That view makes God's election respond to a problem rather than revealing God's ways of accomplishing His "Yes" to humanity.

Barth will listen and look at Jesus from every viewpoint. All else leads to abstraction and becomes elusive. In Jesus, the nature of God's relation to humanity is made possible. He is the human who acts on our behalf to bring us home. Election is personal. Jesus stands on behalf of the many who love and also those who resist Him, eliminating any doubt that His grace is unconditionally dealt out for all.

CONTEXT: *CD* 2.2
Pages in Paragraph: 100 pages (pp. 94–194)

Subsections
1. Jesus Christ, Electing and Elected
2. The Eternal Will of God in the Election of Jesus Christ

TEXT: § 33. The Election of Jesus Christ

OPENING SUMMARY: The election of grace is the eternal beginning of all the ways and works of God in Jesus Christ. In Jesus Christ God in His free grace determines Himself for sinful man and sinful man for Himself. He therefore takes upon Himself the rejection of man with all its consequences, and elects man to participation in His own glory.[1]

SUMMARY:
1. Jesus Christ, Electing and Elected (pp. 94–145)
The bridge between God and humanity is the One unique person of Jesus Christ.

---

1. *CD* 2.2, § 33, p. 94.

To say Jesus mediates between God and humanity is to affirm the possible. He is fully God and fully human and can speak as God to human-kind and as a human to His Father.

In Him, the will of God to be for us is made actual and present—His heart extends to us.

At the same time, our incorporation is made actual by God's choosing to embrace us in Jesus His Son—we are included.

"It is by Him, Jesus Christ, and for Him and to Him, that the universe is created as a theatre for God's dealings with man and man's dealings with God."[2]

Jesus is grace in action. There is no silent Word, no hidden decree, nor unknown beginning of all things.

Jesus encloses all things in Himself with an absolute choice. He is for and with His creation in such a way as also to include the autonomy of all other words, decrees, and beginnings.

Barth investigates the opening statements in John's gospel to let the Bible inform our placement of Jesus in the life of God.

John's gospel begins, "In the beginning was the Word." The beginning is emphasized as existing before all created realities.

One cannot look within time to find the beginning. One must look within God to find the beginning to which we are referred.

Jesus is not outside or alongside God. He is God Himself revealed.

This living Word embodies the communication uniting God and humanity.

Because Jesus is the Creator of all things, who holds all things together, we must recognize Him as the Word of God who speaks and creates.

- Jesus is the decree who elects and is elected at the beginning of all things.
- Jesus is the beginning of our being and all our thinking.
- Jesus is the source of our faith, as we come to know His ways and workings.
- Jesus is the first and final authority with respect to the origin and aim of God's work.

When God elects, He does this in person. He acts by beginning the existence of everything that comes into being other than Himself.

---

2. *CD* 2.2, § 33, p. 94.

This decision to create is a free act of God's inward life spreading outward in love. As God acts outwardly, we see the free expression of His love.

The Father established a covenant with humanity from the beginning. He gave His Son to become a human as the means to fulfill His grace in an unconditional covenant of love.

The Son chose to be obedient to this grace by offering Himself up so that the covenant might become a reality.

The Holy Spirit was resolved, from the beginning, to act in unity with the Father and Son in this covenant with humanity.

The Father, Son, and Holy Spirit made this covenant choice at the beginning. Through it, the glory of God's love was freely demonstrated in God's self-giving for His creation.

Jesus fulfilled the Father's love and reconciled humanity in love on their behalf.

Jesus' election is both an active (divine determining) and a passive (being elected) act for humanity.

As the electing God, Jesus is primary. Jesus being elected can only be understood in the light of His divine determination.

God's election of grace and the contents of that divine election take the form of creation, reconciliation, and redemption.

Jesus is *the* good pleasure of God in action. He is not merely *an instrument* of God's good pleasure or *one among many* objects of God's good pleasure.

Jesus is the One elected for reconciling humanity back to God—the very reason He took the form of a human.

We are called.

We are summoned to faith.

We assent to the divine intervention on our behalf.

We recognize the fact that we are sons and daughters of God. God is our Father.

We open to the communication of the Holy Spirit, who is the Spirit of obedience for us in our adoption.

The election of Jesus is the light of predestination for us. He shines out the electing of God so that we may know we are dealing directly with the electing God, and He is for us.

Unfortunately, we think that God leaves us in the dark to wonder if we are elect, creating all manner of delusions.

The restriction of Jesus to *His human role* misses the point that He is the electing God. We were chosen in Him before the foundation of the world (Ephesians 1:4).

Holding Jesus as merely the first among humans leaves us unsure whether we are elected. This stance misses the fact that *the decision and action of God* were made in Jesus toward us with God's specific lovingkindness.

There is no hidden decision of God that allows us to keep wondering whether God has elected Himself on our behalf.

The cradle, the cross, and the resurrection all point to the choice of God to act on our behalf.

The will of the Father does not elect specific individuals before electing His Son. Jesus does not submit to the justice of God. He *is* the justice of God who makes it actual. There is no hidden absolute decree, only the decision in Christ.

The elect did not belong to the Father before Christ; they belong to Him in Christ.

- Jesus is the electing God.

    We can have an assurance of our election. Jesus has decided it. He has enacted it. He has spoken it to us. Nothing can shake the fact that *God elects us* in Jesus.

- Jesus is the elected human.

    As God, Jesus was appointed to be the human on *behalf of all other humans*. He is not just one of the elect.

    Jesus has authority as the Lord so that others may be elected "in Him." In His election is the assurance of our own election.

Jesus is not only the *object* of election, the one chosen as an elect creature. He is also the *subject* who chooses, the electing Creator.

Before time and before creation, the eternal choice of God invested in Jesus of Nazareth's life, death, and resurrection to fulfill the divine covenant with humanity.

What unites humanity in Christ's election is that He, as God, wills Himself as a man to act on behalf of humanity. His is the original, all-inclusive election.

We become Christians because He first became the Christ—the chosen One of God. We became parts of His body because He became the head. We believe in Him because He became believable as One to trust.

Jesus is the *destiny* of our human nature. He is the possibility of fellowship with God. He is the means of our participation with God by the grace of God.

Jesus is the *cause* of our being lifted into the life of God. We become Christians by being nourished by this grace through the work of the Holy Spirit.

God's glory flows out to the other, to His creature, in incredible, tender grace. He makes the other His own.

God wills His fatherhood to us, and in the same act He wills our adoption as His children. This engagement is how God's grace sets forth His glory.

The New Testament understands Jesus' election as a call to suffering. He was obedient to the point of death. This sacrifice was His choice from the beginning.

> Jesus is the destiny of our human nature. He is the possibility of fellowship with God. He is the means of our participation with God by the grace of God.

Jesus' election means that God intended and executed righteous judgment. In Him, human sin is righteously rejected as He bore the wrath of love against human rebellion.

God's wrath stands against all human abuse and dishonor that leads to death.

However, in the election of Jesus, corrupted humanity is bestowed with the love of God from eternity.

Left in powerlessness, humans become the enemy of God as we submit to the seduction of the enemy of God.

God has rejected all who go the way of corruption. God's wrath, as His purifying love, stands against those who must die.

From eternity, God elects to have His beloved Son stand in the place of rebel humanity. The wrath directed at humanity is transferred to the Son, elected to stand in our place.

The elected One defeats Satan on behalf of all those elected in Jesus, descendants of Adam beloved by God.

God allows His righteousness to proceed against His Son instead of those found guilty. He is the Lamb slain before the foundation of the world.

God pours out His love on those who have rejected Him. He has always loved them. They were ignorant and had no desire for Him. He elects those rejected, who have abandoned Him.

Who is elect? Jesus, He who had to suffer and die, making Himself responsible for those who made themselves His enemy. He takes the consequences of their actions with His suffering and death.

Why does the just God stand in for unjust humanity? Because His justice is merciful. Because He sees through our disobedience to comprehend our need with pity. Because He understands the powerlessness of sinners.

The resurrection and ascension to the Father confirm the steadfastness of God's election.

In faith, we cling to the steadfastness of Jesus' election for us. From this, our joy and comfort are gained.

As we honor Him, we have our own lives. Our rejection is put behind us. He has rejected our rejection.

Next Barth discusses the supralapsarian-infralapsarian controversy.

If we are to say that God has elected to be for humanity from all eternity, can we equally say He rejected from all eternity as well? Is the human created and capable of falling (lapsing), or is humanity created fallen?

The *supralapsarian* position holds that from eternity God determines that some shall be saved and some damned.

By their own fault, humans would fall. Some receive mercy for God's glory, and some are damned to reveal the justice of God.

Adam, and all humans in Adam, had to be brought to the place of actually falling into sin.

In this view, God is revealing mercy to the saved and justice to the damned. The fall had to take place in accordance with its conception of the will of God. God had to reveal mercy and justice, and this is how He had to do it.

Everything else is conceived in light of this plan. God did not create humans and allow them to sin. All went according to plan and humans did fall. Some were saved and some not—all for the glory of God.

Outside (supra) creation, God made humans to be fallen (lapsed). This doctrine is the supralapsarian view of Beza, and probably Calvin, Zwingli, Luther, and others in modified forms.

The *infralapsarian* view has been dominant in Church history. This view also works with a basic plan where God reveals and glorifies Himself. Evil does not enter by chance. The fall is inevitable as an event decreed by God.

Infralapsarians depart from the supralapsarian at the point of knowing. Where the supralapsarians know the plan of God, the infralapsarians do not. Neither do they know the reason for creation and the fall.

For infralapsarians, the acts of creation and fall precede God's act of predestination. This position is supposed to reveal God's mercy and justice in response, after creation. But the origin of sin and the fall is grounded elsewhere. Much is left unknown.

The God who willed that all humans would necessarily fall into sin wills that some, out of His mercy, should be saved. The rest He abandons to punishment, which is to be expected since they have earned it.

Barth holds that it is right to believe that all are sinners. However, this should not be deduced from God's election nor any supposed decree, as though God's action is driven by *the problem* rather than *love*.

How do we properly include divine purpose and human fallenness without collapsing into one or the other?

The divine purpose must be included in God's predestination, along with an honest acknowledgment of humanity as created and fallen. The supralapsarians were wrong about God's choosing, and the infralapsarians about distinguishing the saved and damned.

Supralapsarians held the object of election as the partly elected or partly rejected children of Adam. Their focus is on individuals. Jesus chooses for the elected and has nothing to do with the damned. Jesus' electing is then passed over; the individual becomes the focus.

All parties think of election as a fixed system. In an individual's life, each school affirms God's choice in selecting or rejecting. God's free grace for all is not their gospel. For them, God and humans are both locked into an unalterable system.

All parties agree that when God set up the system, He said a "Yes" and a "No."

Both parties held that election is an absolute, hidden decree from eternity.

The absolute God of eternity is pictured in the form of an abstraction, not the self-affirming and human-engaging Son of God, Jesus.

Barth believes that it is best to articulate the grace of God, revealing His mercy and justice, at the head of our discussion. Only then are we talking about knowing God's will in election. All is in God's hands, not in a reaction to human failing.

The *ordering of God's grace and mercy* must precede any designation of who is accepted and who is rejected. God's will must choose in love before any discussion of the fallenness of humanity.

The *ordering of human reason* wants God to decide based on human success or failure worthy of election to the appropriate ends. But this is not God's way. The infralapsarians have given themselves over to human logic.

The biblical ordering of the story of God always moves from God to humans with whom God initiates covenant. The supralapsarians maintained the *priority of God's action* in election. The infralapsarians collapsed into the logic of *human ordering in salvation* as the focus.

The infralapsarians offered something beyond the rigid determination of God and pointed to something better without discerning it fully.

The infralapsarians left an open mystery regarding God's relation to evil in the world. They respected God's providence and avoided assigning a cause for sin, leaving God to deal with sin in election or reprobation.

The two positions could not be fused into one, although they both deal with important issues.

If we are to lean between a God-focused ground for election and a human-focused one, we must affirm the God-focus of the supralapsarian, even if its God is too rigid. At least we are facing in the right direction.

Barth invites us to detach our supralapsarian view from its problematic foundations.

We must begin with God's primary purposes concerning the world rather than attaching election to decrees, human issues, or abstract decisions.

All things are God's creation. He is Lord over all things. Reality is to be comprehended and understood in the light of His purposes.

He wills the election of humanity in One Man. This Man is the revelation of His glory and the object of His love.

The witness of this man affirms what God means when He says "Yes" as His will. He also clarifies that to which God says "No." This assertion clears the way for living in covenant with God.

God rejects sin with a "No." That is not a "No" in the sense of God's elected will; it corresponds to His love for humans, to whom He says "Yes." He opposes their "no" to Him with His "No" to their sin.

God does say "Yes" to humans in their sinful state as an affirmation of His loving will.

Jesus acts in history to confirm what God has willed. He removes the obstacles that stand in opposition to reconciliation. His death and resurrection include a judgment and a pardon to fulfill reconciliation.

In Jesus, God wills to be the One who comes to help humanity. He is the only One who can give victory over the power of evil and darkness that opposes them and keeps the human opposition to God.

This is Barth's modified supralapsarian position.

1. As the first and last word, the sovereignty of God is assured in Jesus, with no abstract election outside Jesus.
2. Rather than living under a predetermined system, we live entirely under the grace of the One elected for us on our behalf.
3. God's glory is attained by the outworking of His love in Jesus. He brings mercy and justice in our creaturely sphere as the fulfillment of God's eternal intent.
4. Rather than a decree being the last word, Jesus is the first and last Word. He intentionally restores the relationship between God and humanity.

Now we see the God who loves humanity. He makes humans His companions. He gives humans a share in His "Yes" and deals with the "No."

We now see that God does not demand humans to seek Him. He has already come to them. They are not the end and purpose of God's grace. He fulfills from His own heart.

Humans find salvation not as a private end but as a participation in the blessings and victory of the Elect One of God.

We cannot blame God for supposedly willing evil. He has willed concerning evil in the "No" that the Elect One addresses.

God has provided the One who has negated evil on our behalf. This provision implies that we were accused and found guilty. God has acted with justice and mercy for us.

We must remove from our minds the idea of individual election.

We must expunge the idolatrous idea of an abstract, absolute decree made in eternity.

Our corrected view must hold that Jesus is the Elect Man, the object of predestination.

The arguments of infralapsarians were not from faith but from human logic and morality.

The theological Enlightenment came along as the result of exhaustion from trying to think according to faith. Faith was replaced by thinking based on unbelief.

2. The Eternal Will of God in the Election of Jesus Christ (pp. 145–94)

Barth begins by reaffirming his key insights:

1. Jesus is the electing God. He is the acting subject in the act of God's grace.
2. Jesus is elected man. He is the elected object of God's grace.

Jesus is the elector and the elect, bringing an unbroken perfection that cannot be exhausted.

1. On what basis do we make claims about God's electing will?

    Barth holds that the will of God is concretely and specifically known in the election of Jesus. This view will focus on what is actually known.

    In the face of the unknown, we end up fabricating thoughts, trying to make the unknown less unknown.

- It is inevitable that we will ascribe our understanding to the unknown God.
- It is inevitable that we will seek God through our chosen realities that seem more available.
- It is inevitable that we will project our self-made images onto God, with a silence that plunges us into obscurity.
- We will miss the genuine form of the mystery, which we could approach in humble adoration.

The unknown God leads to decreased knowing of the known God.

We ought not turn to philosophical arguments dealing with cause and effect, time and eternity, or phenomenon and idea.

Some read the Bible through lenses and schema that did not derive from the Bible.

Passages in the Bible on the electing God and elected human are not plentiful. However, they are our starting point. All the dealings of God in the Bible work from God's point of view, acting on behalf of elected humanity.

Election is a comprehensive concept: God elects to deal with humanity, which always focuses on His electing action. All that God does is from His decision to live in this relationship. This commitment is steadfast even in corrective wrath and discipline.

Unfortunately, many Christian traditions thought about election as dealing with an individual or the sum of all individuals or general humanity.

This debate distracted from the electing God, whose choice they neglected.

The New Testament casts a penetrating light on the Old Testament, confirming that Jesus has been given all power in heaven and on earth.

Yet, there have been problems in understanding the election of God. Rather than focus on Jesus exclusively, there appeared new horizons hidden beyond Jesus. These refer to some other eternity and other forms of proposed eternal life. These false horizons allowed theologians to take passages out of context and miss the meaning of the whole.

We must not forget that humanity is against God. More importantly, Jesus Christ is God for humanity. He fulfills God's will in dealing with our resistance and our reconciliation.

2. Traditionally, we think in grand but abstract images of eternity and God's will.

God's eternal will is the Alpha and Omega from whom all our thinking about the world and ourselves must begin.

God's will is not obscure, hidden beyond, before, or outside time.

The light of God's good pleasure dispels the darkness of unknowing.

Predestination is revealed. It is not hidden; it is disclosed.

If we do not close our eyes, nothing is kept from us regarding the meaning, direction, and nature of God's will for us.

There is a selectivity on our part as to how we come to know, to have faith. We must question whether we have selected an adequate form and character regarding God to inform our confidence and obedience. Has He given us what we need to believe?

The adequacy of God's goodwill, given in His revelation, is the answer to our questions. It takes an intelligent love of God, worship, and reverence for us to be brought from the darkness to see in the light.

We come to behold the covenant of grace established and maintained by the power of God's free love. God has openly and unconditionally confirmed His faithfulness.

This covenant stands as the decision between God and what He creates, and the basis of all that follows. This covenant is the source of all the order and standard of wisdom that flows in God's relationship to His created reality.

God's covenant is the fixed end toward which all was foreordained as the will of God. That will is Jesus Christ; He is that will, not merely one revealing the will of another.

In the face of God's power and majesty, we ought not tremble. Rather, we know Him, love Him, and praise Him.

We respond as God's glory overflows in the act of His freedom. He does not demand. On the contrary, He illuminates, convinces, and glorifies to awaken faith.

We must leave behind the horror or the peace—we know not which for us—of the absolute decree hidden in eternity.

We embrace instead the absolute decree made in the One Man, Jesus Christ. Our life is hidden with Christ in God's life.

We stand before the mystery of God. There is no cause for anxiety.

We stand with worship and reverence before the One to whom we belong in the mystery of His choice of us.

The distant, detached, decreeing God can only create religion, not faith.

The present, engaged, love-determined God known in Jesus is an invitation to faith.

The active, concrete God known in Jesus opens us to explore His mystery so that we may continually be taught.

Instead of abstract traditions, the election of Jesus is the one thing we must constantly explore.

3. The eternal will of God is to give Himself for created and then alienated humanity.

The incarnation, death, and resurrection of Jesus are the content of God's predestination.

God gave Himself up to vulnerability.

God did this for humanity, created by Him.

God did this for humanity, fallen from Him.

What did God elect to do in Jesus?
- God chose Himself to act. He is not reactive.
- God's faithfulness to Himself originates the election of God.
- He was free and loving in His actions in His election.
- His Word sounded forth in the world of humans.

God accommodates Himself to enter into covenant with us. We stand to gain. God stands to lose.

In a sense, the duality of election and reprobation are fulfilled in Jesus. He has credited to humanity salvation and life. He has ascribed to Himself perdition and death.

On the *negative* side, God has elected Himself as a Friend and Partner of humanity, a surrender of Himself to the reality of that which opposes Him—becoming one of us.

Humanity was tempted by evil.

Humanity did evil.

Humanity became guilty of evil.

Humanity bears the consequences of evil.

Humanity was a compromised servant of the divine will.

Even at our best, we are challenged and not like God.

Humans stand on the frontier of the impossible, in participation but contradiction to all God has willed.

What did God elect for Himself?
- He elected our rejection.
- He elected our suffering.
- He elected to love us.
- He elected to give Himself.

Whom does Jesus elect?
- He elects Judas, who betrays Him.
- He elects Pilate, who sentences Him.
- He elects the cross as His kingly throne.
- He elects the garden tomb to be the site of His being the living God.

In this election, God loved the world, electing the world to be in fellowship with Himself.

God does not seek revenge. Instead, He bears the consequences of human rebellion. He mediates on our behalf.

God treated evil seriously. He was just. He judged, sentenced, rejected, and condemned evil.

God was merciful. He took evil to His bosom. He willed that the rejection, condemnation, and death should fall on Him.

God suffered what humanity ought to have suffered.

The exchange of God with humanity, Him taking our place, fulfilled God's will and cannot be reversed. This event is the great exchange at the core of the gospel.

What did God elect in Jesus? This question addresses the *positive* side of God's election.

In the outflowing of His glory, He communicates the goodwill that He has and shares.

God creates the very essence of good as the glory that is the content of His goodwill. This provision also creates the possibility of evil as a concession, the shadow resulting from light. This kind of existence allows for autonomous power; the place of Satan arises in that space.

The shadow of evil is entirely different from the nature of light.

God does not will evil; He permits it. Evil is a shadow that yields and flees from God's light.

Evil has no status in the divine economy. It exists as that which is excluded and resisted by God's holy will.

Evil can only be the abyss of negation overcome by the "Yes" of God's goodwill intended for humanity.

We do not have a "No" in God's judgment, but the "Yes" is expressed in God's holiness and wrath in love's stance against evil.

We cannot make the twofold nature of "Yes" and "No" into a dualism of equally opposed wills.

Jesus bore human suffering on the cross as a sacrifice for the sins of the world. He is God's "Yes" to the world.

The glory of the resurrection and ascension is the ongoing confirmation that the will of God is being fulfilled.

First, we must know what God wills to give to us, and second, we must know what He intends to remove from us.

The resurrection of Jesus far outweighed the failures of humans.

Election is not part promise and part threat. There is only pure joy.

In divine taking, Jesus removes our sin. In divine giving, He brings us to Himself.

4. God's election takes the form of action. It becomes the history of encounters and decisions between God and humanity.

    God's being and activity outside Himself are an outflowing of His inward being and activity.

    In election, God proclaims His decision. His internal vitality extends to vitalize the world He decides to create and love in freedom.

    God's being as the Lord of creation is acted out in events of encounter that shape history.

    The person of Jesus, who was with God in the beginning, was God's self-giving on behalf of humanity. He makes concrete His union with us in the one person existing as both the Son of God and the human, Jesus of Nazareth.

    Jesus speaks as the grace of God and swoops down to scoop us up to Himself.

    God does not need humanity. However, God wills to be with us, to invest in us.

    God acts as subject in His electing, fulfilling His intent.

    God confirms Jesus as His Son.

He sends Him as His own Word.

God gifts Him to suffer on our behalf.

God raises Him from the dead to share His glory.

In all this, Jesus established the kingdom of God in Himself.

The place of the human is in prayer, obedience, and following.

God has conceded a place at His side for humans to have auton-omy, which His goodness can concede.

The Jews did not recognize their King in the form of a servant. This blindness is a continuing human struggle.

In the act of prayer, genuine self-awareness is born. Proper knowl-edge and action may be attempted, and all fear drops away. Jesus lives this life for us, and we participate in His life of connection.

Humans elect God that we may live in freedom before Him. We make a choice in miniature in response to His awakening choice for us.

He prays that we will be united with Him in joy and peace and fulfill the meaning of creation. He gives us our own sphere and auton-omy by grace, but He does not abandon us there.

Election is God's will in action, where He decides to give human-ity autonomous existence within the enclosure of His grace.

Predestination is an act of God's will and not an abstraction achieved by logic and reason.

Predestination is not something unchanging or unchangeable. It does include God's determination in the process of the world.

God created the world. He is the context of its history. He is the One who encounters humanity with His constant love and freedom.

God's eternal decree is not a single occasion. There was no time when all decisions were made, set in concrete, completed in an eter-nal past.

"God's living action in the present consists only in the execution of this decree, the fulfilment of an election and decision already made."[3]

We focus then not on predestination itself but on the execution of His decision.

We cannot be satisfied with echoes of some note struck in eternity. We can only hear God's voice repeated here and now.

---

3. *CD* 2.2, § 33, p. 181.

Deism is the tragic result of conceiving a distant God who resides in eternity but is not active in our world.

In Deism, God is thought of as inactive in the ongoing process of the world.

In Deism, the world's processes default to predetermined laws.

In Deism, God's will was isolated and predetermined before the world began. But God is no longer seen as present in the world. God is no longer *actually* here.

In Deism, God becomes a principle, a power that controls a stream of events in which we find ourselves.

However, we can only have faith in the God who is present. That is the electing God who is deciding now.

God's decree is more living than any human decree. God's is determined by the constancy, faithfulness, and dependability of the triune God Himself.

God's will is not left behind in time; it accompanies and outlasts our time. It has happened, it is happening, and it will happen.

God's work is completed, but it is not exhausted. It is not behind us; it is still taking place.

God is never an echo. He is always a self-determining sound, stressing God's freedom in the ongoing act of His love.

When we speak of the connection between theonomy (divine sovereignty) and autonomy (human faith), we talk about the life of the Spirit, which preceded human life. The life of the Spirit is not fixed or rigid. It is constant and powerful and never ceases to be a concrete event.

There can be no breaking off from past events. There can be no fixed conclusions that become a static foundation to build on. The decisions of the past have not ended.

God's election was not temporary. It has been eternally in effect as God's personal activity. It has God's enduring authority and power, the very premise for the functioning of human life.

God's eternal decision precedes all the events in the history of the world. All subsequent events take place for the sake of fulfilling God's election for His creation.

Predestination is not concealed from us. It is divine life in the Spirit. It takes place in time as an act that affects us. It is the revealed secret of the whole history between God and humanity.

The revealing of the secret takes place in our midst, in the room that is God's creation.

- ○ It takes place when God's Word is proclaimed.
- ○ It takes place in the existence and guidance of Israel and the Church.
- ○ It takes place in the making right of humanity by God.
- ○ It takes place when we are awakened to faith, hope, and love.
- ○ It takes place even when we do not recognize or understand it.

While the exercise of God's love is never hidden in the world, our ability to perceive it depends on our interest in what is happening.

If we try to be spectators, we remove ourselves from participation and can see nothing. God's "hiding" is a form of blindness on our part.

God remains free. God continues to decide in His freedom. He makes new decisions in time.

Election is God in action always and everywhere. We must start there.

- ○ Others may have a *static* God who stands at the beginning rather than indwelling an activated history.
- ○ Some may have a *quietistic* view that sets aside activity.

Jesus' acting in history demands we proceed with a *dynamic, activist* outlook. This attitude calls us to oppose a static God or election.

Humanity attains freedom in the lived history of the electing God.

The living God predestines only insofar as He deals with the living human He has created.

Predestination happened in the heart of the Father before all time.

Predestination happened unchangeably in the election of Jesus as the work of God in history, in time.

Predestination happens in the living acts of the Spirit.

God wills to reject the evildoer. He also wills to lift this rejection from humanity and put it on Himself.

God does not will the death of sinners. He wills that they turn to Him and live.

It is foolish to say that we do not know how we stand with God or what we may expect from Him. God does not play games with us.

God's will is progressive, a continuously renewed act of the Spirit.

We cannot condition, coerce, or change God's mind as though His freedom can be manipulated or altered by us.

Our choices and actions cannot change His will toward us. The relationship is constantly renewed, but not as volleying between divine decision and human response.

In the Bible, God and humanity appear as partners. They have different capabilities. Each remains autonomous. The relationship is not deterministic but is living and intrinsically loving.

Due to our autonomous state, it would be easy to default to placing the human as superior in our relationship with the unseen God. We must focus on the concrete will of God in the election of Jesus to avoid this dilemma.

This relationship has no synergism. Neither the sin of humans nor their prayers can form a complement to the mystery of God's decision.

There is only a single revelation of one divine mystery. It is the mystery of grace. This intervention is the unqualified affirmation of God's love for humanity. In this way, it is the history between God and humanity.

COMMENTARY:

- Calvinism has made election a cause for fear and confusion. It assumes that some individuals are in and some are going to hell. Barth rejects this as missing the point.
- Jesus is not merely elected as a bridge between God and ourselves.
- He becomes our whole embrace of the Father, by the Spirit in whom we participate.
- Jesus promises to embrace our humanity forever and has fulfilled all to bring us into His embrace.
- Jesus is both the Chooser and the Chosen. "Are you elect?" one may ask. Yes. But only in Him who has chosen to be for us already.
- If we look at Jesus instead of ourselves, we know that we belong to Him.
- If we look at ourselves to question if we are worthy of election, we begin to judge on an improper basis.
- The most significant problem with election arises when we look anywhere other than Jesus to find the source and cause.
- Any hidden decree, act of the Father, or human failure that "necessitates" election leads us off the trail.

CONCLUSION FOR THE CHURCH: The Church has been remiss when it comes to making clear the constancy of God's "Yes" for all humanity. In this paragraph, Barth calls the Church to refocus on the person of Jesus and His stand for us. Jesus is not just a figure in the story of God. He is the whole gospel history in person, its context for meaning.

Jesus is the embodied choice to be the "Yes" of God at all times and places. His "Yes" invites churches to say "yes" to Him and quit being judges of who is in and out regarding the "chosen."

The absolute centrality of God's good news is that God's whole will and ways of working are made evident in Jesus. The Church needs to quit being distracted and to learn to listen and follow Him every week. We must learn to ask what Jesus is saying "Yes" to, so that we may follow in the concrete reality in which we live with Him. There will be a "No" that responds to those things that are off track. They will be revealed as the corrective element within the affirming of the "Yes." God's election in Jesus is His active voice to the Church, calling us to hear and respond, and never imagine ourselves apart from Him.

 INSIGHT FOR PASTORS: The Bible talks about election, and so must we. However, it has been interpreted with anxiety, as though God's decision regarding our eternal destination is out of our hands, hidden in the vaults of heaven. Some construe that our performance will admit us into the company of the elect. Some think God will elect, and we may be a part of the "frozen chosen," the lucky winners.

These unsettling options miss the profound "Yes" in Jesus as God's choice to be for us. They miss His love. It is true that within His "Yes" is a "No" to what is contrary to love. When we say "yes" to one spouse, church, or job, by implication, we say "no" to others. "Yes" always implies "no" to what becomes excluded. God's "Yes" is not a cheap grace; He is committing to our lives being lived in love. This faithful proclamation is the task of a church so His family may be transformed as they accept their adoption in knowing God's election.

The election of God is a personal "Yes." Our place as leaders is to default to the "Yes" of Jesus and let Him engender, even compel, a loving response. We may say "no" to what harms our community and families, but only within the "yes" of love. We do not say "yes" to abuse or power grabbing. Love stops violations in word and deed.

This section calls us to drop the judgments and arguments that arise from human wisdom regarding salvation, sanctification, ethics, and all other considerations that need their proper context in responding to Jesus' election. This stance is not a passive "yes" on our part. It is a reflection on His "Yes." The more we preach, teach, and live within His "Yes," the more our interpersonal connections will attune our lives to the content and intent of His song of love. Any other view of election will lead people away from Jesus, and we will be chasing sheep all day. The sheep need to learn to hear the Shepherd's voice and what it means to answer His choice, confirming they belong to Him.

INSIGHT FOR THEOLOGIANS: The task of theology is to know God and make Him known. Reading the history of theological thinking, it has appeared that election was about God's hidden choices in eternity. In this paragraph, Barth articulates how even someone like Calvin can miss the boat and end up with a system strewn with hidden, abstract decisions. This misguidance sets theological thinking adrift, with heartbreaking consequences. This is not one doctrine among a set of many separated doctrines. Election is the fountain that ushers forth from the loving grace of God. Here we meet God's proactive intention. Election is the expression of the heart, intent, will, and personal commitment—the sheer faithfulness—of the triune God. It takes on manifold expressions from this personal act of election in Jesus.

The critical point is that we cannot separate the will of God from what Jesus has done and is still doing. He is Election in the flesh. He is the choice in action. If the Christian theological academy stays true to its subject, Jesus Christ, it must resist the temptations to construe alternate theories. We were chosen in Him, we are being chosen in Him, and He has chosen us to share His end purposes. There is no question whom He has chosen to be on our behalf.

CLARIFYING QUESTIONS: Does your theology seek to use logic and texts from the Bible to discern who will go to heaven and who will go to hell? Do you think God's will in election is hidden and only discovered somewhere in eternity? *Or* do you see the election of God as known, personally given, unquestionable, and complete in the person of Jesus?

CHAPTER 15

THE CHOSEN CHOIR

§ 34. The Election of the Community

FOCUS STATEMENT: The impact of Jesus' election on His community, and the world, is expressed in this paragraph (§ 34). Jesus, the voice of God, does not intend to sing alone. Jesus does not sing to entertain individuals. He invites humanity to join His choir. We discover its scope in "The Election of the Community."

Jesus created culturally distinct groups to accompany Him. These groups contribute to Jesus' invitation to call the world to join His song. Each group displays the dissonance, resonance, and modulations that Jesus has composed since the beginning.

We will hear ancient themes of Jewish music, filled with lament as they wrestle with God. We will also hear their lyrical law, even when in conflict with the Chief Musician. Nevertheless, these people are never thrown out of the choir.

The image of a rabbi passing on the text of ancient hymns and psalms to a grateful and humble generation makes way for lament, praise, and soulful expressions born in the heart of God.

Later themes of music unveil many forms of spiritual songs sung in many languages and places. These are songs for the scattered. They hum along in harmony, resonating with the hearts of those set free. They have heard the invitation to come and belong. They were chosen for this. They sing with sheer joy for being included, celebrating what is coming.

INTRODUCTION: We continue with the theme of election being grounded in Jesus and now move to explore the election of the people of God. Many want to jump ahead to ask who is elected. However, election is not about individuals being selected and rejected.

Barth follows the biblical progression, seeing God's election of communities of people. This paragraph focuses on the chosen people of Israel and then on the developing elected life of the Church. Together they make up the community of God, people embraced by God's mercy.

We must remember the basic reality: Jesus deals with our rejection in the crucifixion and accepts us in His resurrection. Everything builds on this initial reality. Israel became a visible sign of the resistance to God that God rejects. The Church is a sign of acceptance, responding to God's mercy coming in Jesus' election. The gospel of God's election is not abstract; it is concrete in the story of biblical people, both the rejected and accepted. Election is not hidden and horrible. It is a visible revolution of love manifested in Jesus.

Each of the four subsections in this paragraph discusses election in the text of Romans 9–11. It explores the election of Jews and Gentiles. This biblical reading concludes each subsection and divides as follows:

§ 34.1　　Romans 9:1–5
§ 34.2　　Romans 9:6–29
§ 34.3　　Romans 9:30–10:21
§ 34.4　　Romans 11

▌▌▌ CONTEXT: *CD* 2.2
Pages in Paragraph: 111 pages (pp. 195–305)

Subsections
　　1. Israel and the Church
　　2. The Judgment and the Mercy of God
　　3. The Promise of God Heard and Believed
　　4. The Passing and the Coming Man

▢ TEXT: § 34. The Election of the Community

OPENING SUMMARY: The election of grace, as the election of Jesus Christ, is simultaneously the eternal election of the one community of God by the existence of which Jesus Christ is to be attested to the whole world and the whole world summoned to faith in Jesus Christ. This one community of God in its form as Israel has to serve the representation of the divine judgment; in its form as the Church, the representation of the divine mercy. In its form as Israel, it is determined for hearing, and in its form as the Church for believing the promise sent forth to man. To the one elected community of God is given in the one case its passing, and in the other its coming form.[1]

---

1. *CD* 2.2, § 34, p. 195.

✠ **SUMMARY:**

1. Israel and the Church (pp. 195–205)

Humanity is elected in Jesus Christ. Creation is elected in Him.

In the first instance, the self-giving of God in election refers to Jesus Christ.

In its final instance, God's election refers to fallen humanity rejecting God.

The doctrine of election in the Bible is in no hurry to skip past Jesus. It is not eager to engage the "many people" of humanity. Election focuses on one person.

God's life and function include other humans in the election of Jesus, sharing His service to humanity.

The specific concept of humanity that forms the focus of Barth's concern is *community*. This term covers the forms of Israel and the Church.

Community is the human fellowship that forms the natural and historical environment of Jesus as a human.

This inner circle of the community speaks to "others" who are also included in and with the election extended in Jesus Christ.

The community stands between the mediation of Christ's election and those elected in Jesus.

No community is elected independently of Jesus Christ, and each has a selfless task in serving Him by witnessing to Him.

The Church does not exist for itself. The inner circle is nothing if it does not exist for the outer circle in the world enacted and included in the election of Jesus Christ.

The outer circle is nothing without the inner circle of the Church, which mirrors the mediating character of the One Mediator, Jesus Christ.

The electing God is one.

The elected humanity is one in Jesus.

The community that is the object of Jesus' election is also one.

Each element is connected to the others, originating in the life of God.

In the same act, God deals with the issues of sinful humanity. On the one hand, He deals with the passing form of our existence. On the other hand, He establishes a new and abiding form. His act and its impact heal the past and provide for His future.

Who is Jesus in relation to the community of God?

Jesus is the head of His Church who gathers Jews and Gentiles.

Jesus is the Messiah of Israel, crucified as the judgment God takes on Himself in choosing fellowship with humanity. With His self-giving to

Israel comes mercy and promise. His covenant inaugurates the abiding form of His community.

Jesus is the Lord of His Church. He has risen as a witness to the mercy of God, who has chosen humanity for fellowship to respond to His glory.

Israel is the people of God who resist divine election. In that they rebel against God as a people, they further reveal the passing of the old man who confronts God, and they also are the origin of the Church.

The Church is those who are gathered by God's election, both Jews and Gentiles. As sinful humanity, it sets forth the goodwill, readiness, and honor of God.

As the crucified Messiah of Israel, Jesus shows Himself as the resurrected head of His Church.

Israel reveals the Church in preparation. The Church reveals the determination of Israel as it passes from old humanity, making room for the new and coming humanity in Jesus.

The Jews are not the "rejected" and the Church the "elected." Election is *for* both. What is elected is one community in its two-fold form.

God has taken on Himself the rejection. God has taken on Himself the election. An unbreakable unity has been grounded in God's choice.

Israel and the Church share one history, and it is known through the person of Christ.

If the Church stands against its unity with Israel, it is not the Church. The crucified Messiah of Israel undergirds its election and hence the unity of the whole community of God.

Within the unity of the community of the elect, the Church stands in a second position. The Church proclaims to and comforts Israel.

The Church reminds Israel that the promises of God to them are now made to the world.

Barth pursues this understanding of the duality of Israel and the Church through the lens of Romans 9–11.

In turning to the Gentiles, Paul does not lose sight of the Jews. From his place in the Church, he summons the Jews to fulfill their election. As an apostle to the Church, he is more than ever a prophet of Israel, calling them back.

The community of God has its beginning and basis in unbelieving Israel. In the form of the Church, it has reached its goal, living in completion of what Israel had received.

The Church lives within the covenant God made with Israel.

The eternal High Priest and His sacrifice has been offered once for all. The Church's worship is exercised in faithfulness to Him and lived in spirit and truth as He fulfills Israel's way of worship on its behalf.

The Church lives by the promises given to Israel, placed in the hope of its risen Lord.

This is fulfilled in

the gift of the Holy Spirit,
    the forgiveness of sins,
        the overthrow of Satan,
            the resurrection of the dead,
                and eternal life in God's kingdom.

The foremost and comprehensive thing to affirm is that Jesus is the life of the Church as Christ, the Messiah of Israel in the flesh. He is an Israelite out of Israel.

He does not belong to Israel or the Church; God's elected community belongs to Him.

Confessing Jesus Christ, the Church acknowledges the fulfillment of everything promised to Israel, including everything recorded in the holy books of Israel.

Paul is disappointed with Israel for one reason: they are not rooted in Israel's true hope—its Messiah and His promises.

2. The Judgment and the Mercy of God (pp. 205–33)

In the election of Jesus, God covenants with sinful humanity. He is the judge and partner of those who have turned away from Him.

In this One Human, God takes on humanity's misery. God clothes humanity with His righteousness, blessedness, and power. Judgment and mercy are executed at the same time.

The Church is elected to serve Jesus in His self-presentation, as He summons the whole world.

Israel serves in reflecting the judgment from which God has rescued humanity and endures in Himself on the cross.

God chooses stubborn humans, not obedient ones with something to give Him.

God chooses to suffer the shame and death that follows from taking on the burden of rebels and enemies.

God radically chooses fellowship by electing Israelite flesh and blood to fulfill His purpose. He elects their curse to be the focus of what is dealt with in His blessing offered.

God's mercy meets human misery; by that alone, humans can abide with God.

The hope is that Israel may join in the form of the Church, by the help of its Messiah, within the community of God.

God does not depend on Israel's attitude but rather on His own purposes. Israel depends on Him.

If Israel were obedient to its election, it would undergird and support the Church's witness to God's mercy. Together they would offer praise as one elected community.

In actuality, Israel is disobedient to its election. Its promised Messiah has come. As He had been elected to do, He was offered up by Israel and crucified for Israel.

As the resurrected Messiah, He is received by many Gentiles.

Israel still refuses to confess and to serve in the one elect community of God.

Israel reveals how it is with humans. It exposes the burden of human resistance that God's great love assumes.

The existence of the Jews is adequate proof of the existence of God. The depths of their guilt and rejection reveal the greatness of God's love in reconciling humanity. The shadow of the cross falls on them and points to His love for the disobedient and rebellious.

The Jews cannot separate themselves from the love of God in Christ Jesus. They may be ungrateful, but they cannot overcome the reason to be thankful.

Even in their stubbornness, the Jews stand within the realm of the work of God.

In the Church, we see what God chooses for humanity. He chooses self-giving love.

- He chooses to be a brother and also a leader.
- He chooses to be a servant and also a master.
- He is a physician and also a king.

These reflect God's glory. All this God chooses for our benefit.

God's mercy sustains His judgment. His severity is exercised in kindness. His wrath is pursued in fulfilling love.

This mercy forbids us to fear His judgment without loving His judgment and justification that comes from Him.

The Church exemplifies the form of the elected community of God. It has unity and distinctions within. It facilitates the interim situation between the Mediator and humanity.

The Church is the community of God's resurrection mercy, as Israel is the community of God's crucifixion's judgment. They do not exist without each other.

The Church was hidden in the life of Israel. Thus, the Church began before the ascension or Pentecost.

The natural root of the community of God—Israel and the Church—is the person of Jesus.

God has elected instruments of mercy who reveal the misery of humanity as those taken to the heart of God. The fire of God's love consumes but does not destroy. Instead, it purifies and makes well.

From the crucifixion, we see the fire of God's judgment. This judgment was elected from before the beginning of the world, within the life of Israel. It will be confirmed until the end of the world.

As the final form of the community of God's election, the Church must recognize itself in prototype form in the history of Israel. This connection points to the election of all Israel as a community, not select individuals.

The Church hopes for the conversion of Israel but cannot wait for it in fulfilling its mission. The Church must confess the mercy that embraces the unity of Israel and the Church.

In Abraham, we see that the law was given (Israel) and by faith received (Church). Abraham is the father not only of Israel but of the elected community of Jews and Gentiles.

In Moses and Pharaoh, we see God electing to move His mercy forward. Moses is elected as a friend, Pharaoh as an enemy. Both fulfill God's purposes. However, in the election of Jesus, all fall under the judgment of the cross, friend and enemy. In this way, He shows mercy to all on the same cross.

God's mercy is the logic of election, not the worthiness of human actors.

All are held under His judgment that He might show mercy to all.

There are not two goals in God's intention, one toward hardening and one toward mercy.

In love, God is wrathful against perversity that is contrary to love. He is freely powerful to help in the face of human powerlessness, taking our failing human affairs into His hands to fulfill His love.

The heart of wrath comes from the grace that corrects. The judgment He brings to human failure He fulfills with His intent to save humanity as He bears our ills.

God has borne the history of Israel through to an unexpected end. He has resurrected its Messiah as the head of His Church.

His mercy follows the revelation of God's wrath. The grace of the resurrection follows the judgment of the cross.

God's righteousness displayed in Israel's history consists of the fact that God has manifested His mercy to His people. Through them, this extends to the Church of all gathered people. This mercy is the miracle work of God.

What has been revealed in Jesus as the goal of Israel's history is divine mercy holding them by God's steadfast grace.

3. The Promise of God Heard and Believed (pp. 233–59)

God has made a promise. In Jesus, He has made a covenant between Himself and humanity.

Jesus is the point at which we see God's promise of judgment on what in us has rebelled.

Jesus is also the point where we see the mercy of God, pledging His life to us.

In the gathered, elected community of God, we hear God because that is where He dwells. Jesus is honored in the gathering as God's promise in person.

God has spoken His Word to humanity through Israel. We must be careful and attentive to listen to it as God's Word to humanity and not Israel's.

The promises God makes to humanity cannot be heard, be believed, or create faith *if* they are not taken as God's address to humanity. "Faith itself can only be the perfect, obedient and active hearing of the Word of God."[2]

The Church's task is to point to Jesus, to hear His witness continually. His Word is not open for modification or speculation. Obedience begins in listening.

When the Church becomes self-ruling and self-expressing, it ceases to be the Church. It abandons the will of God.

The community who hears God is the community of Israel's Messiah, determined to live on toward its goal. This community tells the world that God determines them to hear as well.

---

2. *CD* 2.2, § 34, p. 234.

God's aim with Israel is for it to pass on its role in active service and join with the Church. Its command is to "Hear, oh Israel" and bear witness to God's election and its own election in conjunction with the Church.

Overall, Israel has not listened to the promise of its election. Its election has been fulfilled in the Word become flesh.

The death and resurrection of Jesus confirm all that was promised to Israel. But Israel thinks it must put itself in right relationship with God. Thus, it fails to hear. Where it could shine for God's glory, it places itself in a void.

Although Israel cannot hear or believe the promise of God, it is still the people of Jesus Christ.

Israel's disobedience cannot alter the promise of God. Israel cannot invalidate the guarantee of the mercy of God that God alone has established with humanity.

In the form of the Church, the community of God is elected by grace to be God's child and brother. We enter His intimate life as friends because He gives Himself for us.

No one could be as close to us as God has chosen to be. Nothing can separate us from Him. Every human need is met in fellowship with Him.

The Church is the medium of communication between Jesus and the world. It is commissioned to speak to all who stand outside its community.

Through His community who accepts Him, Jesus intends to make Himself heard by the world.

The goal of the history of Israel was the existence of the Church of Jews and Gentiles.

God's making things right has been revealed in the death and resurrection so that every human can live by Him and with Him in responsive faith.

God has called to the Gentiles. They have answered the freedom offered to those awakened from their graves.

Only in relation to Him, who is the meaning of it all, can the law be kept. That is a relation by faith in God's mercy. But Israel pursued obedience by works.

Israel lacked the "work of all works," that is, to rely on God's promise, the mercy of God. It relied on itself, its own running and willing.

Israel is the genuine people of God who cannot eradicate God as their God for the simple reason that their belonging is based on His election, not their choice.

The shadow of Israel's election is that human guilt must be revealed to show that the glory and praise of God's mercy are grounded in His election.

Israel did not recognize the righteousness of God or His mercy. They could not accept that everything that had made them who they were was based on God's gift.

Jesus comes as the fulfillment of Israel's law. One could not propose Jesus has invalidated the gift of the law given to Israel.

Jesus was not the end of the law. He came to end the ignorant adoption and application of its misuse.

If anything, Jesus was the end of sin, making use of the law, controlling it for its own ends.

It is with Jesus alone that the law is concerned as the order of life. He interprets it. He fulfills it. He guarantees its validity.

To be obedient to the law means to believe in Jesus. Refusing to believe in Him is to break the law. Israel resists the One Word of God spoken to it.

Jesus is the manifestation of divine mercy. Israel does not recognize Him as such. He is a stranger to them. To them, He is a blasphemous bringer of new revelations. This blindness reveals how estranged they are.

Saying *Jesus is Lord* is equal to saying *Jesus is God*.

One elected Human is a proper partner for the electing God. We believe in Him and participate in His election. Jesus has satisfied the righteousness of the law as the faithful Israelite.

As God Himself in person, Jesus is the source of salvation. He is the sum of all blessings for all who call on Him.

Scripture creates preachers who will bring the power of its meaning to the Jews.

In the face of unbelief by the hearers of the Word, something happens. God, who initiated the Word of His promise, can bring a final resolving Word.

God confirms His election of Israel in proclaiming the good news of His Word in Christ. Israel confirms its election in its disbelief and disobedience. It can only stand under the judgment and mercy of God.

God has caused Himself to be found by those not seeking Him.

The resurrection of Jesus, the event of Pentecost, and the mission of the Church of both Jews and Gentiles have overcome any excuse. No one may claim to have an inability to hear or understand that God has acted.

The events of the messianic age enter into the sphere of the apostolic age with a conviction. Scripture has made the calling of Israel clear. Israel has failed to respond appropriately. All have come to the Jews as God's mercy.

The electing God has mercy on all sinful humanity. Election is always mercy, not abstract or earned.

4. The Passing and the Coming Man (pp. 259–305)

In the election of Jesus, God appoints a merciful, gracious end and a gracious new beginning for humanity. He dies that we may live.

The old man is passing away. This is seen in Israel. The coming man is seen in the Church. These are both seen in the context of Jesus, the passing of the old humanity in His death and the future humanity in His rising.

In corresponding to Jesus, both Israel and the Church must have a form of death and life, attesting to what is taken away and what is bestowed by God.

Israel depends on God's attitude of mercy; God does not depend on any particular attitude from Israel.

Israel will not take up the message "He is risen," but it cannot help saying, "He is not here!"

God seeks the supreme good of humanity, even in the face of unfaithfulness and ingratitude.

Didn't God see all the unfaithfulness and resistance, even before the foundation of the world? He saw humanity that was passing. Thus, He came as the Man who meets all the dead, even those of the synagogue of death. He brings life to those who dwell in the ghettos.

God's mercy is directed first to the Jews. There will be punishment for old sins, but there is an irrevocable promise in their brother Jesus that cannot be rejected.

God makes Himself the way for humanity to participate in God's eternal work. In the form of the Church, He reveals Himself with a death that is surrounded by life. By announcing the kingdom of God, even hell is shown for what it is.

The Church is the perfect form of community. This is because the message of the Church is the gospel, good news for all who are gone astray or in distress.

God's goal for His community is shining His light of mercy in the world.

God's fatherly disposition through His people is the ultimate meaning of history. Even His warning and punishment are fatherly. Humanity passes through its suffering seasons, like Job, under the fatherly purposes of God.

In the crucifixion and resurrection of Jesus, God benefits humanity.

What is prefigured for the Church in Israel is revealed when the Jews and Gentiles come together. Together, they receive the blessing of the gospel.

The Church is founded on the resurrection of Jesus from the dead.

The Church confesses the unity of God's community. It acknowledges Jew and Gentile together under divine mercy.

Has God rejected His people? No, He has stretched out His hand to these resistant people.

Paul sees his own apostolic office as an active representation of the presence and work of the risen Christ. He, an Israelite, was taken from Israel to be sent with the risen Jesus to the Gentile world.

The one thing in which the elect can glory is that God lives from His purpose—the unconditional nature of His grace.

Has God rejected His people in favor of the Church? No, God has brought a remnant out of Israel to the Church as a realization of Israel's election.

God is the God of all, even those He hardens for His purposes. The election of the remnant and the hardening of the majority confirms all is grace and mercy. None are worthy.

The Word of God has spoken among the hardened. The table is set and remains open with the fullness of God's benefits. The stumbling, the falling, the hardened, and all who miss the point are in the hands of God.

The "rest," beyond the "remnant," are blind to what is sealed and prepared for them. They are not ready for what is prepared for them. They are in a deep sleep regarding the God who is gracious and keeps them in His hand.

The rejection of the Messiah by the Jews has made the Gentiles desirous. They are jealous of the grace of God, to have the blessing that was neglected and rejected. Jesus, the stumbling block for the Jews, has become the cornerstone of the Church.

If the Jews had not handed Jesus up to be crucified, He would not have become the Savior of the world.

Had Paul not been repulsed by the Jews, he would not have become the apostle for the sake of the Gentiles.

Through hardening comes a reflection of the glory of God's love. Because of love, the Father did not spare His Son but gave Him up for us all.

The Church waits for Israel's conversion, for the day that their unity in election becomes an actuality.

Israel's sin opens the door for the fullness of God's mercy, which then pours into the world for the Gentiles. Death is overcome, and the reconciliation of the cosmos is achieved.

God's election, which begins for this one people, becomes the great exchange available to every person within God's election.

If the Gentile Church abandoned Israel, it would be abandoning God and His purposes.

The holiness of Israel and the Church derives from its root. He is the ground and goal of Israel's election. Because this root is holy, the branches will be holy.

By grafting wild branches into the cultivated tree, God goes against the horticultural practice. He grafts the Gentiles into the stem of the Israel tree, which has a holy root.

We cannot follow anti-Semitism, which sees the Jews killing Jesus as disqualifying them from election and leading to their replacement by the Church.

In the resurrection, Jesus cancels the rejection of the Jews and the Jewish rejection of Jesus.

The will of Jesus stands against the will of Israel to eradicate Him. He maintains His intent to be the Messiah of Israel and the Savior of the world.

By His acts of grace, God exposed the impotence of humanity to resist and reject Him.

The Church is not to decide the final goal of God with Israel.

Paul does not build on the arbitrary belief that with God, all things must finally be possible. Paul does not assert a final redemption of every person in an optimistic restoration.

It is impossible to expect too much from God; He is supreme in His promise to humanity.

We must not believe in unbelief. We may believe in the future faith of those who do not yet believe.

Gentiles were united to Israel's Messiah by faith alone. What was needed was accomplished in Jesus Christ.

The term *mystery* embraces the three chapters of Romans 9–11 and the problem of the relation of the Jews and Gentiles in their relation to God's election.

The goal of these chapters in Romans is to bring the reader to stand before the riches of the wisdom and knowledge of God.

Paul asserts that the will of God in hardening the Jews is in anticipation, waiting for the time of joined fulfillment when God's election is complete *with* the Gentiles' inclusion.

The fullness of inclusion dwells in Jesus Christ, not a certain number of people who become qualified. He is the measure of the fullness and wholeness. He is the sum and measure of the elect.

"All Israel" includes all those elected in Jesus Christ, Jews and Gentiles. This gathering is the whole Church together, with Jesus Christ as the stem, Israel as the root, and the Gentiles added later as the branches.

God's mercy is His will and is the source, goal, and medium of all things. God wills one and the same thing. He wills to be Himself. He shows mercy in Jesus Christ for the sake of His elected Israel.

God always loves first. He loves even when He is not loved in return.

Human disobedience is everywhere. Human obedience has not brought us to the point where we have a future and a hope.

No one set out for and arrived at Zion. The Deliverer came and drew them to Himself.

The Jews' disobedience is worse than the Gentiles'. It was exercised amid the revelation of their election. It was carried out despite the covenant between God and them. It consisted of their rejection of the Messiah. This comparison does not make Gentile disobedience trivial.

 COMMENTARY:

- All are elected in Jesus. He bears our rejection. He fulfills our acceptance.
- Election refers to the giving and receiving of the Son.
- Election is not abstract.
- The heart of the gospel does not leapfrog over Israel and the Church to address the election of individuals.
- Specific election can only follow the basis of our election in Jesus and the context of our election in the community of God.
- God's election intends to call humans into fellowship with Him. This invitation is facilitated by life in a community.
- Starting with individual election leads to individualistic and judgmental Christianity.
- Israel and the Church form one indivisible unity. Their unity is found in the Messiah.
- The community of God takes two forms, Israel and the Church, but they have a common identity in the One Messiah.
- Israel is not an afterthought. Barth places them clearly within the doctrine of God as a part of God's loving intention.
- The whole of this paragraph plays out the pairing of:

Israel	Church
Rejected	Accepted
Jews	Gentiles
Judgment	Mercy
Hearing	Believing
Old man	New man
Crucifixion	Resurrection
No	Yes
Passing	Coming
Jesus' election to wrath	Jesus' election to righteousness

- The election of God is provisional and progressive, extending the love of God in continuity toward reconciliation.
- Humanity may resist God, but this does not negate God's love. It is a possible impossibility:
    - God does not pass by some people for any reason.
    - God does not predetermine any people to rejection.
- Jesus is the One rejected on our behalf. He is the One accepted on our behalf.

 CONCLUSION FOR THE CHURCH: The Church exists as a community to mediate the election of God. It is not a franchise to help people find what fulfills their lives independently. The roots of the Church are in Israel. The Church now needs to be seen as continuing within God's human community development, enjoying His covenant life. Israel may be an estranged family, but they are the first human family of God. They are the tree to which we are attached, to live within God's electing purposes. Together, God has one family to bless, and He reconciles all humans to come home.

We can no longer stand in judgment regarding Israel or any other group as rejected by God. Even in being resistant, the way is made for God's outlandish love for the hardhearted and the confused. If we are to stand with God's judgment, it must include both a recognition of the rejection of Jesus and an acknowledgment of His unfailing love for all. Nothing can separate us from the love of God, even when we are resisting.

 INSIGHT FOR PASTORS: The preaching of the Word must include both the Old and New Testaments. The community of God's beloved people includes Jews and Gentiles of every nation. Jesus is the elect One on their behalf. We cannot think of the Church as a building, congregation, denomination (or nondenomination), tradition, or any other segmenting concept. The Church exists as the community of God with *all* His beloved. We must teach our people to think of participation within this whole family.

Focusing on Jesus' election, we are compelled to understand our community mission as participation in God's elected mission. We join in hearing and believing the Word of Jesus. We share in echoing His love to the hard of heart and the hard of hearing. We have a gospel privilege to announce the depth and vastness of the judgment of God's love. We choose our words and tone of voice so that they simmer in the mercy that affirms each person as chosen and beloved by God.

A significant point to take from this section is that the election of *individuals* is not the place to begin discussions on election. Election is entirely grounded in Jesus' act and decision to be for humanity. Jesus' consequential endeavor toward humanity is to elect a community to live out the embodiment of His mission. That is our invitation.

God's mercy does not lead to universalism, but it does reveal a universal love. God still grants humans the freedom to resist. Many do resist and reject, but this cannot stop God from loving them. The human protest, that God must be "fair," is ignorant of God's fierce love. God has been constant from eternity. He created time and space and has been patient with Israel for millennia. Our churches need the patience of God, not Job, to share in God's election, believing God has elected each person we meet as the object of His love.

 INSIGHT FOR THEOLOGIANS: As theologians, we are called to pay attention to the intentions that move God's actions. God does not merely will from eternity. He also chooses to fulfill His purpose in history. This choosing refocuses the *perfections* of God in His eternal being to the specifics of God's *interactions* with His creation and creatures.

God's intentional activity depicts the will of God. This movement includes all that Jesus has elected in the divine mission, of which Israel is a foreshadowing of hope, later fulfilled in Jesus as the Messiah.

To be Christian theologians, we must see the Old Testament and its people as preparation. We must be attentive to God's intentions. These become vividly clear when Jesus steps into the field of history, displaying His mission in light of all that pointed to Him.

We cannot be New Testament theologians and neglect the Old Testament. Such narrow-minded thinking takes Jesus out of context. We miss Israel as God's community in expectation, finding final fulfillment in Jesus' Church. Further, if we investigate God's election in light of individualistic enlightenment culture, we will construct lenses alien to the intent of God. What are we left with if we are blind to the intent of God in His relation to the world?

This section brings into continuity the sensibility of God's judgment and mercy. We may now understand how these conform to God's unlimited, unmerited grace. We need not turn a blind eye to God's judgment. He is constantly dealing with human estrangement and violations from a heart of love. We see Jesus resisting human resistance with divine love. His final word is grace and mercy. We find that this was also His first word. Together, they open us to the unfolding future as a new person in Christ.

? **CLARIFYING QUESTIONS:** Does your theology of election begin with asking which individual humans are elected? *Or* does it start with Jesus' election and how He selects Jews *and* Gentiles as the focus of His reconciling work in His election? Do you recognize a relationship of preparation and fulfillment that includes both Israel and the Church?

The Symphony of God
Adapted for Humanity

Begins Trinity Sunday
No Auditions Necessary

Come as you are
You are selected, accept now!

CHAPTER 16

NO AUDITIONS NECESSARY; ALL ARE WELCOMED

§ 35. *The Election of the Individual*

FOCUS STATEMENT: The big question addressed in this paragraph (§ 35) is who is in and who is out of the choir of God. Jesus decides, invites, and finds a way for all to join. Even the voiceless and tone-deaf are integrated, as are the disrupters and self-interested. He loves the wallflowers and the wailers. Of course, He is happy to have the talented as well, as long as they do not think they earned their way. He cares for every person, as we see in "The Election of the Individual."

No human capability, quality, or intention qualifies one to be in the symphonic choir of God. No musician is simply "endured" with their imperfections. Jesus integrates all to achieve a symphonic outcome that is beyond human imagination.

The invitational sign given by Jesus is one of inclusion. It is boundlessly embracing, even when people walk away. The excluded are self-deselected. He never gives up.

The movements of the symphony reverberate with the magnificent chordal structures of the grandeur of God. However, silence and stillness equally open space for meaningful encounters. The whole of God's inclusive election streams out, like reaching arms, to the multitudes. Under Jesus' leadership, this holy host attains a coherence of sound beyond our understanding of harmony. Individually, each was just a whisper in the night. But now we hear the contributions, as well as the malfunctioning of each human, woven into the symphony's theme of God's freeing love.

INTRODUCTION: This is a long paragraph. Over 25 percent of CD 2.2 is contained in this section. Election is a decision on God's part. God's determination sets the outcome—to include all humankind—into action for each person.

There is a lot of debate (by humans) over who is deemed worthy of God's love and salvation. Barth overwhelmingly affirms that God has chosen to love all. Not all humans act in response to the love of God for them. This situation sets up the discussion for discerning who ought to be called the elected and the rejected. As we will see, all are selected in Jesus. Those who are rejected function under a lie that they can live outside Jesus' choice for them. But Jesus has not rejected or abandoned them.

The question of universalism (whether all are destined to be saved by God) is brought to the table for discussion. Barth denies being a Universalist, but he lives in hope and confidence that God is good and more gracious than we can imagine. We are encouraged to leave judgments to God. We may confidently hope that all are loved and chosen by God to receive His love and companionship because of the supreme act of Jesus. In the end, these are not our judgments to make, but we can look to Jesus to always act from His freeing love.

CONTEXT: *CD* 2.2
Pages in Paragraph: 201 pages (pp. 306–506)

Subsections
1. Jesus Christ, the Promise and Its Recipient
2. The Elect and the Rejected
3. The Determination of the Elected
4. The Determination of the Rejected

TEXT: § 35. The Election of the Individual

OPENING SUMMARY: The man who is isolated over against God is as such rejected by God. But to be this man can only be by the godless man's own choice. The witness of the community of God to every individual man consists in this: that this choice of the godless man is void; that he belongs eternally to Jesus Christ and therefore is not rejected, but elected by God in Jesus Christ; that the rejection which he deserves on account of his perverse choice is borne and cancelled by Jesus Christ; and that he is appointed to eternal life with

God on the basis of the righteous, divine decision. The promise of his election determines that as a member of the community he himself shall be a bearer of its witness to the whole world. And the revelation of his rejection can only determine him to believe in Jesus Christ as the One by whom it has been borne and cancelled.[1]

SUMMARY:

1. Jesus Christ, the Promise and Its Recipient (pp. 306–40)

We now come to consider the election of the individual.

Many theological studies begin with this issue as a problem. Their approach raises questions regarding the ordering of the private relationship between God and specific human beings.

Augustine's inward turn shaped an understanding of the relation between the individual and God to focus Christian spirituality on autobiography—one's inner life. People began thinking of relating to God through the mind, turned inward in reflection.

In Augustine's thought, *some* humans are prepared for grace. Thus, the view arose that God has predetermined to speak to some and not to others. Consequently, it appeared that some individuals were chosen, and others were rejected.

Calvin bought a more decisive determination on God's part. He believed God decided for the human race, and individuals, who would have life and who would have death. Election and rejection became standard fare for those who followed.

Over time, Jesus' place in election and predestination became more and more remote.

Influenced in part by secular individualism, the focus on the individual led to pietism (pure in act) and rationalism (true in thought) in the Church.

The major problem addressed in this discussion is whether we will allow God His free decision in His covenant relationship with humanity or require a fixed system of worthiness in thought or act.

Either God's covenant is revealed and expresses the will of the God who loves in freedom, or we will collapse into an abstract, hidden, and arbitrary deity.

All other descriptions of the election of individuals are inadequate when set against the biblical revelation of Jesus' election on our behalf.

---

1. *CD* 2.2, § 35, p. 306.

The election of the individual fits within divine election. We must begin with Jesus' election on behalf of every human being and then proceed to the elected community of the Church. Through His election of the Church, Jesus determines the witness of His election for each person.

Jesus is personally elected on every person's behalf. Each person is individually elected within Jesus' election.

Jesus precedes all others in His election. He does not deprive them; He provides for all.

There are two *secular imitations* of the election of Jesus Christ:

1. The *concept of the leader.* These individuals fashion a role not on behalf of others but in place of them. The elevated individual operates in an expanding sphere, besides whom there is no "elect" individual. All societal power and authority carry out this person's decisions.

   This person rises from the ranks of the many and becomes inflated over them (think Fascism).

   They usurp all freedoms and responsibilities of other individuals. All power belongs to this leader.

   This leader has nothing to do with election except existing as the mirror opposite. This person is a misrepresentation of the relation between the one and many.

   This leader spoils the many for the sake of the one. However, Jesus gives Himself for the sake of the many. He brings freedom and empowers the many.

2. The *concept of the community.* This "secular imitation" attempts to reflect the intimate relationships of the Christian prototype.

   This imitation takes on two forms. One creates community as a *social mass*, the whole people (think Communism). This form appears to gather people to resist oppressive rulers.

   Fascism, where *nationalistic pride* takes over, represents the second form of "community," with rallying cries of "our nation first." Race, language, and history serve as unifying factors. This form combines with the "elect leader" for a seductive interplay of ideals and power.

   Both Communism and Fascism create a totalitarian state. Here, the unified mass of people and the glue of nationalism combine. The people feel elected. Individual people find themselves only as a part of the whole, replaceable at any moment. The value of persons is forfeited to the state.

In a totalitarian state, the particular person must die to self, so the whole of the people might thrive as a state or nation, swallowing one's particular worth or potential.

All uniqueness, inwardness, and mystery are taken from the person. This move is the opposite of the election in Christ.

For Barth, divine election in Christ is on behalf of a nation as a whole and the individuals as a part of this whole.

There is no need to compromise about the individual when each one is seen as valuable to the community.

In other words, we need not default to individualism or collectivism. Instead, we live within the promise and valuing of Jesus. He holds us together in His election as persons in His community.

We can now see that an "individual human being" is an ambiguous concept in this context. This idea must be clarified concerning whom Jesus elects.

God's grace occurs between Himself and human beings. The community is His medium to fulfill His purpose.

No family or nation is a predestined group. Even Israel is only a transitory form of God's community.

Through particular humans, God fulfills His blessing to humanity. Through these persons, God loves and makes known the many benefits of His covenant and gracious choice. These people are not special; they are simply chosen.

The triune God is undividedly one, sending the particular One, Jesus, to express His ways and works.

Individual persons are summoned to participate in the life of the Church of Jesus Christ. They recognize the election of Jesus Christ on their behalf.

By the Holy Spirit's working through the community, humans are moved to make a free personal decision.

In this case *individual* has a positive, focused sense, as each individual responds personally to God. Contrast this with secular individualism, where people go their own way, abandoning God and fellow humans.

However, election is not about the individuality of a human predestined by God's choice. Its ground is in Christ's choice, not the specific characteristics of a human.

We must think of the individual in an entirely new way. The term refers to a forgiven person standing before God by God's justifying grace alone.

Individuals stand covered by the sovereign God, who transforms and renews rebellious children.

There is no "Therefore" that assumes that the status or accomplishment of a person concludes in God's acknowledgment.

There is only a "Nevertheless," the miracle of God's will. God chooses to make us partners of His covenant apart from our merit. The Holy Spirit makes even those of us who resist usable for the purposes of God.

Burdened and opposed, humans need God's renewal. This state is not necessarily what we feel as we stand before God.

Individuality is not necessarily equated with sin. We merely acknowledge the particularity of each person's uniqueness before God.

The form of individuality addressed and dealt with in Jesus is a perversion of a first sense. This sense rejects the dignity conferred by God. It repels with ingratitude the grace of God.

The second form of individuality is a self-made life. This individuality works in developing the natural disposition of human life, making a claim on God to regard their way of life with a distinction based on human abilities and merits.

In this second mode, humans think that God loves and chooses them as if their will, not God's, was at work joining in covenant connection.

Like the conditional and obligation-laden ways humans relate, this individuality is duty-bound. Jesus rejects this human-willed form of individualism.

Humans may legitimately be individuals before God. But apart from and against God, human individuality can only lead to ruin.

God does not intend this isolation for humans. It is a satanic possibility that God rejects.

Humans choose what God has rejected. This choice, this quest into the void, is made godlessly.

Jesus tells the godless person that He is for them no matter what.

The good news of the community of God is that Jesus Christ knows and has chosen to love each tragic human life, even in this self-chosen isolation, by drawing near to them.

Having separated from God, we are ready targets for authoritarian or collectivist structures of human organization. We are also susceptible to every other abusive, diminishing practice that stalks the powerless and weak.

The urge to move to the shadows and hide in isolation is strong. To reject is to be rejected and to live as a rejected person in self-seclusion.

But in receiving the good news, a person comes to know Jesus Christ. It is a call to a place of belonging.

The godless are still concerned as they suffer their existence in the shadows, aware of the threat, not the overcoming, of their rejection.

The goal of the godless to pursue rejection cannot be reached. The desire to be godless was nullified before the world began.

The task of the community is to reveal the act and intention of God already made actual through His Son.

As God confronted the world who rejected Him, we, too, speak to the world's lost children. These people are not lost according to God's promise.

To each, we may say, "You are the object of God's gracious decision to bring you home."

To be an elected human does not mean that one lives as such.

Living as a rejected person can conflict with one's election, but it cannot annul one's election, which is grounded in Jesus and not in human response.

In Jesus Christ, a decision has been made. He who was rejected on the cross is the One who was elected. Our rejection is met with His election. It has been decided that we can only be elected in the face of our rejection.

We are called to accept Jesus' decision and follow the actual situation of the relationship. We then act with an attitude of discernment that shapes every decision, in opposition to the godlessness that reflects the void life.

For the elect, the old life of independence is replaced by the will to live life together.

God is not talking *about* us; He *addresses* us as those who hear.

We may adopt an attitude appropriate to the address made to us. Our attitude may align with or deviate from the promise.

The Church must address all humans with the promise of God as a personal summons.

The community must speak in the second person, saying, "For you."

This one election in Jesus unites believers who have merited rejection and unbelievers who are granted unmerited election. Both look to the One in whom they are elected and not rejected as the outworking of divine grace.

1. The emphasis must be on faith in Jesus Christ.

Faith is an attitude that acts in loving response to the determination of God in His eternal will. God has oriented humans to Himself, and they positively respond.

The gift of the Holy Spirit facilitates this.

The election of the elect is concretely visible in their faith, as they live in conformity to God. This new status is activated by knowing and loving God, and the believers are awakened to obedience and trust.

Believers cannot confront unbelievers as those who are rejected.

We cannot stand *against* unbelievers, only *for* them, as we address them with the promises made for us all.

2. Election comes only by the grace of God and delivers those who are utterly unable to restore themselves to God.

God watches over those who were born alienated and corrupt in their uncleanness. He draws these to Himself.

It would be impossible to reach out to God if He were not first reaching out to us.

The elect do not always head in the right direction or walk in a loving manner. Everyone stumbles and falls, even to the point of losing their way.

God's grace is profound as He addresses Himself to the godless. He confronts the impossibility of their rejection and makes possible the recognition of His grace that they may treasure it.

3. Election includes the constancy of God's love in the preservation of His people.

The loving Father will not allow those for whom He gave His Son to perish.

God did not help us just to leave us to help ourselves.

Even after responding in faith, believers live in the flesh and must humble themselves before God. Though they struggle, they must cling to the grace in which God is faithful and bears them along.

God will not remove His Holy Spirit from His own; He will remain with them unswervingly.

The entire gospel shines with the constancy of God's preserving love that extends to all.

4. Election in Jesus assures us of our salvation because it is grounded in the work of Christ and not our own.

The question is whether anyone can have certainty as to their election. Barth acknowledges that many answer negatively. But with Paul and Calvin, he affirms confidence in this knowledge if we think properly through Christ.

In Christ, we see the tranquility granted in Christ for us, which gives us confidence.

Concerning the basis, and hence the security, of trust in our election, we must look past our works. We must fix our eyes on the goodness of God alone. Works may strengthen us as evidence that God is at work. But we trust in His lovingkindness alone.

If Jesus is the fundamental basis of election for each person, facilitated by the community of God, then the assurance of the individual has been fully answered. In faith, they take hold of that which is given to them. They then live as the elect by their faith.

2. The Elect and the Rejected (pp. 340–409)

By what criteria or on what basis do individuals become elected persons?

Individuals become elect through a distinction made by God. This relationship is particular to each person, though it is not based on that human's particularities, conduct, actions, or any human qualification.

Human awareness of election is evidenced as a person continues to live in continuity with their election. Their acts become consistent with what God intends for them.

The basis of the elected relationship to God, both in His relation to the human and the human in actual human response, rests in God alone.

The election of the twelve named apostles is established by the Word of God addressing them.

The calling of specific humans in the Old Testament is replaced by every person who believes in Jesus Christ in the New Testament. Each person fulfills their personal election in answering the election of Jesus, who calls them.

In the Church, all are elected, fulfilling specifically what Israel was corporately.

Those who are elected have responded to their distinctive determination by God as particular elected persons. This reply is neither chance nor a necessity. It is the unfolding of God's mystery.

Only God can be who He is. At best, we approximate this authentic life as those who are loved from eternity, living in covenant, and destined for the fulfillment of its promises.

The significant figures of the Old Testament do not speak for themselves. They speak "in the name of God."

In each of those He elects, God confirms Himself as a way of repeating Himself in all His works.

Jesus' disciples are identified as "friends" who have learned through Jesus what His Father is doing.

One who is active in the ministry of reconciliation is an instrument of God's revelation. They walk with God and know they are His friends and children.

Through the community, the Holy Spirit proclaims the election of Jesus already at work. It is a call to a corresponding faith, waking to their election by the election of Jesus.

By hearing the proclamation and believing in faith, these persons are placed in a different relation to God and other persons. They adore, find joy, and are at peace in ways at odds with what others experience.

What distinguishes other persons from the elect is that they do not have the Holy Spirit, meaning they do not listen to what is told to them, and they will not believe.

Devoid of God's mystery at work in their lives, the hostile mind becomes a false witness to life itself. It seeks what is not life.

Rejection would be the inevitable lot of all humans outside of God's election.

The election of Jesus has diverted the threat of destruction from humanity. Jesus has become the rejected human in our place, averting the devastation for all humankind.

The choice to run away as the rejected has been excluded, made impossible, and removed from the menu.

Rejecting God is evil, perilous, and futile.

It is *evil* because it denies what God has done for humanity out of His eternal love.

It is *perilous* because it draws one to the shadow of withdrawal, a hazard for every human.

It is *futile* because it cannot alter the fact that there is only one rejected, and He bears the consequence and punishment for human rebellion and guilt. That is Jesus.

The elect are to be found in the hand of God, answering the call of Jesus. They are free members of the household of God.

The others are also to be found in the hand of God. These have become slaves, living under the curse of God. The expression of their lives is against what God wills.

All humans sin against God. All express their enmity with God in their attempt at self-willing. Apart from Jesus, the elected are no different than the rejected.

The elect work out their election by faith in Jesus. They must simultaneously be filled with gratitude for the removal of the rejection that threatens them. They must remain in solidarity with the godless even while remaining separate from their unbelief.

The Holy Spirit makes possible proclamation and faith. Without the Spirit, the elect would be like those from whom they are distinguished.

Anyone who is now a believer was once an unbeliever. Every elected person has been interrupted with long stretches away from the realm of faith.

We must claim our solidarity with the godless. Only the cross stands between us, and it is the only hope for us both.

In the godless, we see what we were and would be apart from the hope of God's grace. In the elect, the godless see the light of Christ who loves sinners. He calls to them as well.

The godless can only give a false picture of the case. However, their claim that Jesus has rejected them contradicts the accurate picture to which the elect provide testimony.

The true rejected human is Jesus Christ, and He has taken on the rejection of humanity in Himself. In the face of that, human rejection can only be provisional, a potential rejection.

The godless may conduct their lives as rejected. They live as liars regarding God, and His truth rightly assesses their judgment that God stands against their rebellion.

Embracing the elect and excluding the godless are human expectations. But they ignore the reality of Jesus Christ. What is given to the elect may be given to the godless also.

The work of the Holy Spirit in fulfilling the election of humans is a work of God as well. We cannot dismiss what God, by His Spirit, will still accomplish.

We cannot believe that the possibility of belief is ruled out for any person. We cannot accept the rejection of the "godless" because we know the rejected One who could not accept their godlessness.

We have every reason to hold the elect and the rejected together despite their noticeable difference. Both are in the hands of God.

There are two classes of humans, the elect and the apparently rejected. These exist as the community of God and the world.

Reality is not to be found where the two groups face one another as the elect and "rejected." What separates them is their stand toward Jesus Christ. What connects them is the same person. In Him, they are against and for each other.

Only if we disregard Jesus' election for them could we call the others "rejected."

Jesus is *the* Elect; apart from Him are those we might consider as rejected by our evaluations. But in Him, all others become objects of divine grace so that they may not be rejected.

Jesus is *the* Rejected; all others can be only an echo of the curse that has fallen on Him who is in their place. He has made Himself responsible for them.

Jesus is *the* Rejected because He is *the* Elected. In His election, He stands in for the rejected. In His rejection, He makes room for their election.

Although Cain kills Abel, God does not abandon him. Cain hides from God's presence, as his parents had in Eden. Yet God promises to protect him.

In the series of contrasting pairs that follow in the story of the Old Testament, God uses His elect (Isaac, Jacob, Rachel, Joseph) but does not abandon the others (Ishmael, Esau, Leah, Joseph's brothers).

Those who are "cut off" remain in a positive relation to the covenant of God.

Death is God's saving judgment, operating out of God's grace in exhibiting love for humanity. Through death, humanity is cleansed and led to life. The whole sacrificial system had death and life built into its structure, death making way to a reconciled life.

The Old Testament text could not yet speak the name of Jesus. However, the portraits and images there point beyond the human realm.

Only the decision of faith in Jesus can confirm the exegetes of the Old Testament who see that these texts point to Jesus. Once we believe, how could we not see Jesus in these texts?

The meaning of the election of Jesus is as the spotless lamb chosen before the foundation of the world to offer His life in place of the many.

Jesus bears our sin away from the Father. Jesus is like the goat sent into the wilderness, even as He brings us into union with His Father.

In the unfolding story of the Old Testament, the people of God are replaced by kings, who come to represent the people before God.

In the contrast between Saul and David, Saul is a portrayal of the monarch that has made himself independent of the kingdom of God. He is the sinful, guilty, punished king of Israel.

If there were no Saul, making visible the rebellious ways of Israel, the stage would not have been set for King David, given by the grace of God. He points to the One true King.

Saul meets the ideal of human leadership in stature and confidence. David is not recognized as a kingly person, but God is with him. His kingship is hidden from human eyes until the time is right.

David is the humble shepherd who can trust God, lowly in human eyes but sanctioned to do the work of God in caring for God's people.

David, the true king, is first secretly, and then openly, elected as the king of Israel. What was concealed is revealed, as it was with Jesus. Saul was the elect of humans; David was the elect of God.

David, the music maker, is the instrument of God's peace, playing his harp in contradiction to the sword by which Saul lived and died.

David's sin shows that he is a man, made king by grace, not by his credentials or accomplishments. He is king despite his obvious human failures.

Election is separate from human worthiness, displaying the decision of God at work in choosing unexpectedly and undeservedly. It is God's grace alone that supports David.

The kingship of Jesus Christ is that to which the kings of Israel point.

Israel's monarchy is a prototype of the *kingship* and *kingdom* of Jesus.

Israel's *rejected* king is a prototype of Jesus.

Israel's *elected* king is a prototype of Jesus.

Judah and Israel also belong in the story of the duality between election and rejection. This complement is echoed in the man of God from Judah and the prophet from Bethel. They battle with truth-telling and lying. These figures represent the challenges in Judah and Israel.

There is a battle between corrupt, institutional life and the true prophet's word rooted in the freedom of God, even for those chosen to speak for God.

In loving His people, God does not will their sin. He stands against every act of unfaithfulness, sanctifying them through His covenant promises.

God does not depend on human skills in promise keeping but rather loves these disintegrating people with faithful mercy and grace. His ways point beyond the moment to the coming Son, their future hope.

In Jesus, the challenging dualities of the elected and rejected in the Old Testament find their unity, purpose, and fulfillment.

3. The Determination of the Elected (pp. 409–49)

God elects humans for a definite purpose. God has elected and called His creatures according to His good pleasure with meaning, order, and a goal.

The decisive place to understand this determination of God for humanity is in the elect man Jesus Christ. He is the natural and historical demonstration of this way of being. The Holy Spirit calls Him.

The Spirit calls us to live within Jesus' election, to be the kind of person for whom Jesus is elected. This selection is not *so* we will be elected, but for us to be *congruent with* our election into Jesus.

As we share in Jesus' election, we are also part of the elected community, members of this one body. We are elected to share in the ministry of the Church as it shares in the ministry of Christ.

We are elected to be in Christ. This affirmation implies we are elected to be part of the fellowship of other Christians, together inseparably involved in caring for others as Jesus is caring for us.

Humans are elect in that they allow themselves to be loved by God, conforming to His election to love us.

We can never become anything other than, or greater than, one loved by God and beloved as part of His family in Christ.

Our human blessedness comes from participating in God's blessedness. But we do not merely accept and possess it. We are not a dead-end street. God's blessedness goes out from God, working out through us for the blessing of others.

The covenant life of participation we have in sharing God's love and work is active.

What is meant by blessedness, gratitude, and being loved by God is human participation in God's life where God Himself is at work in sharing His glory.

We do not follow our own imagination or inventions. We live from our relationship with Him.

As elected persons, we stand in service of the gracious God. The Holy Spirit summons us. We are commissioned to be witnesses. We are messengers of God.

As Jesus is sent out as an apostle of grace, His whole community is ordered to follow Him. In our election by Him, we allow the light He kindles to shine out through us.

We do not choose or reject anyone in our service with God. We portray who God is, and what Jesus has done for the love of humanity, to share His glory.

We must not regard anyone as if they are not elect, as though God's love did not apply to them too. We must urge all to believe the good news of God's love.

No one is rejected; Jesus has been rejected on their behalf. In response to this news, each person may recognize what God has done, finding confidence in Jesus and the call of love's obligation on their life.

We do not know the final state of all humanity. We must respect the freedom of divine grace. God does not *need* to elect any human, and He does not *need* to elect humankind.

We must avoid abstract statements about the necessity of God electing or excluding anyone.

Whenever an individual is elected, a new person is found in Christ.

God has determined to live by grace for all. "He will face others wrathfully but never contemptuously, with indignation but never with malice, angered but never embittered, a guest and a stranger but never an enemy."[2]

God was in Christ reconciling the world to Himself, and God understands what that means. This reconciliation is our concern as well.

Every person is elected in their own way so that God should be the direction and aim of their life.

It is difficult to derive from the Old Testament the meaning of being elected as a friend, servant, and child of God. The presence of the nonelect casts a shadow over the story, veiling the promises of God.

In the Old Testament, we see a wrathful love, the judgment of the grace of God for the sake of life-giving. The will of God for Israel is lovingkindness.

The puzzling damnation in the Old Testament is subordinated in the New Testament to the lovingkindness of God for humanity. The judgment precedes the acceptance that has the final word.

Jesus lifts the veil on the frontier of the Old Testament.

1. Jesus clearly reveals God's will for the elect, the purpose of election, and the aim of the life of the elect, without the presence of the Old Testament opponents seen as the rejected.
2. Where previously there had been paired images of the elect and rejected persons, Jesus takes both in Himself. He is the answer to human rejection. He is the One in whom all are elected.
3. Jesus is the personal revelation of the reconciliation of the world rejected by God. He reveals the superiority of the electing will of God over the rejecting human choice. The will that refuses is subordinated but takes human sinfulness seriously. The will of God triumphs in Jesus as the limiting of the divine "No" by the divine "Yes."
4. Jesus Christ reveals the reality of life's content for elected persons. Jesus does not act for Himself. He fulfills the will of God for other persons, the lovingkindness of God for the many. He overcomes their rejection and promises their election.

---

2. *CD* 2.2, § 35, p. 419.

The will of God aims at the salvation of all humans. We cannot say all are saved, but there is an unlimited many who are the aim of His will.

Jesus is the unconditional love of God for the world. We cannot make an "open number of the elect" correspond to a "closed set of people opposite the rejected."

We cannot make the "limitless many" the same thing as "all humanity." We cannot propose any freedom of God that is not realized and revealed in Jesus.

Each elected individual is a member of the community of Jesus Christ. Together, they have fellowship with one another because they have fellowship with Jesus Christ, by the Holy Spirit.

The terms *elect*, *beloved of God*, *accepting the gospel*, *awakened by the Spirit*, and *part of the Christian community* are synonyms. There are many more similar designations.

All these are loved by the Father, sanctified by the Spirit, and made clean by the blood of Jesus.

Election means faith in Jesus' faithfulness. It means to be part of His body, the Church.

What an elected person receives from God is never a special task or destiny.

The Church is not an institution for the satisfaction of human needs. It does not provide the means to achieve individual fulfillment. But this may happen in the course of involvement in our community.

Persons elected to life in the Church are equipped and empowered to become useable by the Lord of the Church.

The Church, like Jesus, is sent out into the world—as apostolic.

Apostolic means living in the ongoing work and word of the apostles; we live with the apostles.

We are sent out as disciples. We see this from the beginning with the twelve disciples. They become visible representatives of the community of Jesus. They are commissioned to speak to the world in the context of Jesus' resurrection and ascension.

We see a three-fold correspondence between the disciples and the ministry of Jesus.

- Jesus began with a *prophetic* ministry in Galilee.
- His *priestly* ministry came next in the passion.
- He is finally exalted as *king*.

As the Father sent Jesus, so the Church is sent into the world; the apostolic Church shares in His mission.

Disciples are prophets, priests, and kings because we are made His own.

- The disciples share in Jesus' *prophetic* ministry.

  Because Jesus is the content of the Scriptures, He uniquely makes of the disciples what they are to become—witnesses of Him to whom the text points.

  The disciples speak Jesus' name to reveal the reality of His person. Repentance is turning to Him, who is the light, and away from the shadows of sin.

  We continue with the ministry that was committed to the disciples, that is, to proclaim the gracious command of God throughout the world in the form of the rule of faith. This mission is punctuated with "I am with you always."

  Through the disciples, the world continues to hear the voice of Jesus. The Spirit will be their guarantee, guiding and correcting the presence of Jesus at work in the words and deeds of the disciples.

  Pentecost is the outworking of Jesus' promised presence in bringing the fulfillment of their commission.

- The disciples share in Jesus' *priestly* ministry.

  At the Last Supper, the disciples are commissioned to take the meal and function as priests. They are called to invite others into Jesus' new covenant and to glorify God.

  They confess what has become authentic in their witness, pointing to Jesus as the Son of God, the Messiah.

- The disciples witness to the *King* and His kingdom.

  If Jesus is the Messiah, He is the King, not only of Israel but also of the world.

  The resurrected Lord is the exalted King and calls for faithfulness instead of betrayal.

  Only Jesus is genuinely apostolic; all others point to Him. He is for humanity as no other could be.

  Peter is the supreme example of "for apart from Me you can do nothing" (John 15:5 NASB). The Church today still needs to learn this.

  When Church leadership exhibits pride or arrogance, it means they have abandoned the authority of Christ, and their fellowship with Him is missing. One does not "misuse" Christ's power; one sheds Christ to seek one's own power.

The number twelve is symbolic. It describes the calling of Israel and the disciples, those called out for the nations.

Healing by the disciples is the sign that indicates the triumph of Jesus' kingdom in His resurrection.

The secret of the disciples' mission is that Jesus is with them on behalf of those to whom they are sent.

The apostles portray the life of persons whom God elects. In them, each individual in the Church should recognize their particular calling to share Jesus' meaning and purpose.

4. The Determination of the Rejected (pp. 449–506)

To be "rejected," one must isolate from God, rejecting God's election. Even so, God will be for this person who is against God.

Although God approaches with open arms, this person draws away.

God frees from the burden of guilt and punishment, but Satan's shadow imprisons this person with fear.

God chooses to give blessings, but the joylessness of pride absorbs this person's attention.

In understanding the situation of the rejected, we come to have clarity about the state of the elect.

Where God has chosen to make a covenant of compassion and grace with the elect, God has not chosen to have a "covenant of wrath" with the "rejected."

The elect are willed to be God's covenant people. The "rejected" are those whom God has not willed to be rejected yet who make this choice contrary to God's choice.

God is patient and wise with the rejecting one, so this person will continue to exist.

The person who chooses what God has not willed shares with the elect the gift of creation and God's providential care; God sustains them.

The elect know the rejected as those who do not know the One who has elected them.

The rejected do not know they are rejected or that they have been elected.

Jesus has taken the place of the rejected. He rejects their rejection.

The elected know that Jesus Christ has been rejected on their behalf.

The elected recognize themselves in the rejected, as those accepted because of Christ's election, but are still compatible with the rejected.

Jesus remedies the disorder of the world and the guilt that is its consequence.

"Being with" our rejected neighbor is our only proper assessment of these neighbors. If we judge them, we stand against those for whom Jesus stands. If we take Jesus' relation to them seriously, we must choose to be for them.

The rejection of the rejected can only be past tense; they have been rejected only in their human choice to refuse.

However, the rejected are no longer denied. The rejection of the Rejected One has overcome their plight. His is the final word.

To exist as the rejected is to be only a shadowy form. Certainly, these persons attempt to oppose grace. But we cannot validate this opposition.

We may oppose their godlessness and not remain silent. We do this, treating the rejected as those beloved by God, who opposes their self-destruction.

The rejected have a distinctive nature at the root of their way of being. They stand alongside the elect. They are reluctant witnesses.

1. The rejected stand as those in need of the gospel.
2. The rejected show what is overcome by the gospel.
3. The rejected exhibit the purpose of the gospel, God giving humans a future.

Judas Iscariot is the character most clearly developed in the Bible regarding the problem of the "rejected." The rejected Judas is not to be found in the hostile, alien world to which Jesus came. He is located at His table.

The opponent of the elect is not confrontive to the kingdom of God from the outside. This counterpart stands in the closest possible connection as a friend and disciple. This one betrays the intimacy of being a disciple.

Judas is no less a disciple than the others. He was called to Jesus' mission. He followed Jesus. He was chosen to be a disciple with the others. He alone is from the tribe of Judah like Jesus.

Judas was a genuine disciple, hand-picked by Jesus, and a betrayer of Jesus. One who is elected was seen as rejected.

Jesus knew from the beginning that Judas would betray Him, but this did not stop Jesus from electing him. Judas had a part to play that must be played.

Judas was not hostile to Jesus; he handed Jesus over to the religious authorities with a kiss. Jesus was aware of what was happening and did not stop it. He was chosen to play this part.

From within the chosen, within the Church, Judas starts a stone rolling by handing Jesus over. This handing over moves on to religious leaders, to political leaders, to a hostile world. He is passed from Jew to Gentile, to death itself.

We must confirm that Judas is guilty and that the act was a betrayal. Judas was a great sinner, and it grieved Jesus that this was the case. Judas acts under the influence of the devil.

Judas's act of darkness does not overpower the light. Jesus makes the disciples clean, seen in the washing of their feet. But Judas was not clean. They are mutually to wash one another's feet and clean the most unclean part in each other.

Mary anoints Jesus' feet in Bethany. Her act is consistent with the cleaning and preparation for honoring with extravagance. She is giving her all in discipleship and anointing His body for death.

Jesus allows Mary to use the expensive perfume to anoint Him in preparation for His death and burial. Her devotion to Him shows her heart of caring for others. This is the outworking of meaningful devotion. She is clean in her self-giving.

Judas is not clean. He has ideas other than serving Jesus with the money under his influence. He did not care for the poor; he was a thief. The acts of Judas and Mary point beyond themselves to reveal their character.

Because Judas had not handed himself over to Jesus, he was able to hand Jesus over to his enemies.

Judas "repented" when he saw the result of his action. He had a change of heart. He spoke it out loud. He acted in response, wishing to change what he could by returning the money. Peter wept bitterly after his betrayal. Did Judas do less?

In Judas's act, the sheep sold the Shepherd to be slaughtered. Judas could not make restitution for his deed.

Judas's repentance cannot be complete in his own work. The only possibility is in the movement he started, in which Jesus' sacrifice brings restitution for the sins of the world, including Judas's sin. None of that could be seen immediately following Judas's act of betrayal.

When the money was returned to the religious leaders, they confessed that it was blood money. Thereby, they accused themselves as guilty for their part in Israel's rejection of the Messiah.

Judas died as his own judge and hangman. He took the judgment of God into his own hands. He could not bear the blast of the explosion he had created.

Judas was one of the twelve disciples. Although he did the act, any of the others could have done the same. Each asked, "Is it I?" when Jesus declared that one of them would betray Him, unsure of whom He was speaking.

Jesus had chosen all of them. All had doubts. Jesus established the relationship and sustained it in the face of their doubts and failures—even Judas's. All were cleansed, and Jesus would not give in to the lie that they were rejected, even with all their letdowns and disappointments.

Jesus loved all His disciples to the end with a love that unceasingly embraced them.

The Last Supper and the Lord's Supper run parallel. Foot washing anticipates what Jesus will give to the disciples and the Church. Both demonstrate the place of Jesus in making us clean. The greater was given in His death and resurrection.

In both suppers, Jesus' love is given perfectly, and His presence becomes persistent.

With the bread and wine, Jesus makes Himself the host of the supper that binds Him to His disciples, giving His body as the sign of self-offering.

In the washing of their feet, Jesus binds Himself as the disciples' slave, humbly attending to their bodies.

Foot washing connects with the death of Jesus as service. The Servant offers Himself as Lord.

All the disciples need the foot washing of Jesus in order to be a part of Him, just as they need to be joined with Him in His death and resurrection. Human washing can never do the trick of making us clean as Jesus does.

Jesus stands before Peter and Judas. Both failed and stand equal in their need to be made whole. They both needed the freedom that only Jesus could give.

To what degree is Jesus' work effective for Judas?

- Judas is still one of the elect.
- Judas is still one of the apostles.
- Judas took part in the Last Supper.
- Judas had his feet washed by Jesus.
- Judas needs the forgiveness of sins.
- Jesus loves Judas to the end.

We cannot give a final answer one way or the other.

- Jesus is for Judas.
- Judas is against Jesus.
- The Bible fails to make Judas an example of hopeless rejection.
- The Bible fails to make Judas an example of restoration.

The situation between Jesus and Judas is the case for all other humans. God has elected, and humans have rejected.

In the gospel, we hear of the power of grace and the weakness of humans in the face of it.

Although humans elected Matthias, we heartily affirm that it was Paul who took Judas's place.

Paul fulfills a proper handing over of Jesus to the Gentiles in the preaching of the gospel.

Whereas Judas "delivers" Jesus to the religious leaders as an act of betrayal, the apostles "deliver" (the same word) Jesus to the Gentiles as an act of faithfulness.

There is nothing concerning Judas's intent to justify his actions. His was a purely sinful act. Only a judge competent in this matter could justify him.

God delivers people over to the power of their own work, which results in their destruction.

What is displayed in the revelation of wrath is that God delivers persons, handing them over to themselves in their own destruction. In this way, God intends to make a fresh start, awakening them from the death which they must die.

Those who once *handed* over to destruction, like Paul delivering Christians to be killed and Judas delivering Jesus for destruction, are now *handing* over. They are fulfilling the purposes of God in handing over the gospel, Judas handing over to Paul, and Paul handing over to the nations the gospel of God who saves the rejected.

Before Judas handed Jesus over, Jesus had handed over Himself. This was to fulfill the act that delivers people from sin. All other delivery originates from this self-delivery of God.

The handing over of Jesus by God is the precondition to which our faith is attached. Our act is a dependent release into God's life-giving death that removes our sin. The obstacle, our sin, is removed.

Because Jesus loved us, He gave Himself for us (Galatians 2:20).

The life we now live, we live by the faithfulness of Him who loved us and gave Himself for us.

Jesus let Himself be robbed of His freedom. He humbled Himself and took on the form of a servant.

The beginning point of this handing over of Jesus was God's eternal love. The Father's merciful intention enabled Him to give His Son for humanity and all creation. His goal was to restore them to fellowship with Him.

God will make humans participate in His eternal life as covenant partners, not just in history but from eternity.

God's freedom is so great that He could freely give His love in this humbled manner.

God is so faithful and constant in the freedom of His love that He would act as He did in His self-delivery to deal with our situation.

He took our place.

He deprived His own freedom by becoming like us.

He set up His kingdom of lovingkindness so we would have eternal life.

He made Himself responsible for us, cleansing us from sin and liberating us from guilt.

"He gave Himself up 'for us,' 'for me,' as it says in all these passages."[3]

This event was not chance, tragedy, or fate. It was the will of God for us.

What stands between God and humanity must be removed according to God's justice and righteousness. Only God can deal with the condemnation and punishment, and only He can bear it.

We are set free because God wills this for us as His gracious gift. In omnipotence He overcomes.

Jesus stands in our place and is for us. He is the owner and Lord of our life. He is the head of His Church. He has determined to be for us beyond our imagination.

If we resist His being for us, we can only be working against ourselves. This self-destruction is what Jesus has stepped in to disturb.

When God hands over anyone to His wrath, it is always accompanied by the possibility of a saving aim.

We must recognize that we, too, belong with all the failed and rejected figures of the Bible, worthy of wrath as those who resist God.

Having faith in Jesus' work, we cannot consider those handed over by God to be lost. We know the intent of His will.

---

3. *CD* 2.2, § 35, p. 492.

The apostles are in the business of handing over what God has handed over to them. This practice starts a long history of handing over into other hands. The origin is in God Himself in a positive self-giving.

The apostles are given authority to act because of the origin of their message. They have become servants in passing it on. They echo what God has delivered to them in His very life and being.

The apostolic tradition is a human transmission of what God has given, now as a reproductive activity.

In His Son, God spoke from eternity to accomplish in history the delivering of His love. This speech crosses the abyss between God and humanity. In this way, God in person still speaks effectually to humanity.

What stood in the way has been removed so that we may enjoy God's covenant relationship.

Humans, in their own words, place before other humans the love of God available for them. The apostles are not philosophers or thinkers about God; they are eyewitnesses encountered by the Word of God.

The human handing over of God's Word comes with the same vulnerability to suffering that Jesus felt in being handed over to humanity.

The Word of God may be rejected, evaded, or invalidated by humans. The divine tradition may be reduced to mere human tradition.

The Word that cannot be reversed or overcome is that Jesus is the victor. The news of the divine tradition points to Him. The news awakens new faith.

The apostles are made powerless in themselves. The power of the gospel becomes the superior power to repeat God's acts of making all things new.

In the final assessment, we acknowledge that Judas served the devil in the sphere of human history. He confirmed the rebellion of humanity against God.

We must acknowledge that the more profoundly we understand the guilt of Judas, the more we comprehend that his deed aligns with what God did in this matter of handing Jesus over.

God willed to give Himself over, intervening for the benefit of humanity and against the rule of Satan. Jesus cleanses Judas and all humanity of guilt.

Judas, like Adam, was a divine creation, made to be alongside God as a covenant partner. Judas was a creature who went into assault mode against God for selfish reasons.

At the most significant point of sin, the most remarkable application of grace abounds. Where the law condemns, the grace of God discloses His gospel.

God endures the assault and liberates humanity from delusion and cutting itself off from God.

In Judas, the serving of the will and ways of God and of Satan coincide. The "No" becomes the "Yes" of God; the betrayal becomes the handing over for the reconciliation of humanity.

The apostolic tradition of God's handing over would not exist apart from Judas and his act of handing Jesus over.

In the circle of election, Judas stands on the left and Paul on the right. Jesus stands in the middle as the prototype of both.

Jesus has entered the prison of those who, in death, are rejected. They become objects of His gospel in the power of its proclamation for all.

Concerning divine rejection, the New Testament fulfills the shadowy picture of divine election in the Old Testament.

All the great rejected persons of the Old Testament live again in Judas. These are elected from out of their rejection with a promise never taken away.

Judas must die. Jerusalem must be destroyed. Israel's right to exist must be extinguished. But the power of divine deliverance is *for* Judas, Jerusalem, and Israel. Their rejection is severe. These events do not alter the fact that God's promise is valid for them as well.

God desires that believers will come as rejected persons who have become what they are—elected.

God has not willed any to be rejected. The elected persons in the New Testament are rejected persons elected in and from their rejection.

The power of election rests in Jesus, who died and rose again. He is elected for all, taking on the rejection of all.

 COMMENTARY:

- Jesus is the elect individual who is for all individuals.
- Jesus stands in for all: the accepted and those who reject God's acceptance.
- In a world losing respect for Jesus, we quickly default to a human leader who will stand in for our group to take Jesus' place. This situation becomes true in churches, in politics, and in the market. These leaders are secular replacements, brought in after we have rejected the election of Jesus.
- In the world that rejects Jesus, the gatherings of humans in secular spaces welcome new forms of "community." These gatherings appear as political parties, interest groups, or rallying around any idea that validates the idea of being a great nation or having superior ideals.

This replacement mentality has shaped much of human history. Jesus is abandoned for new heroes and their vision.

- An actual "individual" who is separate from all others is an impossible idea. We are all connected.
- God lives with a grand "Nevertheless" that overcomes our reasoning and affirms that His love wins in the end.
- All are elected in Jesus. We know His love never fails.
- The Church is a sent people. We are not sent apart from Jesus and the Spirit. We are elected to share in the mission of the One apostolic person, Jesus.
- Judas, like every human, is elected and used by God in spite of himself. We love to judge Judas. But God gave Himself over to Judas before Judas handed Jesus over to complete the work Jesus came to fulfill, to stand in for the elected on the cross.
- We can no longer think about the individual and election by starting with the human and considering who is elected. We must consider all in the light of Jesus' determination to be for them in their "individuality" and let His judgment determine the result.

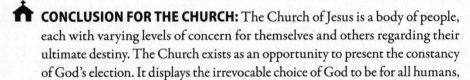 **CONCLUSION FOR THE CHURCH:** The Church of Jesus is a body of people, each with varying levels of concern for themselves and others regarding their ultimate destiny. The Church exists as an opportunity to present the constancy of God's election. It displays the irrevocable choice of God to be for all humans, in that He chooses to be their God, particularly, not just as part of humanity.

Many neighbors will not walk through the door of a church because they already feel excluded. Often, the elect insiders give signals of God's preference for the good people. This belief is contrary to the gospel. The Church is the called community. It is intended to extend a confident affirmation that God loves all people—Jesus is the proof of that. This Jesus is the core of the calling of the Church to be out in the streets and trails, in stores and subways, treating all as the chosen of God, beloved without reserve.

INSIGHT FOR PASTORS: In addressing the issue of election, the role of a pastor is to look to Jesus for the answer. With the question "Am I elected by God?" we may confidently say that God has elected to be for every person. We may accept and live joyfully in response without fear. If a person confesses their sins and asks whether God will reject them, we may again say that Jesus is for them and wins the day. Rejection is not God's judgment. Rejection is human distrust of God.

If a person says that they have rejected God or even the idea of God, we may chuckle (with God) at their stance. God leaves room for humans to reject His love and companionship, but God never rejects back. Like a person holding their breath, they only deny that which sustains them.

Pastors would do well to infuse their people with a sense of being sent with Jesus to hand over the meaning of life itself. We are not trying to convert people as much as restore connection with the love that made and sustains them. We are selected, elected, and resurrected from our rejection. We are awakened to the presence of Jesus' eternal choice to be for every woman and man of every race, age, creed, status, and hobby. The alarm we ring is to wake the sleeping to life, not scare them into deciding to save themselves. Jesus is the saving presence who gives life. He is with each person as the personal presence of love that knows and embraces specifically.

 INSIGHT FOR THEOLOGIANS: This is a valuable section from which we learn to take the road less traveled. In a theological discussion on the individual's election, it is easy to default to a specific person and ask how we determine whether they are elected. It seems so logical. But Barth teaches us to start at the beginning and never divert from this proper point of departure.

Election begins and ends with Jesus. Since election is God's will in action, this informs all our theological thinking. This being the case, we can ask what Jesus' election enacts and fulfills in our theology. If we desire to start with the judgments of God and the wrath poured out on sinners, that says more about ourselves than God. If our sense of justice leads us to think that God has limits to His love, we must think more deeply about where we got our sense of justice.

Barth sees justice, and even judgment as provisional, whether of people, individuals, or Jesus on the cross. The actual end of justice is achieved in overwhelming love. Can people live contrary to their election and bear the consequences of challenges to God? No doubt. But we may not read our interpretations into God's intentions. Proper listening begins by understanding the election of God in Jesus fulfilling the justice of God and its restorative implications.

God's choice precedes and overcomes the many courses of human tragedies and successes. Reading general history, or the story of a person, to see whether God was electing certain kinds of people is like reading tea leaves. Those are subjective evaluations based on limited and biased assessment. Good theology cannot be seduced by such reasoning. The election of God is the good news of the gospel, and it is suitable for everyone.

❓ CLARIFYING QUESTIONS: Does your theology seek to discern who God loves and who goes to hell based on the blessings and curses in a person's life? *Or* do you have a firm sense that election is all about Jesus, especially that He extends His choice to be for and with every person? Can you live with the tension that Jesus elects all, and only humans leave Him, which never changes Jesus' election of them?

CHURCH DOGMATICS, CHAPTER 8

"The Command of God"

CHAPTER 17

FINDING HIGH FIDELITY IN THE LOVING HARMONY OF GOD

§ 36. Ethics as a Task of the Doctrine of God

FOCUS STATEMENT: This paragraph (§ 36) is about ethics. Ethics is usually about human behavior. Barth contends we need to start our ethical discussion with God's behavior in Jesus. Otherwise, we will abandon a *theological* ethic entirely. We can only learn human ethics as a responsive fidelity achieved through knowing the God who has been faithful to us. Thus, we must discuss "Ethics as a Task of the Doctrine of God."

High fidelity means faithful to the original, with little or no distortion. In this case, the ethics that flow from God will be the focus of our attention. With traditional ethical discussion, humans turn to questions of human good behavior. Barth seeks to avoid distortion in the interplay of God's music and human harmonization. For Barth, we must first learn to listen to the loving melody of God.

Barth refuses to sabotage how we do theological thinking. Consequently, we must understand God's being and speaking for a proper conception of theological ethics.

The leading "ethical problem" for Barth is that humans want to build on human understandings of what is "good." However, each human has different sensibilities as to what is good; there is no standard beginning note. Additionally, our styles are so *different from* and *indifferent to* each other that we create chaos and pandemonium. Barth clarifies the problem and establishes God's dynamic starting point.

Jesus is the first note of the gospel. All else responds to Him. If one does not learn to listen and correspond, one will divert from the good. The law is best conceived and heard as a response to the gospel, which is equally expressed in Jesus.

Jesus is also the improvisational response, the vibrant expression of the laws of music. In Him, the unity of Jesus' melodic gospel and responsive practices draws all humanity into His holy harmonics. When the law is aligned rightly with the gospel, the law is the outworking of love, sounding forth with the loving harmony of God.

INTRODUCTION: We now begin chapter 8 of the dogmatics. In *CD* 2, we have looked at the knowledge of God (ch. 5), the reality of God (ch. 6), and the election of God (ch. 7), and now we turn to the command of God on ethics. It clarifies how we understand that God makes Himself the context of human responsibility. Barth vigorously steers readers away from seeing the word *ethics* as referring to what humans do in right behavior. We must focus on Jesus as God's expression of loving command who opens the way for human response.

For Barth, the gospel is ethical. God's election creates a human response. God has made Himself a covenant partner. Obedience involves living within God's covenant of love. This relation is not conditional. It is an unconditional response that restores us according to God's love and allows His love to transform us. His love, not our choice, is at work.

CONTEXT: *CD* 2.2
Pages in Paragraph: 42 pages (pp. 509–51)

Subsections
1. The Command of God and the Ethical Problem
2. The Way of Theological Ethics

TEXT: § 36. Ethics as a Task of the Doctrine of God

OPENING SUMMARY: As the doctrine of God's command, ethics interprets the Law as the form of the Gospel, i.e., as the sanctification which comes to man through the electing God. Because Jesus Christ is the holy God and sanctified man in One, it has its basis in the knowledge of Jesus Christ. Because the God who claims man for Himself makes Himself originally responsible for him, it forms part of the doctrine of God. Its function is to bear primary witness to the grace of God in so far as this is the saving engagement and commitment of man.[1]

 SUMMARY:
1. The Command of God and the Ethical Problem (pp. 509–42)

God has established a covenant between Himself and humanity. Two concepts work together to articulate this covenant:

1. God's *election of grace* for humanity, through which God is made knowable in Jesus Christ as both God and human.

   God's very existence is known in His covenant with humans. He is Creator and Lord of the covenant.

   God's relationship with humanity is crucial for our understanding of God, who has put Himself into this relationship.

   Although humanity has no place in the doctrine of God, Jesus Christ does. Therefore, His compassion and faithfulness expressed toward humanity reveal the nature of God's life in relationship with us.

   Election precedes creation, and so we will discuss election as the basis for ethics before we discuss humans as created partners.

2. The doctrine of the *divine command* is the second component of God's covenant.

   God has elected in freeing love to rule over humanity, calling them into His service, to empower them to be witnesses to Jesus and to make His glory known.

   Having heard what *God has chosen*, we then question what God specifically *wants* from humans.

   God is determined that we be *persons* in this covenant relationship, not just objects to be controlled.

   God desires human obedience. God claims us for Himself and His service. God is the only competent judge as to the measure of human satisfaction of this obedience. And we are measured against God.

As we engage the issue of our human response to God's command, we must remember we are still in the sphere of God's gracious election on our behalf.

---

1. *CD* 2.2, § 36, p. 509.

God has determined to be for us. Our self-determination includes the decisions and actions we make in an obedient, responsible covenant partnership.

This response is the law of love and means to live in the light of the gospel. The law cannot stand independently and be good news.

The gospel always precedes the law; through it, grace informs human response.

The evangelical indicative of God's grace ("I have loved you"), which is God's persistent way of being, becomes transformed into the imperatives of law ("You must act like you are loved"). This ordering brings forth the freeing response of humans within the impulse and limits of love.

The covenant is not exclusively about what God has done for humanity. God calls to humans to submit to His law of love in obedient action.

At every point in discovering God, we become aware that there is a demand on our lives because this God is the God to whom we belong.

We must apply the term *ethics* in our own particular *theological* way.

Generally, ethics addresses the basis and possibilities for human action. It explores what ought to be repeated to serve as an example for others. It discerns the value of what may be considered "good" in human action.

Ethics in philosophy deals with principles of what is moral as a directive for customs and habits.

Moral law should not be confused with natural law, meaning that which seems the *natural thing to do*.

Morality does not denote conformity to what *everyone else* is doing.

Morality does not suggest mere conformity to existing *laws of the state*.

Morality is not mere agreement with *what seems right* for a particular time and place.

Proper ethical questioning asks about the rightness and value of these other approaches that have been accepted uncritically. It must ask the fundamental question as to what makes conformity to these laws good and what makes noncompliance evil.

This approach leads us to ask from the point of view of the good, not from an individual or general mode of human action.

Dogmatics serves ethics by providing the starting point for the good, which is God.

God is the starting point for every ethical question and answer.

We begin with the revelation and acts of the electing grace of God. God's grace is the answer to ethical problems.

God's grace calls humans to Himself. It makes humans whole from their sinful ways. It allows them to answer God's command to leave the past behind and be realigned for future action.

We exist as persons in that we act. The goodness of our acts is judged in continuity with our actions.

God has decreed Himself as our covenant partner. The ethical question points to our response to God's grace and asks who we will be in answer.

Many ethical systems arise from the human desire to judge between good and evil. The human wants to *give* the answer as a judge, not *be* the answer in obedience.

Jesus shows us the fulfilled Adam, created to correspond with obedience. The first Adam became "ethical" when he became independent in his judgment of good and evil. This event is also called the fall.

Jesus does not *give* the answer to ethical questions; He *is* the answer. God's choice for goodness is seen in the intention and action of Jesus for humanity. He is the answer in action.

The default of ethical thinking usually builds on the perceptions and culture rising from human insight. Christian ethics begins with the living God. He cannot merely be added to those other proposals.

The Christian God is already the *whence* from which ethical thought is considered.

We may not become apologists for a Christian ethic by accepting other systems' frameworks of thought and then trying to justify Christian thought within them.

> God is the starting point for every ethical question and answer.

Theological ethics cannot be created; they are commanded to us. Three types must be avoided:

1. We must avoid apologetic approaches that reason from within *another framework* and abandon God.

   Those who follow an apologetic approach in forming theological ethics comply with what is not demanded—making sense from human logic instead of God's gracious revelation.

   We are not required to appeal to "human moral nature" nor an independent human capacity to discern evil.

   Any "common sense" in ethics must be heard from divine wisdom revealed in Jesus Christ, not derived from knowledge belonging to and controlled by humans. Basing common sense in humans would be a move to "natural theology," a traitorous exchange applied in ethics.

2. *Separating the theological sphere* of thinking from the philosophical spheres opens the door subtly to shift one's allegiance to human interests.

Separating the spheres of thinking but finding specific meeting points between them appears to be friendly. It seems to preserve both approaches in their own fields of thought. But theological ethics is reduced to a special form of general ethics.

There are four issues to note:

a. A new *source* for thinking is found in humans, with a Christian religious consciousness that sounds like Schleiermacher's human sensibility for God. It defaults to the human even when using the term *revelation* for its insights.

b. A new *locus* is found in the church as a community of those who think Christianly. However, the church remains a human community in its speaking. It neglects to point to the Lord, who is the proper locus.

c. A new *principle* replaces the personal command of God as the power that operates in believers. This move defaults to rational self-determination in the guise of Christian ideals or the influence of the Spirit.

d. New *content* is given to the vision of being theological, importing a moral view onto the idea of the coming of the kingdom of God. This approach may also selectively choose to adopt the "positive aspects" of Jesus. It masks the self-interest that is at work.

The idea of morality easily becomes human self-directing. Humans think according to their sense of what is reasonable. This idea of morality lives in a sphere apart from Jesus.

The proper starting point for theological ethics is enclosed in the command of the grace of God.

- It has a sound source in Jesus, not in human reason and experience.
- It speaks from a person, not philosophical principles.
- It must have a scope that engages all the motives, problems, and concerns of all other ethics.
- It must listen to the other forms of ethics with a comprehensive understanding that is critical, corrective, and uncompromising.
- It must not allow a replacement of the command of the grace of God.

3. The Roman Catholic manner coordinates a universal human morality with Christian morality, making them equal partners, interconnected in a personal union, but with an imbalance. The *natural power of human morality* is the pivot point on which all is centered.

Barth imagines a building with moral philosophy as the foundation and first floor, and moral theology as the upper story built upon it.

For moral philosophy, the human "natural light of reason" is the stairway from the first to the second floor. Each step is a moral principle built on a rational principle within the staircase of the laws of logic.

To ascend the staircase, one pursues the imperatives, following the moral principles of prudence, justice, fortitude, and temperance. These are relative human goods that can only echo the ultimate good of God.

For moral theology, the upper floor contains the Bible, the tradition, and the teaching of the Church. This free library inspires moral behavior, healing the ills of humanity.

One who regularly visits will find the work of reason and grace working in parallel. Together, they move the seeker toward a personal expression of the good beyond original sin.

God's grace on the second floor perfectly completes the natural human endowments of thinking and willingness gained from living on the first floor. For Barth, this has foundational problems.

This two-story construction is a combination of Aristotle and Augustine. The whole building has an imposing, classical structure.

Within this structure, the command of God lacks the significant role that it ought to play.

The Roman Catholic view builds on the harmony between nature and supernature, depending on reason and revelation, drawing on God and human insight.

What is intended to be God's grace and command is commandeered and made compliant to the moral intuitions of the human. While the fall has impacted human apprehension of God, Catholics believe that enough remains to inform basic intuitions. This confidence is misplaced.

Further, the human is conceived to have a reasonably functioning free will to follow God. It is a natural capacity for God, not given by God's unique grace. The light of natural reason enables moral formation "with the help of God." It proposes a process to restore what is present in human nature, which was created by God.

In this structure, moral theology cannot exist without the foundation of moral philosophy. It builds, not on the grace of God, but on the reason of the human, who is capable of knowing and doing the good.

Theological ethics must begin with divine act. We cannot develop a theory based on creaturely creativity in consideration of the nature of our human being.

We must remember that God does not find an existing partner in the human; He creates a partner.

The Roman Catholic use of *analogia entis*, the analogy of being, begins with the human and adapts as it goes, speaking of God with a form of ignorance.

We do not have an aptitude for God. His revelation graces us. We apprehend God's self-giving, which cannot be seen as cooperation if that implies we have a part to contribute.

We do not have a "free will" that may allow us to find God, pursued with an optimism that our search will be fulfilled on our terms. Our natural will blocks out the will of God. We naturally fulfill our agendas and build our utopias as we turn away from Him.

Barth's complaint—not only with Roman Catholic ethics but with ethics in general—is that they are distracted and dominated by a human point of view.

What is in the foreground blurs what is in the background.

To say God is the Lord over humanity implies that humans are to be obedient.

Obedience is a human problem. It is a problem of every human. To be human means to act. Every action involves choosing. This acting involves what I ought to do and, more generally, what *we* ought to do.

When we begin with the God who elects humans, we adopt a new starting point. We are not allowed to return to the usual ethical questions and answers.

We begin with the question of human obedience. Every human action stands before the God who commands as part of His election.

There is no human action that does not in some way respond to God's command. Thus, it either has the character of obedience or disobedience.

We cannot begin by asking whether God and His command are good.

The good is not our considered choice. It can only be chosen as that which is determined in obedience to God's command. Thus, we can only choose to live ethically in correspondence with having been chosen.

We cannot look for God's thinking to fall in line with human ethical thinking.

What is good has been shown to humans (Micah 6:8). We cannot redefine it for ourselves.

We are engaging this subject of the good as a positive science. Our quest is to understand God and ourselves in His context.

Theological ethics may not be reduced to a set of rules, affirmations, ideas, demands, or descriptions.

Christian ethics often end up with a law-making agenda not dissimilar from other forms of ethics. This fabrication is not to be confused with God's command.

We must start from the fact that what is said to humanity is good and then cling to what is given.

As God, Jesus sanctifies us. He is also the human sanctified on our behalf. In Him, God has acted *toward* us, and as human, He has acted *for* us.

In Jesus, God has judged human sinfulness and has also restored humans to His image. His is the only image we need.

In Jesus, we have the image of God who reconciles us, illuminates us, and consoles us with God's grace. In Him, we also have God's law, as He binds us to God's grace and obliges us to respond to Him.

This call is specifically to walk with Jesus. He is the One who loves in freedom and calls for active love in response. Whether one knows and believes or not, we all belong to Jesus Christ.

Our investigation must begin with His command and action.

Jesus has fulfilled obedience on our behalf. We can add nothing to Jesus' obedience.

Our simple question in Christian dogmatics is whether our actions are a glorification of the grace of Jesus Christ, or to what extent.

Obedience to God's command is the only good. All other attempts are grounded in the human, who moves toward inhumanity outside of Christ.

"Know thyself" can only be a summons to rebel against the grace of God.

Proper ethics must be Christian ethics. True Christian ethics must be theological ethics. In a scientific form, there is only one ethic: theological ethics. All else is human speculation.

2. The Way of Theological Ethics (pp. 543–51)

Our understanding of God shapes our understanding of ethics.

In giving humanity His command, God makes Himself responsible for humanity. His command is the execution of His care and commitment to its fulfillment. He calls humans to live under this care and so to find its fulfillment.

The correct actions and responses on the part of humanity have already been fulfilled in Jesus Christ in His Word and work. Our part is to *confirm* His action on our behalf.

The point of the *whence* of our discussion is to get to the root of our theological thinking to create a theological ethic.

Consideration of God is smothered quickly when we pounce on questions about what *we* should do and what seems right to *us*.

The human quest for "the good life" replaces God's intention for us when we begin with the wrong questions.

For Schleiermacher, theological ethics was the work of the Church and other human institutions to "purify" the institutions and activities of humanity. His concern was for human action in the spheres of life, developing a Christian personality, and moral practices in society.

He believed that shaping the human moral will, and the activities structured from this human process, would usher in the kingdom of God. For Barth, these schemes appear to build upon supposed human capacities for God but do not originate from allowing God to do His work.

Deriving a Christian doctrine of virtue from will, cognition, emotions, and life practices may be refreshing and practical, but this is sourced from Plato. It has no right to be affirmed as originating from Christian thought or the life of God.

Once God is out of the way, all proposals become worthy of consideration.

Making the problems of human conduct the measure of all things will overtake the framework for the investigation of all things.

Humans ask questions that theology must answer, including the following:

- How do I become a Christian person and act like it?
- What does it mean to have Christian conduct in my activities?
- If I act like a Christian, what difference will it make in my life?
  - Will I have more vitality?
  - Will I have better social status?
  - Will I be more financially successful?
  - Will I improve the place I live?
  - Will my marriage and family life improve?
  - Will I contribute to the arts and sciences?
  - Will my work and play take on new meaning and enjoyment?

We put these questions to God, but it is the human who is to be questioned. How will we act in the face of the revealed command of God?

Theological ethics consists in clarifying our thinking to remember that our conduct is always answering the command of God.

Human-based theological ethics act as a travel-information booth, inviting questions from those who stop by. It would be better to ask questions of those who pass by regarding their response to the command of God.

The Word of God intends to make something new of a human person. Therefore, we must not get stuck thinking we need to make something of the Word of God.

The first task of theological ethics is to understand and present the Word of God as the subject who claims and commands us to sanctify humanity. Sanctification is God's goodness making us whole in response to Him.

Humans act as hearers of this Word, and their goodness is in acting as hearers of this Word. This is called obedience.

When humans act responsibly toward God, they are doing well. This responsible act is called *commitment*.

When we act freely in response to God's Word, we answer the goodness of God in our own reply.

For humans, doing good is an outworking of being a Christian, meaning knowing and living as one accepted by Jesus Christ.

This knowing that makes one a Christian is an acknowledgment that Jesus has elected and called this person into covenant with Him.

All goodness is shaped by God being good. Therefore, both the eternal and temporal events of Jesus are good and revealed as such.

The human is not good. Only God is good. The good can never be found in an abstract concept of the good (especially because it is based on human perception). God is not abstract, nor is His goodness.

God has determined in His goodness to turn toward humanity. God has determined to make Himself responsible for humanity. God still intends to live His goodness in this self-determination as an act of His compassion for humans.

The ruling principle of theological ethics is that God is revealed in divine action, in the reality of an event that occurs.

We cannot build a comfortable space to examine the command of God in isolation or separation from God.

In His command, God gives Himself. By His command, humans hear God and are made responsible. Divine action always precedes human activity, and the latter is judged by the former.

For now, we must see the extent to which God directs theological ethics. Later in *Church Dogmatics*, we will discuss the divine command as directed to humans.

- As His command, the Word of God reveals the reality of God.
  - This determination is displayed in the act of *creation* as the kingdom of nature.
  - His command manifests the pretemporal will of God in action, especially regarding our being determined for God.
  - His act precedes our ethical response.
- The Word of God reveals the reality of God in the act of *reconciliation* as the kingdom of grace.
  - This command manifests the cotemporal will of God in action, speaking about our relationship with God.
  - The One revealed God acts on behalf of humanity as true God who elects. The One actual human is elected in our stead for God in the One man Jesus.
  - His will invites our corresponding response.
- The Word of God reveals the reality of God in the act of *redemption* as the kingdom of glory.
  - This command manifests the posttemporal will of God in action, speaking about our ongoing relationship with God.
  - His grace is the reality we are living into.

True humanity, we must insist, is found uniquely in Jesus Christ. He has taken all human sin and dealt with it.

In His resurrection, Jesus has fulfilled and revealed the divine image in glory with God in heaven.

We must understand humanity from Jesus Christ.

- Jesus is God's creature.
  - In Christ, humans are the creatures of God.
- Jesus is the human pardoned by God.
  - In Christ, humans are sinners shown grace.
- Jesus is the expectant heir of the coming kingdom of God.
  - In Christ, humans are heirs of the kingdom of God.

When looking at Jesus to understand ourselves, we are not looking in a mirror for our likeness. We are looking to see ourselves as God sees us in Jesus, who shows us the truth of our being.

The command of God cannot be known in abstraction or by dividing up nature, grace, and glory. The divine command can only be understood in its relations between the three.

God lives in the freedom of His love, displayed in His perfections, and revealed in His election. Consistent in every way, He is for humanity by the Word and work of His grace.

I know the urge to talk about our part in ethics. But we must get clear on who God is as the covenant partner who has made the way for us. Only then may we live within the actuality of life for us, with us, and with him who constantly calls us to Himself.

 COMMENTARY:
- Ethics is not just about human morals and right behaviors; it is first about the goodness of God's ways with the world.
- God fulfills all divine goodness by showing up in person, not by sending principles.
- God's command is not a conditional decree; it is His choice to love. He does what He commands—loves! His command is election in action.
- Obedience is hearing and acting correspondingly from a loving heart.
- The question "What is the right thing to do?" is always the wrong question; it defaults to human logic and judgment.
- The question "What is the loving thing to do?" is much more adequate, but it must respond to God's vision of loving that calls us to obedience.
- Ethics focuses on action, not on mere thoughts. We must look to where God acts out His grace.
- Jesus is the answer to the ethical quest.

- God alone defines the good.
- Human ethics are equivalent to human sin. They involve the human in self-reflective judgment.
- There are many ways to miss the starting line in ethical thinking, including apologetics, philosophy, and religious modes of thought.
- The source of theological ethics is in the "Whence?"—which is Jesus.
- The goal of theological ethics is in the "Whither?"—which is Jesus.
- Only when we hear Jesus will we act appropriately.

CONCLUSION FOR THE CHURCH: The Church needs to stay focused and grounded. In the same manner that a proper understanding of the Church begins with Jesus as its head, the study of ethics starts with Jesus as the One who acts in such a way that He fulfills obedience. He also ignites us to be transformed, to do what is consistent with His love in action.

We must stop beginning with situational questions as to what we are to do. This route inevitably puts the Church's attention on human wisdom. We end up doing what is right in our eyes, which is the beginning of significant problems. The more the Church knows Jesus and His gracious love, the more it will act like Him. The more a church lives with positions and arguments, judging and shaming, the more swiftly Jesus will be left outside the church with the people He loves, for whom He died. We must fix our eyes on Jesus, or we start living out Adam's fall.

INSIGHT FOR PASTORS: Humans often come to church to learn how to be better people. They want to improve, be happy, or find fulfillment. They are looking for answers and strategies. They are intent on learning what they can do to make a difference. Barth is calling us to be leaders in a different direction. He proposes that we need to wake up to the love of God already present and let that awakening change us.

God's love alone can change our thinking and behavior. Nothing can change God's covenant love for us. His covenant is to bring love to us so we can live in the power of being made new. This transformation happens by being with Him who is for us and with us. Real change can only occur when we accept the love of someone we cannot help but love back. When someone wants to change us, we feel we are not accepted as we are. We resist. God's command is not a statement of "You'd better change or else." It is more like this: "I have loved you with an everlasting love and done all to bring you home. I have made you My own. Now joyfully and freely live within my love."

Barth's insight concerning ethics for pastors is to stop trying to improve people. Instead, help your people open to the covenant embrace of God (we will call that obedience). When we fall in love with someone who loves us, a change in behavior will appropriately be the outcome of love, not from anxiety about getting it right.

 INSIGHT FOR THEOLOGIANS: As a disciplined theologian, Barth is challenging our sensibilities about how to do theology that impacts human lives. When the word *ethics* appears, we naturally think about what we are to do or tell others to do, as individuals, communities, in politics, medicine, or obedience to human laws. Barth stops us dead in our tracks and says we cannot do that.

To do proper ethics is to know that God has unconditionally made humans His covenant partners. No human act can change or improve God's love for humans, especially sinners. God's covenant, and therefore His command, is free and entirely offered as a gift. Nothing can be done to earn it or lose it.

So, what does God want? An unconditional response. He desires we live from love as covenant partners shaped by mutual love, with a God-sized investment made known in Jesus. Theology that discovers the pervasiveness of God's presence, as a partner who will never give up, will be able to fulfill the theological task of being made new in Christ. Any view of the cross or the life of Christ that thinks from conditions being met (legal) will miss the point. The gospel is the outworking of God's audacious love that never gives up. Ethics is a form of acting as though God's loving presence is all that is needed for us to be faithful to God and true to ourselves. Ethics is the gospel walking at God's speed in everyday life with Him.

 CLARIFYING QUESTIONS: Does your theology seek to address injustices and hurtful actions and then create guardrails to keep humans within what God will accept? *Or* does your theology look at ethics as an unrestrained and undistracted exercise of awakening to the love of God? Does your ethical thinking bring you to explore the ways God is deepening your love for God, neighbor, and self?

CHAPTER 18

FOLLOWING THE CONDUCTOR'S GESTURES

§ 37. The Command as the Claim of God

👀 **FOCUS STATEMENT:** We continue with the theme of ethics in this paragraph (§ 37). "Ethics" naturally looks at what humans are to do for exemplary behavior. In this section, Barth transitions to acknowledging the claim God has on our lives. This focus takes the form of "The Command as the Claim of God." His command is for us to love Him and one another.

God is the conductor in command, and we are His orchestra and choir. The conductor's job is to bring the music to life. In this section, God brings His love to give meaning to life and our behavior in response to His commanding gestures. These commands are not against the will of the orchestra. They lead in the performance of a masterpiece with a confident call to move together. One person brings together the diverse instruments and voices to create a satisfying whole.

The conductor's interpretation instills in the performers a sense of dynamic response. Each plays their best, yet the incitement and excitement are inspired by the One who leads them together, and the music itself. The conductor does not control each person, yet He constantly leads them, bringing the many into harmony. He compels a response facilitated through the shared language they have learned.

The hands of the conductor direct the mood, movement, tempo, entrances, and exits. Wordlessly, the conductor creates a bond. For Barth, this initiating work of God is the source of divine ethics. God directs with grace and mercy, leading humans with love and freedom. His command constantly calls for listening obedience that evokes response.

This conductor-performer relation is a carefully choreographed exchange. It works because those who know and follow the conductor's commands live with a joyful correspondence. They are free in their response, doing the very thing they do best. Following is not against anyone's will, even as the will of the conductor directs. The others willingly follow within the scope of the leading.

INTRODUCTION: In exploring theological ethics, Barth now establishes the *reason* why God claims our lives. He finds this basis in God's being and acts. The foundation of God's claim is that He is God. He is the ultimate authority, the One who loves us and calls us to freedom. This freedom is achieved by being obedient to His command.

The *content* of God's claim is found in Jesus. He claims us as our Lord. He loves and is gracious to us. He calls us to respond to His command and to claim Him as our Lord. Having extended goodness to us, He calls us to participate in His goodness.

The *form* of His claim comes in the person of Jesus. He directs God's address to us. He came to earth, calling us to belong to Him and live with joyful obedience in accepting His love. His command is to accept the call to love the One who loves us. This claims our lives to playfully live out His love toward God and others as He guides us.

Barth is adamant that theological ethics begins with God. This venture begins by acknowledging God's goodness. All else is a response.

CONTEXT: *CD* 2.2
Pages in Paragraph: 79 pages (pp. 552–630)

Subsections
1. The Basis of the Divine Claim
2. The Content of the Divine Claim
3. The Form of the Divine Claim

TEXT: § 37. The Command as the Claim of God

OPENING SUMMARY: As God is gracious to us in Jesus Christ, His command is the claim which, when it is made, has power over us, demanding that in all we do we admit that what God does is right, and requiring that we give our free obedience to this demand.[1]

---

1. *CD* 2.2, § 37, p. 552.

SUMMARY:

1. The Basis of the Divine Claim (pp. 552–65)

The command of God is to cleave to God.

This command to cleave to God implies that God claims our lives in love.

God is the power over all things, the very touchstone of reality. To not acknowledge and act in response to God's authority is to submit to harm for oneself and others.

- *It might be said* that since God rules over all, every person is subject to Him. It is best to respond to the truth and not pursue a lie. God's reality and authority will go on even if we deny it.

  Humans are not mere objects, determined by the laws of nature; we are determined by God to be made His own. In our freedom, we decide for God in response. We are not equals, but those submitting to the God who holds the universe.

  To submit to God, who loves us, is to submit to freedom. To pit power against power is to be enslaved. To submit to God is to find the proper freedom for which we are made. We correspond to God's decision to be for us as the basis of His claim.

  Humans will never be free when they default to their own power or their chosen dependence on what *they* may choose—including religion. This pursuit gives illusory freedom and power that gives way to all manner of superstitions.

  God will not force us to obey. If we were forced, it would not be obedience.

- *It might be said* that God is the essence of the good. He claims humanity for Himself in that we have participated in His good from the beginning.

  When humans do good, they are stumbling toward God, directed toward adhering to God's life.

  That God claims humanity for Himself shows that He is good. But this is not a basis for His claim for human obedience.

  However, humans do not find the good in themselves. We do not will to do the good or, out of our resources, seek God. We pursue our own good and abandon God's good on the warpath to our independence. There is nothing *in us* that compels us to seek God.

- *It might be said* that God is an all-sufficient being and what He chooses is the good. When we seek this good, claiming to follow Him, we end up selecting that which is good from *our own ideal* good.

If God gives His goodness to be chosen by the human, then the *human* will do the choosing. Humans prefer what satisfies themselves and not God. God would merely be *inviting* humans, not *claiming* them.

The God in whom we may believe has called us. We come to recognize the force of His command. We must realize this in freedom.

The force of God's claim does not come from *our* belief. God makes a claim, and humans accept it.

God's goodness comes as light into the space of our existence. We see it as light and irresistible power from the good and for the good. God is good, even when we are in the dark. God's goodness claims us in coming to us.

From being the One true God, He derives His authority. This status is the basis of His claim, the validity of His command, and the freedom in which we are bound to be obedient to His will.

In Jesus, we know the gospel as God's commanding grace in action. In Him, the law comes as the freeing response to His grace. He has completed the will of God in giving God to us.

Jesus assumed our humanity and became one of us. Through Him, we have been adopted into God's life. We are brought into brotherhood through Jesus to share God's good existence.

Jesus has taken our self-will and godlessness, suffered our punishment, and accomplished what we could not. He fulfilled the faith that obeys the command of God on our behalf. We endorse His faith with our own.

We live in light of the faithfulness of the Son of God, having faith in the fact that He first believed in us. What remains is to let our eyes rest on Him and follow Him.

Following becomes our faith. His work matters: our faith is in His work.

God's claim is addressed to all humanity. We may run from it, but we cannot hide.

This humanity of ours is positioned with Adam; we stand in the image of God, mirroring God's being. At the same time, we are warped and wayward, attempting to be equal to God.

The God who creates us aims at the completion of what He started.

Despite human failure, God shows us favor. In this way, God maintains His glory, authority, and majesty.

God's glory is shown in that His love achieves its goal in the end.

God is gracious, but this does not make Him soft. He never wavers in His sovereignty, including His purpose for humans.

To accept God's grace is to admit His sovereignty. We respond with obedience to His personal authority. He is goodness in person.

Jesus, in the grace of God, exemplifies the primary and original image of humanity in response to God's sovereignty. He is free and complete in His relation to God.

Jesus is obedient. He is neither subject to fate nor subordinated to be ruled.

In Jesus, we see the free human in obedience to a free God. Only this can be faithful obedience.

In Jesus, we see that the basis of the divine claim is in His Father. We come to understand the validity of this relation to God and the necessity of compliance rather than resistance.

God's will is always consistent with what He has already done for us and in us.

The grace of God was determined in heaven.

The grace of God was enacted and professed on earth.

The grace of God summons us from the rebelliousness of Adam.

The grace of God calls us to respect God, attend to His Word, and follow His will.

From the indicative of God's way of grace comes the imperative of human response.

God's grace never stands alone. It always summons humans to attend to the fact that God is gracious to them.

Repentance is our term for the human turn to love and respect God obediently.

Jesus, as the living form of the gospel, is clothed with the law. Faith does not abolish the law; it establishes it as a response to grace.

The Church cannot proclaim the law of God except as the gospel applied.

When the law is treated independently of God's reality, it becomes hollow and weak and loses its authority. It loses the free obedience that God intends.

Everything else we are to say about God's command must stand upon and make visible the gospel as the power of the law.

2. The Content of the Divine Claim (pp. 565–83)

Barth begins by quoting Micah 6:8. What is critical is that God has shown what is good, what the Lord requires, which is to do justly, love mercy, and walk humbly with God.

We should be suspicious of human attempts to provide opinions and calculations about what God wants and claims from humans.

The content of God's claim extends from His command. The command is the outworking of God's grace as the gospel takes the form of law. Its basis is in God's goodness.

We are called from our impulsive inclinations to submit to God's claim in the form of grace.

God's command is not arbitrary; it is the work of His will. There is not a vacuum in knowing what He will call from us moment by moment, as though we are left to ourselves to interpret.

There is no abstract divine claim separate from God's concrete claim, no set of rules.

God's grace has teleological (end goal) power. God has a good end in mind that He will fulfill.

God is not self-limiting, held back from the world. Grace is not a suspended potential awaiting release.

Jesus has taken on flesh so that God's grace is the grace of real, actual humans.

The goals that humans set for themselves as children of Adam are invalid. All the impulses of our lives that follow our own will are doomed.

Within God's divine decision, humans are not their own masters.

The divine decision will establish the basis for a human confirmation of God's will. We are to be holy as He is holy.

The *basis* of the divine claim is made visible in Jesus: He is obedient; the cause is realized in His action on our behalf, that we might live in Him.

The *right* of the divine claim is realized in the obedience of Jesus, He who alone shows what God rightly wills for us.

The *goal* of the divine claim is embodied and manifested in Jesus to show us our future in Him.

Jesus lives what is good.

Jesus lives what is required.

Jesus shows us grace, making known what God desires.

Jesus does justly.

Jesus loves mercy.

Jesus walks humbly with God as God.

All *other demands* in life are to be measured as true or false, judged by whether they proclaim the life and rule of Jesus.

In obedience, we respond to Jesus willingly or not at all. He claims our hearts to bring us into harmony with the will of God.

The will of God is being fulfilled wherever one bears the character of loving Jesus and actively lives according to His commandments.

The will of God is often fulfilled outside the Church better than inside. This situation is not because of any natural goodness in humans. It is because Jesus is still the Lord of the world. He has servants even where His name is not known or is forgotten.

Jesus calls us to follow Him. This invitation means to be with Him, to accompany Him on His way wherever He may go.

Jesus does not teach a way of life or a program of self-betterment for us to follow.

The kingdom of Christ exceeds the sphere of Israel and the Church. Even the kingdom of the world belongs to Him and not the devil.

The sphere of history was created so that the grace of God might abide in space and time, dwelling in person with His own specific, concrete presence.

God gives Israel His law. It is not a general law for humans; it is a specific ordering of Israel's life as His people.

There is nothing abstract about the law, as some set of general regulations.

God's rescuing from Egypt is the specific act of God that underlies the corresponding reply of the Ten Commandments as a covenant response.

What Israel should do is connected to who Israel is. Having no other gods is reflective of covenant faithfulness to the One God. The people of Israel are maintained in the acts of this law to love God and neighbor.

Israel is called the son of God, created and ruled as God's special people. Jesus fulfills and completes this sonship.

Jesus is the Promised One who alone will keep and fulfill the law.

The holy and merciful God confronts His people in all their unworthiness.

Through God's people, He speaks to all humanity, revealing what He wants of them.

Jesus is the fulfillment of the Old Testament covenant for failing humans.

Jesus is the New Testament fulfillment of the new covenant: loving God and neighbor, loving one another—fulfilling the whole law.

When we hear "the claim of God," we should think of God's grace come to us.

God's grace *wills* His covenant with humanity.

God's grace *creates* His covenant with humanity.

God's grace *determines* that humans should live as His covenant partners.

Therefore, God's grace brings human action into correspondence with God's action.

God has determined that human action should bear the image of God.

As creatures live in uniformity with their Creator, they experience eternal life, God's own life.

The covenant of grace is the fundamental relationship between God and humanity.

Sin is living in deviation, in turning away from the way to eternal life.

Obedience is our reflection of God's grace.

This reflection informs the life of imitation. We put off what does not correspond to grace, and exercise mutual kindness.

This lifestyle cannot be a human-created imitation. It is uniquely and firmly related to the gracious attitude of God operative in Jesus.

To accept God's claim as correct is to stop all resistance and hostility toward His actions. Instead, one engages God's gracious action with contentment and joyful participation to love God in His action.

We are to accept as true the fact that we do not belong to ourselves.

There will always be persons who, in *hostility* toward God, want to belong to themselves. They think God is a thief, trying to take their life from them.

Others have an attitude of *indifference*, unable to see who cares for them, blind to the kindness of God, and unaware of the consequence of their inaction.

Finally, there are those who *willfully* look away from the sphere of grace and seek a way of escape from God.

However, it is right to be God's possession. Having seen God's gracious dealings with us, we recognize that it is good for us.

What are we to do in the face of God's claim?

- We must accept that God only meets us compassionately.
- We must acknowledge that God is the One who comes to help us out of our misery.

- We must recognize that He sees us and judges us apart from what we deserve: death.

Why do we submit in the face of God's claim?

- In discovering the grace of God's dealings in Jesus Christ, we find that we are lost and alienated.
- We discover ourselves awakened from death by God's power as a miraculous, free act.

How do we submit in the face of God's claim?

- Having been confronted by how God has stood against our opposition to His love, grace, and mercy, we must accept the profundity of what He has done for us to quell our noisy opposition.
- He saved us when we were lost in our displeasure at His claim. We accept Him for all His undeserved goodness.

What are we to do?

- We must drop our *hostility* and admit He does what is beyond our power. We must let Him do what only He can do.
- We must drop our *indifference* by which we are left blind in the fog. We must let Him invert the situation and give courage where we live with a fear that keeps us reserved, self-interested, and inattentive to others.
- We must drop our *willfulness* that wants to reverse the situation, to claim what we want.

All of the opposition that humans carry in their hearts resists God's mercy.

To do what is right is to accept the summons of God and what He has done for us.

"We can sum it all up by saying that what God wants of us and all men is that we should believe in Jesus Christ."[2]

The essence of faith is to accept that God's action on our behalf is right and to set our mind on Jesus because He has already set Himself to be for us. Our faith aligns us with His reality.

---

2. *CD* 2.2, § 37, p. 583.

3. The Form of the Divine Claim (pp. 583–630)

As we discuss the form of the claim of God, we are referring to how the command of God encounters humanity.

God's command is imparted by God. His command speaks in a form that will address specific recipients.

All objects and statements contain a command. "Commands" demand our attention, consideration, and understanding to ask us a question and await an answer.

Truth statements compel us to agree with their conclusions. These form our intuitive conceptions of reality, stamping themselves on our thinking.

Some commands are more compelling in that they relate to the necessities of life, like eating, drinking, and sleeping. These demand an answer to their call.

Other commands are forced on us by education or custom, layers of the spheres in which we participate. We also have self-imposed commands that limit, guide, and direct us.

All humanity stands under a plethora of commands, all claiming attention and conformity.

All these many forms of commands are different from God's command.

God's command is a permission that grants definite freedom.

Other commands do not give us release into freedom. They constrain us, holding us fast and binding us. Each command represents the powers and authorities that constrict humanity.

All these other commands express the suspicion that it might be dangerous to release humanity. Liberty entails becoming vulnerable to abuse.

The commands created by humans fill others with anxious fears: fears of isolation, shortage, weakness, and of what one might possibly do unintentionally. Fears hold humans in a grip.

The command of God sets humans free with permission. It meets us with trust, not distrust. It appeals to courage, not fear. It will breed trust, not mistrust.

To stand under the influence of other commands is not to be refreshed. It is to surrender to the temptation to eat from the tree of the knowledge of good and evil. That pursuit of divine likeness is merely disobedience. That is the story of the fall, with all its repercussions.

That Edenic disorientation from God brought humanity into the sphere of harassment. Judgments were required for the human on every side on every day, and there is no rest.

God's command does say, "Do this," and "Don't do that," yet it is of a different character.

- Do this so that we may live again by God's grace.
- Do this to confirm God's rejection of our rejection by Jesus on the cross, bringing forgiveness.
- Do this because we have been born anew into the image of God.
- Do this to live in the freedom into which we were called.
- Do not continue in a life echoing from the fall of Adam.
- Do not live in contradiction to the grace of God.
- Do not live in the captivity of fear and judgment.

God's command always speaks concretely, like other commands, but as permission.

God's command sets us free. We are released from continual judging.

God's command wills us to make use of the permission given by God to be what we are.

The *ought* of the command of God is to be done with the seriousness of joy.

The perfect law is that of freedom. We come to hear as hearers ought to hear: willing and ready to act in freedom.

In choosing to follow the desire to glorify self, we walk out the door toward death. While in a living body, we are dying as we cut ourselves off from the source and sustainer of life.

There is only one way back to life. We must look to Him. He frees us from the desires to serve what is other than the freeing will of God.

Turning from life-draining alienation, we find God's life-affirming grace. This grace is the law of the Spirit of life.

The law of sin and death has been taken away, that which accuses us as sinners and keeps us enslaved to guilt and the fear of judgment.

Attempts to escape by our own power only bind us more fully in self-righteousness. All this amounts to idolatry—replacing God.

New freedom comes to us in the form of belonging. We belong to the Other, who died and rose on our behalf and now lives with and for us.

For the liberated person, there is no condemnation. Living as though there is no condemnation is what is required.

The first Adam, who perverted the human relation to God in self-willed error, is condemned.

But the second Adam was condemned to bring acquittal for humanity, which is realized by belonging to the risen Christ. He restores what was lost in the first Adam.

Having been set free from the condemnation of the law, Jesus has set us free for obedience. We turn from the spirit of bondage to receive the Spirit of belonging. We cry out, *"Abba*, Father!" as the basic command of God.

God's command orders us to be free. Divine permission is given to us; consent is not given from anywhere else.

God unmasks all false permissions by revealing the truth. He exposes the deception of those whose lies make us slaves.

What is called *free will* was a trick that reduced humans to slavery. Thinking themselves free, humans turned from the love and obedience that brings life. They turned to a destiny with oppression and torment. Belonging to God was traded in for bondage under a tyrant.

He stands against the domination of our self-deception and destruction, cravings disguised in the form of our own lusts and desires.

God's command keeps us from withdrawing into ourselves. All other commands force us to come back to ourselves again and again. We attempt to become judges between good and evil in our secluded independence.

The command of God takes up our proper cause—fulfilling life within the decision of God to be for us, making it our choice.

When we live with anxiety and fear, we become burdened. We attend to the threat that confronts us. We contemplate all the ways this state might become a catastrophe.

Anxiety is a little fear wanting security in the face of an uncertain future. An anxious person cannot admit real fear.

Fear is inflated anxiety. People in the Bible fear Jesus based on their misguided thoughts. Fear is caused by faulty thinking. It is an anticipation that assumes defeat.

Fear and anxiety are the opposites of freedom. Looking at the future with fear, we are not free in the present. We are missing real love.

We need not deny the presence of actual threats or the insecurity of the future. But we need not be their prisoner.

With freedom, we do not anticipate or try to control the future. When conflict arises, we see that there are possibilities and not impossibilities.

The command of God calls us to not be anxious or live in fear. This urging is the gospel, and this is the law!

If we persist in choosing anxiety and fear, we have failed to see God's permission and command, to know that God is for us. The Father knows what we need and cares for us. We need not be anxious.

Jesus, the only One we must fear as judge, is the One who raises and restores us.

Another pair of words that command us are *abide* and *stand*.

In all its forms, *abiding* is accomplished by the grace of God.

Standing is also a position that locates us within God's care and command.

Abiding and standing are possibilities given in Jesus Christ.

When abiding and standing in Jesus, fear and anxiety are excluded.

The place of abiding and the ground of standing refer to grace, faith, and apostolic proclamation.

To be "in Christ" is to abide in Him. It is not a step down the road to other possibilities.

The only other option in life from abiding would be going elsewhere.

In describing the divine claim, we are standing against *legalism* and *lawlessness*. Both claim authority and freedom other than in Jesus. One is an impersonal principle, and the other is an anarchy of the self.

Apart from faith, we submit either under a condition of *legalism*, an obligation that is not a permission, or *lawlessness*, a permission that is not an obligation.

If we let go of the grace of God, we will fabricate illusions about our permissions and our obligations.

The free life of the children of God comes in the work of the Spirit, who stirs their hearts to cry out, "*Abba*, Father." These become children who are no longer slaves to fear.

Obedience to the command of God is *spiritual*—that is, the work of the Spirit facilitates it.

Jesus' obedience is key to learning about the outworking of permission, spontaneity, and freedom.

Jesus reveals the will of God because it is His will. As we look at Him, we come to be called the children of the same Father.

Jesus is free to act in love for other humans because He exercises His will as the free love of God.

With this freedom, God covenants with humanity. Jesus is the first and normative covenant partner of God. He gives this term its meaning.

The command of God is spiritual. It is not ideal. It is a reality fulfilled in Jesus Christ. He is the ground, content, and form of the divine claim.

God has turned to us in this person. We accept the offer of His covenant, sealed by Him. He is the form of the command of God directed toward us. His work extends to all humanity. We all belong to this person and not to ourselves, and our work is to confirm that this is true.

We live in unity with Him, who is hidden, present in faith, and withdrawn from sight while we remain in this world.

We still require instruction. We endure living by the grace that is continually extended to us.

What has been done for us in Jesus is not yet disclosed fully. What we are in Him is still coming.

Our life in this world is lived with waiting faith, ruled and claimed by Him here and now.

All distinctions of other lords must be seen as not being this One true Lord. Alongside Him, we cannot trust anyone else.

If it is not Jesus' call that summons us, we cannot be rid of anxiety and fear.

Within our decision for Christ, everyday decisions repeat and confirm our decision for Christ.

We will know freedom is simultaneous with God's command.

"The command of God is 'personal' because it claims our obedience in relation to this definite person, Jesus Christ."[3]

The divine command is not impersonal; it has a personal character that requires a personal response in the form of a decision.

We are a part of His body, of which He is the head. We exist in Him and respond accordingly to stay alive. Cut off from Him, we are dead.

Our minds become oriented to and aligned with the mind of Christ. Departing from that stance is enmity and disobedience to Him.

Our personal choice to respond to God's command must be repeated and confirmed with joy continually.

Each day comes with freshness as we find that we belong to the One who loves us.

The story of the rich young ruler is a picture of a negative response to the divine command in contrast to the disciple's positive response—the disobedient and the obedient.

Even in disobedience, the young man is in the kingdom. It is impossible to be expelled from the kingdom of God.

The rich young ruler sought eternal life and was sure he must do something to get it. He knew Jesus had the answer. He came to the right person but in the wrong way.

---

3. *CD* 2.2, § 37, p. 609.

The question that comes from Jesus can only be answered by obedience or disobedience. This response is the way Jesus is Lord of His kingdom, within the covenant He made with humanity.

This rich young man seeks a way to eternal life.

Two things are clear:

1. This person has heard the command of God. He has already heard the answer to the question he asks.
2. The range of authority of the One he questions extends to the whole sphere of hearing God's command.

Jesus sets the external aspects of obeying the law before the man, the things one can witness. These acts of obedience assume the internal aspects of loving God and honoring Him.

The rich man comes to Jesus with confidence that he has already passed the test. But he is delusional. Having kept the commandments, he has not understood them.

He has the clear conscience of a disobedient man. He is still a rebel, determined to go his own way.

The commandments that speak to his external life want to speak to him internally. Speaking of loving neighbors, they intend to call him back to God as a covenant partner.

Actively loving neighbors is a test for the real point of whether one belongs to Jesus. To look at the external form of the command of God and miss the centering point of loving the One who loves us—that is to fail the test.

From the point of view of this fettered man, he knew the commandments. He judged and acquitted himself based on his selective rendering of its intent. But he was still in bondage to himself. He measures himself by law and not the love of Jesus.

Jesus does not unmask the rich man's fallacy; Jesus loves him even in his disobedience. To follow the law would be to let himself be loved. He does not love his neighbor or belong to Jesus. But Jesus loves him.

Jesus urges the rich young man, beginning with, "Go and sell."

Selling requires parting with what belongs to him. This man lacks the power to relinquish his belongings to become a covenant partner with God. One might say he belongs to his belongings.

The young man cannot answer the obligation of the gracious God. He is not free to love God or neighbor.

He fulfills the outward obligations so that he can feel good about himself. He misses the real meaning of being bound to the living God and acting accordingly with freeing love. He is captive, even though he feels so self-satisfied and pure.

The man's urges instill a love of money, fear of losing it, trust in its power, and hope for a good life on his terms. He has faith, hope, and love, just misplaced in another lord.

God will not tolerate this other lord that sabotages His grace. Jesus sees that he must be freed from the domination of this other lord.

Jesus opened the prison door of this prisoner. The man was unable to shed what bound him. Jesus still loved him.

Next, Jesus exhorts the rich young man to "Give to the poor."

As a covenant partner of God, he should meet his neighbor as God met him, with grace and compassion.

God is rich and gives what He has without expectation of return. This gifting becomes a call to us to share with our neighbors.

In giving what we can to the poor, we testify that we have been liberated from our allegiance to money.

Jesus did not want to take what belonged to this man; He wanted him to give away what did not belong to him, except as a child of God.

The final appeal by Jesus to this man was, "Come and follow Me." It is a call to stay with Him.

"Follow Me" is the meaning of the second half of the commandments given to Moses when they are fulfilled in action.

The freedom to be for one's neighbor is the freedom to be for Jesus as a covenant partner with God.

And so, this man went away sad. However, we cannot understand this event as purely negative.

The incident happens within the sphere of the kingdom of Jesus. The man confessed his lack in walking away. But Jesus is free, only bound to be with the poor and outcasts with the riches of God.

This man has all he needs except the fullness of life with Jesus. But does Jesus abandon him?

We do know that Jesus is there for the rich who are poor in their hearts; they are included in those whom He loves.

God embraces humanity even when He is misunderstood, resisted, and scorned.

Wherever one is in the abyss, one will encounter Jesus and find Him pursuing those who are lost.

"Who then can be saved?" is a hinge passage. The answer is that with God, all things are possible. Saving is not within the power of humans; it is entirely the work of God.

Human capacity does not include the power to be obedient to God. Even the disciples lack the ability to be obedient to God. All stand in need of grace.

What makes the disciples different from the rich man is that they are aware of and trust in the possibility of God saving disobedient humans. In this, the impossible became possible.

The question arises for the disciples, and maybe us: "What will become of us?" They were not always joyfully obedient.

The answer they get back announces Jesus' provision of life both now and in eternity.

Jesus promises to provide for all people, including those bound in anxiety and those set free. He moves in a sphere beyond where humans conjecture what is possible and impossible.

 COMMENTARY:

- Theological ethics must be appropriately oriented to the God who commands, responding to the command which He extends to humanity.
- Ethics, in this context, cannot be equal to "What must I do?"
- Because God is present in human life as the One who loves in freedom, all that we call ethical must be derived from this point of departure. It must fulfill God's kind of loving and freedom.
- Ethics begins as an attitude of knowing that God has claimed us for His own. We accept this and live as those who belong to Him. This alignment may be viewed as accepting our adoption or accepting our identity. We become new persons as we give ourselves over to the One who loves us.
- If we choose to see ethics as "situational," this can *only* be appropriate as attentiveness to being situated as the beloved of God.
- This attentiveness means living in Jesus and being situated as a covenant partner who desires to be faithful to our partner. It cannot be about taking on a set of rules, expectations, or ideals.
- We may not simply evaluate the situations of our lives that we think require our ethical decision. All our decisions must be correlated with the love of God that has claimed us as His own.
- Barth has confidence that God's love is greater than human performance or right choices. The rich young ruler provides an example

of one who comes face-to-face with Jesus and walks away when he could have "made a choice" to follow Jesus. However, for Barth, the choice of Jesus toward this confused person is greater than human misguided choices.

- Barth's ethics makes God's love and grace the standards of what is good, right, true, and loving.

 CONCLUSION FOR THE CHURCH: Church is a place where many send their children to learn to be good. But what are they expecting? Usually, they hope they learn to be moral and well-behaved. They desire compliance with what is acceptable in the community. The ethics of Jesus were to be about His Father's business. If this meant that others disapproved, He was not daunted. Jesus was unstoppable when it came to following His Father's will. This is the call for the Church in its form as a community reflecting divine grace. All must begin with, proceed with, and end with a deep passion for knowing the living God, and let the reflection be the fruit of this love as the character of the community.

When churches want to be "relevant for today" or "practical in their programs," they run the risk of building an ethic on the morality or faddish wisdom of the day. This kind of ethics is not theological. It does not help the church in being the Church of Jesus Christ. Jesus was not issue-driven or committed to a set of rules. He aimed for the heart in response to the call of God to love extensively and exhaustively. This chapter calls the Church back to the transformative experience of abiding in Christ with listening ears and walking with Him to reflect His presence.

 INSIGHT FOR PASTORS: This paragraph is a challenge for pastors to delve deeply, to embody the message and actions that reveal who God is. This section addresses what claim His love has on our lives as a community and as persons within it. It is not a matter of rules for loving marriages or Christian parenting. It is not a matter of getting people saved so they go to heaven. It is much more profound.

What Barth is talking about here is that we go from belonging to ourselves to giving ourselves to God. This belonging extends far beyond marriage, making new friends, or joining a new work community. Those can be life-transforming. But they still maintain a sense of self-directed investment that *we* manage. Barth calls pastors to unleash the love and grace of God for His people so that every part of life is claimed, infused with the love of God. This transformation calls people to an all-in, joyful response of belonging from which actions flow unreservedly. The more people are claimed by God's love for them, the greater the transformation of a community into the life of love. Even for the resistant, we offer the unleashed grace of the kingdom to affirm that Jesus will take no prisoners, but He will always hold on to sons and daughters whom He will never let go (and He has a big embrace).

 INSIGHT FOR THEOLOGIANS: Barth's ethics are difficult for those trained in the Western tradition of philosophy and theology. Those systems argue by looking back to the Greek philosophers and all those who follow and build on human foundations for thinking. It is so "reasonable" to think from a human point of view in ethics. It is natural to go looking for wise principles for ethical reasoning. We want thinking that leads to "godly" actions in the challenging situations of life. Barth will have no part in that if it is to be called theological ethics.

With Barth's unique take on the discipline of theological ethics, we must begin discussing the God-human relation by focusing on who God is in shaping the relationship. This refocusing is what Barth wants to accomplish in this paragraph. If we cannot hear the command of God, recognize His claim on human lives, and know the profound presence of God's freeing love in His command, then we have missed the point. This focus on Jesus is not unlike Barth's resistance to natural theology. He wants us to listen to God and not assign human ideas and values to God. Herein we narrow the scope to ethics. Barth resists ethics that project human notions of right and wrong, goodness, and right behavior onto God or concepts of "the good." The opposite approach is to work from the nature and givenness revealed in the person of Jesus. In this manner, we grant God the right to define and will the right and the good. We pursue that which is consistent with His will. Only in understanding the law of God that calls us to love may we develop theological ethics at all.

 CLARIFYING QUESTIONS: Does your conception of theological ethics begin with humans and ethical principles, possibly even derived from the Bible? *Or* does your idea of theological ethics begin with God? Can you believe that you are called to live each day responding to His love that already embraces you?

CHAPTER 19

GOD'S SONATA, SOUNDING FORTH A NEW MOVEMENT

§ 38. The Command as the Decision of God

FOCUS STATEMENT: With a burst of exuberance, this paragraph (§ 38) accentuates the themes of love that define the command of God. The God who sounded forth the symphony's opening movement now unfolds a thematic invitation to all that follows. The fullness of God's movement memorably calls for a symphonic response, inviting human life to play together.

One must listen attentively. Themes such as command and law may fool us into thinking of legalistic human structures. However, God's loving choice shapes us so that we hear "The Command as the Decision of God." God's decision reverberates with goodwill and translates into love's freeing expressions. This echo is the goodness of the gospel speaking to the spectrum of human interactions.

The image is one of a person lost in new modes of musicality. What fills the air defies what has been heard before, even as it draws themes from it. As the symphony draws to a close, it rises to unveil a new day coming.

INTRODUCTION: Barth has focused his theological ethics on being attentive to God and His intentions. God's part is vital in shaping the human ethical response.

Now Barth reveals examples of the command of God in the Bible. He exposes the heartfelt decision of God to expound His covenant love. God's commanding presence touches on every aspect of human being and relating. God provides no general rules for humanity to interpret in their own way. His call is to live in personal response to Him.

In this section, we encounter great texts, such as the Ten Commandments, the Sermon on the Mount, and the community exhortations of Romans 12–15. These provide brilliant riffs on the themes of God's command.

God is personally active in His decision to be for humanity. He commands a human response to His love. God is calling out our best selves. This restoration can only happen for those who live in love within God's choice. *He* has decided to be with us and for us. *Our* ethical life is an answer to the call to engage love personally.

CONTEXT: *CD* 2.2
Pages in Paragraph: 101 pages (pp. 631–732)

Subsections
1. The Sovereignty of the Divine Decision
2. The Definiteness of the Divine Decision
3. The Goodness of the Divine Decision

TEXT: § 38. The Command as the Decision of God

OPENING SUMMARY: As God is gracious to us in Jesus Christ, His command is the sovereign, definite and good decision concerning the character of our actions—the decision from which we derive, under which we stand and to which we continually move.[1]

SUMMARY:

1. The Sovereignty of the Divine Decision (pp. 631–61)

God's command is a claim. A claim comes from the outside. God's command works on the heart in relational renewal.

With God's command, humans are claimed to be changed from what they were to what they might be.

With external claims, the human is left to decide whether to respond to the claim. Obedience or disobedience is the human's choice alone.

Humans cannot evade the claim of God on them. God has made a decision.

The human choice may be in conformity or contradiction to God's will, but it does not change the will of God.

Obedience is a surrender to this will of God.

---

1. *CD* 2.2, § 38, p. 631.

God's command does not require *us* to create the relationship through which we belong to God. We cannot create this relationship.

We do confirm the grace of God toward us. Grace is the activity of God that creates the relationship. We acknowledge God's will in response to what God has freely given us.

Jesus is the content of God's command. He is the One who loves as the commandment commands.

Jesus is the claim of God on our lives. He has acted on our behalf to reconcile us to God, claiming us as His own.

God's will and law are to love. We either conform to it and bring praise to God's love, or we refuse and blaspheme God's great love.

Our life consists of a series of decisions that we make. We make decisions, and He judges. We will not be our own judges.

We know that God tests, searches, and reaches into the hearts of humans. A person in covenant connection does not see this as a burden. Instead, it proves that God cares and is in the process of correction.

We cannot escape God's testing, but the important thing is to not want to escape.

We are encouraged to act in a manner consistent with who we are in Christ.

Christians are tested through suffering. This challenge develops steadfastness and fellowship with the sufferings of Jesus.

Christians ask what is pleasing to the Lord, who judges goodness, righteousness, and truth in distinction from their opposites.

All we ever ask is how righteousness stands between Jesus and us.

Faith is to have a heart found pure by God and consistent with our walking with Him.

The concept of responsibility gives us precise insight into the human situation as we stand before the almighty God.

Responsibility takes place in a relationship. One willingly responds in an encounter with God, unceasingly answering the divine command.

We are never alone, and we do not belong to ourselves. We are not abandoned to ourselves or any alien power that would call to us.

In living out the will of God, our prime human directive is to live in covenant partnership with God.

Our lives are lived in this core of responsibility before God, whether or not we know it. We live each moment responsible to God. Each daily act is a miniature moment of our final standing before the judge responsible for our whole lives.

Only Christian ethics has an idea of responsibility, meaning to stand before Christ in all things.

Non-Christian views of life may have some sense of making a claim on a human's life to be responsible. They betray their stance in having no true sense of the basis of the obligation to be responsible. It can only be a diluted form of justice with no solid foundation.

Moral reflection is an outworking of the idea of responsibility. It is an examination of our compliance or noncompliance to the command of God.

What should we do? We should be holy in the way that God is holy. In that case, the will of God would have been realized in our lives. We would keep the covenant as faithfully as God does.

Humans do not know what they ought to do. In craving to be like God, they have a self-interested desire to discern between good and evil.

Humans have lost their desire for divine grace. This situation is the essence of the fall and results in human separation from God.

We cleave to what Jesus has accomplished for us through His death and resurrection. He prepares us to live within His act of making us whole.

The way forward is shaped and guided by an attitude that attends to Jesus' act and actions on our behalf.

When we ask Jesus what we ought to do, we implicitly become obedient. We cannot look to a set of teachings or principles to follow. We follow the voice, not disconnected laws to command us.

In our humility, we may ask:

1. *What* ought we to do? Any answer we give will be repeatedly questioned.

    The command of God has provided proposals and convictions to consider and meet God's demands. We are prepared to question all the previous answers and schemes put to us or provided by us.

    At this point, we need the grace of God. We pray, seeking what is established in the death and resurrection of Jesus. Jesus accepts us as we are.

    Instead of looking to our merit, we must lay aside our attempts at controlling life and say we are sorry for the way we have treated the grace of God.

    With humility, we approach God as those who are ignorant and prepared to be transformed by God's work.

    We set aside all we have known of goodness and the need to "be right" in our opinions. We release our standards and ideals, rules and regulations, and surrender even the good ones. We may hold these in reserve.

These external and internal guidelines we have set up for ourselves no longer have a valid, boundless claim on our lives.

All other commands are, at their best, refracted light from the command of God. But they shine through imperfect prisms.

When we ask what *we* ought to do, as though there are possibly new and better answers and modes of thinking, we abandon God.

The Church is most faithful when it is *linked* to the past but not *tied* to it. With those who have gone before, we search the Scriptures and orient our lives around God.

The Church weakens and dies when it is tied to the past. It becomes enslaved instead of freed into God's future opened by the Bible.

The practice of regular repetition and renewal is the law of spiritual growth. It brings us into continuity with God. God's steadfastness creates space for new expressions of our freedom.

The critical problem in asking "*What* ought we to do?" is that it takes us to answers formerly rejected.

If asking "What?" comes from anxiety, it will distract us from discovering what is truly valuable in the command of God.

2. What *ought* we to do? This quest is not about knowledge for the sake of knowing.

We do not seek the divine truth; it seeks us. It demands of us to know the truth as the rule and norm of our conduct.

We are not directed to options we might *consider* but to what we must *obey*.

To speak of *ought* is to consider what we will to do based on what is required.

If our will is not free and joyful, it is disobedient to God.

Proper obligation arises when our will meets the divine will in Jesus as our Lord, and we desire to belong to Him.

We do not act as those estranged from God when we ask what we *ought* to do. We affirm Jesus as our representative and operate within the sphere of His authority.

3. What ought *we* to do? In our moral reflection, we may consider our part in the interaction.

We are to be human. We are to be covenant partners. Barth offers some self-limiting considerations.

    a. Asking what *we* ought to do is a personal question, meaning we are asking specifically what we as *one* person ought to do.

        It is easy to talk about human conduct in general. There is an urge to remain a spectator, interested in what others ought to do. But we are summoned personally.

    b. In this reflection, we do need to consider who we are in the context of others. What I do is related to others. I am always included in the "we" of human action.

        My God is our God. His command applies to us all. We are always summoned in community. We are in solidarity with humanity; we are never alone.

        We are distinct, but not detached.

    c. This *we* is qualified as those who are elected in Jesus Christ.

        This body of people knows we belong in it together and seek an answer about what we are to do in compliance with His command that we have come to know. We know God knows about us.

4. What are we to *do*?

    It is good to be curious about what we are to do. But we cannot pursue generalized studies, such as psychology or history, to gain perspective. They lack focus and specifics. They have pursued an investigation regarding ethics that seeks their own questions, which pretend to be ethics but merely fulfill their own theories.

    Ethical reflection adopts an awareness of what has gone before in our decisions and what will follow.

    We also look forward to the future in anticipation. We utilize subconscious and conscious reflection to consider what to do in light of the divine command.

    As we stand before God with these considerations, we ask not only what to do but also who we are to be.

    We know whose we are and what He commands, so we cannot live in a neutral sphere of influence.

    We are not responsible *for* an idea but *to* a person. Our ethics need to be an ethos, the very characteristic of living with this person, and not a mere theory.

2. The Definiteness of the Divine Decision (pp. 661–708)

In establishing an understanding of theological ethics, we began with God's decision as to the context and starting point.

The inescapable verdict of the divine judge has addressed the specifics of good and evil in our decisions.

Through the giving of Jesus Christ, God has claimed our obedience.

The atonement of Jesus is enacted to make God responsible for our lives.

The love of God intends to be for us, and therefore God wills to be responsible for our infractions.

The human response to God's love is gratitude.

He wills to have us as His own and to be our God.

God has granted all creation a manifoldness. All He creates bears the expression of His wide variety.

Similarly, our human existence is known and enjoyed in its uniqueness. This existence was granted from the freedom of God's personal life.

Human lives are contingent, dependent on His will and action.

For our part, we clarify that we are God's creation. We point back to Him as the source and vitality of all we enjoy as a gift.

God's law is incomparable. It is not like human law with general principles that find specific applications yet to be determined.

God always addresses us with specific meaning and intention. His will is expressed in His command. He is particular in His decision. He has foreseen everything and left nothing to chance.

In their various positions, most people live with general rules and make judgments for their own applications. Humans become the final judges in one form or another, justifying their own will.

God's command is a demand with specific content that touches every part of our lives. It addresses us and calls for action.

We are not to be judges, measuring against "the idea of the good," based on what humans develop through their encounters with life.

The idea of the divine command acknowledges that humans have a Lord over them. Our moral life is rooted in His personal will.

The human "good" is radically different from God's command. Neither the categorical imperative of Kant nor conscience can replace the command of God. Both become arbiters in our decisions in a humanly formed manner.

Our consciences may receive the Word and command of God and participate in God's knowledge as He gives it to us. In that case, we are thinking from God's point of view (eschatologically) and not from the human (anthropologically).

Only in integrating our existence with that of Jesus Christ can we conceive the human conscience as an organ of the divine will. We participate in His good on His terms.

God's Word is not given *by* conscience but may be given *to* it.

Normative concepts, such as the categorical imperative or the idea of the good, all default to human judgment and discretion.

Another form of abuse is to take ideas like the kingdom, God's glory, the love of God, righteousness, or holiness and turn them into normative concepts where we fill in the concepts with our own interpretations and judgments.

All these titles (the kingdom, the love of God, etc.) are other names for the command of God.

However, God's command is God's alone and is definite. Our choice is to obey or disobey.

God wills something specific from us. This willing excludes other possibilities. Each command, as well as our decision in response, is a personal decision.

It is futile to object that God has not given His command with clarity. God is present in the world and to every person. We hear as we belong to Him.

The question is not whether He speaks but whether we hear.

We are commanded from the Bible. Through it, we recognize the concrete command that encounters us.

To be assured of the divine command, we must shed light on two points:

1. The biblical divine law is always a concrete command.
2. This commanding must be understood as relevant to us who were not initially addressed by it.

The first is an exegetical question. When encountering God's command in the Bible, we easily think we are dealing with universal legal codes or rules that are valid across all time.

God's command is not limited to certain texts in various contexts, but extends to the whole from which they belong.

The content of the Bible is replete with ethics. God desires humans to act in a specific way, as a father desires of his child.

We must recognize that God rules as the Lord God, embodying His grace, directing His child in such a way that there is no question as to what is required.

The Ten Commandments are an example of a specific, contextually determined command.

The prohibition regarding eating from the tree of the knowledge of good and evil was specific, to stop humans from becoming independent judges.

Becoming independent of God is prohibited. Humans were made to correspond to God. With separation comes death. This turning from God is the model of all future sins.

The five books of Moses are full of specific divine commands. These are specific commands, not general rules.

The New Testament is the same. The gospels depict God giving specific commands to Mary, Joseph, the shepherds, and so on.

The disciples are given specific commands. Story after story unveils concrete commands by Jesus.

Jesus does not give general principles for living; He gives specific commands. If we turn His personal commands into broad principles, we turn away from the living and acting Jesus.

In place of universal laws, we have a person.

It is important to keep these series of specific commands as primary in our thinking about the whole Bible. The living Lord commands as He goes about His work. Humans correspond with obedience or resistance.

We are not called to assimilate general rules. We are not left to decide how to apply the rules.

We are called to keep securely before us what God has called us to do.

"In the command of God we are face to face with the person of God, with the action and revelation of this person, with God Himself."[2]

The commands of God, which are normative for humans, are made in personal encounters.

God always precedes us with His knowledge as to what is beneficial, presenting it with steadfastness so that humans may obey the particularity of what He commands.

The fact that God's command is set in context in history does not mean it is meaningless elsewhere.

God is a specific person. He has a particular character to His will, revealed and known in the person of Jesus.

---

2. *CD* 2.2, § 38, p. 676.

We can say that God has a way and a plan that the writers of the Bible recognized.

Understanding the meaning of God's will is not eliminated as we consider the specifics of God's history.

In the story of God's covenant of grace, we see God's mercy at work to draw humans to Himself in Jesus.

Jesus becomes a human to execute the divine order against human sin. He fulfills the order to make humans pure, free, and blessed. He gives Himself over to death that humans might have life to the full. This act provides the meaning that inspires all the commanding and forbidding in the Bible.

In one person, Jesus carries the rejection of human sin and the election of humans by grace. This self-giving fulfills the will of God and prepares humans to proclaim God's merciful and loving intention.

The Bible proclaims that God wills one thing, the completion of His election of grace.

This will informs the history of God with humanity, becoming its theme and content. Humans are called to adapt to and correspond with this history.

God ratifies His covenant with humans by giving commands. Humans accept the covenant by agreeing to the commands.

When Jesus commands and forbids, He discloses His Messiahship and summons humans to share in the imminent coming of God's kingdom as active participants.

Some biblical texts do take the form of a general command. The question arises to what degree we will interpret them out of context and miss their meaning.

Do we best interpret texts in their contexts or our contexts in light of these texts? Most prefer the latter, which isolates the text from its origin. These become rootless rules with autonomous significance.

This method of separating commands from their context as God's ideals is convenient. It gives the law a meaning, even apart from God. Therein lies the problem. A good deal of the good becomes an adaptation to human ideals.

The Bible was not intended to be a venue for ethical principles displayed for human consideration.

The biblical texts bear the task of witnessing to God, especially Jesus in the New Testament.

Humans hear the personal address of God in the context of the Church. To hearers, the texts do not lose their particularity nor their connectedness to others.

Everything required of a person is contained in the biblical summaries of His will. We take them and live them in the context of the Church in a personal manner.

The summaries of laws are never intended to replace a person hearing God's address.

We must hear the proclamation of the command of God from generation to generation. This attentiveness trains our ears to hear the living God. He speaks to every person with the voice of the Good Shepherd.

God is always the backdrop of our relating. He deals with humans through an immediacy that infuses each moment. This awareness ignites human obligations, fully called into action.

Within the framework of this relationship, the texts of the Bible refer us to this interlocking way of being.

The Ten Commandments illustrate the point. Their original presentation took place in a direct encounter between God and a human, Moses.

This very particular situation required a human fitted for the situation and called to its task. Moses represents the people as he receives God's commands for the ordering of life for these people.

Moses is to pass on to the people what he received from God. Before Moses can do this, the people sin with the golden calf.

These commandments belong to the life and culture of the people. They are to direct the concrete life of the people, shaping their lives in the presence of God.

The commandments are interpreted by their immediate context as pertaining to real-life situations.

The Ten Commandments call the people of God to be set aside. They are to reflect the election of God by which He has called them to Himself.

The sphere that is addressed is not the inward life of the human but is the sphere of life with God and the community of God.

The commands state prohibitions of that which violates the community in relation to God and other humans.

The honoring of God by His people is the theme of the first four commands.

The other six commands are about honoring the community, protecting it from strife and self-destruction.

The giving of the Decalogue is *the* big event in the life of Israel.

In every way, Israel is to listen to the living voice of God through His messengers and this law.

The Sermon on the Mount clarifies the command of God in its connection with the kingdom of God come in Jesus Christ.

The whole of the Old Testament law is fulfilled in Jesus. It was founded by Him and is now fulfilled by Him through a life of obedience, summoning all humanity to cling to His obedience, lived on their behalf.

Jesus rules as the mediator between God and humanity. He concerns Himself with the problems of human life and the maintenance of daily existence.

The Sermon on the Mount announces the kingdom of the new humanity in Jesus. He is the new Adam who brings the new kingdom.

Jesus inaugurates the covenant of grace, fulfilling the purpose of the law and the Ten Commandments.

The Sermon on the Mount, like the Ten Commandments, announces that something new has come.

The Ten Commandments are a preface to the covenant of grace. The Sermon on the Mount is its postscript.

In Jesus, God has accomplished freedom for humanity. Freedom is given to God's people in the form of the Church.

The Sermon on the Mount declares the coming of the kingdom of God. It has arrived in the middle of all other human kingdoms and countries, even within the sphere where Satan does his work.

God has all other kingdoms in a checkmate, although they do not realize it yet. Thus, they will not concede their power.

It may seem like the kingdom of God did not come. Perhaps it only drew near or was merely a possibility.

But this kingdom is a present reality. Jesus has made it so, indwelling all human spheres with His authority.

The new reality is not created *by* us but is made *for* us. Jesus has reinterpreted the dark text of our lives according to His gracious purposes.

The kingdom has appeared. The Lord of the covenant has become the neighbor of humans and all human spheres. The covenant is completed.

The law has been brought to its fulfillment. There is not a new one in place of the old one. The old one has become newly expressed.

God has determined for human life to be the fulfillment of all commands. He does this as the commander who embodies the commands.

Righteousness in the Bible is not a state or a decree; it is a way of being in action. This action brings restoration, making right a wrong state of affairs, or healing a suffering relationship.

One can also conceive of righteousness as the act of a judge who, as a competent helper, secures a right where there had been a wrong.

This setting right is the aim of the Sermon on the Mount. What had been outward forms of correction in the Old Testament delves now into the inner life of humans to include all of our humanity.

Jesus has come to fulfill the law. The promises are completed in Him. Humans do not now need to move in self-assertion, to strive toward righteousness. It is all captured in the ability and validity of Jesus saying to us, "I know you."

The righteousness outlined in the Sermon on the Mount comes from the realization of being known by Jesus and living by His mercy.

What affirms one's righteousness is not upstanding performance nor our confession of Him. What matters is His confession of us: "This one belongs to Me." This is grace extended.

In arrogance and disillusion, those who aspire to live by human strength think they are whole but miss the narrow gate.

By God's gracious election, we are permitted to live life in Him and with Him.

Because the kingdom has drawn near to us in Jesus, we become new creatures entirely as a gift.

We see new persons changed by Him:

- Jesus in His own people
- Jesus in His disciples
- Jesus in those who hear and do the word of grace addressed to them
- Jesus in those who have assimilated the righteousness of the kingdom, which Jesus is and proclaims
- Jesus in all to whom He *gives* a share in what He has accomplished
- Jesus in those who have *received* their share as a gift

These are the children of God. Their newness and goodness have not been achieved by themselves.

The children of God do not learn a way of "give and take." The golden rule that is the goal of the covenant is "take and give." They grow as children receiving from their Father in heaven. They love and pray for others in continuity with their Father, deepening who they already are.

There is no weight of obligation for the child, only the flowing fruit of thankfulness, which is a gift.

Grace must be lived out. One blessed by their Father in heaven is always ready to give what is good. So, we ask, knock, and seek Him. Coming to Him, we are doing the will of God.

What we need most is the Master Himself. Apart from our relationship to Jesus and what the Father constantly gives us in His Son, we would either become legalistic Pharisees or lawless publicans.

The heart of the Sermon on the Mount is that it takes us to prayer. We enter the order of grace and never leave it again.

We must never forget that the only One who actually fulfills the law is Jesus.

The demands of the sermon hold up a mirror for us to see ourselves honestly before Him.

The life reflected in Jesus can become possible for those who hear and do the word of Jesus.

The mercy of God has an impact on humans because of what is revealed and operative in Jesus.

The sermon opens a new perspective for the people of God seen within the kingdom of God.

What was promised has been made concrete in the kingdom of grace, which is made active in the Son, Jesus Christ. The law was a preparatory language that has been translated into personal presence.

The requirements of the Old Testament are not made obsolete by the Sermon on the Mount. We needed the preparation and the fulfillment. But we see new dimensions and a radical new depth.

The sermon reveals that the law of God is to be lived from the grace of God, beginning to end. It is this grace that demands a new life in personal fidelity and freedom.

The kingdom of God and its covenant of grace have become objective, actual, and observable in Jesus.

Without the insight of grace, the divine law is open to distortion and misunderstanding. When humans replace the claim of grace with the arbitrariness of human works, what results is a history of brokenness and transgression in relationships.

Moses disclosed human opposition to the law in human failings and disobedience. The Messiah reveals the fulfillment of the law in the obedient death and resurrection of Jesus.

Jesus reorders the life of the people. He brings forgiveness for their sins, and the new beginning for life with God embodied in Himself.

Barth sees, with and beyond Martin Buber, that the sermon not only takes us back to the mountain of the Ten Commandments. We ascend into the clouds, to know the heart behind the voice, to the very eternal personal being of God. Buber thought this was maybe too much to see in the sermon; Barth thought it about right.

The rest of the Old and New Testaments are not made unnecessary by the Sermon on the Mount. They guide the Church continually to Jesus. The Church is not left alone with private interpretations of the texts.

The giving of the Sermon on the Mount and other significant texts is best seen as an outpouring of the Holy Spirit, taking the original events to a new and proper fulfillment for the people of God.

Humans need not exceed nor try to measure up to the standards of the life of the Messiah as we wait for His return. He will always be the One who gives the law, is the law, and is the fulfillment of the law.

By the given law of the Spirit of life, we come to distinguish the voice of the Good Shepherd. We must learn to hear that voice afresh to hear and follow the will of God concretely.

The Ten Commandments and the Sermon on the Mount are not general truths or merely classical documents for the masses. They are not examples of general ethics that may be removed from their contexts and goal in pointing to the living God before whom they place us.

These texts guide humans to live within the covenant of grace to shape humans in relationship to God.

These texts prepare the way for the opening of the heart. The aim is ever-refreshing obedience marked by grace.

The triune God is not a formless spirit. His face bears the features which emerge in these texts. So, too, we begin to see the features on human faces which bear the distinctive marks of being in relationship to this God.

The Bible displays that the command of God is always concrete. This was the first point regarding the divine command.

We turn to the second point. Here we affirm that the divine, concrete command speaks to us and our concerns as well as its original context.

The Bible enables us to hear the will and work of God in His self-revelation.

The Bible reveals:

- God has entered human history, meeting with people in specific times and places.
- Considering His covenant of grace, God said "Yes" and "No" to specific attitudes and actions.
- God has come as speaking subject to these humans as the object for hearing His election of grace.
- God and these humans are linked together in the person of Jesus Christ.

- God has entered the historical process with these persons. He leads them to the goal of the covenant of grace and the fruit of its outworking.

The Bible stands as a witness in court. It asks us to accept its truth as a decision in response to what we have heard.

The Bible speaks of God's commands, for here and now. It hopes to get our attention. In recognizing the facts, it aims to engender our faith.

The Christian Church assumes that the Bible's claim to credibility will be accepted, and its witness approved as true.

We are deceived if we think that we are alone. We are not abandoned by God, compelled and competent to be our own judges. We are not to utilize the command of God in our own way.

If we have all the truths of the Bible as we have been arguing, but do not have the living, commanding God, then we have an impossible situation for God and humanity.

We must hold that God is not far from us; He is near.

Humans are not far from God; we are near. We are members of the community of God. We have been called as members of the body that is freed by faith in Him.

Any command of God or compilation of human morality that becomes general and abstract can only be a shadow or caricature of the living God's command displayed in the Bible.

God's good is given in the covenant of peace, electing humanity in grace, and bearing the name of Jesus.

We are commissioned to share in God's work. This is true for every person, place, and time. This commissioning is not a self-appointment.

Who God is and who we are in compliance with His will are not hidden. We know what is good and what is required of us.

Where God meets the human, He requires specific things.

- The Bible states what God commands and forbids concerning our relation to Him.
- Having heard, the Bible calls us to make a concrete decision, shaped in response to our Lord who stands before us.
- Not only does the Bible instruct and guide, but it also mediates God's presence.

The Lordly Word fulfills His work through the biblical Word.

Jesus stands over the whole world as Lord, whether or not He is recognized and loved.

- He is the Lord of each person.
- He is present at all times and in every situation.
- He confronts every aspect of our lives.
- He speaks through the Bible to fulfill His work in us.
- The Bible tells us *that* God commands us, *how* He commands, and *what* He commands.

The Bible, as a Word of command, is personal. That is how we are to understand the Bible. It is not an impersonal collection of ethical principles and examples.

If the Bible reveals the reality of God in His works, we cannot avoid hearing it as the Word of His command.

When we speak of the Bible, we refer to the God who speaks. The human authors speak not on their own behalf but as witnesses to God's revelation.

The Bible is the living speech of God.

- By its speech, we are set in a relationship between God and humanity.
- We are set in a concurrent relationship with the biblical witnesses.
- We hear the command as they heard it.
- Through their witness as they heard it, their God becomes our God.
- God's command is given to us as we hear it.

We are not identical with the original witnesses, but we share their listening and task.

We must allow ourselves to be addressed as those to whom it was given then and there. We must also accept that it was meant for us.

While we might regard the Bible as the normative Word of God, we often live and think as though this were not the case.

That God is the judge of our actions is true whether we know it or consider it true.

God's election of grace embraces us. His living command, through which He attracts us to Himself, awakens us to obedience, sanctifies us, and makes us partners of His covenant relationship.

3. The Goodness of the Divine Decision (pp. 708–32)

Goodness refers to God's specific form of goodness, not some general idea.

There is a unity in the character of God's goodness that contains rightness, friendliness, and wholesomeness. God must also define these words.

The good command of God will be discerned from the revelation of the God revealed in Jesus.

As we explore the unveiling of God's goodness in God's command, no other idea of what is good, or a command, ought to be considered. God's good command unravels and disqualifies other concepts of the good.

To say that God and His command are good implies that God's being precedes the good. Having established this, we can say that the good is the outworking of His command.

God is motivated in His command by His friendliness and goodwill.

God intends to impact human welfare and salvation. He considers the whole scope of life and what will bring eternal joy in His presence.

Rightly declared in alignment with God's perfections, we can see that God's decision and command are good news, the gospel.

God is not against humans in any way. He is for them. In this, His glory is shown.

When we begin to judge ourselves, we must assess how we are aligned with God's goodness in His command with all His friendliness and goodwill.

God's sovereignty will always imply particularity. Universal truths have nothing to do with the will and command of God.

God has an intention toward each person. He finds each one in their situation. He reaches them in the details of their lives.

God's goodness is expressed in kindness that commands and forbids in every situation.

To say His goodness is rich is to say it is never identical. It is always particular and therefore manifoldly diverse as applied in each situation. Yet it is held together in a bond of peace, never split up, as it operates from a united whole.

In every case, God loves what is right. His manner is friendly. He always wills to bring a wholesome outcome.

God does not create disorder or chaos.

God creates fellowship and the connection of all.

God *forms the interconnection of the many separate parts* of His creation into an integral whole. This integration is the context for the life of each person as part of the whole.

1. God's will *may not be atomized.* The decision of God is not numerous, in some way tied to the many needs and urges of each individual person. God's decision flows from the *one goodwill* of God.

The inner voice we hear is not the command of God. Inner voices *do not* fulfill God's idea of the good, however friendly they may sound to us.

Human rules and regulations contain inconsistencies and contradictions.

In the long section starting at Romans 12:1, Barth investigates the command of God in action.

These chapters outline the will of God as it shapes the conduct of a congregation responding to God's command.

Each person in the community is to act for the good of their neighbor and the community.

We are called to be like-minded toward one another according to Jesus Christ, glorifying God with mind and mouth.

Christians are to fulfill all obligations by loving one another. In this way, they build up the Church and fulfill the law. They are motivated by the will of God, not by fear.

We must receive one another because Christ has accepted us all. In Christ, all are called to thank and praise God with reciprocity in building up the body.

In the command to love there is a unity of intention as well as a diversity of expressions.

The will of God is both a comfort and an encouragement. From God's mercy, we are moved to become the body that extends the grace of God to one another.

For Paul, the divine command is the gospel. It lives from grace extended to the unworthy and calls them to respond to the command to love and obey the One who loves them.

We are to give all of who we are, every part, possibility, and function. We must realize that our life is a living and sacred gift desired by God.

Only Jesus can offer reasonable worship to God as a priest. He alone brings us into correspondence with God.

Not everyone participates in Christ's divine service, offered on their behalf. Even so, it is still available to them.

To *participate* is to believe and trust Jesus' work on one's behalf and know His person by the Holy Spirit.

These persons serve God with deep thanksgiving. They serve Christ in the Holy Spirit. They seek the kingdom of God with righteousness, peace, and joy.

The inner unity of their life in God is the source of their outward unity with mutual love.

2. God's good command *takes human diversities and unites them* within His life.

Throughout history, "generally recognized principles" have not been the source of unity for humanity.

Principles require interpretation. These become individual interpretations that draw each person to their own conclusions.

This individualizing movement is like a centrifugal force at work, as it forces the person away from the unifying center and into an individualistic interpretation.

For each person, self-interest moves them away from Jesus and one another unless it fulfills a self-interest. Each searches to better their viewpoint, resulting in outcomes of jealousy, breakdowns in relationships, and competitive parties.

We are confronted with the question as to how there can be unity beyond all the diversity.

When we humbly stand under the judgment of God, we stop judging one another.

Humans are made to be free by this Lord and to be free for Him. Through this freedom, we come to have fellowship with one another in His love.

While humans seem far apart in the diversity of their individuality, humanity does exist in a web of relationships.

In these developments, a common responsibility emerges when neighbors acknowledge one another.

The command of God is always a command for freedom in connection and companionship with the other. No exit is provided to escape this calling.

God always provides opportunities for what is right, wholesome, and friendly with one another. Longstanding conflict depends on abstract complaints that fuel the distance. There are natural differences to work through. These should be engaged for the greater goal of peace.

Under God's command, we are always on our way to fellowship with the other.

We are each called as members of the human family to invest in making an honest contribution with our gifts. All are called to build up the common life and not destroy it.

Barth notes that the exhortations of Romans 12–13 are not addressed to the private lives of Christians. It is about the life of Christians in relation to one another.

The summation of this life together is to follow the law of love, which fulfills the whole law.

This vibrant love is awakened by the Holy Spirit and guided by Him with a flame of passion for serving with joy. The whole life of the community is directed to the service of its master.

Love lives in the community. Therefore, service is its natural outcome.

All that Christians owe the world is to love one another. When love is alive among Christians, God's good work will go on in the inner circle and extend to the whole world.

The Church cannot exist in separation from the world. It must stand for all who are caught up in the world.

Having been reconciled to God, Christians now accept their part in the ministry of reconciliation.

God is patient. He will give humans time to recognize His grace, and the Church time to proclaim it.

Leaders of the state may function as servants of God.

The Church lives within the graceless order of the state, revealing its ultimate meaning and purpose, living its own characteristic life that bears witness to grace.

The Christian life of love includes involvement in the work of the state. But the Church must remain the Church, following the causes of its Lord, and fulfilling the law of love.

The Church is constituted by those who are weak and those who are strong. It is diverse on many levels. It creates the prism of humanity present in the Church, all needing grace and called to service.

The soundness of our faith is shown in our concern for peace and building up the Church and our neighbor's faith.

3. God's good *command unifies each person*. When we are not at one with ourselves, we will not be at one with one another.

When we lack inner stability and steadiness in ourselves, we lack constancy in our relationships.

Being in harmony with self and others cannot be seen as preparing to be right with God. God's presence and address bring harmony to self and relations with others.

Humans live with an inner conflict when resisting the command to love.

In the pursuit of fighting for oneself, one fights against oneself. One realizes their greatest fear: being alone.

When then turning to others, our own disquiet and turmoil accompany us. Internal conflict becomes relational conflict. This dynamic is what we call the law of sin and death.

The law of the Spirit of life does not divide; it unites and connects as it is heard and accepted. It "unites the individual in himself and then makes him an instrument and messenger of this harmony to others."[3]

Moral principles have the opposite effect. They awaken desires excluded by God's command. They employ human attempts to take control.

God's command releases humans from the position of opposition.

- It begins by telling the human they are not their own master.
- It opposes the foolishness of human attempts to control one's life instead of accepting grace.
- It demands that one live according to the fact that God is for us.
- It sets one within the peace of God's acceptance.
- It grants the ability to live a life maintained and protected by God.
- It commands us to live in peace by the law of the Spirit of life.

We must learn to recognize the concept of individual persons only when considering the community. "Private life" as such is not the concern of Paul in Romans.

Humans are wholly mortal in the flesh, entirely susceptible to life in contradiction to God, which leads to death.

Humans are also indwelt by the Holy Spirit, who raised Jesus from the dead and gives them hope.

Living in the human tension between the flesh and the Spirit, we need exhortation and renewal to conform to God's life and will. We live in a tension that requires ongoing attention.

---

3. *CD* 2.2, § 38, p. 727.

Christians are called to leave their disharmony behind by the work of the Spirit.

By the love of the Spirit, Christians are called to live and act in peace with themselves and one another.

Christians are to act outwardly as they are inwardly, despite conflicts. They are to take responsibility in the world.

Who is the Christian? The Christian is one who belongs to the Lord. Inwardly and outwardly, we are messengers of His peace.

 COMMENTARY:

- Barth is invested in discovering the claim of God that brings actual change to human lives.
- Rather than a set of actions, Barth unfolds the command of God as a call to belong to Him with all our being. This approach departs from all other forms of ethics. It addresses our being in relation, not in compliant performance.
- As we remember Him in our acting and being, our willing is shaped as a response-ability.
- The prime directive for God is to have humans as covenant partners who live and love by the will of God.
- For Barth, ethics is a way of showing up, walking with God every day, and acting like those who correspond in life together.
- Barth affirms God's grace as His making Himself responsible for us.
- We do not add any merit to our righteousness; we simply and profoundly live a life of gratitude.
- Independence is not a choice for the people of God; that was the outcome of the fall.
- The Bible mediates the command of God as His personal presence, so that God speaks to His people by His Spirit.
- The ethics proposed by Paul are always expressed in relationships, in a life of interdependence, and not judged as an act of an individual.

 CONCLUSION FOR THE CHURCH: Barth is developing a strategy to renew the body of the Church. This possibility happens by reorienting churches from self-focus to operate within the personal sphere of the living God. In this section, the behavior of the Church is realigned with the One who has decided from eternity to be for His people. This adjustment takes as a specific form the command of God to love God, neighbor, and self. We must begin by living in the orbit of God's personal presence.

Barth's concern in this section is that ethics has become principle- and rule-oriented. Thus, it misses the essential dependence of the Church on its head, Jesus Christ. The content of God's ethical venture is expressed in God's covenant; it addresses and claims His people as His own. He expects them to act as covenant partners in personal interplay. We are partners with God, having been claimed by God. In all our ways and actions, we are to acknowledge that we belong to Him. Only in relation to Jesus, by the Spirit, can authentic, ethical life be nurtured.

 INSIGHT FOR PASTORS: Although parents often send their kids to church so they will become "good," this individualized and externalized expectation misses the mark. The trajectory of that thinking is one of self-improvement or living by the rules. Barth, in this section, hopes to make a major shift from becoming a better Christian by oneself to growing as part of a community where we learn to live with mutual love in the sphere of God's embrace.

Pastors must take care never to preach principles of controlled behavior that are not bringing us to live face-to-face with Jesus and to be led by the Spirit. We are not to do the "right" thing according to book knowledge or traditions that have lost their orientation and context. Instead, because we are loved, we love. Because Jesus is with us, we act in a manner appropriate to resonate with His love. We do not ask, "What would Jesus do?" but "What are we to do because we are walking in His presence?" He is present, not a distant memory. Ethical training involves depending on the presence and command of God to love others every day. We can tell stories that illustrate; we just cannot make them into concrete norms that violate the wisdom of learning to listen to Jesus by the Spirit.

INSIGHT FOR THEOLOGIANS: As theologians, we need to be consistent in beginning with Jesus. This means not interpreting all the exhortations of the Bible and systems of ethical thinking to be good. Those become systems of human control and management that serve human goals. They are human prescriptions, not God's mobilization to bring us to live within His service.

The God revealed in Jesus does not work within the parameters of human usefulness. That is an illusion of human control seeking the good. The theologian must disillusion ethical thinking that furthers human agendas. Instead, we are called to attune our thinking to be personal, contextual, and entirely driven by the present actuality of God's will to do the good and loving thing. We discover by listening to Jesus. Then we pray for insight regarding the wholesome and friendly thing to do.

We are encouraged to envision anew a realistic theological ethic. This point of view acknowledges that God is speaking, taking specific forms of engagement that fulfill His unconditional love. Our theological thinking points to and places us before the known God. From that vista, we apprehend what is unknown, as the fresh claim of love blows in each situation.

? CLARIFYING QUESTIONS: Do you feel the urge to summarize the exhortations of the Bible and follow "Christian principles"? *Or* does your theology immediately turn your attention to the living presence of Jesus, to listen and discern what good and loving thing He is doing here and now?

CHAPTER 20

GOD'S GRAND TRANSPOSING

§ 39. *The Command as the Judgment of God*

 FOCUS STATEMENT: In this final paragraph (§ 39) of *CD* 2, Barth focuses on God's intent to bring humanity into harmony with His eternal life. His intent is His loving judgment; thus, "The Command as the Judgment of God" plays out God's freeing purposes.

Jesus has shifted humanity from its *dissonance*, with its clash and tension with God, back to *harmony*. To be in tune would achieve an agreement for appropriately belonging together.

Jesus' life and ministry transpose us to a whole new key, attuned to what was previously inaccessible.

In this final section, humanity is moved to take the harmony offered by God. He provides unheard-of resonance for humans. His resounding, echoing character brings the life of God's future into our present. Or, one might say, humans are transposed into God's eternal key.

Transposition involves moving a piece of music to a new level. For this section of Barth's development, we hear the human's life as a sinner in *dissonance* brought into harmonic *consonance*. Beyond that, the symphony becomes an invitation to the life of freeing joy. This is called *resonance*, echoing out from the harmonic consonance. Jesus prepares us for reverberation into His musical future. And the Holy Spirit tunes our ears to hear and our feet to dance.

INTRODUCTION: This is a short finale to *CD* 2. It maintains our focus on knowing the God revealed in Jesus, who loves in freedom. As the final focus, it resounds with the judgment of God's love for humanity. The word *judgment* can sound legal, but try to hear it as the outworking of God's eternal love to restore what failed in the God-human relation.

God's love unreservedly creates space for honest relationships. This honesty requires a candid acceptance of human sinfulness and self-will. It also necessitates an acceptance of God's profound acts of forgiveness and restoration. The presupposition in God's judgment is that God justly works in Jesus to treat us as His own, acting for the good of all. The execution of His judgment is in the death and resurrection of Jesus. He deals with our failure and brings God's forgiveness. The purpose of God's divine judgment is to bring new life with Him.

||||| **CONTEXT:** *CD* 2.2
Pages in Paragraph: 49 pages (pp. 733–81)

Subsections
1. The Presupposition of the Divine Judgment
2. The Execution of the Divine Judgment
3. The Purpose of the Divine Judgment

📖 **TEXT:** § 39. The Command as the Judgment of God

OPENING SUMMARY: As God is gracious to us in Jesus Christ, He judges us. He judges us because it is His will to treat us as His own for the sake of His own Son. He judges us as in His Son's death He condemns all our action as transgression, and by His Son's resurrection pronounces us righteous. He judges us in order that He may make us free for everlasting life under His lordship.[1]

✠ **SUMMARY:**
1. The Presupposition of the Divine Judgment (pp. 733–41)
God deals with humanity in His command, both in His claim upon us and His decision regarding us.

God's command is a definite event, not an abstract idea. Its character is one of judgment. This event includes a verdict with a sentence that has been fulfilled.

In the *eternal decree* of God, we find the beginning of all the works and ways of God in the election of grace.

God's *divine judgment* brings us to the flip side of this decree. The verdict is God's decision in the face of God's judgment, which is to be for us.

In the atonement, we see the judgment of God at work.

---

1. *CD* 2.2, § 39, p. 733.

This insight into God's command directs our attention to the center of Christian truth.

- God wills the reconciliation of the world with Himself.
- God judges humanity in His command.
- God causes reconciliation to become a fact.
- God is in His act of reconciliation, fulfilling all His ways and works.

We are now prepared to explore *how* God is God in all His encounters with His creation and creatures.

God must judge humans. We are measured, weighed, and assessed.

Real humanity is disclosed as God judges our true nature with His ultimate competence in His task as the Lord.

In the end, God judges humanity because He treats us as His own.

Humans can never measure up when judged by God's yardstick. We will always stand condemned and found wanting.

- We are incapable of making ourselves anything other than what we are.
- God has already received us into a relationship with Himself.
- We now belong to God and stand under His providential care.
- God makes us responsible as His possession under His command.

Only in the context of God's original and true love does the possibility of judgment come.

Even in anger, God's judgment is always a demonstration of God's burning, passionate love.

God does not will to be without us. He wills to be with us and do what love commands.

If we do not hear the "Yes" of God's command given in love, we do not hear Him at all.

Having been loved by God before we could choose, we act to confirm His decision.

If we do not listen, we have every reason to fear judgment.

God's love and faithfulness, grace, and compassion, are manifestations of the seriousness of His love.

God has given us Himself in Jesus for a direct relationship with Himself. There is nothing more to give than everything.

We follow Him as we go with Him into God's judgment. He is the reason we can go without fear. He has taken to Himself that which over-comes humans.

Jesus allows the judgment on us to overtake Him. We may now stand with Him; His glory covers our shame and judgment.

To obey is to accept the invitation to belong. We may rejoice as we sub-mit to the embrace of this One judged in our place.

All of us have been given over into Adam's death. We are all condemned in him. Jesus has fulfilled the sentence of death on our behalf.

God fulfills His judgment in Jesus. The One who is judged is His eter-nally Beloved.

What is accomplished in Jesus Christ is that God has given His Son to be the sinner who must bear wrath, condemnation, and death. What stood in the way has been destroyed so that we might live for God.

In love for us, the Father has made us His children by making His Son our Brother.

We deserved to be abandoned, but He has claimed us as His own.

We have benefited from the whole love of God fulfilled in Jesus, who removed what separated us and gave us what we lacked and needed. Our task is to hold on to Him.

We are joined as a family in the household of God as those who belong. There is only joy, not fear, in the face of God's judgment.

2. The Execution of the Divine Judgment (pp. 741–63)

In being confronted by God's command, humans are clearly in violation. We may want to claim ignorance of the command, as well as how it speaks to us, or to deny that it has any claim on us.

The proof that humans are sinners is that they deny or dismiss the charge of violating God's command.

God hates this lie we tell ourselves and that we defend our detachment. We also develop a propensity to hate or resist God and our neighbor instead of loving them.

Honesty includes a recognition of the problem that precedes our ability to respond to it.

However, our ignorance and resistance do not hinder God's command that is in full force for all humans. Resisting love leaves us as violators, choos-ing rebellion and alienation.

Consequently, we become useless in living out God's love. We are lost in ourselves and estranged from Him.

We would like to have nothing to do with Him who has done all for us.

We resist seeing ourselves as God's property and behave as though we belong to ourselves.

Our resulting state is one of unfriendliness, unresponsiveness, willfulness, and lovelessness.

We stand aloof. We think we know better than God. We maintain the right to judge good and evil from our perspective. We believe we are better off on our own than living in the freedom of the children of God.

When we're called to responsibility, we take flight. We are not prepared to be honest with what God asks of us, much less fulfill it.

How can we stand with such a bold contrast when God commands us from His goodness, which is right, friendly, and wholesome?

God honors us, whatever our attitude may be. But we do not accept His sovereign command.

This dilemma makes sense of the execution of God's judgment for us. We have failed to live the one thing He asks. The blackest sin is to deny we are sinners.

The secret of the command of God is that it flows from grace.

Grace is like a light in the darkness for a blind person. We cannot speak of colors to a blind person; color is a dimension unavailable to their natural senses.

We cannot escape the darkness or see the colors of grace until we recognize our blindness and receive the gift of sight.

God judges in such a way to reveal our sad state *and* God's glad grace that precedes and completes His restoring work for us.

The execution of God's judgment is the death of Jesus.

Jesus is righteous in our place. He is obedient for us. He acknowledges our sin. He drinks of the bitter destruction that follows our offense. He has done this for us.

- He bore our guilt.
- He suffered the wrath of God on our behalf.
- Because He confessed and atoned in our place, our sins are forgiven.
- In Jesus Christ, God has found us as we are.
- By His goodwill, He now sees us in His Son.

In place of every weak theory of God comes a powerful theory in practice—namely, our actual relationship to God.

- All that God originally had to say to us is said to Him.

- What we have to say to God is properly expressed by Him.
- We now repeat what is said in the conversation between God and His Son.

In Jesus, we are each addressed as a sinner, a lost child. We also each confess ourselves as a sinner, embraced as we are by Him.

That I myself should reject the name sinner is made impossible. It is nailed to the cross. It can only die with Jesus.

Divine judgment has been executed as God gives His command and is gracious to us in Jesus Christ.

By the Son, the Father speaks to us. By the Son, we speak to the Father. By the Spirit, we are brought into unity with the Son.

Now, we are readied to live as those who are in the wrong, still expecting every good as we live with an honest confession.

We ought to fear nothing more than our attempts to return to denial again.

Still, we must speak to be reminded of our sin and guilt. We talk about the judgment of God, who in His love and mercy addresses the fundamental problem of humanity concerning God.

The *first* word of divine judgment points to our alienated state of being. This reality is revealed in the act of Jesus addressing this fracture. The goal is to restore us from our helpless state.

The *second* word of divine judgment is that God in His love puts us right with Him. Having seen our sorry state, His grace acquits us and brings forgiveness.

We must never forget that God's judgment alone brings forgiveness of our sins and our justification.

God's command is given to us. Do we respond with joy in obedience? No. In varied ways, we revolt, resist, and turn away.

We are transgressors before God, and as such, we are in need of God's grace.

It is not God's intent to enslave humans in the state in which He finds them. He does not constrain or batter us with His holiness or our lack of holiness.

God commands those who are already elected, loved, and blessed by Him. We are His covenant partners, whom He will earnestly seek and restore.

God's faithfulness always overrides our unfaithfulness.

Humans are rebels against God's command. At the same time, humans are the objects of God's love. Being beloved came first and endures throughout.

God also knows us in a state beyond being sinners. We are known as the object of God's fidelity, despite our infidelity.

God maintains His claim on us. He stands against all claims of Satan and the false claims we have regarding ourselves.

God's supreme justice is at work despite our shortcomings. We are justified, made right with God, by His fellowship with us, not by His standing against us.

Forgiveness does not mean forgetting. Forgiveness does not mean the sin is reconsidered not to be a sin. Honesty about sin is still needed.

If sin does not grieve us, and we do not maintain a sense of responsibility toward God, then we misunderstand forgiveness.

Sin "being forgiven" means God does not primarily look on us with our sinful intentions and actions.

God's forgiveness means seeing us through His love for us, honoring His covenant, and being faithful to His perfections.

God does not allow our sin to carry the day with Him. Neither does He see sin as our primary essence or condition because He cancels sin. He sees us as snow white because He makes us that way.

The forgiveness of sins is total acceptance of sinners, a radical reversal of the actual being with which we stand before God without excuse.

God cannot lie, so He cannot call what is evil good. But by His powerful compassion, He can make that which is wicked good. He can make the sick whole. He can make the weak glorious. He can make the dead alive.

Simultaneously, we remain totally sinful and totally righteous.[2] These two states of being do not cancel or exclude each other.

We may affirm that our being righteous is more significant than being evil, as they stand in opposition. God can create good out of evil, but never evil out of good.

We can only understand the justification of sinners from the actual event of the execution of divine justice.

The resurrection of Jesus is the divine proof that sinners may stand before God and be proclaimed righteous.

Jesus was the bearer of our sin. He took our place before God. He accepted God's sentence and our punishment.

As our representative, Jesus died for sin. As our Lord, He rose from the dead, accomplishing the task of making sinners right with God.

---

2. See Jeff McSwain, *Simul Sanctification: Barth's Hidden Vision for Human Transformation* (Eugene, OR: Pickwick, 2018).

Jesus stands before the Father at the cross, burdened with the weight of sin and guilt for every person. The love of the Father sent Him there. The Son is faithful to be sent there by His Father and for us. He includes us.

This God remains faithful to the transgressor. He remains faithful to Himself. He remains true to His promise in Jesus. He is committed to receiving us, free from condemnation.

God gives us what is secured in Jesus: condemnation for our transgression and adoption through our election in Him.

In knowing the truth of our being, God opposes evil with His "No," and despite all that has gone wrong, He says "Yes" to humans.

Decisive help is given to humans who have nothing to bring to God.

- Jesus covers our shame and nakedness.
- Jesus gives us His righteousness and acceptability.
- Jesus speaks for us.

Sin and guilt only persist when humans do not live by the forgiveness granted to us and do not let Jesus speak for us.

We must keep before us the fact that "Jesus lives, and I in Him" as our most honest truth.

We must understand justification with proper Christ-focused depth and breadth.

If we think we can be free other than by God making us free, we will not be free.

The secret of Easter day is that Jesus is the fulfillment of God's reconciliation.

The Holy Spirit is the secret of bringing us to share in what happened between the Father and Son on Easter day.

The work of theology must always transcend itself so that it becomes a theology of the resurrection, meaning it draws us into a life of prayer with the resurrected Lord.

In prayer, we are unleashed to live in dialog as a dear child of the Father.

The life of faith is in Jesus Christ, and this is life in the truth. We live according to the judgment of God, who overcomes the lie and grants us the truth of His freeing love.

3. The Purpose of the Divine Judgment (pp. 764–81)

God wills to have humanity for Himself. This affirmation is the fundamental presupposition of God's judgment.

God's judgment elects humans to be in a covenant relationship with Himself.

The judgment of God does not leave us unchanged. It is the secret of every hour in human life.

In walking this way, affected by the judgment of God, one has a new orientation and subsequently is a new being. One can never be the same or go back.

God is persistently faithful and unflustered, resolute in self-will.

We do not forget that we are accused and pardoned. This awareness prepares us to accept who we are and who we are becoming.

Regardless of our attitude and interpretation, we are judged by the command of God. This verdict means we are directed to love by the grace of God.

We are sinners caressed by divine forgiveness. This condition is our everyday existence.

To be judged by God's command means to be directed, corrected, and reoriented by it to live sustained by the grace of God.

We are called to faith. This change of mind means to be oriented to the facts, not to have an unexamined belief. Faith engages objective reality; it is not a subjective wish or ideal.

Faith is the corresponding of our thoughts and attitudes to the judgment and grace of God. We agree to be directed by God's grace. These affirmations become explorations into the nature of reality and its meaning for us.

Faith is our acknowledgment that God is doing right by us. We live before God, and with God, both judged and glorified as those He has made His own. Sin means departing from this relation.

We believe when we consider and confirm God's judgment in what we do. We do not merely listen as spectators to an ideal theory.

Faith is never a matter of human capacity or competence. It never originates in humans. It answers God. It is lived with gratitude.

Faith is a gift of the Holy Spirit, but it is engaged as a conscious and intentional act of the human. One still acknowledges God's judgment that we are forgiven sinners who live by grace.

When we are referred to God's grace, we must respond "yes" without hesitation.

Faith is always born in an act of repentance. This change of mind is not a moment of choice but is an awakening, the conforming of our lives to correspond to God's grace each new day.

We walk in the light of each day, believing we are forgiven and given to walk in obedience. This is a life of repentance.

Humble obedience is what God wills of those judged by Him:

1. Know the reality of sin by knowing that it is forgiven. Otherwise, the truth is shaped by some other judge or form of judgment.

   What we know apart from forgiveness is in error.

   The Penitential Psalms speak from the perspective of recognized sin and God's forgiveness.

   Repentance is more than remorse, self-accusation, and despair. It is an awakening to the goodness of God that deals with our sin and God's forgiveness. God's kindness leads us to repentance (Romans 2:4).

   Sinners who are not forgiven simply do not know or admit sin. Their energy will be focused on defending their own honor.

   We cry for mercy only when we know we are lost. Then we find that God has already accepted and redeemed us.

   We pray, "Forgive us our trespasses," as those who know they need forgiveness. We are at the end of ourselves and open to believing in Him.

   - To believe is to admit that God wants to make a new beginning.
   - To believe is to consider ourselves as belonging with those who need help and can be helped by God's mercy.
   - To believe is to act as one who might pray and gain insight and hearing and healing from the One who directs.
   - To believe is to accept the conflict within us while believing God is with us as our friend.
   - To believe is to consider the protective response of God if we begin to seek our security elsewhere.
   - To believe is to resist our own unfaithfulness in the face of God's faithfulness.
   - To believe is to be directed to works of repentance and obedience to good works, which are pleasing to God.

   All transformation comes in acknowledging the fact that we are to live surrendering our self-centered dignity and power.

   Good works are the fruit of repentance and not from our own activity.

2. Learn to recognize sin so that we may be confident that we are forgiven.

   Without an accurate knowledge of sin, humans will ignore it, see it as a character defect, or forget it exists.

   Where God's condemnation is heard, His pardon is heard as well.

Only in establishing the lordship of God over a human does justification do its work of freeing us from our contradiction to God's mercy and grace.

God takes us seriously in a manner not accessible to self-knowledge. He arranges Himself by our side. He takes up our cause. He liberates us.

Our knowledge of sin requires that we recognize that God is right in His Word.

The transformation of forgiveness begins a new relationship as we are our authentic selves before God.

- To believe is to turn from our own opinions about good and evil and to stand in God's truth.
- To believe is to turn from our own cleverness and to obey the works that can be done under the Lordship of Jesus.
- To believe means turning from our laziness and turning to the joy and readiness that comes from knowing God's goodwill.
- To believe is to know the place of those who know mercy.

Faith is the birth of a new person who can and will do what is pleasing to God.

God's purpose in His judgment is to direct people toward the life He has promised. This includes preparation and the exercise of a new life. This is called sanctification. It is God's work in transforming us to His mode of life.

When we speak of eternal life, this pertains to human life invested with God's glory.

- This is a life God has granted to create fellowship with Himself.
- This is a life within God's openly revealed love, echoed in His corresponding freedom.
- This life is proper to God and shared by humans as unshakable, indestructible, unceasing, and unlimited.
- This is a life in which God sees Himself. He sees us as humans. He is not able to be seen by humans. Outside Him, we do not truly see ourselves.
- This is a life of participation in God's joy, which was always the purpose of human life.

- This life is already waiting for us here and now, but we can only rejoice in a disjointed way. It has doubts and passing moments of joy that give hope.
- This is human life in harmony with the life of God, His angels, His people, and all of creation.

God saw and willed harmony from before the foundation of the world.

Everything displayed in the history of God's covenant, including His command and the judgment reflected from it, is a preliminary form of human life in preparation for eternal life.

In faith, we accept the outcome of God's purposes and grasp the provision of God's orientation of us toward eternal life here and now. Eternal life is present, even as it is concealed.

We are made free for eternal life here and now, but we do not yet live it. Every act of God moves us toward this freedom.

We live in the morning glow of a promise already fulfilled and yet waiting to be recognized and grasped.

He is our hope. He saves us from eternal death. He prepares us for eternal life, daily dying to self and nourished for faith in Him.

Sanctification is the work of God preparing humans for life with God.

Faith is the human answer to God's work, bringing us into correspondence.

Too often, we look in vain to fulfill our own sanctification. These are more of a sunset of our attempts rather than the sunrise of God's new day.

Those who live with trust in their own ability, focused on this life, end up trying to have faith in themselves.

Our sanctification is the ground on which we stand. It is the horizon before us that is our frontier. It is the air we breathe.

Our life finds meaning in sanctification by God. It is as concealed as it is real.

The voice of the Good Shepherd speaks to us.

Theological ethics reveals God's command, given to humanity by God through Jesus.

Jesus is a holy God and a sanctified human in one.

- In Him, God commands, and humans obey.
- In Him, we have the command of God; and through Him, God has claimed us as His own.
- In Jesus, what is hidden is revealed.

- Jesus already lives the life to which we are connected.
- To say we are sanctified is to acknowledge that we are what we are only in relation to Him.
- Our faith in Jesus adds nothing to all that is fulfilled in Him. We can only confirm and accept His reality.
- We accept Him. We participate in Him. We live as those who are His.

The voice of the Good Shepherd demands that we die to the old person and live in His life as a new person.

No other voice can transpose us from disobedience to obedience in the form of repentance. No other voice can win our hearts. No other voice can make us believe.

Jesus does not speak from afar. We hear Him when He speaks our name to us.

In obeying His voice, we are set free. To remain in disobedience is to stay in shame and hiding.

In this faith, we are holy, set aside for God and His life with us.

This faith gives glory to its object, to Jesus. We live a full life as an echo of His call.

- Jesus calls to us.
- We hear Him and at the same time receive His Holy Spirit.
- Consequently, Jesus' relationship with His Father is awakened and repeated in us.
- The Father knows us. We know Him. This corresponds to how the Father knows Jesus and Jesus knows His Father.
- Living within this relationship of correspondence is living in the Holy Spirit. We are sealed within the certainty of the resurrection. We are prepared for eternal life.

Life in the Spirit is a joyful, humble life lived courageously. Knowing we are the children of God, we have confidence that we are brothers and sisters of Jesus, in the family of His Father.

We listen to the call of God and respond to it with an attitude of thankfulness and worship.

In hearing and responding, we confirm that we are accepted.

We act now as those on whom the dawn has come. We live and breathe and pray in the givenness of grace.

The One who teaches us to pray intercedes for us in His Spirit. The Father hears and answers Him, and with Him hears and responds to us.

We will never tire of praying for the grace of prayer itself, yearning for more as we joyfully cry out, "Come, Creator Spirit!"

 COMMENTARY:

- Judgment is a complex subject. In this section, we must keep in mind that God's love is the only motive that informs God's command as judgment.
- When we judge that we want to marry someone, it is a "yes" to them that is a judgment of "no" toward all others.
- A doctor judges our physical state to bring health and avoid disease. Health and healing are for our good and must deal with what ails us. This echoes God's judgment.
- Grace is a judgment. It is the starting point of God's ways and works. It requires God to condemn what destroys and deal with it, as He did on the cross.
- In this chapter on judgment, we need to see that it is all ultimately restorative.
- Barth is emphatic regarding the human need to recognize our sin. This honesty is not to create guilt; it is to be truthful about who we are apart from God, accept God's gift freely, and come home forgiven.
- The judgment of God falls on Jesus. In Him, we see the cost of our condemnation. We also see the new life that we have in Him.
- God has willed a harmony from the beginning and is still attuning humanity to His intentions.
- It is a norm of human life to accept lies about God, each other, and ourselves. These lies must be crucified.
- God wills friendship, and we have failed this in many ways.
- God's judgment involves two sides of the same coin: sternness toward sin and grace for belonging.
- God desires life in harmony. Jesus comes singing a new song and asks us to join in.

 CONCLUSION FOR THE CHURCH: Calling people sinners is unpopular. In this section, Barth advocates for an honest acknowledgment that we are sinners and forgiven. To not recognize we are sinners is to imagine we do not need God. To not affirm that we are forgiven is to live in fear. The Church needs to understand both the depth and impact of sin and the grandeur of God's grace and forgiveness.

This section is about judgment. As with all doctors, diagnostic assessment comes from a desire for health. Accepting that there is an actual problem precedes willingness to treat the problem. We need a change of mind to accommodate required changes for health. Health ultimately comes from God. As persons and as church communities, we must recognize that we are inclined to go our own unhealthy way. We easily neglect God, or worse. Only by recognizing that God has come to free us will we turn back to God. Then we will be set right in all the consequential relationships. God has made us right with Him (justification) so that we may walk as children of His family and kingdom (sanctification). This relational health is the ethical goal of the Church in consonance with God so that we resonate with Him in all our attitudes, activities, and relating.

 INSIGHT FOR PASTORS: Some pastors are accused of going light on sin. They emphasize the love and grace of God. We must appropriately convince and remind people that they are sinners. We are not bad; we just fail at loving God, neighbor, and self. We can tell the story of Jesus to understand how human alienation destroys relationships and how God stands against diseased humanity. God rightly diagnoses the disease that is killing us. We never need to stop telling the truth about this condition. We can be bold in love.

We can also boldly affirm that God's judgment is the treatment plan that restores humans. We never lose the old disease. However, we can live freely, dependent on God's grace and forgiveness to enjoy a future with Him. In fact, grace is the reality that brings each person to know they are a beloved child.

This section calls for pastors to preach that all people belong to God. But we still have the DNA to run away from God. This combined truth leaves us humble and grateful. We confirm what God has done in bringing His children home, with a belonging that shapes who we are intended to be from now until eternity. Our goal is to help our congregation live as God's dynamic community, belonging to Jesus by the Spirit and living in the love of the Father. The diverse and unified community shares and exhibits the personal life of the kingdom of God. We pray the Spirit makes it so!

 INSIGHT FOR THEOLOGIANS: As theologians, we helpfully correct mistaken views about God. Few doctrines are more detrimental to the gospel than thinking that God is against humanity, especially sinners. We need clarity that can affirm both that we are sinners and that grace abounds all the more.

God's justice addresses the reality of human existence. When we say we are totally depraved, it is true insofar as we are not plugged in, like an appliance without power. We are without God by inclination. However, we can never escape the sphere of God's care. The power of His love frees us to live again.

God's command sounds something like, "Come home to Me." This statement is not so much a law that needs interpretation and clarification. It is a direct call to come home to where we belong. Theology that works within this call is less abstract and philosophical. It is personal and direct. Our response is an acceptance of the summons to come home. God's command is invitational and relational, compelled by the dynamics of God-human relating, as God says, "Come." This recentering insight is the theological equivalent to Einstein's shift in the field of science. We move from seeing everything in distinction (many parts) to now apprehending everything with relativity (field theory). We no longer talk about a single person as an individual separated from God. God's presence is intractable, so we can never be alone. We need Barth's theology that welcomes the richness of the transforming crescendos and diminuendos as we journey together with God and one another as sanctified sinners.

? CLARIFYING QUESTIONS: Does your theology measure human performance by God's eternal laws and render judgments based on human compliance? *Or* does God's ultimate judgment proceed from the cross as a "No" to human sinfulness, accentuated in His death, awakening us to His "Yes" in human restoration, accomplished in the resurrection?

PART 4

VOICES VALUING
CD VOLUME 2

The Doctrine of God

THE VALUE OF *CD* 2 FOR BIBLICAL STUDIES

Chris Tilling

Chris Tilling is lecturer in New Testament Studies at
St. Mellitus College, London, and visiting lecturer in theology
at King's College London. He is author of numerous works
on Pauline theology, including *Paul's Divine Christology*.

In my own field, facility in theology is not always as valued as it should be. "Better to let the chips fall where they may and let the theologians put the pieces back together again." And while this mindset contains a grain of truth, it forgets how theological the practice of reading the Bible is. Theological commitments are involved in how one prioritizes and understands cause and effect, how one negotiates the nature of time and history, and, naturally, how one undertakes the task of understanding in reading. It is difficult to corner off theology as an archaism, unimportant to "proper historical work" when trying to understand texts that speak so often about God in a way that presumes a measure of coherence. Whether reading Romans 1 or Mark 15, theology is built into the warp and woof of the analytic and critical task. Even methodological naturalism implies commitments vis-à-vis theological truth-claims. So biblical scholars, especially those who are sure they *aren't* doing theology, often *are* doing theology. Just badly. And this, in turn, can undermine their ability to interpret biblical texts.

So how do we develop a theological facility that supports the historical-critical task? *CD* 2 is just the right medicine for biblical scholars like me who know they need help. This is so for at least two reasons.

First, there is Barth's sophisticated theological engagement with Scripture. Not only does he practice extensive biblical exegesis in his "Doctrine of God," but his reading of the Bible, particularly of Paul's letters and the Johannine literature, helped define key steppingstones in his developing theological vision. His theological work was thereby deeply indebted to critical biblical scholarship. Of course, his exegesis wasn't without its problems in *CD* 2 (arguably especially in relation to the question of Israel), but the seriousness with which he took Scripture in his theological work remains a benchmark. And this is so because *CD* 2 presents the kind of theology that *demands* patient and extensive scriptural analysis.

This is to be contrasted with at least three tendencies in the contemporary theological scene.

1. There is a propensity to shallowness that is disguised by layers of fashionable hermeneutical novelties. It results in predictable assertions about the *reader* that tend toward boring moralism and do not facilitate or require substantial engagement with Scripture.

2. Then there are tendencies to biblicism, especially in popular church and conservative circles. "The Bible said it; I believe it" approach tends to work by plastering over difficult questions and ignoring critical biblical scholarship. It then takes up a defensive rather than creative posture.

3. Finally, there is a tendency to speculative theology that has little to do with robust exegesis of Scripture beyond plucking out a few verses here and there. The result is an atomized "proof text" approach to the Bible that merely serves up nuggets as launch pads to random metaphysical conjectures. It thereby pirouettes away from the deep structures and patterns within Scripture's bumpy witness.

CD 2 is effectively a broadside against such trends, ancient and modern. Barth's project in § 25–27 ("The Knowledge of God") involves interrogating the unevangelized metaphysical commitments of speculative theology. Here we do not find highfaluting philosophical guesswork that tends to leave many biblical scholars rather cold—and suspicious. What is more, § 32–35 ("The Election of God") presents a theology that not only plumbed the tradition but moved beyond what had come before in new and creative ways. As such, it pushed readers back to Scripture to reassess received exegetical understandings. Therefore, there is little resemblance to naïve biblicism or preachy hermeneutical posturing. It should be remembered that *CD* 2 was penned before and during the Second World War. And in this time of unique upheaval and challenge, Barth modelled the pursuit of a scripturally robust and engaged dogmatics with almost unprecedented energy and depth. Yet he was persistently conversant with the wider tradition and biblical scholarship that provided claims that demanded exegetical assessment—in this way, reading *CD* 2 facilitates the ongoing conversation between systematics and biblical scholarship that many of us are still trying to cultivate.

But there is another aspect to Barth's theological engagement with Scripture that delights a biblical scholar like me—namely, his emphasis on Christology. This brings me to my *second* point: Barth pursued his creative task in a way that honors that which is central. The key to reading the New Testament, unless one deliberately wants to mislead, is *the centrality of Jesus Christ*. To canvas the obvious: Hebrews is all about the centrality and priority of Jesus Christ throughout. Paul's letters are the same in this regard. Thus, Paul said that for him "to live is Christ and to die is gain" (Philippians 1:21) and that he considered everything as rubbish compared to the surpassing value of knowing Christ Jesus his Lord (Philippians 3:8—there's the center of Paul's theology, if you're looking for it; not "justification by faith" or some elaborate overarching narrative that has a nice space for Jesus as a subpoint.) The Gospels aren't primarily about the reconstruction of putative communities or lessons in morality, but are biographies *of Jesus Christ*. Revelation is the "revelation of Jesus Christ" ... and so on. I trust the point is made. Barth, too, presses the centrality of Christology in both his account of theological epistemology throughout *CD* 2 and then into his beautiful account of election.

So these are two general reasons why I, as a biblical scholar, appreciate Barth's doctrine of God: it is full of fruitful theological engagement with Scripture that demands patient exegesis, and it is centered on Jesus Christ. But I can be more specific, so now I will present for your reflection two exhibits, speaking primarily as a scholar of Paul's letters when reading *CD* 2.1.

Exhibit one: theological epistemology. Barth's theological epistemology in *CD* 2 is profoundly Pauline and emerges from his reading of Paul. God reveals God (see, e.g., 1 Corinthians 1:21–2:16) and the "primary objectivity" speaks of *God's* knowledge, including within it a "secondary objectivity." So, Paul speaks of God's knowledge of us (Galatians 4:9; 1 Corinthians 8:3). What is more, in theological knowledge, God remains the Subject for Barth, and so it is not our possession—as also for Paul (1 Corinthians 8:2). And for both Barth and Paul, theological knowledge is grounded upon the revelation of Christ, not apart from it (Galatians 1:11–12; 1 Corinthians 3:11). Nevertheless, such knowledge, while true, remains penultimate to

> Though writing in response to very different circumstances and out of very different philosophical axioms, the theological epistemologies of Paul and Barth overlap in astonishing ways: both are Trinitarian, relational, eschatological, Christological, and participatory.

the advent of Jesus Christ (1 Corinthians 13:9–10, 12), and in this way it demands not the appreciation of spectators but the love and devotion of disciples (1 Corinthians 8:3, 6, etc.). Though writing in response to very different circumstances and out of very different philosophical axioms, the theological epistemologies of Paul and Barth overlap in astonishing ways: both are Trinitarian, relational, eschatological, Christological, and participatory. Reading *CD* 2 is a tremendous way to calibrate theological epistemology in ways that reflect central Pauline intuitions.

Exhibit two: Paul's gospel. Too many scholars default to an impoverished theological vision when reading Paul, albeit with varying degrees of sophistication. Often, they assume a theological account that, to a greater or lesser extent, emerges from within modernity and makes particular sense only in those terms. As such, it offers "common sense" accounts of human agency, the individual, metaphysics, and more besides. This in turn encodes words such as *justification*, *faith*, and *law*, among others, which are then read back into Paul's Greek, leading to interpretative problems. In its less sophisticated versions, Paul effectively becomes a cipher for a theology that thinks there are two eternal "destinations" and that God makes *possible* a way of escape from the judgment that awaits those who aren't perfect. This escape can only be actualized by the human individual as they exercise faith in a particular understanding of the atoning work of Christ. The result is that Paul is taken to baptize such sloppy theology because the New Testament reader naively thinks that they have objectively found all this in his letters; they merely "let the chips fall where they may." And because this account of the "good news" is thereby supposedly given the stamp of Scripture's approval, it becomes *God's* view of matters, which then generates a host of other, more sinister problems. Not only is this kind of theological account of Paul's gospel widespread in the church at the popular level, but it also infests the imagination of sophisticated and learned engagements with Paul in numberless commentaries and accounts of Paul's theology.

But Barth was a better reader of Paul than this. He recognized, with a particular force that still needs urgent attention, that Christ's centrality is a bomb underneath this theological gruel. Numerous scholarly readings of Paul also need their theological frameworks evangelized by the gospel of Jesus Christ. For Paul, as well as for Barth, the actual comes before the possible, and this is particularly important in grasping Paul's account of the gospel. It is, in the first place, *a story about Jesus Christ with Trinitarian contours*. For Paul, God sends Jesus Christ in unconditional love (Romans 5:8).

Christ thereby assumes the enslaved and sinful human condition (Romans 8:3; 2 Corinthians 5:21) to the point of death on a cross. However, Christ's death is not the end as God raises Christ from the dead by the power of the Holy Spirit (Romans 6:4; 8:11). Christ is raised "at the right hand of God" where he "is also interceding for us" (Romans 8:34). But in the second place, and this is where the first ripples of that aforementioned bomb start to be felt, *Christ's story, for Paul, is our story too.* And so Paul says, "I have been crucified with Christ" (Galatians 2:20), and not just him: "we are convinced that one died for all, and therefore all died" (2 Corinthians 5:14). "Our old self was crucified with him" (Romans 6:6). This means that all are included, and *actually* so, in the death of Christ. But there is more. For "we know that the one who raised the Lord Jesus from the dead will raise us also *with* Jesus" (2 Corinthians 4:14), and "if we died with Christ, we believe that we will also live with him" (Romans 6:8). This is why the "much more surely than" and "grace abounding all the more" logic of Romans 5 means what it says, and why Paul writes, "Just as one man's trespass led to condemnation for all, so one man's act of righteousness leads to justification and life for all" (Romans 5:18 NRSV; cf. 11:32). The *actual* comes first for Barth and Paul. Thereby they showcase the beauty, universality, and vitality of the gospel. Thus, they theologically relocate and Christologically ground our confident response to Christ in faith.

All of this is woven deeply into Barth's reworking of the doctrine of election in *CD* 2.2. Just look at how often Paul's texts pepper Barth's small print in § 33–35! Barth has captured the heart of Paul's account of the gospel herein. Writing as a Pauline scholar, I think Barth was absolutely right to insist on the primacy of the election of Christ and our election *in Him*. This is also why Paul's language of *predestination* makes sense, not as ammunition to speculate about a God behind or above Jesus Christ, but as key to Paul's pastoral efforts to encourage Roman followers of Christ (see Romans 8:29–30). Barth grasped this dynamic with peculiar force, and for that reason, he remains one of the most important resources available for understanding Paul's letters, for "the doctrine of election is the sum of the gospel because it is the best of all the words that can be said and heard" (§ 32; translation mine).

THE VALUE OF *CD* 2 FOR SYSTEMATIC THEOLOGY

David Guretzki

David Guretzki is executive vice president and resident theologian at Evangelical Fellowship of Ottawa, Canada, and author of *An Explorer's Guide to Karl Barth* and *Karl Barth on the Filioque*.

Anyone can make statements about God. One person might claim God is the force that energizes the universe. Another might state God is an ancient grandfatherly figure who occasionally, or never, checks in on us earthlings. Still others contend God is a being who maintains distance from mere humans while eternally contemplating his own beauty and perfection. All these claims—and many others—have been made about God. The problem: Which is correct? Or better: Are any of them correct?

Traditionally, systematic theology tries to bring together, in coherent and consistent ways ("systematically"), all that can be said about God. But any attempt to provide a coherent representation of God may ironically have absolutely nothing to do with what God is actually like. Tolkien painted a compelling literary picture of the world called Middle Earth, yet—as far as we know!—it does not actually exist. Thus, a fundamental question for systematic theology is, *How do we distinguish between personal opinion, projections, or fantasies about God from what God is really like, if in fact he exists at all?*

Barth's *Church Dogmatics* 2, "The Doctrine of God," is a logical progression from *CD* 1, "The Doctrine of the Word of God," or the doctrine of revelation. In *CD* 1, Barth argues that theological claims about God must be evaluated against God's self-revealing. What does this mean? A simple analogy might help.

Most reading this essay have never met me and do not know me personally. If I asked a random reader to write a short biography about me based only on having read this essay, it would be impossible to put together a coherent, let alone complete, biography about me. Beyond surmising I'm a male theologian with possibly some Polish heritage, any point beyond that would be speculation. Why? Because I haven't revealed anything personal about myself in this essay. Thus, the degree to which you could accurately write my biography depends directly and proportionally upon how much I share with you.

Similarly, in *CD* 1, Barth makes the point that a systematic theology, a biography of God, as it were, must be judged by one criterion: Does it align with God's self-disclosure? In other words, a doctrine of God can only be based on God's self-revelation. *CD* 2 is Barth's attempt to do just that.

Barth argues in *CD* 2 that, based on the self-disclosure of God in Jesus Christ as witnessed to in Scripture and in the church, two things about God may be asserted.

First, God is *free*. That is, God is not compelled by anything or anyone outside himself to reveal him. God reveals himself to us on his own accord. He would not have had to reveal himself, but that he did is evidence of his freedom.

Second, God is *love*. That is, by freely choosing to reveal himself to us in the human person of Jesus, he shows that God is a God who *desires* humans to be in relational fellowship and communion with him. We would not make the mistake, in other words, of concluding that a purely self-contemplating, self-isolating, or nonpersonal God is loving.

In *CD* 2.1, Barth also makes an extremely important contribution to systematic theology by entering the long-standing theological debate over whether God can be known in any way other than through self-revelation. One method sometimes offered by theologians is to seek knowledge of God in nature or creation, which, not surprisingly, has been called "natural theology."

Barth denies the fruitfulness of natural theology in learning about God, arguing that any theological inquiry into anything other than God's self-revelation would violate God's self-giving love and freedom. Accordingly, seeking knowledge of God in ways other than in his self-revelation is analogous to writing the biography we talked about earlier by hiring a fact finder to investigate my backyard or analyze a painting I produced, without ever just talking to me. You may choose to use that method, but in so doing, you bypass the option of asking me freely to tell you about myself. And without personal connection to or dialogue with me, there is no compelling way for you to conclude whether I am a loving person because love can only be experienced and confirmed in relationship.

Not all agree with Barth about natural theology, but the value of Barth to the debate is noteworthy. To align with Barth's mode of systematic theology yields one portrait of God while seeking knowledge of God through nature yields another. Although the two methods may produce some overlapping conclusions, it is clear that the former method can conclude some things that the latter method cannot.

In *CD* 2.2, Barth engages in what many have considered one of the greatest contributions to systematic theology in the past half-millennium, his doctrine of election. In the history of theology, fiery debates have raged over whether God elects some to be saved and others to be damned. Here Barth offers a novel way through the debate by again building on the assertion that if God is to be known, then our knowledge of him needs to be based on what God has freely revealed.

Barth's complaint is that historically theologians have too often viewed election as if it were a decree of God that occurred sometime in eternity past and therefore beyond knowing or understanding. Consequently, election becomes a "secret" God has hidden from us—a secret that may or may not line up with what he has otherwise revealed about himself. The implication is troubling: What if everything we know about God by his self-revelation is a cover-up for what otherwise may be an arbitrary, spiteful, illogical, scheming, electing God who wants to deceive us into thinking that he is truly love, only to damn us all in the end?

Contrary to election as a hidden decree of God, Barth offers an alternative model of election in *CD* 2.2 that insists God's electing activity must be part of the revelation of his character, not relegated to an inscrutable ("hidden") decree in eternity past. Barth argues that God's electing action is centered on Jesus Christ, who is the perfect, visible, historical revelation of the Father. For Barth, election is not hidden but visibly open to inspection in Jesus Christ. Barth thus concludes that Jesus of Nazareth is both the deity who elects and the human who has been elected to be the Saviour of the world. As Barth puts it, Jesus is both the subject and object of election, the One who elects and the One elected.

Viewed this way, the doctrine of election is not a doctrine hidden from human knowledge but a doctrine at the centre of the gospel itself. Indeed, Barth announces, "The doctrine of election is the sum of the Gospel."[1] Why? Because in election we not only find out that Jesus Christ, the One who reveals the Father, is the One who lovingly and freely chooses humans,

---

1. *CD* 2.2, § 32, p. 3.

but he is also the One chosen first on behalf of all humans throughout time and history, and thus the only One through whom humans are able to come into communion with God. This is good news indeed!

In summary, what is the value of *CD* 2 for systematic theology?

First, Barth insists upon a basic "rule" of systematic theology in which the only claims about God that should be accepted are those shown to align with how God has revealed himself. All other claims are speculation.

Second, Barth demonstrates that any doctrine that cannot be spoken of from the perspective of Jesus Christ, who is the perfect self-revelation of God witnessed to in Scripture and testified to in the Church, stands outside a truly systematic account of a self-revealing God. Here Barth reclaims the doctrine of election by grounding it in Jesus Christ, the One who both elects and is elected for human benefit and salvation. To follow Barth is to affirm that Jesus Christ is a primary focal lens for all systematic theology.

> To follow Barth is to affirm that Jesus Christ is a primary focal lens for all systematic theology.

Third, it is difficult to conceive of any future systematic account of election that does not consider Barth's novel approach to the doctrine. Future theologians may or may not be convinced by his Christocentric doctrine of election, but they certainly cannot ignore it. If they reject it, they will need to offer a convincing alternative that does not relegate election back into the category of "hidden decrees of God," which can only be asserted but not actually aligned with how God has revealed himself in Jesus Christ.

THE VALUE OF *CD* 2 FOR PASTORS

Earl F. Palmer

Earl F. Palmer is pastor at large through Earl Palmer
Ministries, Seattle, Washington. He has pastored the
University Presbyterian Church in Seattle, the Union
Church of Manila, the First Presbyterian Church of Berkeley,
and the National Presbyterian Church in Washington,
DC. He has served on the Board of Trustees of Princeton
Theological Seminary, Board of Directors of New College
Berkeley, Board of Governors of Regent College, and Board
of Trustees of Whitworth University, and is the author of
many books to enrich pastors and the people of God.

Karl Barth, professor of theology at the University of Basel, Switzerland,
writes in the preface to volume 2 of *Church Dogmatics* in the year 1942 and
alerts readers to the atmosphere he faced ten years earlier with the rise of
division among the people. He states:

> We were plunged into the Third Reich and the German Church-
> conflict. From that time the affairs of Europe and finally the whole
> world hurtled with increasing violence into the crisis which still
> engulfs us. By the very nature of things I have not been able to devote
> the last ten years solely to dogmatics, as was my intention in 1932. Yet
> dogmatics has been ever with me, giving me a constant awareness of
> what should be my central and basic theme as a thinker.[1]

Barth felt compelled to address the evolving crisis. This leads me as a
pastor to ask: Where do pastors today turn for guidance in teaching and
leading the church? I find that Barth's work takes us to the heart of pastoral
work informed by theology that leads to God's decision of grace.

    In this writing, I hope to clarify for pastors the central basis from which
Barth builds the doctrines of the gospel in *Church Dogmatics*. He asserts

---

1. *CD* 2.2, preface, ix.

that the doctrine of God gives direction for how the Church can face the challenge of establishing a solid foundation upon which to form its beliefs and to act. Barth uses the word *election* to help us understand God's decision on our behalf and the importance of God's decision as the guidelines.

THE ORIGIN OF GRACE IS GOD'S DECISION

Barth starts with a clear affirmation that the doctrine of election is essentially God's gracious will. He begins by stating the struggle, and titles the first section "The Problem of a Correct Doctrine of the Election of Grace."

> The doctrine of election is the sum of the Gospel because of all words that can be said or heard it is the best: that God elects man; that God is for man too the One who loves in freedom. It is grounded in the knowledge of Jesus Christ because He is both the electing God and elected man in One. It is part of the doctrine of God because originally God's election of man is a predestination not merely of man but of Himself. Its function is to bear basic testimony to eternal, free and unchanging grace as the beginning of all the ways and works of God.[2]

What is the source of the doctrine of God's election decisions? Karl Barth is both brilliant and wise as he takes the reader on a journey through several defining possibilities in finding the meaning of the doctrine of predestination. He states that the doctrine must be based in its origin. As written by the apostle John:

> In the beginning was the Word, and the Word was with God, and the Word was God. He was in the beginning with God. All things came into being through him, and without him not one thing came into being. What has come into being in him was life, and the life was the light of all people. The light shines in the darkness, and the darkness did not overtake it. . . . And the Word became flesh and lived among us, and we have seen his glory, the glory as of a father's only son, full of grace and truth. (John 1:1–5, 14 NRSV)

Building on the prologue in John's gospel, we understand that God is in the beginning when the Word was made flesh and dwelt among us. This knowledge helps us grasp the importance of God's decision in the very

---

2. *CD* 2.2, § 32, p. 3.

beginning, when He ordained Himself to come alongside humanity. In freedom, He chose to set us free. And for us, in spite of ourselves, this act of grace has allowed us to know the living God through Jesus Christ.

Barth makes a humorous yet crucial point when he describes our search for who the living God is:

> The truth is that we continuously stumble across that name in matter and substance. We stumbled across it necessarily. For as we proceeded along that path, we found that that name was the very subject, the very matter, with which we had to deal. In avoiding the different sources of error, we saw that they had one feature in common: the negligence or arbitrariness with which even in the church the attempt was made to go past or to go beyond Jesus Christ in the consideration and conception and definition of God, and in speech about God. But when theology allows itself on any pretext to be jostled away from that name, God is inevitably crowded out by a hypostatized image of man. Theology must begin with Jesus Christ, and not with general principles.[3]

The stumbling leads us to Jesus Christ. *Barth establishes the doctrine of the Church on God's decision to make Himself known in the person of Jesus Christ.* For me, as a pastor, this has been the basis of the theology that has guided my ministry.

With this in mind, Barth posits that God's prior decision was to become man so that we might know Him and His love for us. Herein lies the truth for guiding our decisions and behavior. This leads to the subject of predestination and prompts us to seek out the source of the doctrine of God's election decisions.

THE TEACHING OF THE CHURCH MUST HAVE ITS SOURCE IN THE ORIGIN

In the section titled "Foundation for the Doctrine," Barth takes the reader on a journey through several defining possibilities that underwrite all theology in finding the meaning of God's two decisions: to be God and to be human. The challenge for the pastor is always to be faithful to what God has revealed as attested to in Scripture. Barth highlights, as mentioned earlier, that there is a common feature when the Church attempts to go beyond Jesus Christ:

---

3. *CD* 2.2, § 32, p. 4.

The Christian church lives on earth and it lives in history, with the lofty good entrusted to it by God. In the possession and administration of this lofty good it passes on its way through history, in strength and in weakness, in faithfulness and in unfaithfulness, in obedience and in disobedience, in understanding and in misunderstanding of what is said to it. . . . The concrete significance of this is that dogmatics measures the Church's proclamations by the standard of the Holy Scriptures, of the Old and New Testament. Holy Scripture is the document of the basis, of the innermost life of the Church, the document of the manifestation of the word of God in the person of Jesus Christ. We have no other document for this living basis of the church; and where the Church is alive it will always have to reassess itself by this standard.[4]

The decisions are prior, destiny decisions. Therefore, they are described as predecisions. For Barth, all dogma rests on the basis that in the time before we were to know God, God decided to provide the foundation for our beliefs and actions for the good of humanity. He continues to establish his point by addressing questions. He asks us to reflect on four ways that ways of doing things through the Church emerge and, in so doing, instructs us to focus on the origin of such.

(1) Does the doctrine best develop along the lines of the tradition of the Church? He answers negatively.

[The] Church tradition cannot be the subject and norm of dogmatic effort. We need to ask what is the true origin of every doctrine. On the contrary, in this matter, we must ask even of the best ecclesiastical tradition what is true origin, and to what extent it may or may not be properly adapted in this respect to serve as an ancillary.[5]

Doctrine cannot just be what the Church wants; doctrine must be based on its origin in Christ. God limits Himself and makes Himself one with Himself. In so doing, He gives Himself to man—an action not merited by man. I read from this citation that, as a pastor, I must be careful not to put God in the place of supporting my own idealism.

(2) He then sets before us the usefulness of doctrine. Barth reflects on whether this doctrine is useful for the cure of souls. He is saying that being

---

4. Karl Barth, *Dogmatics in Outline*, trans. G. T. Thompson (New York: Harper & Row, 1958), 10–11, 13.

5. *CD* 2.2, § 32, p. 36.

practical is not enough. He states, "But at a deeper level we must enquire into the foundation of the doctrine in the divine revelation quite independently of its value and usefulness."[6] He reinforces the concept: "The true origin cannot be dominated by ecclesiastical/religious tradition."[7] God's revelation in Scripture provides the essential guideline.

Barth writes that "it is not simply a matter of proceeding to develop the doctrine along lines which allow the tradition of the Church to rightly prescribe and lay down in advance the theme and program of its exposition."[8] He clarifies further: "We must enquire into the foundation of the doctrine in the divine revelation . . . and the doctrine must then be constructed and expounded in accordance with that foundation. Only as that is done will the fact and the extent of its didactic and pedagogic value and usefulness really emerge."[9] As a teaching pastor, I have learned to focus on the decision made by God and hold the doctrines accountable to the decision of God.

(3) The third possibility Barth brings up is that of basing the reliability of doctrine on "datum of experience, presumed or actual."[10] He asks, "Is it right to go to the Bible with a question dictated to us by experience?"[11] He warns us that if a doctrine is grounded by experience, then it is dependent with reference to man in general. So as not to negate the importance of our personal relationship with Christ, Barth adds, "Thus the divine election does indeed determine and ordain the plenitude of the private relationship between God and every individual."[12] The gospel honors the importance of human experiences based on the concrete love of God at work in human lives. The saving event is always an event because of God's action.

Barth's position has guided my role as pastor and helped me focus on the gospel in teaching and preaching. It helps me remember not to use my experiences as the primary teaching point and to resist the temptation to fall into the over telling of my story. Yes, the experiences we have of God's grace are illustrations of truth, but the truth is rested in the source of grace and the witness in Holy Scripture and the experiences of real people with the Lord Jesus Christ. What He says and what He does are congruent.

(4) The concept of God as "omnipotent will, governing and irresistibly directing each and every creature ascending to his own law is another

---

6. *CD* 2.2, § 32, p. 37.

7. *CD* 2.2, § 32, p. 36.

8. *CD* 2.2, § 32, p. 35, 36.

9. *CD* 2.2, § 32, p. 37.

10. *CD* 2.2, § 32, p. 38.

11. *CD* 2.2, § 32, p. 38.

12. *CD* 2.2, § 32, p. 43.

foundation that presents and one which must be taken seriously and all the more carefully avoided."[13] Barth reminds us that "God is prior to everything else. Otherwise He would not be God.... He is the Almighty and in His almightiness He is free.... But here error can also arise ... supposing God's power is irresistibly efficacious power in abstract naked freedom and sovereignty as it were."[14]

Barth explains more on this naked freedom and sovereignty statement. He argues:

> If we allow God's self-revelation and the testimony of Scripture to prescribe our concept, then the Subject of election, the electing God, is not at all the absolute World-ruler as such and in general. We cannot, therefore, understand the election as one of the main functions of world-government exercised by Him, nor can we deduce it from, or establish it as a consequence and application of that one basic principle.... God is not at all the absolute world ruler as such and in general.... God is the One whose freedom and love have nothing to do with abstract absoluteness or naked sovereignty.... The true God is the One whose freedom has determined and limited Himself to be God in particular and not in general.[15]

Karl Barth points out the hazard of naked freedom as if it is in our power to impose on others without the restraint of Scripture. He makes clear that God does not institute government. This translates into a warning for those who want to claim that God has put a particular individual in a place of absolute power. The exercise of authority needs to be checked and balanced by the greater revelation through Jesus Christ as the source of truth and grace.

So, what is Barth teaching? As a pastor, I have been inspired by the highwater mark of Barth's theology. It now comes sharply into focus and reminds me of his commentary on the second article of the Apostles' Creed: I believe in God the Son:

> "Tell me how it stands with your Christology and I shall tell you who you are." This is the point at which ways diverge, and the point at which is fixed the relation between theology and philosophy, and the

---

13. *CD* 2.2, § 32, p. 44.
14. *CD* 2.2, § 32, p. 44.
15. *CD* 2.2, § 32, p. 49.

relation between knowledge of God and knowledge of men, the relation between revelation and reason, the relation between Gospel and Law, the relation between God's truth and man's truth, the relation between outer and inner, the relation between theology and politics. At this point everything becomes clear or unclear, bright or dark. For here we are standing at the centre.[16]

GOD'S DECISION FACES UP TO THE SINFULNESS OF MAN

This brings us again to the place of Jesus Christ. The passage reads:

The election of grace is the eternal beginning of all the ways and works of God in Jesus Christ. In Jesus Christ, God in His free grace determines Himself for sinful man and sinful man for Himself. He therefore takes upon Himself the rejection of man with all its consequences, and elects man to participation in His own glory.[17]

This belief moves us to the center and explains the sacrifice of Jesus Christ on the cross of Good Friday and the victory over death on the third day, Easter.

The opening sentence in "The Election of Jesus Christ" is like a bolt of lightning on a clear night. Barth begins this all-important section as follows: "Between God and man there stands the person of Jesus Christ, Himself God and Himself man, and so mediating between the two. In Him God reveals Himself to man. In Him man sees and knows God."[18]

Barth sketches in a few but totally encompassing words. These words "in its simplest and most comprehensive form the dogma of predestination consists in the assertion that the divine predestination is the election of Jesus Christ."[19] That essential simplification is the best introduction to the all-important theme of the Holy Bible fulfilled in the man, Jesus of Nazareth. Now we know the basis of our worth and our belovedness with its widespread implications. Again, to emphasize: this is God's choice and revealed in Jesus Christ. Barth has helped me throughout the years of ministry to accept the reality that all of us have our failings and to accept the fact that God's decision is in our favor. With this in mind, as a pastor, I can present hope.

Barth does take on the idea that in the midst of the election, God's decision is that humanity is given the freedom to make choices, recognizing that

---

16. Barth, *Dogmatics in Outline*, 66–67.
17. *CD* 2.2, § 33, p. 94.
18. *CD* 2.2, § 33, p. 94.
19. *CD* 2.2, § 33, p. 103.

humanity would make bad choices. What determines the outcome? As for humans, our freedom is also a part of God's choice. "Man was willed and chosen by God with his limitations, as a creature which could and would do harm . . . by the misuse of its freedom."[20] Barth continues with this discussion to clarify: "We will take evil seriously for what in its own way—but only in its own way—it is allowed to be on the basis of the eternal divine decree. But we will not make of the two-fold nature a dualism [between good and evil]."[21] With the encouragement from Barth, I can teach/preach that the greatest power resides in good.

To give the total picture, however, we must grapple with the idea that there is a disproportion in man's poor use of freedom. However, Barth continues: "We are no longer free, then, to think of God's election as bifurcating into a right and a leftward election. There is a leftward election but God willed that the object of this election should be Himself and not man."[22]

Karl Barth was very familiar with the letter to the Romans, where St. Paul raises the question, "Who is to condemn?" I interpret this question as, "Who has the right to say the last word?" Paul answers, "It is Christ who died, or rather, who was raised, who is also at the right hand of God, who also intercedes for us" (Romans 8:34 NRSV). God disarmed evil in the eternal "Yes" of Jesus Christ. With this, we are to remember that all humans are beloved by the election of Jesus, very God and very man. The last word undoubtedly belongs to Jesus. It is not up to man to judge. As a pastor, I have to remind myself and others of this truth.

Barth's teaching about the gospel is front and center. He invites every one of us to meet the eternal man Jesus and to know His presence in our lives. We are given the gift of belovedness, and with this, we are told to share this love with others. Pastors are wise to remember that this is the greatest commandment and a most important tenet for our beliefs and actions. In the calling to be a pastor, it is best for us to recognize how to follow Jesus faithfully and pay attention to the witness of His life. To do so, Barth strongly advises to test the church's dogma against the prechoice that God made through Jesus Christ on our behalf.

A PERSONAL TESTIMONY

This thinking of Barth has influenced me to be a teaching pastor who focuses on the centrality of Christ and to present the gospel in a way that the

---

20. *CD* 2.2, § 33, p. 169.
21. *CD* 2.2, § 33, p. 171.
22. *CD* 2.2, § 33, p. 172.

listener can discover for him or herself the Jesus of history. I remember that through Jesus God revealed His decision to take upon himself our failings. I don't ever want to forget that He calls us "beloved," and in so doing, He has set us free to love one another and share His grace.

With the freedom that God gives us, it is critical for pastors to make choices according to His will. This concept translates into being aware that the authority of the pastor rests in the authority of God, whose decisions set the stage for my role as a servant leader. As a pastor, it is my calling to understand God's decision on our behalf and to teach from that perspective of truth and grace. The overall lesson I have learned from Barth is to keep my focus in teaching on the centrality of Christ and what that means for me and for those in my surround. His grace remains as the origin—then, now, and forever. Although we do not fully understand this, we know that He has determined Himself. In so doing, we are in His hands as the "Creator, Reconciler, and Redeemer"[23] in life and in death.

> The overall lesson I have learned from Barth is to keep my focus in teaching on the centrality of Christ and what that means for me and for those in my surround.

It has been my privilege to be a pastor among those of differing views on the way the church makes decisions and/or how to move into action yet not get lost in the list of agendas that divide. Barth, in *Church Dogmatics*, has helped me to keep the focus of Christ as the main teaching point and not get sidetracked with the peripheral issues. I commend the lessons from Barth as the guiding principles for serving God as he intended for us to do in our calling to ministry.

---

23. *CD* 2.2, § 33, p. 171.

THE VALUE OF *CD* 2 FOR ORDINARY PEOPLE

Wyatt Houtz

Wyatt Houtz is an ordinary person and a software
developer in Woodinville, Washington. He is a contributor
to the PostBarthian, https://postbarthian.com.

HOW I LEARNED ABOUT KARL BARTH

I first learned about Karl Barth from friends I had met at church. I enjoyed
reading theology as a hobby, so they invited me to their weekly theology
discussion group. They were familiar with all my favorite theologians, such
as Jonathan Edwards, John Calvin, and Augustine of Hippo. They were particularly enthusiastic about an unfamiliar theologian named "Bart."

Each week this "Bart" was mentioned many times, so I looked him up.
I could not find "Bart" referenced in any of my theology books. The closest
name I found was "Karl Barth." If the "h" was silent, then this would be the
"Bart" I was looking for. But all the references to Barth I saw were negative—
opposite of how my friends spoke of him. My friends later confirmed that
"Bart" was "Karl Barth." They explained that the negative comments
were started decades ago by a few influential evangelicals who could read
German and attacked Barth before translations of his books were available,
and people have been repeating these same petty things to this day.

I asked for a second opinion of Karl Barth from some other theology
enthusiasts that I had known for a long time, and I was surprised to hear
them dismiss Barth (as my church friends predicted) for petty reasons such
as Barth's writings were too long, too difficult to read, and didn't have any
pictures! Another complained that Barth had moral failures in his personal
life, eliding similar personal issues that Edwards, Calvin, Augustine, and
many other theologians have had. I adopted these petty criticisms for a time
because I received them from *people I trusted*.

HOW I CHANGED MY MIND ABOUT BARTH

Sadly, many ordinary people will never read Karl Barth due to petty criticisms
of him by people who have never read him. Thankfully, my church friends
had patience with these criticisms I parroted and encouraged me to read Barth

firsthand. I resisted for a long time, until one day I found volumes 2.1 and 2.2 of *Church Dogmatics* in a glass case reserved for old books at a used-book shop. The books were too expensive, but a few months later I providentially received a half-off coupon in the mail and decided to return to the store and buy them.

I began reading the *Church Dogmatics* 2.1, "The Doctrine of God." It was challenging at first. *Church Dogmatics* was formatted differently than the other systematic theology books I'd read. It included many small-print paragraphs with untranslated Greek and Latin sentences that I had to skip over. Nevertheless, it didn't take long for me to realize that Barth's theology wasn't all bad. Like a rock hound discovers a gem after the hard labor of digging, like a hiker who encounters a waterfall after hiking far up a trail, I read. I admit that I didn't change my mind entirely about Barth until I had read several more volumes of the *Church Dogmatics*, but it was *CD* 2.1, followed by *CD* 2.2, that set me on the right path. In the end, I remember being overjoyed to admit to my friends that they were right and I was wrong about Barth.

I learned two big ideas from the *CD* 2 that have been exceedingly helpful to me as an ordinary person. The first is Barth's rejection of natural revelation in *CD* 2.1, and the second in *CD* 2.2 is his reconstruction of the doctrine of election around Jesus.

CHURCH DOGMATICS 2.1

In *CD* 2.1, Barth argues that it is not possible to obtain knowledge of God from studying the natural world. Therefore, attempts to learn about God by looking inward or by observing the natural world inevitably result in an idol, and idols closest to the truth may be the most dangerous. We may not say anything true about God unless God first speaks to us, and God has only done so through Jesus. What is God like? Karl Barth's answer is Jesus. May God be known by studying triangles, biology, philosophy, religions? Barth's answer is *Nein*! I've been thinking about Barth's response for years, and I still struggle with it. Must we still say *"No!"* to what we learned from Auschwitz?

Barth's rejection of natural revelation has garnered criticism and dismissal without seriously considering how simple and direct his insight was. For instance, Wayne Grudem writes, "His [Barth's] radical rejection of natural revelation has not gained wide acceptance; it rests upon the unlikely view that Rom. 1:21 refers to a knowledge of God in theory but not in fact."[1] Ironically, Barth's small print analysis of this very same verse (which is ignored by Grudem) was what impressed me the most about Barth's argument.

---

1. Wayne A. Grudem, *Systematic Theology: An Introduction to Biblical Doctrine*, 2nd ed. (Grand Rapids: Zondervan, 2020), 122n6.

One of my favorite counterstatements is by Flannery O'Conner, who was responding to another author when she said, "Raven is too given to *natural* religion and I distrust folks who have ugly things to say about Karl Barth. I like old Barth. He throws the furniture around."[2] O'Conner is right. Sometimes temple tables need to be flipped.

CHURCH DOGMATICS 2.2

The second great insight I learned from Barth is that election is the sum of the gospel. Election is a scary topic that circles the black hole of hell. Are we all orbiting the edge of a black hole, with some of us being pushed into it by God, or do people freely choose to dive into the singularity? Barth escapes this insolvable enigma with the simple realization that election is about Jesus. Jesus alone is simultaneously the rejected One and elected One. Election is transformed into the good news that Jesus was rejected (i.e., crucified) and elected (i.e., resurrected) not only for us but the entire world (1 John 4:14). Barth's analysis of Ephesians 1:4 was particularly clarifying; the object of election is not unknown but is specifically known in Jesus.

Sadly, many have hastily dismissed Barth's doctrine of election with a couple of proof texts and say that "to talk about God choosing a group with no people in it is not biblical election at all."[3] Statements like that can be easily dismissed by anyone who has read the first page of *CD* 2.2.

CONCLUSION

After I had finished reading *CD* 2, I learned that Barth had written this magnificent volume after being deported from Nazi Germany for his support for the Confessing Church and during a time that his brother Peter and son Mathias had died. As an ordinary person, I've learned so much from Karl Barth, despite the unfair criticism of him I've heard from other ordinary people. I've seen many beautiful vistas hiking through the trails of the *Church Dogmatics*. It's hard work, with many obstacles, but worth the effort. Enjoying Barth requires throwing the furniture around when resistance is encountered, but in the end, I believe that ordinary people who venture into Barth's theology will find a best friend.

> Enjoying Barth requires throwing the furniture around when resistance is encountered, but in the end, I believe that ordinary people who venture into Barth's theology will find a best friend.

---

2. Flannery O'Connor, *The Correspondence of Flannery O'Connor and the Brainard Cheneys*, ed. C. Ralph Stephens (Jackson: University Press of Mississippi, 1986), 180–81.

3. Grudem, *Systematic Theology*, 824–25.

THE VALUE OF *CD* 2 FOR MENTAL HEALTH

Andrew Howie

Andrew Howie is consultant psychiatrist and Fellow
of the Royal Australian and New Zealand College of
Psychiatrists, Auckland, New Zealand. He is author of
"Ethical Approaches to Dealing with Impaired Health
Practitioners" in *The Oxford Handbook of Psychiatric Ethics*;
"Cultural Values, Religion and Psychosis" in *International
Perspectives in Values-Based Mental Health Practice*; and
"What Does It Mean to Be Well?" in *Stimulus: The New
Zealand Journal of Christian Thought and Practice*.

Barth makes no explicit mention of mental health in the *Church Dogmatics*.
He acknowledges the concerns of health as a field separate from his own
concern.[1] Barth does not want to close his eyes to these concerns; rather, he
wants to establish a proper foundation for inquiry into the basis and content
of what theology has to contribute to human flourishing. In *CD* 2, Barth's
focus is first on God, establishing an understanding of the God revealed in
Jesus to affirm God's self-giving, and only secondarily reflecting on practical
human implications. This agenda in *CD* 2 provides a basis for mental health
to operate within a context that discerns and corrects an adequate science
in understanding God to provide insight into the responsive mental life of
the human.

While *CD* 2 is about the doctrine of God, it has important implications
for human health. Barth recognizes that a proper understanding of God
includes God's concern for humans. For him, "Health means capability,
vigour and freedom. It is strength for human life. It is the integration of

---

1. *CD* 3.2, § 46, pp. 431–32: "There are undoubtedly correspondences and connexions, agreements and relationships between psychical and physical conditions of sufficiency or lack, health or
sickness, strength or weakness, soundness or degeneration, between psychical and physical actions and
passions, conditions and experiences, achievements and omissions. They form a whole field of undeni-
ably genuine human living reality. It is the business of non-theological science, of psychology, physiol-
ogy and biology, to establish and evaluate these facts. From the standpoint of theological anthropology,
we have least reason of all to wish that the facts were otherwise, or to want to shut our eyes to them."

the organs for the exercise of psycho-physical functions."[2] Understanding the human must not begin with observing the human divided into distinct parts. A proper anthropology must begin with comprehending the whole person as uniquely seen in Jesus Christ. Jesus reveals the complete unity of humanity and divinity, creating a life of freedom. Barth deals with the reality of God, known in Jesus Christ, to reveal God's decision to claim humanity for fulfilled personal connection. Barth saw the need for an authentic assessment of the God before whom humans stand. Not only do we come to know the Creator, but we discover the roots of distress and dysfunction. The alienation has actual and imagined aspects, so inappropriate thinking and behaving arise due to not understanding this God.

Therapeutic roles within mental health seek a proper engagement with the specific, concrete, real circumstances, of other persons who present, transiently and functionally, in the role of patient or client. One "industry standard" for psychiatry, the *DSM 5*, diagnoses, codes, and classifies mental health disorders by asking whether a clinical syndrome identified by specific diagnostic criteria causes significant distress or dysfunction.[3] Any such assessment has a large subjective element on the part of the patient and therapist and leaves lots of room for clinician discernment. However, it points to the idea that a functional (adult) human being engages rationally and socially in interconnected ways. Knowing and adequately encountering other persons is critical for mental health. Barth focuses on the divine-human encounter, and this has implications for human function and dysfunction.

Barth's theology posits and engages with God as a subject, the initiator of the encounter. This God, seen in Jesus Christ, testified to in Scripture by the power of the Spirit, creates, reveals, and sustains humanity, first community and then the individual. The healing of suffering, distress and dysfunction are endorsed in Jesus' ministry as signs that God is with us. The challenge for us is to discover the implications of how human believing leads to human flourishing and not to suffering in the distressful consequences of an impaired relationship with God and humans. Dogmatics, for Barth, is a corrective science to remedy errors and realign restored thinking with reality—particularly in the church's understanding of God. This thinking, however, occurs within an epistemic context. In affirming any thing, object, principle, or set of consequences as "good," we thereby affirm (1) its axiological salience, (2) to some degree, the empirical *a priori* of its existence, (3) any

---

2. *CD* 3.4, § 55, p. 356.

3. American Psychiatric Association. *Diagnostic and Statistical Manual of Mental Disorders*, 5th ed. (Washington, DC: American Psychiatric Publishing, 2014).

internal consistencies implicit in its mode of being, (4) its telos (e.g., its being conducive to the good life), and (5) the presuppositions of our affirming it, the "hinges," the life context within which we make any given affirmation. Impaired mental health can disrupt each of these domains, through the pervasive disruption of thought, affect, and behaviour in psychosis, through the comparatively less disruptive though potentially distressing "neuroses," through the obliteration of cognition or the dementias and other brain disorders.

Barth invests the reality of human knowledge with the assertion of God, Father, Son, and Spirit as the context for human functioning.[4] His method requires a necessary empirical *a priori*, discovering the authentic nature of the other in actual history as his starting point.[5] He works from a Christocentric logic to align with the personal functioning of God and the corresponding dysfunction of humans.[6] His goal is a life of love, lived ethically before God in a responsive life of freedom.[7] All of this hangs within a history of thinking that is focused on our own experience, which requires corrective and constructive thinking to bring proper functioning in the God-human relationship.[8] This approach does not exclude human relating; it is the context of meaningful, authentic life together.

Both Barth and mental health professionals are concerned with human engagement with reality. In psychoses and neuroses, appreciation of reality, its content and evaluation, vary, as do the impacts on interpersonal relations. Barth is concerned with a loss of encountering the reality of God. Barth asserts that disconnection profoundly affects relationships and one's sense of reason, purpose, and capacity to overcome the distress of dysfunctional relating with God and humans. Obviously, these are not direct in correspondence but raise critical questions for human flourishing and dysfunction. Dementia lies outside the scope of Barth's work. Still, one might wonder about personality disorders like narcissism. Barth depicts one face of this state in the potentially disastrous misconception of the "elected leader." He describes this person as one who develops an unhealthy connection with a codependent community. As a harmful character, "the leader is the individual who in some fashion unites in himself the fulness of the election of grace, so that he is the elect, not on behalf of, but in place of others."[9] The "elected

---

4. *CD* 2.2 chapter 6, "The Reality of God."
5. *CD* 1.1, chapter 1, "The Revelation of God."
6. *CD* 2.2, chapter 7, "The Election of God."
7. *CD* 2.2, chapter 8, "The Command of God."
8. *CD* 3.4, chapter 12, "The Command of God the Creator."
9. *CD* 2.2, § 35, p. 311.

leader" takes the place of Christ but also reveals the problem within the person themself. There is much to be learned in the dynamics of disfunction, as Barth saw played out in his context, probably thinking of Hitler.

Disordered mental health impacts a person's social roles and impersonal relations. Barth is concerned with one's sense of connection and disconnection from God and neighbor. Barth has a vision of human flourishing based on the life of the God who loves in freedom, which makes this way of being a reality for God's creatures.

While God may seem hidden, Barth presents a revealed God, even in God's hiddenness. We humans, in our fullness of being, are hidden from one another. We are blind to who this God is and how to relate in loving and freeing ways. In a fear-based environment, people hide. Proposals from thinkers like Martha Nussbaum reflect a world of hiding that erodes our mental health and relational capacity.[10] Her model of human flourishing is contested, but she calls for a vulnerability that diminishes hiding. Human flourishing comes with vitality in bodily health and integrity; senses, imagination, and thought; emotions; practical reason; the freedom to affiliate with others; the ability to live in relation to nonhumans (animals, plants, the environment); play; and control over one's own environment. These require vigor in a unity of experience that does not withdraw from fear or attempt control. There is security, courage, and connection.

If one were to consider Nussbaum's categories through the lens of Barth's Christocentric thinking, it might bring a unity of thought with a diversity of applications. This move would correspond with Barth's ethics in the final section of *CD* 2, which avert from principals and think of life in a personal response to the love of Christ. This recentering removes the shame and anxiety of human judgment regarding failure. Nussbaum calls for vulnerability to move toward health and honesty in regard to our neediness and weaknesses. Barth displays a God who invites this honesty and vulnerability. This honesty, paired with the security of the love of God, opens the possibility of freedom as the outworking of love that is not categorized but lives in dialogical interplay.

Barth establishes a context that embraces the heart and soul of humanity, lived in the grace of the God who loves in freedom. This focus revives what is lost in contemporary mental health, which looks at distortions in the personality, how individuals think, feel, and behave, whether from

---

10. Martha Nussbaum, *Hiding from Humanity: Disgust, Shame, and the Law* (Princeton, NJ: Princeton University Press, 2006).

physical or situational sources. The quest to relieve distress and the causes of distortions is symptomatic in its starting point, searching for explanations in a scientific manner that may miss the complexity of the situatedness of relations.

As expressed in Barth, Trinitarian theology sets the quest in the context of a God who makes room for adequate interpersonal relations. Not all religions have a roomy God. Barth's God, known in the whole person of Jesus, provides a God who loves in a manner critical for mental health.

Barth makes visible what M. Scott Peck envisions as love, leaning toward or extending to another to help and not hinder. Peck says, "Love is the will to extend oneself for the purpose of nurturing one's own or another's spiritual growth."[11] Barth grounds our loving in the love of God extended toward us in Jesus. This proposal becomes the ground of becoming whole in Christ, a proper, dynamic, personal context for personal and spiritual health—for Barth, this understanding includes our mental aspect; it may not be separated from our being as whole persons.

God's election—God's choice to be for us and with us—deals with human distress and dysfunction.[12] Whether the distress is suffering from trauma, abuse, impaired thinking, or the dysfunction of human relations, health means finding relief and proper function appropriate to each person's life in relation to the other. For Barth, this not only includes God; it begins with God as the being who is Creator and Sustainer of all our contexts of loving. Human flourishing is not an individual human quest; it is the fruit of being restored to our Maker and consequently to all God's created works, including humans.

For Barth, the end of suffering for humanity is met on the cross. God's sacrifice of love, holiness, and all God's perfections reveal the scrambledness of humankind in its alienation and isolation, as well as the fulfillment of restoration and belonging.[13] This divine proposal contrasts with hope in humans having the means of overcoming human distress and suffering. Human agendas often end up as a collection of attempts by dead white males with reductionist theories. The flourishing of humanity by human rescue strategies has far to go. This deficit is true, both within the academy and for the populace, who are still clouded by fears of appearing broken to those who peer at their lives.

---

11. M. Scott Peck, *The Road Less Traveled, Timeless Edition: A New Psychology of Love, Traditional Values and Spiritual Growth* (New York: Touchstone, 2003), 81.

12. *CD* 2.2, chapter 7, "The Election of God."

13. *CD* 2.1, § 29–31, on the perfections of God.

All mental health theories make helpful contributions to aspects of human encounters and strategies for ethical life together. Ethics are the outworking of the good in service to society and its members. But each culture has its own sense of the good and the place of the individual within it. Cultures themselves are burdened with dysfunctional ways of relating. As the clinical director for Māori mental health, I encountered this when my patients endured me for some time but then got frustrated. The Māori have an intuition for whanaungatanga (connectedness) that I did not have ingrained in my work. Once I recognized I was out of touch, I had to ask, "How am I getting this wrong?" The elders had to acclimatize me to this rich, embodied, formative connectedness aspect within the fabric of their community to work within their categories. The command of God to love may seem general, but it has specific outcomes every day. These are not following the rule; they are responsive to persons in need.

Mental health has the opportunity to be personally and spiritually embracing of cultural distinctions, not in principle but in the context of the God who loves freely and unconditionally. At the same time, we can address the particulars of our situations as a shared compassion with the heart of God. This perspective calls us to belong to the family of God and treat each person with dignity and respect. In doing so, we respond to the command of God to love appropriately in each situation as a participation in God's love in action.

Barth calls us not to look firstly at the world or human wisdom for answers to our struggles. As my confirmation class taught me with a story from the Very Reverend Owen Baragwanath—when a boat full of servicemen with him as chaplain, was caught in a heavy fog, and they feared crashing on the shore, the call from the captain, who saw a church on the shore, was to "keep your eyes on the cross on the hill, and we will be ok." The *CD* do not tell us what to do to provide mental health for the tragedies of human mental health. But they position us to respond to the One who loves in freedom, orienting our work to the command to love. This focus creates the secure base for attachment that facilitates healthy attachments with a love of the other and self simultaneously, as proposed by Bowlby and developed by Ainsworth.[14] Churches can activate this secure love of God when rightly living within the grace and love extended to this community of care. When fear rules our emotions, we will default to fight or flight in self-preservation.

---

14. Mary D. Salter Ainsworth, Mary Blehar, Everett Waters, and Sally Wall, *Patterns of Attachment: A Psychological Study of the Strange Situation* (Hillsdale, NJ: Lawrence Erlbaum Associates, 1978), 22. See also Tim Clinton and Joshua Straub, *God Attachment* (New York: Howard, 2010).

In a loving, listening mode, which Barth promotes, we enter by the Spirit to share God's revealedness by being present as extensions of God's calm, loving context, creating a secure environment. This mode of operation shapes the body of Christ as a functional family, drawing life from its head with gratitude and then creating an atmosphere with a generosity of spirit that nurtures health.

The world of mental health is not alone in its challenges. Unfortunately, issues of faith, spirituality, and theology are a diminished part of the mental health conversation. However, churches and those who are people helpers also need insight. We need to understand why people are afraid of the church and God. We need to critique and correct our intruding agendas that derail the hope and help of God made known to us. We need to listen better to discern what is missing of the love of God in the specific person who is in front of us. We need rich dogmatics and sensitive spirituality to inform our development of providing mental health. We need a receptivity to the best of theology that speaks and heals. We need to develop the best mental health practices to address dysfunction with the love that frees specifically in each situation.

In conclusion, mental health deals with issues we bring to each encounter, to ourselves, with our community, and in our encounter with God. We even have to deal with our concerns in our encounter with *CD* 2. It is an invitation to discover the rich, personal context that calls for constructive reflection on what mental health hopes to achieve and what is missing. Even more, it is an invitation to see that the triune God is interested in the whole person as seen in the person of Jesus, who comes to make wholeness actual in our place and time.

THE VALUE OF *CD* 2 FOR SPIRITUAL FORMATION

James Houston

James Houston is on the Board of Governors and is professor emeritus of spiritual theology, Regent College, Vancouver, British Columbia. He is author of numerous books and articles on theology and Christian formation.

In volume 2 of *Church Dogmatics*, Barth presents Jesus as the One who loves in freedom, the unique image of hope in our thinking about being formed as Christians.

Barth presents the freedom of Jesus as the Son of God being who He is in all His acts. The uniqueness of God is His person, whereas other gods are false, as worshiped by Buddhists, Hindus, and Muslims. They are all nonpersonal. Formation requires personal engagement.

The biblical God is personal as He proclaims, reveals, and manifests divine love. Out of love, in freedom, He created all things: the cosmos, then creatures, and in climax, human beings, to bear His image and likeness—the *imago dei*.

What then is freedom? For far more than actions being without restrictions, God reveals His freedom as the incomparable outworking of His love. God made this revelation most fully through the incarnation when God became man. John the Evangelist cites seven times the claim of Jesus to be the I am. This revelation is far more than a list of divine attributes. It is Jesus' claim to be God, opening the mystery of the triune God as the Son of God. As John recites, Jesus, as the Truth, makes us free (John 8:32, 36). Only in Him are we truly free to be formed as persons.

Barth then proceeds to unfold the being of God, who loves in freedom. He provides for us the perfections of love in grace, holiness, mercy, righteousness, patience, and wisdom. Such is the length, depth, and height of the divine resources. In Christian formation, we are given to become "like Jesus," transformed by encountering Him in the perfections of His love.

We may affirm that good instruction was devised by Ignatius of Loyola in the sixteenth century. He promotes the four attitudes: uncompromising iconoclasm in support of the second commandment; encouragement of image worship as mediators of supernatural grace; defense of images as a valuable means of instructing the unlearned; and concentration on images of Christ Himself as the unique image of the invisible God (Col. 1:15).

Thinking in the context of this Catholic tradition, one may wonder how Barth and von Balthasar, as the Protestant and Roman Catholic, interfaced as colleagues at the same university of Basel. Loyola's teaching, to be like Jesus, is fine and helpful, but Barth's teaching on Christian formation is far more profound.

Barth further affirms that God has elected to be for and with all His creatures. He delves into this mystery as the essence of the gospel and proposes that we are to be transformed in the light of His election.

How can we understand this? This cannot be humanly explained. It is simply received in faith, hope, and love of God. Barth goes on in this second volume to trace the continuum of the election of God's people from Israel in the Old Testament, to the promise of the coming of the Messiah, and to the incarnation of Jesus Christ as the Son of God. In turn, after the resurrection, Jesus promised His disciples the advent of the Holy Spirit, as the *Paracletos*. The Spirit's work continues to deepen and further the work Jesus had begun with His disciples in every possible way. In this dynamic engagement, we become spiritually formed, like Him.

Barth concludes this volume with the revelation of God being humanly received as the command of God. This section engages what it means to be ethical. With election, there is also sanctification. God is free to love us, and we are free to desire to be like Him. Gospel and law cannot be separated, for as God made His covenant with His people in the Old Testament, so God still reveals Himself today to His people, as both law and gospel. This calls forth a transforming response. Thus, gospel ethics display a faithful, stable, unique way of life that transcends all other ethnical cultures and customs.

> Barth speaks to our life of Christian formation by taking us back to its very source in Jesus.

In the light of God's prevailing love, particularly in old age, we need solemnly to remain faithful to the end of our lives. Tragically, we see too many prominent Christian leaders become distracted from Jesus and fall into sexual sin. They have preferred the embrace of a woman's bosom instead of being like the disciple John, leaning on Jesus' bosom. John was formed in the intimacy of hearing Jesus praying to the Father His High Priestly Prayer.

With all its intimacy and security, John hears Jesus pray, "My prayer is not that you take them out of the world but that you protect them from the evil one" (John 17:15).

We need to affirm that we can never appreciate God without His embrace of humans. And so, Karl Barth very appropriately said, "There is no such thing as godless humanity." If God is not there, humanity is not there either. We need to listen more, though some of us find it very difficult to listen to Karl Barth's *Church Dogmatics*. We should be listening to pastors like Eduard Thurneysen, who was a friend of Karl Barth, and whose theology of pastoral care interprets Barth pastorally. So too Barth speaks to our life of Christian formation by taking us back to its very source in Jesus.

THE VALUE OF *CD* 2 FOR SCIENCE

Ross Hastings

Ross Hastings is Sangwoo Youtong Chee Professor of Theology, Regent College, Vancouver, BC, Canada. He is author of numerous books on Trinitarian theology, including *Echoes of Coinherence: Trinitarian Theology and Science Together.*

Science does not even merit a mention in the index of *CD* 2.2. This is not surprising given that Barth has concerns with natural theology and the met-anarrative of scientism, a naturalistic, materialist worldview in which science exerts a hegemony over theology in an idolatrous way, as if it had no philo-sophical presuppositions or theological commitments. Yet throughout his corpus, he acknowledges the importance of the sciences while insisting at the same time they cannot have the final word on matters to which divine revela-tion speaks. For example, in response to his niece's question about evolution, Barth skillfully advises towards awareness of the category difference of "cre-ation" and "evolution"—creation as the revelation of an act of God relevant to all that is and of its relevance to the covenant of God with his people, in the genre of a saga; evolution as a hypothesis based on observation.[1] By way of further example, in his next volume, Barth freely admits that many forms of anthropological understanding derived from sociology, psychology, biol-ogy, existential philosophy, naturalism, and evolutionary science hold some significance, for "in their limits they may well be accurate and important."[2] Yet he is adamant that true humanity cannot be understood apart from the Creator. Barth insists that if "we think of man in isolation from and

---

1. Geoffrey Bromiley, trans., *Karl Barth Letters: 1961–1968* (Grand Rapids: Eerdmans, 1981), 181, 184. This seems to presage Stephen Jay Gould's advocacy of noninteractive disciplines or NOMA (nonoverlapping magisteria) although differently motivated and conceived. As I have indicated, "Torrance found in the theology of Barth the construction of a unitary approach to reality, an approach he found also in Einstein. Barth was not aware of this, but apparently seemed pleased about it when Torrance informed him of this (see T. F. Torrance, *Transformation and Convergence in the Frame of Knowledge* (Grand Rapids: Eerdmans, 1984), ix)." Ross Hastings, *Echoes of Coinherence* (Eugene, OR: Wipf & Stock, 2017), 105n23.

2. *CD* 3.2, § 44, p. 122.

independence of God, we are no longer thinking about real man."[3] For Barth, humanity exists because of the election of God and only in relationship with God. Outside of this relationship, humanity ceases to be human.[4] In *this* volume, however, prior to these assertions, may I suggest that Barth not only outlines the doctrine of God in such a way as to *allow* for the sciences in their proper place, his majestic description of the triune God as the One who loves in freedom *inspires* the study of the sciences.

Having noted his reserve with respect to science, the epistemological/ theological framework that Barth lays down in the volume contains all of the elements of a theology that can be properly though asymmetrically coinherent with science. It has been contended, if somewhat controversially, that modern science prospered within a Christian cultural context.[5] The reasons for this relate to belief in its doctrine of God and of creation. On the one hand, the clear distinction between God and creation overcame the fear of creation that prevented science in pantheistic and animistic contexts. On the other hand, a good creation made by a good God assured the scientist of its order, making creation amenable to logical study.

Furthermore, a creation into which God himself entered in the Son confirms the goodness of creation and renews the cultural mandate to care for the creation, which must necessarily involve science. The historically empirical nature of the revelation of God in the Son also provided encouragement for empirical study so crucial to science. A revelatory Son who could in his humanity be seen and touched (1 John 1:1–3) provided a paradigm for creation that must be seen and touched to be known, and which cannot be known in advance of such experimentation. Unsurprisingly, almost all of the elements of this doctrine of God and of creation are implicit in this second volume.

The following are exemplary:

1. EPISTEMOLOGY

The first paragraph of this volume reveals the closest one can get to an epistemology in Barth, and it is crucial to the relationship between theology and science. Indeed, as I have argued in my book *Echoes of Coinherence*,

---

3. *CD* 3.2, § 44, p. 123.
4. *CD* 3.2, § 44, p. 123.
5. This is the well-known Foster hypothesis. See Michael B. Foster, "The Christian Doctrine of Creation and the Rise of Modern Natural Science," *Mind* 43, no. 172 (October 1934): 446–68; and "Christian Theology and Modern Science of Nature (Part I.)," *Mind* 44, no. 176 (October 1935): 439–66. It has been challenged by Peter Harrison, who exhorts care especially with regard to how Newton is interpreted in the hypothesis.

epistemology (and ontology which determines epistemology) in theology and in the sciences is a point of mutuality, even though its application in each discipline may differ according to the subject. In both disciplines, critical realism rather than logical positivism is the acknowledged epistemic. That is, we know not *a priori* but *a posteriori*. Or to express this another way, understanding cannot be separated from faith (or interpretation or prejudice). In the early pages of this volume, Barth expresses that he learned this way of knowing God "at the feet of Anselm of Canterbury."[6] This is a key concern for knowing in theology in *CD* 2.1.

Here Barth draws the distinction between the primary objectivity of God, which cannot be abstracted from his own self-giving, and his secondary objectivity in the "sign-world used by his self-revelation to" humanity.[7] What Barth refers to as sacramental objectivity is to be found in the humanity of Jesus Christ. Following Barth's famous phrasing, the possibility of the knowledge of God is grounded in and only in the actuality of our knowledge of him in Jesus Christ. In this first paragraph, he deconstructs both natural theology and Roman theology precisely around the matter of the distinction between the possibility and actuality of our knowledge of God. In both systems of thought, he sees "an underlying cleavage between God's being and His action."[8] He does not discount the place that revelation through natural theology has prior to the reception of the positive revelation given in the incarnate Christ in the gospel or of its place once this our knowledge of God in Christ has been obtained. T. F. Torrance will build on this in expressing his theology that is deeply coinherent with science, grounded in the incarnation.[9] Barth, however, is more concerned with establishing the nature of divine revelation in Jesus Christ, and given the power of the natural theology of Nazism, one can understand this. This is not to say that Barth did not respect science.

2. THEOLOGY AS SCIENCE

One evidence of this respect is that Barth refers to theology as a science in this volume.[10] It can only be called such if it need not submit to standards

---

6. *CD* 2.1, § 25, p. 4.

7. *CD* 2.1, editors' preface, p. vii.

8. *CD* 2.1, editors' preface, p. vii.

9. Alister McGrath, *T. F. Torrance: An Intellectual Biography* (Edinburgh: T&T Clark, 1999), 208.

10. *CD* 2.1, § 27–28, pp. 204, 258. See Barth's dialogue with H. Scholz, "Wie ist eine evangelische Theologie als Wissenschaft möglich?" in *Zwischen den Zeiten* 9 (1931): 8–35, reprinted in G. Sauter, ed., *Theologie als Wissenschaft* (Münich: Chr. Kaiser, 1971), 221–64. Barth insisted over against

valid for the other sciences. Yet, in calling it a science nevertheless, he insists that "theology brings itself into line."[11] Barth elevates theology above the other sciences primarily because his definition of science is *kata physin*, to seek views in correspondence with, according to the subject, and the subject in the case of the theological science, objectively speaking, was the transcendent and immanent God. The fact that divine revelation in the Son by the Spirit was subjectively speaking the way in which ecclesial humans come to know the Subject leads Barth to state confidently that "theology is on firmer ground than all other sciences."[12] By the same token, to wish to have theology spoken of as a science says something about Barth's acknowledgement of his respect for science (*scientia*) and of the correspondence regarding the nature of knowing in each.

Barth's section on "The Hiddenness of God,"[13] which speaks to the limits of our human knowledge of the God who is "known only by God,"[14] could speak correspondingly to the search for truth in science, and might invoke in both theologians and scientists the intellectual virtue of humility. Barth was not minimizing the revelation we have been given of the immanent Trinity, which he thought must correspond to what is seen in the economic Trinity, that is the revelation of the Father in Christ through the Spirit, but the word *correspondence* was carefully chosen over against coalescence, as in Karl Rahner, for example. It also preserves the reality that there are as yet undisclosed mysteries in the eternal Godhead. Astrophysicists, despite their amazing knowledge of the cosmos and its origins, acknowledge humbly that they do not know what dark matter (the source of gravity) and dark energy (what drives the expansion of the universe) actually are.[15] Barth also speaks in this section of the reality that our knowledge of God in its "viewing and conceiving is adopted and determined to participation in the truth of God by God himself in grace."[16] Participation in the truth, whether it be in the realm of science or in theology, is participation in the One who is the truth.

---

five qualifications, the foundation of what it means to be *science* involves one criterion only, that *of the adequacy of a discipline to its subject matter.* There is a more detailed discussion on theology as a science and the qualifications that allow this in *CD* 1.1, 9–11.

11. *CD* 1.1, § 1, p. 11.

12. *CD* 2.1, § 27, p. 204.

13. *CD* 2.1, § 27, p. 179–203.

14. *CD* 2.1, § 27, p. 179.

15. This does not mean that the "mystery" should not be probed, for it is the very essence of good science not to invoke God into the gaps. In theology, the category of mystery relates to what is unrevealed and may not be revealed until the end (John 1:18; 1 Cor. 2:9), although the mystery card must not be used to justify sloppy thinking.

16. *CD* 2.1, § 27, p. 179.

All theology and all science are thus engraced. I would to God that all practitioners might live in this awareness.

3. THE ONE WHO LOVES IN FREEDOM / THE BEING OF GOD IN ACT

The manner in which Barth expounds "The Being of God as the One Who Loves in Freedom"[17] is both sublime and hugely influential for theologians reflecting on science. Under the heading of God as the One who loves in freedom is "The Being of God in Act." This refers to the reality that in the acts of his revelation of himself as Father, Son, and Holy Spirit, he is who he is, not something different from who he is. This is true in his self-revelation to humanity, creating fellowship between himself and humans—that is, the economic Trinity. However, this is true because he "is this loving God without us as Father, Son, and Holy Spirit"[18] in the eternal, immanent Trinity. His eternal relations within the Trinity of generation, filiation, and spiration constitute who he is. Barth will insist that "the being of God is in act" infers that the identity of the Son was always oriented from eternity toward the creation and the incarnation (he was *incarnandus* before he was incarnate). The salient point here is that God's free act of love expressed in creating the universe was not the result of need within the Trinity (aseity is preserved[19]). It was an expression of his freedom, an *ekstasis in communio*, an outflow of his love and volition, not a reproduction of his essence (Athanasius). Similarly, his reconciling of a fallen humanity and creation in Christ was an act of freedom and love, as the gospel confirms.

Barth's understanding of the freedom of God in creating, as well as the agency of the Son and the Spirit in creation, has a great deal to say about the creation and the science of origins. It infers that creation has been granted its own freedom to be and to act, to *be* in a way that is distinct from the being of God, and yet with a freedom that is a derived and relative freedom, a freedom in God's freedom. This real but relative freedom of the creation provides at least one window for accounting for creation's agency and involvement in its own creation under the providence of God. This has importance for the big bang theory and theory of evolution. The *concursus* of the divine freedom and that of created entities in Barth allows both for the participation of the cosmos in its own creation (fecundity) and God's gentle guidance of the process.[20]

---

17. *CD* 2.1, § 28, pp. 257–321.

18. *CD* 2.1, § 28, p. 257.

19. *CD* 2.1, § 28, pp. 301–4.

20. This point has been expressed more fully in W. Ross Hastings, "Divine and Created Agency in Asymmetric Concursus: A Barthian Option," in *Divine Action and Providence*, ed. Oliver Crisp and Fred Sanders (Grand Rapids: Zondervan, 2019), 115–36.

In addition to the freedom of matter to be itself and to participate in its own origin in Christ, the very nature of what matter is seems to echo something of the nature of God as *being in act*. I was recently listening to a lecture by quantum physicist Arnold Sikkema from Trinity Western University, who made the startling statement that an electron is what an electron does. This is true of quantum particles also. He notes, "According to quantum field theory, each particle is continually sending and receiving real particles to and from other particles, which is how they feel each other; these are called mediating bosons. And, central to their ontology, each particle's individual existence involves a continuous emission and re-absorption of virtual particles."[21]

4. RELATIONAL ONTOLOGY

Barth's understanding of the God who loves in freedom is really answered in the doctrine of the Trinity, which he expounds to some extent in this volume. This suggests the notion of a relational ontology in God, and elsewhere Barth will speak to an ontology of relations in humanity. It is not too far a stretch to suggest that he might have approved of conceiving of all matter as reflecting a universal relational ontology. John Polkinghorne confirms this when he speaks of "the most striking discovery of intrinsic relationality in physics," the phenomenon referred to above as "quantum entanglement."[22] Einstein and two of his students (Podolsky and Rosen) noticed that "quantum theory implied that two quantum entities which had once interacted with each other could, in consequence, be in a state in which they retained a power of instantaneous influence on each other, however far they may become separated."[23] This phenomenon is thus known as Einstein's EPR (Einstein–Podolsky–Rosen) effect, which showed that once two quantum entities have interacted with each other, they remain mutually entangled.[24] Although Barth did not move in his ontology of relations into affirming a full-blown view of *perichoresis*, what has been affirmed by those who did so is well expressed by Graham Buxton, for example:

> It is precisely because God embraces creation's "frail contingent reality within the everlasting power of his divine presence" that we should expect trinitarian theology to offer a cogent *analogia relationis*

---

21. Arnold Sikkema, personal email, April 15, 2021.
22. John Polkinghorne, "The Trinity and Scientific Reality," in *The Blackwell Companion to Science and Christianity*, ed. J. B. Stump and Alan G. Padgett (UK: Wiley-Blackwell, 2012), 528.
23. Polkinghorne, "The Trinity and Scientific Reality," 528–29.
24. Polkinghorne, "The Trinity and Scientific Reality," 73–74.

(analogy of relations) between the creator and his creation. God's own ecstatic perichoretic life finds expression in the creation that he has brought into being, the creation that he unchangeably and unconditionally loves and blesses. Creation is open precisely because God himself is open; it is free—in the contingent sense—precisely because God is free; alive and surprising because God is inexhaustibly living and creative in his inner being.[25]

5. THE BEAUTY OF GOD

The climax of Barth's consideration of the *perfections* of God, his preferred term over *attributes*, is a consideration of the beauty of God. The editors of this volume of *CD* state that "The richness and beauty of Barth's treatment of these themes (the perfections of God) gives substance to his own claim that dogmatics is the most beautiful of all the sciences."[26] Barth's own comment in this regard is most exhilarating for a theologian, but it also has repercussions for the scientist:

> At this point we may refer to the fact that if its task is correctly seen and grasped, theology as a whole, in its parts and in their interconnexion, in its content and method, is, apart from anything else, a peculiarly beautiful science. Indeed, we can confidently say that it is the most beautiful of all the sciences. To find the sciences distasteful is the mark of the Philistine. It is an extreme form of Philistinism to find, or to be able to find, theology distasteful. The theologian who has no joy in his work is not a theologian at all. Sulky faces, morose thoughts, and boring ways of speaking are intolerable in this science. May God deliver us from what the Catholic Church reckons one of the seven sins of the monk—*taedium*—in respect of the great spiritual truths with which theology has to do. But we must know, of course, that it is only God who can keep us from it.[27]

He then goes on to speak of Anselm of Canterbury, who makes an "occasional allusion" to the beauty of theology. Barth states: "The *ratio* which *fides*

---

25. Graham Buxton, *The Trinity, Creation and Pastoral Ministry: Imaging the Perichoretic God*, Paternoster Theological Monographs (Eugene, OR: Wipf and Stock, 2007), 128. The citation is from T. F. Torrance, *The Christian Doctrine of God*, 218. This reference to the openness of God is not necessarily an affirmation of open theism, but rather an affirmation of the relational openness of God to his creation, human, animate and inanimate.

26. *CD* 2.1, editors' preface, p. viii.

27. *CD* 2.1, § 31, p. 656.

quaerens intellectum has to seek is not only *utilitas* [useful]. It is also *pulchritude* [beautiful]. When it is found, and as it is sought, it is *speciosa intellectum hominum (Cur Deus Homo* I,1), *a delectable quiddam (Monol.* 6)."[28]

The scientist who is given insight into what creation is and who is, in fact, a priest of creation, giving creation a voice, is privy also to great beauty, and there is no room for a sulky face in this great discipline either. The line between aesthetics, or art, and science is a very fine one indeed.

John Polkinghorne speaks of the wonder of the fact that the intelligibility of the universe is evident from mathematics, which is "the key for unlocking scientific secrets." The correspondence of reality to mathematical formulae arising from within the human mind is indeed remarkable. Polkinghorne states that in fundamental physics, mathematics is an actual technique of discovery. Equations that account for reality are actually sought out and looked for. He states, "Time and again we have found that it is only equations possessing economy and elegance of this kind that will prove to be the basis for theories whose long term fruitfulness convinces us that they are indeed verisimilitudinous descriptions of physical reality." Then he cites Paul Dirac, whom he considered very highly, and one of the founding fathers of quantum theory, as having once said "that it was more important to have mathematical beauty in one's equation than to have them fit experiment."[29]

Not that he undervalued empirical findings. But Dirac was just convinced that ugly equations could not answer to the reality of what was going on in matter, in creation. Metaphysics and mathematics must fit the physics, and that usually means beauty. In my own research days, it was common to hear organometallic or organic synthetic chemists speak of certain synthesis or synthetic pathways as "elegant" and even of molecular structures determined by X-ray crystallography as beautiful. The astronomer looking into the telescope sees beauty in the Milky Way. The cell biologist looking down the microscope sees beauty and economy in the organelles and the overall structure. The beauty of the Trinity defines beauty, and it is no surprise that it emanates into creation.

In sum, the second volume of the *Dogmatics* may not say much about science directly, but it provides the space and the groundwork for science and theological reflection on science that can move us beyond respect for the non-overlapping magisterial and move us into a way of seeing them as coinherent in the triune God and his incarnate Son, Jesus.

---

28. *CD* 2.1, § 31, p. 656.
29. Polkinghorne, *Science and the Trinity*, 63.

THE VALUE OF *CD* 2 FOR THE ARTS

Jeremy Begbie

Jeremy Begbie is Thomas A. Langford Distinguished Research
Professor of Theology, Duke Divinity School, Durham, North
Carolina, specializing in systematic theology and the interface
between theology and the arts. He is author of numerous books
on Trinitarian theology and the arts, including *Theology, Music
and Time*; *Resounding Truth*; and *Music, Modernity, and God*.

Barth is not known for his enthusiasm for the arts, but in fact, he was well
informed in many of the major art forms—especially painting, music, and
literature. In the *Church Dogmatics*, he writes at length about Mozart, for
whom he had a lifelong, perhaps even obsessive, devotion. However, the most
important thing Barth offers to the world of the arts is not his comments on
this or that piece of art (though there are plenty of those) but a theological
framework, a way of thinking about the arts oriented to the gospel.

As all readers of Barth know, his longing is to see theology oriented
around Christ from beginning to end and thus as Trinitarian through and
through. Volume 2 of the *Dogmatics* is concerned with knowing God and
with the reality of God—and this God is none
other than the God who has disclosed himself cli-
mactically in Jesus Christ. Barth's genius is to spell
out with a burning determination the implications
of this divine, self-revealing dynamic.

> Barth paves the way for a theology of beauty seen as a quality of God's own Trinitarian love, played out for us in Jesus Christ, a beauty which we and the created world can share in and reflect.

How does this relate to the arts? Religious language and the arts have often gone together. These
days it is not hard to find people claiming that
through, say, music, they have a sense of the "sacred," of the "transcendent,"
of the "spiritual"—whether or not they have a specific faith commitment.
Studies have shown this is widespread in many cultures and applies to many
art forms. What are we to make of this? Barth, I think, would want to say
something like this: "This kind of experience may well point to God in some
way, perhaps even be a sign of God's focused activity. But as Christians,

we will surely want to know the extent to which we are in touch with the true God, the God of Jesus Christ. Otherwise, we run the risk of deluding ourselves. Moreover, since the arts can be used for good or ill, we run the risk of enlisting God for harmful ends." Barth's passion is to prevent us from fooling ourselves about God and—as it happens—anything else we might want to think about in relation to God, such as the arts.

How, then, can the Barth of *CD* 2 help us engage with the arts in a more God-oriented way—that is, in a way that constantly looks to Jesus Christ? I highlight four ways he has helped me do just this.

First, he has helped me see that when it comes to thinking about the arts in Christian terms, it is *who God is and what God has done (and is doing)* that needs to occupy my attention before anything else, not my eagerness to express myself, the quality of my aesthetic experience, or my keenness to make judgments about other people's art. The great drama of salvation centering on Christ, crucified and risen: *that* is the context in which I need to set the business of making and enjoying the arts. Outside the theatre of the gospel, I will always be prone to fashioning idols—out of my creativity, my playlist, my favourite artist, my experience of aesthetic rapture, or whatever.

Second, Barth has helped me see that *God is not a static object to be gazed at*. To speak of knowing God is to speak of being caught up in a movement, the self-revealing momentum of God-in-action. Many attempts to speak of the revelatory power of the arts gravitate toward questions like: "How does this poem reveal God?" or "How does this film give me a sense of the divine?" That approach suggests poems and films are a little like people, active agents with built-in powers to change things. Barth turns all this around. *God* is the primary actor, and God does not sit still. So more often, we ought to be asking questions like: "What might God be *doing* and *saying to us* through this song, through this video, this film?" (And that might turn out to be a word *against* what the art itself is telling us.)

That leads to a third point. Barth has helped me see that God's self-revelation is always *purposive*—God is in the business of altering and transforming things toward an end, above all, wayward human beings like you and me. God reveals himself not merely to provide information (though that's part of it) but in order that we can know him through Jesus in the power of the Spirit. And to do that, God needs to reconcile us to himself (the subject of *CD* 4). In this light, we will begin to ask more often questions like: "How does this film bear witness to, and perhaps even convey a sense of God winning us back from the darkness of sin, from the self-made holes we dig for ourselves?"

Last but certainly not least, Barth has helped me rethink *beauty*. It's hard to avoid talking about beauty when we get involved with the arts. Yet when we start thinking about what beauty is and what makes something beautiful, in Barth's eyes, a particular danger looms large. We elaborate a grand theory of beauty and then try to supplement it with theological truth—we try to add Christian icing to a premade philosophical cake. As we might expect, Barth thinks this will likely land us with another Tower of Babel. If we're going to think about beauty—and especially about the beauty of God—we need to take our bearings not from some ready-made aesthetics, however venerable, but from the way the triune God has actually given himself to be known.

So, in *CD* 2.1, Barth offers what at first seems a striking and unusual reflection on God's beauty—a corner of the *Dogmatics* many seem to miss, by the way.[1] For Barth, divine beauty is one of the "perfections" of God, an aspect of his glory. There is something about the "form" of God's glory in his self-revelation that awakens "joy, desire, pleasure and the yearning for God,"[2] something that *attracts* rather than repels us. And the beauty of God is just that—the attractiveness of God's self-revealing in Jesus Christ. Many believe Barth could (and should) have gone much further than this, tying beauty even more closely to the cross and resurrection and spelling out how beauty can characterize the created world as well as God. Perhaps they're right. (Barth's friend Hans Urs von Balthasar went on to do just this.) But as so often with Barth, he doesn't spell everything out or give you all the answers. He sets you on a course and says, in effect, "Off you go."

When it comes to beauty, then, Barth reorients us to Jesus Christ as the self-revelation of God. And this is sorely needed today. Sadly, so much Christian talk of beauty in the arts is little more than a celebration of sentimentality and prettiness. Barth paves the way for a theology of beauty seen as a quality of God's Trinitarian love, played out for us in Jesus Christ, a beauty that we and the created world can share in and reflect. In Jesus himself— the One conceived and empowered by the Spirit, born in a stable, hounded to a shameful death, vindicated by God on the third day and exalted as a "spiritual body" (the stuff of the earth made new)—in him creation's beauty has been brought to its culmination, and divine beauty has found its most glorious demonstration. There can be no greater measure of beauty than that for the arts, or indeed, for anything else.

---

1. *CD* 2.1, § 31, pp. 650–66.
2. *CD* 2.1, § 31, p. 655.

AFTERWORD

I continue to appreciate those who have made this series possible and practical. This second volume owes a debt of gratitude to Jeremy Begbie, who has inspired me to think of theology through the arts. His work was an inspiration for the musical theme that provided amplification for God's work in revealing to us with a musical voice that invites us to join in the symphony.

My brilliant daughter Abigail has taken complex concepts, discussed at length, and made them into musical invitations to illustrate each chapter. This exercise has provided for me a work of translation that widens the horizon. Wyatt Houtz has contributed an essay, given feedback, and has created helpful images of the *CD*, for which I am grateful.

My wife, Cindy, has been that stellar person behind the work who has made the journey possible. Her love and support sustain me.

I have received extensive feedback from my Australian friends, Marc Anderson, James Baker, and James Chaousis. Their feedback has challenged me to greater clarity and encouraged me to value the work for lifelong learners, pastors, and theological students. Anna Lyn Horky continues to provide extensive editorial and technical support, for which I am eternally grateful. Katya Covrett and Matt Estel have been kind and encouraging companions in making this monumental task a reality.

The essayists have added their voices to the symphony, bringing insight from their multiple disciplines, for a wonderful grand finale to the volume. Thank you! They have added to the orchestra of disciplines engaged in this conversation. I could spend significant time commending them to you, but their work exudes its own brilliance that needs no further accolades.

This volume is longer than the last. I pray that you have been prepared from the beginning to engage more deeply in the thoughts of Karl Barth. I aim to keep the topic connected with the grandeur of the original text, yet distilled to a leisurely pace for enjoyment and comprehension. Some may think I have made statements too simple. This book is not an end in itself; it is an invitation to swim in the deep waters of the *Church Dogmatics* themselves. If I have made errors in my distillation, I hope it provides space for healthy clarification and conversation.

This volume has been a marathon. I have run daily and pressed on for the goal. I am pleased to offer it as a gift, not only in understanding Barth but the triune God to whom Barth brings our full attention. May you finish with a song in your heart.

God sings.

God invites.

God chooses to call you to sing along.

May this book resonate in you as you hear God's voice anew.

Marty Folsom
August 2021

FURTHER READING

THEOLOGY

Bromiley, Geoffrey W. *Historical Theology: An Introduction*. Grand Rapids: Eerdmans, 1978.

Gorringe, Timothy J. *Karl Barth against Hegemony: Christian Theology in Context*. Oxford: Oxford University Press, 1999.

Hunsinger, George. *Reading Barth with Charity: A Hermeneutical Proposal*. Grand Rapids: Baker, 2015.

Matczak, Sebastian A. *Karl Barth on God: The Knowledge of the Divine Existence*. New York: St. Paul, 1962.

Nimmo, Paul T. *Barth: A Guide for the Perplexed*. London: Bloomsbury, 2017.

Willimon, William H. *How Odd of God: Chosen for the Curious Vocation of Preaching*. Louisville: Westminster John Knox, 2015.

SPECIFIC SECTIONS IN *CD 2*
Perfections

Holmes, Christopher R. J. *Revisiting the Doctrine of the Divine Attributes: In Dialog with Karl Barth, Eberhard Jüngel, and Wolf Krötke*. New York: Lang, 2007.

Price, Robert B. *Letters of the Divine Word: The Perfections of God in Karl Barth's Church Dogmatics*, edited by John Webster, Ian A. McFarland, and Ivor Davidson, vol. 9, T&T Clark Studies in Systematic Theology. London: T&T Clark, 2011.

Election

Colwell, John E. *Actuality and Provisionality: Eternity and Election in the Theology of Karl Barth*. Edinburgh: Rutherford, 1989.

Dempsey, Michael T., ed. *Trinity and Election in Contemporary Theology*. Grand Rapids: Eerdmans, 2011.

Hausmann, William J. *Karl Barth's Doctrine of Election*. New York: Philosophical Library, 1969.

Neder, Adam. *Participation in Christ: An Entry into Karl Barth's Church Dogmatics*. Louisville: Westminster John Knox, 2009.

McDonald, Suzanne. *Re-Imaging Election: Divine Election as Representing God to Others & Others to God*. Grand Rapids: Eerdmans, 2010.

Ethics
Biggar, Nigel. *The Hastening That Waits: Karl Barth's Ethics*. Oxford: Clarendon, 1993.
Haddorff, David. *Christian Ethics as Witness: Barth's Ethics for a World at Risk*. Eugene, OR: Cascade, 2010.
Migliore, Daniel, ed. *Commanding Grace: Studies in Karl Barth's Ethics*. Grand Rapids: Eerdmans, 2010.
Nimmo, Paul T. *Being in Action: The Theological Shape of Barth's Ethical Vision*. Edinburgh: T&T Clark, 2007.
Webb, Stephen H. "Karl Barth and God's Freedom." In *The Gifting God: A Trinitarian Ethics of Excess*, 98–104. Oxford: Oxford University Press, 1996.

HANDBOOKS
Burnett, Richard, ed. *The Westminster Handbook to Karl Barth*. Louisville: Westminster John Knox, 2013.
Hunsinger, George, and Keith L. Johnson. *Wiley Blackwell Companion to Karl Barth*. Hoboken, NJ: Wiley, 2020.
Jones, Paul Dafydd, and Paul T. Nimmo, eds. *The Oxford Handbook of Karl Barth*. Oxford: Oxford University Press, 2020.
Webster, John, ed. *The Cambridge Companion to Karl Barth*. Cambridge: Cambridge University Press, 2000.

ONLINE RESOURCES
Center For Barth Studies, Princeton, https://barth.ptsem.edu/
Karl Barth Archive, Basel, https://karlbarth.unibas.ch/de/
Barth Literature Search Project, http://barth.mediafiler.org/barth/index_Eng.htm
Theological Studies: Karl Barth, https://www.theologicalstudies.org.uk/theo_barth.php
Karl Barth Resource Guide, https://issuu.com/ptsem/docs/barth_resource_guide